A History of Philosophy in America

A HISTORY OF PHILOSOPHY IN AMERICA

1720–2000

Bruce Kuklick

CLARENDON PRESS · OXFORD

OXFORD

UNIVERSITY PRESS

Great Clarendon Street, Oxford OX2 6DP

Oxford University Press is a department of the University of Oxford.
It furthers the University's objective of excellence in research, scholarship,
and education by publishing worldwide in

Oxford New York

Auckland Bangkok Buenos Aires Cape Town Chennai
Dar es Salaam Delhi Hong Kong Istanbul Karachi Kolkata
Kuala Lumpur Madrid Melbourne Mexico City Mumbai Nairobi
São Paulo Shanghai Singapore Taipei Tokyo Toronto

Oxford is a registered trade mark of Oxford University Press
in the UK and certain other countries

Published in the United States
by Oxford University Press Inc., New York

First published 2001

First published in paperback 2003

British Library Cataloguing in Publication Data

Data available

Library of Congress Cataloging in Publication Data

Data available

ISBN 0-19-825031-2

ISBN 0-19-9260168 (pbk.)

1 3 5 7 9 10 8 6 4 2

Typeset by
J&L Composition,
Filey, North Yorkshire

Printed in Great Britain on acid-free paper by
Biddles Ltd., Guildford & Kings Lynn

For Marya, Stan, Casey, and Jake

Di patrii . . . servate nepotem

CONTENTS

For he who'd make his fellow-creatures wise
Should always gild the philosophic pill!
Gilbert and Sullivan, *The Yeomen of the Guard*

Introduction

This book sketches the history of philosophy in America, but I have been aware of many conceptual difficulties in the project. 'Philosophy' is a contested notion, and so is the notion of its 'American-ness'. Finally, such a history involves a package of ideas about the quality of thought.

By philosophy I mean more or less systematic writing about the point of our existence, and our ability to understand the world of which we are a part. These concerns are recognizable in the questions that thinkers have asked in successive eras, and in the connections between the questions of one era and another. For instance, in the eighteenth and nineteenth centuries, thinkers asked: what is the individual's relation to an inscrutable deity? How can human autonomy be preserved, if the deity is omnipotent? After Charles Darwin published his *Origin of Species* in 1859, philosophers asked: how can human freedom and our sense of the world's design be compatible with our status as biological entities? Early in the twentieth century academic thinkers wanted to know: if we are biological organisms, enmeshed in a causal universe, how can we come to have knowledge of this universe; how can mind escape the limits set by causal mechanism? By the second-half of the twentieth century, professional philosophers often assumed both that we were of the natural world and that knowledge demanded a transcendence of the natural. They then asked: how is knowledge possible? What are the alternatives to having knowledge?

For three centuries Americans have pondered these concerns by relying on the formulations of the people whose views are examined in this book. These people, for better or worse, have elaborated the frameworks used in grappling with issues of human destiny. Just as intellectuals today worry about how to 'get right with theory', and consider it important, so did Americans in the past worry. Just as intellectuals in the present believe they have the sort of detachment from ordinary concerns that gives to their ideas a truth apart from any locality, so did the thinkers I treat in this book. But just as intellectuals today operate in a restrictive cultural context that must be considered in appraising their views, so must we also consider that context in the past.

Thinkers have often, though certainly not always, been connected to institutions of learning, and their beliefs have tended to be complex and even to hinge on expertise shared by few. What philosophical exposition meant to these scholars was often at variance with what Americans looking for enlightenment expected. Americans have *needed* to have speculative questions addressed intelligently, but when pursued in some settings philosophy risked losing the audience that had called philosophers into existence in the first place. Philosophy is a subtle and demanding exercise but has to establish some productive and positive relation with its cultural environment if it is to remain healthy as a practice. Its history is most interesting when the audience is so demanding that philosophy is oversimplified, or when philosophers are so independent as to dismiss the desires of a putative general audience.

In focusing on *American* philosophy, the book makes implicit claims about thought and life related to a peculiar Western polity and, by the nineteenth century, the United States. Much philosophical exchange has existed across national boundaries, and it is not clear that anything unique characterizes American thought. At times it heavily depended on philosophy abroad. That dependence was itself conservative, reflecting the priorities of the guardians of high culture in the United States. Britain, Germany, and France have been consistently prominent over the last 300 years, and almost nowhere else has been significant. Americans, however, have been ambivalent about philosophy overseas. They have sometimes assumed that whatever the Western Europeans say must be correct, especially if it is almost unintelligible. At the same time European ideas were mistrusted, as if the foreign philosophers were diplomats, trying to outsmart the United States. This book chronicles the changing appropriations.

Simultaneously, standard features of philosophy in this country stand out. Philosophers have displayed their upbringing and schooling in America. In the period before the Revolutionary War, divines often looked upon the 'new learning' of Europe with distaste, and the greater religious coloration of their thought resulted from self-consciously attempting to purge thinking of the evils of the old world. In the nineteenth century the close association of thinkers in Scotland and America revealed both their dislike of England and their inferiority as its intellectual provinces. In the twentieth century the strength and freedom of the United States, especially in the period of Nazi dominance, made America an attractive destination for European intellectuals and dramatically altered philosophy at home; during the period of the Vietnam War suspicion of the United States also affected thought.

The study of the history of philosophy finally requires complex judgements of quality, which are both questionable and necessary. Some philosophers must be understood because they were influential in their own time or thereafter; a few must be studied because their ability shines through the ages; perhaps most will have as many detractors as defenders. The historian threads through the maze of claims and counter-claims and gives the reader a sense of the debate and of the options at any given time. This is not easy.

My strategy has been twofold. First, I have been selective in my emphases rather than encyclopedic and exhaustive. To foster this aim I have stressed a number of thinkers as representative—for example, among theologians Nathaniel William Taylor over Joseph Bellamy, Leonard Woods, and Edwards Amasa Park; among metaphysicians Josiah Royce over Alfred North Whitehead and Paul Weiss; among instrumentalists, John Dewey over George Herbert Mead; among public intellectuals, Richard Rorty over Herbert Marcuse, Sidney Hook, and Noam Chomsky. I want to suggest how we should approach the topic; not how we should treat it definitively.

Second, my goal has not been to put forward a list of great thinkers from whom we still have something to learn, or to establish a canon of thought. I have rather depicted student–teacher relations, conventions of argument, and constellations of problems that endure over generations; and the cultural setting and institutional connections that make up an *enterprise* of philosophy. I have described traditions of thought and the intentions of thinkers within a social matrix. I am not certain that a causal relation always exists between this matrix and the thinking—in some cases I am persuaded no such relation exists—but I am convinced that better sense is made of the thought when I locate it in the culture; the latter is relevant to philosophy.

From the middle of the eighteenth century American thinkers have been attracted to idealism, that speculative view that existence is essentially mental. The belief that the world is encompassed in individual consciousness—subjective idealism or solipsism—was regularly noted in America only to be disparaged. But Kant's position, that the physical world did not transcend consciousness; and Hegel's, that the world was an aspect of an absolute mind, usually called objective or absolute idealism, both had their followers in America. Some thinkers have also defended communitarian idealism—that one or another aggregate of finite minds defined reality.

I have explored how these beliefs developed. The most important substantive theme of the book is the long circuitous march from a religious to a secular vision of the universe. In America this march has taken a longer time than in other Western cultures. One might presume that the march would diminish the role of the mental, often a term only a step away from the spiritual or religious. But despite the growing emphasis on the non-religious, the deference to one or another kind of idealism has meant in America that realism (the view that physical objects at least exist independently of mind) has often been on the defensive, although a constant option. The eccentric journey away from religion has meant only the slow growth of what is often thought to be realism's cousin, materialism—that monistic position opposed to idealism stipulating that the mental world is reducible to the physical. More to the point, idealism and a defense of science have often coincided. Philosophers have regularly conceded that scientific investigation could easily but erroneously combine with materialism. On the contrary, however, they have usually argued that only some sort of idealism can preserve scientific priorities. Moreover, the varieties of idealism have a strong voluntaristic component: the will, volition, and propensity to act have been crucial in defining the mental or the conscious.

A subsidiary theme concerns social and political philosophy. Part of this argument is definitional, and is the crux of Chapter 2, Philosophy and Politics. Like other commentators, I have ultimately identified philosophy with an orientation to the spirit. But I have drawn out the implications of this definition: socialized in a more religious culture than that of European thinkers, American philosophers were gripped by issues of faith into the twentieth century, and thereafter continued to focus on related matters. They ordinarily dismissed the world of political behavior as irrelevant to what they were doing. As William James advised Josiah Royce about philosophical pursuits, 'We are all isolated. . . . Books are our companions more than men.' A few extraordinary politically oriented thinkers identified with pragmatism in the twentieth century test the rule, but for the most part politics has not shaped American philosophy.

PART I

Speculative Thought in America, 1720–1868

In the eighteenth and most of the nineteenth century, people in America known formally as philosophers were part of a wider dialogue that had three major components.

Most important were parish ministers, primarily in New England, who wrote on theology and participated in a conversation that embraced a religious élite in England and Scotland, and later in Germany. These clerics expounded varieties of Calvinist Protestantism. Jonathan Edwards was the most influential and talented member of this ministerial group, which later included Horace Bushnell and Ralph Waldo Emerson. But these two lived at a time when such thinkers were deserting their congregations and turning away from traditional Protestant doctrine. Because these sages were unconnected to institutions of higher education, I have sometimes called them amateurs, although this term embraces a wider collection of individuals, some of whom were less religious, or were on the fringes of the emerging system of advanced academic training in the late eighteenth and early nineteenth centuries.

The second major component of American speculative thought was located in one part of this system, the seminaries that grew up in the Northeast, the old Midwest, and the South throughout the nineteenth century. Often independent entities unconnected to American colleges, these institutions were, aside from law and medical schools, the only places where an aspiring young man could receive instruction beyond what an undergraduate received; they arose to train a professional ministry. The specialists in theology at these centers gradually took over the role that the more erudite ministry had played. Leonard Woods of Andover Theological Seminary; Henry Ware of the Harvard Divinity School; Nathaniel William Taylor of the Yale Divinity School; Charles Hodge of the Princeton Theological Seminary; and Edwards Amasa Park of Andover belong to this cadre.

The divinity-school theologians controlled the major power bases in the nineteenth century. They trained the ministers and determined much of what was published. Their outlook tended to be more narrow and sectarian than that of those speculative thinkers who were not professors of divinity, but it is difficult to argue that they were not the intellectual equals of those outside the divinity schools.

A final group was actually known as philosophers; they were the holders of chairs in mental, moral, or intellectual philosophy in the American colleges of the nineteenth century. Their function was to support theoretically the concerns of the divinity-school theologians and the most serious ministers on the hustings. The philosophers were invariably ministers and committed Protestants themselves, but in addition to showing that reason was congruent with faith they also studied the grounds of social order and politics, and commented on the affairs of the world. Often the presidents of their institutions, they had captive student audiences and easy access to publication. Such worthies included Francis Bowen of Harvard, James McCosh of the College of New Jersey (Princeton), and Noah Porter of Yale.

This philosophical component of the speculative tradition was provincial. Until after the Civil War, American colleges were small, sleepy institutions, peripheral to the life of the nation. Their leaders, including philosophers, participated in the shaping of public discourse but were generally undistinguished. Their libraries were inadequate, their education mediocre, and the literary culture in which they lived sentimental and unsophisticated. Europe barely recognized these philosophers, except when they went there to study. Yet the philosophers found senior partners in transatlantic correspondents and were on an intellectual par with the other Americans previously mentioned.

The intersecting dialogues among amateurs, divinity-school theologians, and college philosophers extended from the time of Edwards to the latter part of the nineteenth century. There is a quiet aspect to this 150-year period, but a complex development of ideas occurred.

Those scholars on the edges of the collegiate and seminary world were more creative and innovative in their use of ideas than those inside institutions. The new ideas that appeared in the academy usually had ancestors outside colleges or seminaries. For a long time the non-institutionalists had less clout, but throughout the nineteenth century the divinity-school thinkers slowly lost their audience, and the collegiate philosophers gradually gained power in public forums. But, the college thinkers were intellectually unprepossessing in the middle of the nineteenth century. After the Civil War, amateurs sought in various informal venues to overcome the stagnation in higher education. An institutional and intellectual revolution that shapes the second part of this book aborted the efforts of the amateurs. The first part of this book deals with the thought of Jonathan Edwards and his descendants, and then traces the movements that led to the reformation of speculative views toward the end of the nineteenth century.

1   *Calvinism and Jonathan Edwards*

Calvinists in America

In the seventeenth and even into the eighteenth century, ministers dominated New England—Massachusetts, Connecticut, New Haven (initially a separate colony), and some of the early New Hampshire towns. Their intellectual focus was the Bible, whose meaning had been determined by the European Protestant leader John Calvin, and Calvinist Protestants adhered to the 'federal' or 'covenantal' theology. According to it, two agreements, or covenants, that God made with man were essential to understanding history. As the Bible's first book, Genesis, related, God placed Adam and Eve in the Garden of Eden, where they could live forever in happiness and tranquility provided they obeyed his law. God could have prohibited any sort of behavior, but since he simply wished to test human obedience, he forbade eating the fruit of a certain tree. This arrangement was called the covenant of works. If Adam and Eve obeyed—if their works were good—all would be well. No sooner had God issued his command, however, than the couple violated it, and were banished from the Garden.

Because of Adam's disobedience, God first punished him with death. Adam was also demeaned by the ills that flesh is heir to as premonitions of what was to come, and was threatened with the everlasting torment of the damned in the fires of hell. Indeed, after Adam disobeyed, all his descendants were destined to sin like him and therefore to die. Finally, as a result of the Fall, God in his infinite mercy made a new arrangement called the covenant of grace. He said in effect: it is now impossible for individuals to be obedient; they will sin no matter what. But if they confessed their iniquity, and recognized their corrupt nature, then, after their physical death, they would not be punished eternally but rewarded with something even better than the Garden of Eden. The coming of Christ revealed the meaning of this new covenant of grace: if individuals had faith in Jesus, they would be redeemed. God knew, the Calvinists argued, that people would continue to sin and would never merit salvation. They would never be obedient as they could have been before the Fall, but they could recognize their wickedness, and could be saved by God's grace, his mercy or goodness. The central event in the Christian life was the gift of grace. By a supernatural act God infused sinners with a consciousness of his glory and love, and enabled them to turn from the idolatry of self. Grace mysteriously transformed human selfishness and overwhelmed and humbled Christians.

The American federal theology was a variant of the Calvinism codified by the Dutch Synod of Dort (1618–19). That synod defined the essentials of Calvinism in opposition to the heresy of Arminianism, after the school of Jacob Arminius, who emphasized the ability of sinners to respond to the giving of grace, to do good or evil as they chose. At Dort the Calvinists stated that human beings, by nature, were totally depraved and could in no way merit salvation by anything they did; some were unconditionally elected to receive grace, which was irresistible when given and never taken back. Calvinists rejected the Arminian concept that sinners might regulate grace.

These doctrines were intricately connected and presented complex problems for those charged with rationalizing belief. In America divines emphasized the responsibility of individuals for their behavior even when they were evil by nature. God controlled events, but humanity was accountable for what it did and subject to moral judgement. These dilemmas were themselves entangled with issues of clerical authority and church membership. The New England version of the federal theology stressed that the believer had to *prepare* to receive grace.

In the early seventeenth century, the Massachusetts ministry recoiled from emphasizing purity and salvation by grace alone. Because grace was undeserved, it could make no demands on sinners prior to its receipt, and anyone could claim it. But if salvation were impenetrably transacted between God and the individual, no churchly authority could monitor the dispensation of faith or require virtuous behavior. This 'enthusiasm' or 'antinomianism' even implied that the Bible was peripheral to God's connection with the individual soul. Confronted by these supposed consequences of the covenant of grace during the so-called antinomian crisis, the New England clergy asserted its essential role in discerning grace and regulating admission to the church. The ministers delineated a conversion scheme that ascertained the genuine nature of spiritual influxes. Preparation for salvation enabled the unregenerate to ready themselves for the possible receipt of grace. They could use 'the means of grace'—the best example was biblical study—despite the fact that these means in no way limited God's power. Preparation was lifelong and involved at least a period of introspective meditation and self-analysis in the light of scripture, whose interpretation was in the custody of the ministry. The soul moved through a series of stages centered on a self-examination intended to arouse a longing for grace.

Critics might conclude that preparation made grace contingent on appropriate behavior: the saved merely met the criteria that the clergy established. How different was this from Arminianism, the view that individuals might do good on their own, or the covenant of works, that they might earn their way to heaven? On the contrary, the ministry held, preparation could be demanded of all, yet be nothing more than a hopeful augury. The practice obligated everyone, no matter how impotent the unaided human will. Not incidentally, preparation implied a place for the ministry as guardian of 'the means', as well as of the social order. The question was whether individuals could predispose themselves to grace when God could always deny mercy. The prepared heart was *almost* necessary but *never* sufficient for salvation.

Through much of the seventeenth century, the theological doctrines of grace and divine sovereignty were not construed as equivalent to the philosophical idea of determinism—that all events were embedded in a causal chain. Our nature as willing agents and God's omnipotence presented problems but were not contradictory in the seventeenth-century world order. Preparation for salvation was a duty that could, in the order of time, be justly urged on everyone. Then, at the end of the century, Isaac Newton in *Principia Mathematica* (1687) and the *Optics* (1704) formulated an epoch-making understanding of the physical world. Although a religious thinker, Newton renewed the scientific and experimental credibility of the atomic theory of the universe. Newton's laws of motion and gravitation demonstrated the orderliness of God's universe and had repercussions for religious thought. For Newton, God's efficient causality ruled the world and might abrogate individual responsibility, while paradoxically the triumph of the new scientific ideas promised greater human control over the environment than was previously conceivable.

Newton changed the intellectual culture of Calvinism. From the viewpoint of the Americans, if preparation were at all helpful, it might be dismissed because it compromised God's omnipotence as Newtonianism defined it. By the eighteenth century some Calvinists felt that the covenant of grace did not simply suppose an unbridgeable gap between the regenerate and unregenerate. The covenant made it necessary for God to take the heart immediately and by storm, disregarding the sinner's previous state and acting outside the normal causal order. Thus began a history of revivalist preaching, in which the minister harvested converts and assisted the sinner in conquering the insuperable obstacles in the way of coming to

Christ. The exploration of preparatory techniques now had to reconcile Calvinist doctrine and Newtonian determinism.

From the mid-eighteenth until the end of the nineteenth century the central issue for American thinkers was the connection of God's supremacy to human freedom. God did not author sin and was not to be blamed for the failure of the covenant of works. He was still almighty and causally sovereign. Although God gave faith and was to be praised for the covenant of grace, people were answerable for their own salvation. Jonathan Edwards came of age in this speculative world.

Edwards's Early Writing

Edwards was born in East Windsor, Connecticut, in 1703, the son of an important minister and the grandson (on his mother's side) of the famous revivalist preacher of western Massachusetts, Solomon Stoddard. In his youth Edwards spent much time at Yale College, a small and struggling school for the Calvinist ministry. He studied there first as an undergraduate, next for two years as an advanced student, and then for a year as a tutor in the early 1720s. Most important for his development was the college's acquisition of an outstanding collection of books sent from England by the Connecticut colony's agent, Jeremiah Dummer. The Dummer collection made Yale's library the best in North America, and gave Edwards direct contact with late seventeenth-century European thought. In his years in Weathersfield (where the college had moved during a three-year dispute) and New Haven, Connecticut, Edwards absorbed the major works of metaphysics, the scientific and empirical learning of Newton, and the most influential philosopher associated with Newtonianism, John Locke. Locke's *Essay Concerning Human Understanding* (1690) was a crucial text for early modern philosophy and the formative document in Edwards's development.

Historians of philosophy have conventionally argued that Locke successfully challenged the earlier ideas of such thinkers as René Descartes. Both Descartes and Locke assumed that the individual was competent to grasp truths but that the only sure basis for knowledge was given—the momentarily and immediately present. These instants of consciousness and the building blocks of knowledge were somehow internal data, ideas. For Locke they were of two sorts, sensation and reflection. Sensations were produced by the reactions of the sensory nervous processes—what people saw, smelt, or heard. Reflections were the images of previous sensations produced by the mind's memories, imaginings, thoughts, and dreams; or the mind's rumination on its own activities of thinking, imagining, dreaming, and so on.

Locke and Descartes were metaphysical dualists who believed in two sorts of substances, mind and matter. And they were each 'representational realists' for whom knowledge of material substances was mediated through mind. An independent world caused the contents of consciousness, but the human grasp of this world came through the mind. For Locke, commentators later held, the secondary qualities of objects—for example, colors and tastes—existed only in perceivers' minds: these qualities were the effect of the object on the perceivers. Without perceivers there would be no secondary qualities. The primary qualities of objects—for example, extension and solidity—existed in the absence of perception and indeed defined material existence.

For Descartes, mind displayed itself in these instants of consciousness, and reflection on its own activity revealed certain principles—innate ideas—applicable to the world outside mind. Against this Cartesian rationalism, said commentators, the mind for Locke possessed no innate principles enabling it to cogitate, a priori, on the nature of things and could not arrive at truths about the world by itself. The mind for Locke was only the medium in which the momentarily given presented itself. Knowledge came from the immediate contents of the mind, called phenomena, experience, or discrete ideas.

Thus Locke was an empiricist urging Newtonian-like observation as the basis of knowledge, against the Cartesian belief that mind alone could provide that basis. The empiricism of Locke's *Essay* provided the speculative rationale for Newtonianism. The impingement of atoms on the sense organs caused the experience on which knowledge of the world solely depended. The eighteenth-century understanding of nature did not rely on armchair rumination; it was subservient to empirical fact.

From a later perspective, Locke's dismissal of innate ideas led to the manipulative attitudes associated with science. Ideas were presented to human beings. How then could the existence of the non-phenomenal, the external, objective world be postulated, as opposed to the subjective, internal world of appearance? Descartes insisted on indisputable truths about the world that the mind possessed independently of experience. Locke sanctioned only the experienced, and no one experienced the non-phenomenal; we were involved in the practical consideration of assessing the connections among phenomena. Consequently, as the textbook history of philosophy was written, Locke's empiricism was tantamount to an anti-absolutistic perspective on knowledge and even paved the way to skepticism.

To see how this was so, we must see how Bishop George Berkeley took two steps and denied an underlying matter or material substance. First,

Berkeley argued, Locke could not distinguish between primary and second-ary qualities. Neither existed outside the mind. Second, Berkeley revised Locke's doctrine that knowledge was gained through the two sorts of ideas, sensation and reflection. For Locke, sensations conveyed knowledge of the physical world; ideas of reflection conveyed knowledge of mind itself. For Berkeley, these two sorts of ideas existed, but they were not different ideas of human beings. Those ideas that made up what the vulgar might call the external world were God's (Locke's ideas of sensation); they were imposed on human beings and beyond their control. Those within control were weaker copies of God's ideas (Locke's ideas of reflection); they emanated from human beings as finite spirits.

For Berkeley only minds and their contents existed, and he became known as an 'idealist'. Primary qualities did not exist outside the mind, and an external object did not cause sensations. Such objects were ideas in the mind of God.

Hard on the heels of Berkeley, David Hume argued that it was illegit-imate to suppose spirits—either human or divine—behind the ideas. He construed mind itself as a series of ideas. Only the disjointed phenomena of experience existed. Knowledge about a world of enduring objects was impossible. Practical belief was based on subjective impressions and good only so far as we could comfortably act on it. Skepticism and rela-tivism were the inevitable result if we searched for an absolute basis for knowledge.

This appraisal of Locke and his role in the history of thought has merit. In the early eighteenth century, however, Edwards read Locke in the con-text of the metaphysical discussion that Descartes dominated. The Dummer gift to Yale also included works by philosophers in the Cartesian tradition, and writings of English idealists who, reacting to Descartes and Locke, attacked materialism and dualism. None of these philosophers was oblivious to the scientific advances of the seventeenth century, but all developed philosophies giving mind the dominant role. Conceptual, a pri-ori reasoning that led to conclusions about the world's structure was com-mon. The new science was interpreted not as implying materialism, uncertainty, or skepticism but rather as asserting the primacy of mind. As Newton himself intimated, physics described the immaterial structure of God's will working incessantly. When read in this context, Locke's *Essay* was less certain in its empiricism and filled with evasions, hesitations, and ambiguities, although it never comforted rationalists. Locke was crucial to Edwards, but it was a vacillating Locke, many of whose ideas could be con-troverted, redefined, or given a religious interpretation.

In 1829, long after Edwards's death, one of his many editors prepared the first publication of a series of extended notes on 'The Mind' that Edwards had begun writing in the early 1720s, after having read in the Dummer collection. Just in his twenties, Edwards fashioned from his reading of Locke an anti-materialist philosophy. Philosophy and theology were intertwined for Edwards. The former characteristically expressed man's reason, and could to some extent ground what was legitimate to believe although it was no substitute for belief. The Bible offered a vision that philosophy alone could not have devised. Theology, on the other hand, meant the systematic study of the speculative problems confronted in accepting Christianity. It too did not yield belief, but the theologian might use philosophy to untangle some of the conundrums of revelation. In his youth Edwards wrote what I would call Christian philosophy: he espoused views that would be congenial to the theologian's task, but was not concerned with Calvinist divinity itself, nor with the burdens of faith. He had an intellectualist interest in religion.

Initially accepting Locke's distinction between primary and secondary qualities, Edwards also redefined the primary qualities. Apparently for Locke the primary qualities of matter inhered in the small, hard atomic particles of the Newtonian universe. Edwards argued that the primary qualities reduced to solidity. Then he asserted that solidity was resistance, the power to resist annihilation. So for Edwards, atoms, the material substances, were reconceived as centers of energy. But such centers of energy, being constant and active, depended upon God; or rather, matter was nothing but the actual exertion of God's power or the expression of the law or method describing the exertion of God's power. '[T]he substance of bodies at last becomes either nothing, or nothing but the deity acting in that particular manner in those parts of space where he thinks fit. So that, speaking most strictly, there is no proper substance but God himself . . . .'

In contrast to Berkeley, to whose work Edwards's is always compared, Edwards distinguished secondary and primary qualities. The secondary qualities existed in the human mind, and in this sense were mental. Human beings knew them immediately. But as the effects of substance on people, the qualities had no reality outside the perceiver. Primary qualities existed outside the human mind and constituted the fabric of the external world. Solidity distinguished substance *independently* of human perception. But, against Locke, the primary qualities were also ideal; they were independent of individual minds but not of God's mind and expressed his active will. '[T]he substance of all bodies', wrote Edwards, 'is the infinitely exact and precise and perfectly stable idea in God's mind.'

Edwards did not rest with this position, which changed in subsequent early writings. Locke and Edwards argued that the secondary qualities existed only when perceived and were less a part of the world's structure than primary qualities. Could this belief be defended? Locke also rejected direct knowledge of primary qualities, or solidity and resistance, existing independently of human minds. The existence of such qualities could only be inferred. Edwards now contended for direct knowledge of these qualities existing outside finite minds. Human beings at once encountered 'the infinitely exact . . . idea in God's mind'; they directly grasped what was called the world of material substance. Inference was unnecessary to discover the existence of primary qualities; they were experienced just as the secondary qualities were. Moreover, secondary qualities were as much a part of the structure of things as were primary qualities. The secondary qualities, too, existed outside human minds but not outside God's mind. People confronted both sorts of qualities as they really existed.

Edwards consequently discarded the representational theory. Both primary and secondary qualities were directly known. He also discounted the dualistic claim that material substance existed independently of mind. Edwards was thus, like Berkeley, an idealist—material substances were interpreted to be mental in nature—but he dissented from the type of idealism associated with Berkeley. The human mental world was not a weaker image of God's ideas. When individuals knew anything, they experienced God's ideas directly.

Edwards believed in *creatio continua*. He rejected the idea of an 'unmoved mover', who originated the world's motion and observed it at remote distance. Instead, Edwards conceived God as an inexhaustible reality, an emanating light, communicating itself as the sun communicated its brilliance. The material world was not merely an idea of God's, but his eternal disposition, his will to display himself. The cosmos was not an act or state of the divine consciousness, but God operating at every moment, expressing himself in finite modes and forms according to a defined purpose.

Edwards availed himself of a powerful analogy. The world was like the moment-by-moment image in a mirror. The mirror-world depended on the objects it reflected. The images were not derived from or intrinsically connected to the immediately preceding or succeeding images. All were contingent on the objects, just as God's activity produced the world from nothing. Ideas in God's mind were the origin, source, and only cause of experience.

Strictly speaking, God's ideas did not cause finite ideas. The finite were fragments or parts of God's ideas. Although finite ideas could not be equated with God—he was not the world—he willed a dimension of himself as the world. Certain ordered aspects of God were the universe. The human mind, in particular, was just another composite of these ideas of God's. If his ideas were construed one way, they were the material world, the world of sense, of enduring objects, of structured experience. But the very same ideas could be construed as reflecting on the world. In this construal the order of the ideas would be different and would typify what was known as minds—our perceptual mental world. God's mind revealed itself to us as two different orderings of ideas. So Edwards wrote: 'All existence is perception. What we call body is nothing but a particular mode of perception; and what we call spirit is nothing but a composition and series of perceptions, or a universe of coexisting and successive perceptions connected by such wonderful methods and laws.'

Locke distinguished two sets of qualities of objects, one of which existed outside the mind. Berkeley denied that either sort of quality existed outside the mind but acknowledged the felt difference between what went on 'in our heads' and the 'perception of the world'; he used Locke's dichotomy between reflection and sensation, and contrasted two different sorts of ideas, the individual's and God's. Edwards disallowed both dualisms. Both secondary and primary qualities existed outside finite minds but not outside God's, and finite ideas were not weaker images of God's. To explain the felt difference Edwards urged that the aspect of God revealed to human beings could be organized in two different ways. One way was the world minds knew; the other way was the minds knowing the world.

Ministerial Career and World-View

Edwards's earliest philosophical ruminations were more or less coterminous with an agonizing period in which he understood his coming to self-consciousness in terms of the formulas of Calvinism. He struggled under the weight of his own sense of sin, 'an infinite deluge', 'a mountain over my head', 'an abyss infinitely deeper than hell'. Grace involved a dialectic of self-abasement and self-aggrandizement, which even if not granted in a revival setting, was an overwhelming and cataclysmic undergoing that simultaneously humiliated and uplifted Edwards, changing his relation to the world, his felt encounter with life in the 1720s. 'The appearance of every thing was altered; there seemed to be . . . a calm, sweet cast, or appearance of divine glory, in almost every thing. God's excellency, his wisdom, his purity and love, seemed to appear in every thing; in the sun, moon, and stars; in the clouds and blue sky; in the grass, flowers, trees; in the water, and all nature.'

Soon thereafter, in the late 1720s, he started assisting his grandfather in Northampton, Massachusetts. In 1729, after Solomon Stoddard's death, Edwards became chief minister in this, the greatest pulpit west of Boston.

He had a powerful mind that was naturally drawn to the perplexities of Calvinist theology but was primarily the pastor of a large flock. In the 1730s he achieved a reputation throughout the colonies when he orchestrated the success of revivals in Northampton and other communities later known as the Great Awakening. As a pastor, Edwards had often witnessed the way parishioners came to Christ and ruminated on the events. His intellectual studies gave way to the concerns of a revivalist ministry, interpreting the complexities of religious doctrine for his congregation, and its experience of the contemporary world.

This interpretation was essentially premodern. The Bible held the key to making sense of a universe that was filled with daily wonders, portents of things to come, omens of judgements on the wicked, and—somehow—the fruition in history of God's plan as Calvinists had defined it. The scream of an owl at night represented the misery of devils residing in eternal darkness. In 1745 the Catholic French defenders of Cape Breton, an island in the Gulf of St Lawrence, surrendered to their Protestant English attackers. Edwards, who steadfastly believed that the Church of Rome was the force of the Antichrist, wrote that the surrender was 'a dispensation of providence, the most remarkable in its kind, that has been in many ages'. The Catholic defeat was a sign of what was to come, for the Bible book of Revelation taught him that the papacy would fall in 1866, presaging a glorious time for the true church beginning about 2000. The Bible was for Edwards the authoritative text for understanding the world, and although he subjected it to much explication, in his eyes it could be read in only one way.

While this cognitive style made Edwards a figure of positive significance in New England, the rigidity in his outlook could be offensive even in colonial America. The Great Awakening split New England intellectual life, pitting Old Calvinists, a group committed to pre-Awakening adaptation to the social world; and revivalists, led by Edwards, who emphasized doctrinal niceties. In the late 1740s, after a bruising battle with his congregation over its failure to appreciate the demands he placed on it, Edwards was forced from his pulpit. He left forever the sort of calling that had kept him in touch with ordinary parish life, and in 1751 accepted a position further west, on the edge of the wilderness at Stockbridge, Massachusetts. He ministered in part to the Housatonic Indians, but his primary focus was a defense of his religious convictions, which depended on an examination of the functioning of the human mind. Spending thirteen hours a day at his desk, if a student's testimony is accepted, Edwards turned inward on the frontier.

Popular Newtonian ideas gave credibility to a mechanistic and material view of the universe, which was combined with a new sense of the human ability to manage the physical world. To Edwards this elevation of the human prospect sounded suspiciously like Arminianism, which stressed the ability of individuals to do good on their own, or worse, but he believed that scientific ideas need not support Arminianism, or any of the positions that threatened Calvinist divinity in what later looked like crab-like movements to a human-centered universe. As a theologian, Edwards embarked on a heroic endeavor—to reinterpret early modern Europe's science and philosophy in a way that would make them compatible with his inherited spirituality. The measure of his success was his agenda in philosophical theology, which stood unchallenged in America for well over 100 years. No other divine in the American or European learned world came close to Edwards, and his achievements are even greater if one considers the impoverished and provincial cultural milieu of his native New England, and the other premodern components of his thought, located in his peculiar Biblicism, revival preaching, and portentous historical reasoning. The unusual force of his intellect, his writing ability, his diligence, and his discipline remain astounding.

A final measure of his success was the manner in which, among the educated, the corpus of his work on philosophical problems of theology—a relatively small amount of his total writing—became the heart of much study in America, a process that began even during Edwards's lifetime. This same corpus even claimed the attention of the Europeans. Dugald Stewart, a preeminent Scottish philosopher of the late eighteenth and early nineteenth centuries, wrote that in 'logical acuteness and subtilty' Edwards was the one American metaphysician who did 'not yield to any disputant bred in the universities of Europe'. The post-Kantian German philosopher, J. G. Fichte, referring to the same material, spoke of Edwards as 'this lonely North American thinker'.

When Edwards returned to the philosophical questions of religion after his long period as an active minister, he revised his early speculations. His orientation was not just Locke's theory of knowledge but the legitimation of religious experience. Instead of writing philosophy of interest to Christians, he wrote Calvinist theology.

The Religious Affections

Edwards's sustained attempt to explore the drama of the spirit matured in his 1746 book, *Religious Affections*. How, he asked, was true religion signified and how could its signs be distinguished from the false? Edwards wanted to know the marks of grace, and how we might mark off the regenerate from those feigning salvation. His argument assumed that grace was revealed not so much in cognitive apprehension or intellectual understanding as in the

affections—in the feelings, emotions, and impulses to action. Edwards ultimately opposed the reification of mental substance: there were not two different things or 'faculties' at work in consciousness. But he did believe that
understanding differed from feeling. A single mind had different capacities,
united in any actual mental activity. Moreover, Edwards did reject the
notion that the mind had more than two capacities. The will, often regarded as a distinct faculty, was not separate from the affections. Willing was
subsumed in the broad class of feelings. Thus Edwards began the *Affections*
by preliminarily distinguishing the head and the heart, the understanding
and the feelings. Although grace always altered the understanding, the cognitive capacities, it was primarily an aspect of the affectional nature.
Gracious affections denoted real Christianity and were typified by the
unselfish feelings of the pure in heart; they were at bottom independent of
learned understanding of Scripture:

It is evident, that religion consists so much in affection, as that without holy affection there is no true religion: and no light in the understanding is good, which
don't produce holy affections in the heart; no habit or principle in the heart is
good, which has no such exercise; and no external fruit is good, which don't proceed from such exercises.

The world was from moment to moment God's ideas, but in appraising
human knowledge, Edwards started with the view that sensation and
reflection conveyed knowledge. Knowledge of the physical world, Locke
held, came through ideas of sensation produced by the five senses; sight
and taste were the most important in Edwards's examples. Knowledge of
the mental world came through ideas of reflection, those gained from the
mind's active power to think about—or reflect on, be conscious of—the
mind and its activities.

Sensation and reflection, for Locke, gave the mind the 'simple' ideas, the
unanalysable experience such as the sensation of color or the feeling of
thinking, basic to all knowledge. Moreover, Locke argued that reflection
resulted in the actual existence in the mind of the idea reflected on. To
entertain an idea meant that its truth was seriously considered; to recall a
painful event meant that it was re-experienced; or to think about the feeling for a loved one entailed actually having the feeling of love, of loving the
person. Ideas of sensation merely 'copied' external objects; ideas of reflection 'duplicated' their originals.

In examining Locke, Edwards here revised the doctrines of sensation
and reflection implicit in his early writing. Against Locke Edwards argued
that *both* sensation and reflection entailed the experience in the mind. He
carried forward his earlier notion that minds and the physical world were

different organizations of the same material. Consequently, he contended in the 1740s that sensory knowledge, as well as reflective knowledge, was direct. Sensory ideas resulted in the actual sensation in the mind. In experiencing a brown chair, individuals directly appropriated the chair; in tasting honey, they immediately experienced a sweet substance. Just as an idea of reflection existed in the mind, the sensed idea existed. As an idealist, Edwards believed that the external world was an idea in the mind of God and mental in character. To know this world in sensation, human minds in part grasped what was said to be external to them, just as they made actual to themselves any reflection they comprehended. For Edwards, genuine knowledge in sensation or reflection—he called it 'apprehensive' knowledge—directly confronted mind and nature; and he isolated that knowledge in which apprehension clearly resulted in behavior and called it 'the sense of the heart': the taste of honey attracting the palate; the desire to sit in the brown chair motivating an action; the pain or misery causing aversion; the love leading to the object of love.

In natural man the sense of the heart was selfish; it was directed to goods gratifying the self disproportionately to its place in the scheme of things. When God gave grace, he changed this sense; it acquired an appreciation of the self's rightful (and consequently insignificant) role in the world. The heart then valued the glory, beauty, and love of God. But this altered sense could not be derived from man's natural faculties; it was above nature, a supernatural gift.

Edwards gave varying accounts of how God gave grace. When a person received grace, said Edwards, God instilled a new principle that changed the sense of the heart. The transformed sense enabled a person to have 'a new simple idea', a novel apprehension. Natural man could never have such an experience, so Edwards allowed that the idea was supernatural. Accordingly, to explain gracious experience was like explaining color to the blind. Ideas achieved through grace, however, were empirical; the regenerate experienced them. The saved apprehended the divine beauty, their rightful place in God's glory; they had a new relish for God:

If grace be . . . an entirely new kind of principle; then the exercises of it are also entirely a new kind of exercises . . . which the soul knew nothing of before, and which no improvement, composition, or management of what it was before conscious of or sensible of, could produce . . . then it follows that the mind has an entirely new kind of perception or sensation; and here is, as it were, a new spiritual sense that the mind has . . .

I say, a sense of heart; for it is not speculation merely that is concerned in this kind of understanding: nor can there be a clear distinction made between the two faculties of understanding and will, as acting distinctly and separately in this matter. When the mind is sensible of the sweet beauty and amiableness of a thing that implies a sensibleness of sweetness and delight in the presence of the idea of it.

In a fashion, sinners could understand that the new simple idea was of a certain sort. Sinners could know that it derived from a peculiar principle. Such 'notional' knowledge differed from the apprehensive knowledge of those who received grace. The difference was *like* that between knowing that honey was sweet and actually experiencing honey's sweet taste. Notional knowledge of the truths of religion was possible but insufficient. People must also have supernatural religious experience, a sensible appreciation of religion.

In a limited way salvation was achieved through reading the Bible, for it possessed the necessary knowledge of God's plan, and scriptural meditation was one of the usual means of grace. Such notional knowledge might 'be needful to prepare the mind for a sense of . . . spiritual excellency', and this knowledge could give the sinner 'a preparatory sense' prior to the receipt of grace. But only grace inspired the correct interpretation of the Gospels. To the extent that empiricism was a distinct position in the middle of the eighteenth century, Edwards was an empiricist. But he also believed that the supernatural was conveyed in experience; he was an experimental Calvinist.

The passive elements in Locke's notion of mind concerned Edwards. In Locke's account the simple ideas of sensation and reflection could not be organized into the patterned world of objects and events. Edwards emended Locke to give the mind constructive powers, certain dispositions or habits. These habits were real tendencies to systematize ideas. Simple ideas occurred under certain circumstances, and the mind's activity 'asserted' or 'rearranged' them so that they corresponded to the way they were really arranged and enabled purposive action to occur. Without this activity the simple ideas would be formless. The mind's activity allowed people to function on the basis of their ideas, placing the ideas in a context larger than what was given.

In this interpretation, grace entailed a new habit of mind. Humanity was naturally disposed to misconstrue the self's place in things. The new supernatural habit was the power of repeating or reproducing in human apprehensions the actuality of divine being. Grace did not imply a novel simple idea such as color, but rather a new way of re-cognizing old apprehensive ideas. A disposition of God himself infused the minds of the elect. They had a principle permitting experience of the world as it truly was.

Grasped in a new way, the life and work of Christ provided the redeemed with the apprehensions to discern God's beauty. God became visible in history in Jesus, who concretely represented God's majesty. God related to individuals through human experience, and he became, through Christ, the reason for behavior. For the elect, Christ, the personal wisdom of God, was the telos of history. Without Christ, history was confusion, a jumble of events passing without order or method, 'like the tossings of the waves of the sea'.

In part, Edwards's psychology was dualistic. He distinguished head and heart, understanding and affection, and his religion was voluntaristic. However, he opposed faculty psychology; the affections for him were the understanding externalized to possess what was understood; and the understanding was the affections internalized to know what was felt. More important, Edwards's innovation consisted not so much in his psychology as in the role of this psychology in his revised grasp of sensation and reflection. Edwards's integrated conception of mind stemmed not so much from his ideas on will and intellect as from his assertion that both reflection and sensation resulted in apprehensive ideas, direct experience of the mental and physical world.

For Edwards, Christian practice evidenced gracious affections. But such practice was not simply behavioral change. It was impossible to know certainly if someone had received grace. The sinful heart might always deceive. Sinners might not be just hypocrites but also self-deceivers. None the less, the saved would act differently, and in describing this grace-infused behavior Edwards most clearly collapsed the distinction between reflection and sensation, between inner and outer, affection and understanding, mind and the world.

Why did Christians behave differently? For Edwards, they experienced the world differently; they viewed things more as they really were; they knew more truly their place in the scheme of things. Selfishness distorted their vision less, and consequently they acted in a good and not a depraved way. For Edwards seeing (receiving gracious affections) was believing (having faith). Christian love was a function of apprehension. The Christian experienced the world differently and therefore behaved differently. Or rather because individuals conducted themselves in a Christian manner, it could be inferred that they perceived the world differently. 'To speak of Christian experience and practice, as if they were two things, properly and entirely distinct, is to make a distinction without consideration or reason.' Religious truth, for Edwards, synthesized internal reflection about the world and the external sensation of it. Religious affections were doings inspired by adequate experiential knowledge, just as selfish conduct was contingent on distorted or incomplete experience. Human life mutually defined mind and world. For Christians the world was the peculiar ways they acted. Experience led to (or was) virtuous reflection. The life of the saint was an entelechy defined by conduct that shone in its undefiled intention. This life signified true religion:

Many hypocrites are like comets, that appear for a while with a mighty blaze; but are very unsteady and irregular in their motion . . . and their blaze soon disappears, and they appear but once in a great while. But the true saints are like the fixed stars, which though they rise and set, and are often clouded, yet are steadfast in their orb, and may truly be said to shine with a constant light.

The nature that gave us knowledge of the world in sensation was just visible spirit, or reflection incarnate. Spirit—the mind's power to reflect—was invisible sensation, disembodied nature.

Freedom of the Will

Calvinists believed that humanity was depraved, requiring supernatural grace for salvation. Non-Calvinists parried that individuals were then not responsible, that Calvinists ruled out free will, and that, consequently, God was the author of sin. For the Arminians, the will was not determined. People could be good if they chose; they could respond (or not respond) to grace. Although Calvinists believed that an individual needed grace to repent, they none the less stressed the will's freedom. In Stockbridge Edwards wrote systematic works showing that Locke and Newton might fortify Calvinism. His greatest effort, *Freedom of the Will* (1754), was the most famous philosophical text written in America through the nineteenth century; Edwards starkly contrasted individual responsibility and divine omnipotence, and tried to show them compatible. He argued for determinism but, as the full title of this book indicated, did not mean to controvert freedom. Rather, he contended against 'the *modern* prevailing Notions of that Freedom of Will . . . supposed to be essential' to moral agency, virtue and vice, reward and punishment, praise and blame.

Before Edwards, Calvinists and their opponents had not thought through consistently what we now understand to be entailed by the demands of determinism and freedom. As late as 1690, when his *Essay* was published, Locke juxtaposed a determinist understanding and an incompatible indeterminist notion. *Freedom of the Will* demonstrated in what sense a determinist could believe in responsibility and freedom.

Edwards contrasted freedom—what he called moral determinism—with constraint—natural determinism. People were free if they did as they chose. The bride who said 'I do' at the altar was free—she did as she wished.

The prisoner behind bars was not free if the will to leave the cell could not be effectuated. How individuals got to do what they wanted was immaterial. Edwards argued that the will, like everything else, was enmeshed in a causal nexus. The will had a cause, but that it was caused had nothing to do with appraisals of freedom. The question of freedom arose when we asked if a want or desire could be carried out. If it could, someone was morally determined but free. If it could not, someone was constrained (naturally determined) and not free.

Edwards also held that when free choices were made, people always chose to sin, and he illuminated this position by distinguishing between moral and natural ability. Sinners were naturally able to change their ways. They could, if they wanted to; but they did not want to. They were morally unable to do so and would certainly sin. Edwards's doctrine of natural ability and moral inability at times intimated that moral determinism did not involve causality. For to argue that the sinner always sinned need not entail that something caused the will. All it need entail was the perfect prediction that, given a choice, natural individuals would sin. Might it then not be that the will was self-caused, the efficient cause of its own acts? That it had an inherent power to make a non-sinful moral choice? Was the will morally determined only in the sense that it was certain to sin?

Such a reading of Edwards cannot be justified because it allowed that the sinner might have done otherwise. This power, some theorists maintained, was essential to free will. The bride at the altar had to be able to say 'No' were she given a second chance, be her character and circumstances the same. She had to be able to act contrary to the way she had acted if she were really free. For Edwards this was unacceptable. For his critics it was necessary to genuine freedom: Edwards's distinctions between natural and moral determinism, and natural ability and moral inability, did not provide an authentic understanding of human action.

Edwards claimed that the alternative to his position was incoherent. The requisite notion of his adversaries was a spontaneous self-determination of the will, a liberty of indifference. But, Edwards argued, moral accountability and responsibility meant predictability and behavioral regularity, a knowledge that in certain circumstances someone would act in a certain way. Unreliable conduct was just what was characterized as irresponsible. If the will had a spontaneous power, then no connection existed between cause and effect, between motives, dispositions, wants, or desires and what one did. Such a power did not simply justify irresponsibility but more accurately legitimated an unintelligible belief. A will whose choices were unconnected to motives was no will at all. Action based on such a will would be the hallmark of the irrational.

In an argument discussed repeatedly in the next 125 years, Edwards said that the self-determination of the will was contradictory.

The will itself is not an agent that has a will: the power of choosing, itself, has not a power of choosing. That which has the power of volition or choice is the man or the soul, and not the power of volition itself. . . . To be free is the property of an agent, who is possessed of powers and faculties, as much as to be cunning, valiant, bountiful, or zealous. But these qualities are the properties of men or persons; and not the property of properties.

If the will were self-determined, an act of the will prior to the act in question determined that act. But the same analysis might be made of the prior act. Then, urged Edwards, the analyst must at last reach a previous cause that was not an act of will, but a cause from which the entire sequence followed. In that case the will was not self-determined. Alternatively, it must be concluded that every act, even the first, was the effect of a prior act. That conclusion, wrote Edwards, was contradictory. Suppose a traveler to an exotic land reported that he

had seen an animal which he calls by a certain name, that begat and brought forth itself, and yet had a sire and a dam distinct from itself . . . that his master, who led him and governed him at his pleasure, was always governed by him and driven by him as he pleased; that when he moved, he always took a step before the first step; that he went with his head first, and yet always went tail foremost; and this, though he had neither head nor tail . . . it would be no impudence at all, to tell such a traveler, though a learned man, that he himself had no notion or idea of such an animal as he gave an account of.

Freedom was having a will. Having a will meant possessing overriding habits, inclinations, desires, motives, and so on. God could not create free beings unless he created them in such a way that their actions would be morally determined. Human beings, through this moral determination, were certain to sin.

Edwards's position should be construed in light of his idealism. The will for Edwards was conventionally internal and consisted generically of volitions—intents, wants, desires, and feelings. In this sense, the will was coextensive with apprehensive ideas as they connected to activity in the world, Edwards's sense of the heart. His proposition, 'The will is as the greatest apparent good is' was first of all a descriptive and not a causal account. The will was not so much a faculty of the self as a way of depicting the structure of human volitions. Certain sorts would follow certain other sorts, and in standard cases certain events in the physical world would follow certain sorts. Neither the apparent good nor anything else besides the will's own pleasure determined it; the will was neither autonomous nor determined by something external. Rather the will corresponded to its object, the apparent good. Each volition was an apprehension, the world as it appeared in our affectional contact with it at a given moment. The will was that part of the world with which we immediately engaged. For natural humanity it was a coherent body of apprehensions that led to selfish behavior, or rather selfish behavior incarnated in apprehensions.

The will synthesized the sensation and reflection revealed in action. Volition was the mind's fiat, a disposition to act founded on the way the world appeared. But the 'letting it happen', for Edwards, occurred in a sphere beyond our immediate control, conventionally called the external world. He distinguished between volition and external voluntary action, between fiat and behavior.

For Edwards, will and act were mysteriously linked. Human wills never efficiently caused external events. Only God efficiently caused them. But for his own purposes God, in certain circumstances, appropriately linked the (internal) volitions with the (external) behavior that satisfied them. Freedom consisted in the effectuation of the will—the occurrence of the appropriate events in the external world. The prisoner was not free because the opening of the door of the cell did not follow the desire to open it. The bride at the altar was free because her saying 'I do' followed her desire to say 'I do'. But in each case God connected the willing and what followed. The bride was ultimately no more the efficient cause of her saying 'I do' than the lock on the cell was the efficient cause of its not opening.

For this reason, Edwards wrote that distinguishing natural and moral determinism depended not 'so much in the nature of the connection, as in the two terms connected'. If one billiard ball hit a second, the second moved away from the first. God established a regular order that licensed the inference that the first caused the movement of the second. But the only efficient cause was God's will in action, causing the second to move after it contacted the first. Causation in the natural world (from thing to thing) and in the moral (from volition to action) was the same. In each case no efficient causal connection existed. Events in the natural world (in certain cases) occasioned other events. And (in certain cases) volitions occasioned actions.

Human beings were naturally able not to sin. If their wills were disposed to do unselfish acts, such acts would follow—just as selfish acts followed from selfish volitions and just as some sorts of occurrences in the natural world followed from other sorts. But human beings were morally unable to behave unselfishly. They would certainly sin. Given the motives, it could be accurately predicated that selfish acts would follow. In this sense Edwards's moral determinism was, indeed, not causal. For a sinful will did not (efficiently) cause sinful events. Moral determinism entailed only the perfect prediction that sinful events would follow from a selfish will. But from this doctrine of moral inability it could not be inferred that the will was self-determined, an efficient cause; or that people could act contrary to the way they acted.

What of the connection among volitions themselves? The will for Edwards was just a series of volitions, of perceptual impulses, and of motives to action (feelings, wants, desires). Each of these, he held, linked to the one following it. One determined the next, a given motive determined by its predecessor. But determination was again not efficient causation. The train of volitions was connected only in the way events in the natural world were connected. Given the predecessor volition, the successor could be certainly predicted. Given an occurrence of a certain type, God willed that an occurrence of another type would follow. The motive dominant in the will at a certain time was such that God efficaciously caused its succeeding volition. God produced a given volition on the occasion of a preceding volition. There was certainty in the serial appearance of the members of this chain of volitions, but no one of them ever (efficiently) caused any of the others. Edwards's analysis combined the efficient causality of the deity and what he called philosophical necessity—the certainty of the connection between volition and volition, or volition and act. The realm of human freedom lay in the 'occasional' nature of this kind of necessity: specifically with the moral determinism that connected volitions and volitions, and volitions and acts; and the natural ability that postulated action if motive were present. In effect, Edwards preserved freedom by maintaining two distinct spheres—that of the infinite (with God's efficient causality) and of the finite (with occasional causality). This dualism did not obscure the fact that only God was causally efficacious, nor did it falsify the fact that humans had free will any more than the truth that fire burned.

Edwards in American Thought

Despite his position in Stockbridge, Edwards was a well-known figure and his abilities highly regarded, and in 1757 he accepted the presidency of the College of New Jersey (Princeton). The College was then a tiny school oriented to the evangelical ministry, but the call nevertheless indicated Edwards's justified eminence among the religious leadership in the northern and middle colonies. Shortly after he took up his new position, he was inoculated against smallpox, testimony to his confidence in medical science. But the disease attendant on the inoculation took an erratic course, and he died in March 1758 at the age of 54.

By that time Christian thinkers in America and Scotland were already appropriating the ideas of the *Religious Affections* and *Freedom of the Will*, among other writings, to defend Calvinist theology. Followers were explicating, promulgating, and defending his ideas. His views of human depravity and freedom, and their relation to experimental revivalism, were the core of learned debate in the colonies. Edwards bequeathed the central question to succeeding generations of American thinkers: how is the lone believer, at the mercy of a cosmos that was spiritually enigmatic, to assert a moral freedom?

At the same time that Edwards's theorizing extended the writ of robust Christian philosophy, it hardly acclimatized the erudite in America to an intellectual milieu that, in Europe, was rapidly moving away from the premisses of the Bible. In clinging to Calvinism as Edwards had fortified it, the ministers, divines, and philosophers who followed an Edwardsean path were proceeding away from the armies of modern intellectual life. When intellectual life in the nineteenth century moved into realms that even Edwards did not anticipate, his American epigoni would be left almost helpless.

2   Philosophy and Politics

When the Puritans arrived in America in the early seventeenth century, they brought not only their strong theological orientation but also tenacious communal impulses, utopian hopes, a sense of being chosen, and a belief in social and religious exclusivity and uniformity. Hostile to the market world of the seventeenth and eighteenth centuries, their modest economic interests fashioned a distinctive society. In England, similar religious reformists compromised with governing tendencies in an increasingly heterogeneous and tolerant culture. In America, the Puritans pursued their ideals with fewer constraints. They tried to create a social order far from the dominant one that they had left behind or, indeed, even from what they had experienced and lost. The culture they made was militantly antimodern, moving in the opposite direction from what they had abandoned in old England. In the absence of competing pressures and with new authority in America, New England uniquely resisted forces shaping the other colonial experiments in British North America.

The clergy's active attempts to shape public life evidenced this impulse. The chief Puritan stronghold, the Massachusetts Bay Company, was a virtual theocracy, and as a leading historian of colonial America has argued, governance of the colony was 'the puritan dilemma'. The problem was to do good in a world that had irrevocably gone wrong. The leaders strove for just rule and, even though religious commitment took priority over political life, they accepted political imperfection as necessary. In the sense that they embraced the burdens of real politics, the early Puritans were thus worldly and to that extent accommodating. By the early eighteenth century, however, the liberalism that had emerged in Boston signaled the end of a hegemonic religious polity, and the later triumph of Edwards's ideas in theological circles during and after the Great Awakening distanced devoted Calvinist thinkers from the political.

Edwards's views accentuated the significance of the individual's connection to the deity and de-emphasized the role of the Christian heritage. Edwards highlighted abstract thought, and diminished the power of those ministers who had been dominant before the Great Awakening and who had acknowledged the problem of living in a world that could not be reformed. Edwards and his followers were not unengaged with their polities, and did thoughtfully reflect on the cultural world around them. But they were suspicious of social amelioration. Edwardseans railed against human wickedness yet were more concerned with its divine meaning, which could best be understood by cloistered study than by political involvement. Politics was to be understood not through empirical study, but through a preconceived interpretation of the providential meaning of the Bible. Consideration of the public sphere was grounded in the explication of personal spirituality. There was, in the inheritance of this theological–philosophical position, an inclination to comment on the world from the perspective of the eternal, and to comment on it in a way that stressed the solitary person, surely corrupted by nature but unencumbered by tradition.

The high tide of Edwards's influence in New England was coterminous with the growing movement in all the colonies to separate from the mother country. From the 1750s to 1800 politics occupied the public life of British North America, and scholars have long puzzled over the fact that the colonial leadership minimized overt religious concerns, and that even in New England the political class was bereft of explicit reformed sentiment despite the undisputed importance of the Calvinist ministry there and the impact of Edwards. The connection between New England theology and colonial politics in this era may not defy explanation, but historians consider the connection as a problem to be elucidated, the subject of much complex interpretative debate. The central point of this chapter is that whatever the substantive connection, the sensibility of the theologians of Edwards's lineage differed fundamentally from that of the politicians.

The Puritan debates that came to fruition in the work of Edwards were the one sustained intellectual conversation produced in the colonies in the seventeenth and eighteenth centuries, but America hardly had a common culture. The middle and southern colonies shared with New England a Christian heritage with a focus on the issues of reformed Protestantism but lacked entirely the intense ministerial interest in theological conundrums. During the Revolutionary and Constitutional periods statesmen such as George Washington who guided the course of the new nation would often blandly assent to conventional Protestant verities for public consumption. But only one signer of the Declaration of Independence—the Presbyterian educator John Witherspoon from New Jersey—was a clergyman. In New England (and indeed the other colonies) leaders such as John Adams occasionally expressed a low estimate of human nature and a cautious attitude toward progress that can persuasively be attributed to the Calvinist cultural context, but even in Massachusetts and its neighboring colonies the high theology that was so overwhelming in the life of the religious leadership was almost absent in the statesmen. The fact is that the scholar has to look for explicit theological, and sometimes even religious, ideas in the work of the Founding Fathers and their political opponents, and has to look for distinctive Calvinist expressions of support for, or opposition to, the new politics.

American Republicanism

Instead, the public men of the era embraced the ideas of the European Enlightenment. They dismissed the inherited doctrines of Calvinism, and stressed, albeit prudently, the possibility of incremental reform in human life that wise politics could achieve. The American leaders were rationalists in their view that anyone with the perseverance to examine the world carefully and to reflect on this experience could arrive at fundamental truths; these truths could not be honestly gainsaid. But 'reason' for them was not defined as intuition or a priori deliberation but as calculating practicality about the present and historical exploration of the past with a view to using the results of the exploration in the present. The titles of some of the central writings of the political theorist Thomas Paine—*Common Sense* and *The Age of Reason*—suggest the place of the basic postulates held by him and his peers in what has been termed the era of the American Enlightenment.

Some of these colonial statesmen explicitly rejected Protestant Christianity because it offended this idea of reason. The virgin birth, the miracles of Jesus, the tale of redemption, the notion of a Trinity, and the resurrection of Christ were dismissed as unworthy of critical inspection. The many inconsistencies in the Bible itself underscored these shortcomings for the Founders. Instead, the perusal of the harmonies of the natural world led them to conclude that a benevolent and orderly deity had created the cosmos. Indeed, this deity was often said to have a clockmaker's mind. There had to be a first cause of nature, and it was only reasonable to assume that this cause—God—reflected the same lawlike principles that were inherent in the organization of the world. This Deism did not deny a veneration for the author of all things, and sometimes Enlightenment figures expressed a providential Deism—a belief in a God whose overarching justice was shown through experience. But it was just as frequently argued that after establishing a benign world, the creator did not much intercede in human affairs. The religion of the Enlightenment had little time for a God who directly intervened in our lives and diminished the otherworldly concerns of Christianity. Deism also heightened moral impulses directed to our relations with our fellows and even had an optimistic strain that emphasized positive human growth. Finally, the American Deists understated their claims for public consumption. The most radical leader among the Deists, Paine, was idiosyncratic in loudly espousing anti-Christian views. Some of these leaders—Benjamin Franklin and Thomas Jefferson, for example—might deny the truth of Reformed Protestantism, yet easily acknowledge it as a desirable form of social control. Other leaders who shared Paine's disbelief in Christianity and his vision of a kindly yet distant God could even construe his sometimes bitter denunciation of mainstream religious sensibilities as culturally dangerous.

The application of 'reason' had brought about advances in the natural world. Men such as Franklin, Jefferson, and Paine had absorbed popular expressions of the physics of Isaac Newton, which indeed underlay Deism and the idea of a clocklike universe. Perhaps genius had to uncover the laws of nature, but by the end of the eighteenth century they were open to the understanding of all. Patient investigation of the world revealed the simple principles on which it operated and enabled individuals to make further discoveries, or put these principles to work for human benefit. In America such ideas were widely associated with Franklin's discovery of electricity. Similar advances might occur in the world of human endeavor and led to a novel grasp of political life.

The Founding Fathers developed the view that it was reasonable—though also congenial—to assume that the creator made people—or at least most white men—equal. By nature individuals had a constellation of rights intrinsic to their character as persons. Such natural rights were fundamental in any society in which human beings existed; their maker endowed them with such rights. Differences in station were expected and permitted, but only variations in talent, industry, and frugality justified such differences. In any event men should, in the order of things, be provided with an equal voice with other men in determining how society should be governed. Only a government based on the voices of equals could protect the rights or liberties with which human beings were born. The Founders, however, were by no means levelers or radical democrats and defined 'the people' in a limited sense—women, slaves, and Indians hardly counted; and the role of the people in governing was restricted. At the same time, the American statesmen were sure that political authority ultimately lay with the people, though they feared this truth. This restrained but persistent faith in the people was the cornerstone of emerging political beliefs in America.

The conclusions drawn from such beliefs were sustained not only by practical experience of the colonial political world and Enlightenment rationality, but also by historical knowledge. The Founders were educated readers of the classic political commentaries of the Greeks and Romans, and knowledgeable of the republican experiments of the city states of early modern Europe. Codified historical experience was as important to them as what they were learning in leading the colonies in the mid-eighteenth century. In drawing from the well of history, the Founders were often reinforced in their apprehension of the masses and occasionally strengthened in their misgivings about the possibility of progress. Yet history also taught them that a republican government—that in which elected rulers represented the people—could best secure the virtue of a culture. A society was better off trusting the people than any smaller, and thus more selfish group, such as a king; aristocrats; the commercially interested; or politically hungry cliques concerned with power.

Society and government must be distinguished. Society was the natural outcome of the human condition—the relationships that derived from collections of human beings living together, raising their young, and cooperating in common endeavor. In contrast to these joint, implicit responsibilities, government was a negative instrument only necessary to the extent that matters went awry; its powers were minimized and, in the natural course of things, largely unnecessary. The American élite was basically satisfied that England had served the interests of the people through the mid-eighteenth century and preserved the liberties of the colonies. The British monarchy might sit uncomfortably with the nascent exposition of New World political ideas, but in practice the system worked.

What had gone wrong in America to impel her leaders to consider breaking their ties to the British Empire by the 1770s? Despite their self-conscious empirical rationalism, colonial thinkers never approached either the natural or the social world with an innocent eye. Just as deistic understanding was a presupposition of their thinking, so too did they believe that the social nature of human beings had been rendered more complex by a more explicit contract between ruled and rulers that eventuated in government. In ideal circumstances, the resulting polity reflected the existence of the rights that God had engendered in human individuals.

Presuppositions also shaped their grasp of their specific circumstances. The Founders embraced the views of some dissenters in England earlier in the eighteenth century. These Commonwealthmen or radical Whigs had developed a pervasive and hostile critique of an English society that eighteenth-century fiscal innovations had debilitated. The growth of the monetary power of the monarchy destroyed the ideal of balanced government between king, Lords, and Commons and led to a situation where the crown bought and sold offices, expanded its power, and ground down the citizenry. The Commonwealthmen looked back to a time of imagined civic virtue and worked for the restoration of what they took to be a natural scheme of governance, overturned by evil and degenerate men.

This nightmarish vision was a constant minority view in English politics, yet the ideas of these Whigs were more widely accepted in political circles in the New World, although the Americans initially lacked the visceral distaste for English politics that the Commonwealthmen regularly expressed. None the less, colonials came increasingly to view England as a nation of rapidly deteriorating virtue and liberty. This belief was corroborated at the conclusion of the Seven Years War. The French and Indian War, as it was known in America, effectively ousted the French from the New World in 1763 and lent new authority to the British Empire. King George III determined that the colonies should bear part of the cost of this triumphal venture. In the next ten years the Mother Country appeared to verify American fears about the corruption of English society by putting into effect a series of legislative acts pertaining to the colonies. Victorious in England, the evil opponents of the Commonwealthmen had now shifted their focus, it seemed, to America, where they wished to place a yoke of tyranny over the colonists.

The Commonwealthmen, however, had only wanted to restore England to the rightful balance between king and aristocracy. In the New World the Whig analysis went deeper and developed into a distinctive American political position. The leadership in the colonies now forcefully set forward ideas about how the British system in North America must be reshaped, how it must be made to conform to their enlarged notion of a republican polity. In addition to a greater role for the people, the Founders emphasized liberty of individual conscience, religious toleration, resistance to tyrants, and reform of the legislature. More important, the Americans denounced the hereditary English political institutions. What was the basis *in reason* for the rule of a single unelected person? And how could logic legitimate the privilege, wealth, and political power accorded to an aristocracy of *birth*? The philosophy of natural rights taught that men were born equal, and, so, men such as the Founding Fathers could now question the foundation of English social order.

In place of this order, the colonials proposed a variety of different schemes. The precise form they were to devise for themselves was a matter that experience and argument would decide in the period from 1774 to 1812. The common denominator was 'American republicanism'. It was at least agreed that power had somehow effectively to be lodged with 'the people', no matter how restrictedly they were defined. The people would choose their governors, with any necessary adjustments. The masses might elect the leaders who would represent them; in extreme cases democracy—an even more direct rule of the people—was advocated. To this concern for popular representation was added a set of views about the decadent state of England and the causes of its decline. Americans were persuaded that any kind of hereditary privilege was evil, and that it was essential to fragment interest groups or to subordinate them to the public good.

By the mid-1770s republicanism was a powerful force in America. Many believed that English rule had to be overthrown and the independence of the New World asserted, and that reasons had to be given for the decision. These republican themes were best exemplified in the document that formally brought war to the colonies, the 1776 Declaration of Independence, primarily composed by Jefferson.

The ideas of the Founders about the political economy of the new United States were, however, less transparent than this. Historians have found a conflict in American republicanism between the values of the person and the group, individual freedom and the good of larger human entities. But the Founders none the less assumed that the preservation of liberties went hand-in-hand with the interests of the commonweal, and their doctrine held not only a concern for individual conscience but also for a national community. After the British surrender in 1783 sentiment regarding the public interest established a consensus among many republicans—the Federalists—who feared the growth of individual liberty. They successfully argued that the new Constitution of 1787 would protect national interests from the private excesses of the earlier Revolutionary period. The mission of the stronger state that the Federalists envisaged reflected the need for an established order and the worries of theorists such as James Madison and Alexander Hamilton concerning Jefferson's and Paine's egalitarian ideas, which were more pronounced during the Revolutionary War itself.

Rather than looking at how to divide the 'liberal' or individualistic from the 'communitarian' or nationalist strands among the Founders, we can see how accords evolved in the Constitutional period from a common philosophy of natural rights: the creator had made a world that respected individuals within the context of human societies. Natural rights theorists brought together opposing beliefs of theoretically *laissez-faire* liberals and antagonists dedicated to a collectively virtuous polity. The Founders were a shifting coalition of political leaders testing their thinking by governing the new nation as adherents of natural rights views; they put forward ideas of political economy that brought together liberal and communitarian perspectives.

Political Theory and Philosophy

The second half of the eighteenth century was a watershed in the career of philosophy in America. Argumentation about the political world had not been central to theology in the seventeenth and early eighteenth centuries, but a ministry committed to maintaining its social importance had not excluded such thought. Edwards led many divines to a heightened emphasis on doctrinal purity in terms of which politics and society had to be examined, and did so at just the time that a group of leaders unconcerned with Protestant doctrine was assuming a position of power. *This* group was politically active and inclined to write about politics. Moreover, it believed that political thought was rooted in the actual give and take of the political world and close observation of it: past and present experience of politics was central, as was the shrewd assessment that defined what was rational. Political theory was not a product of contemplation, nor of matching the rules of the polity to biblical truth, nor of deducing what ought to be done in the polis from a religiously based ethics; political theory rather arose from engaging in politics, from an understanding of political behavior. During this time Paine wrote *Common Sense* (1776); Jefferson, *Notes on the State of Virginia* (1781); Hamilton, Madison, and John Jay *The Federalist Papers* (1787); and John Adams *A Defense of the Constitutions of the Government of the United States of America* (1787–8), to name only the most famous.

As the English statesman William Pitt, who was a defender of the American revolutionaries, said of them in the 1770s: 'for solidity of reasoning, force of sagacity and wisdom of conclusion, under such a complication of difficult circumstances, no nation or body of men can stand in preference to the General Congress assembled at Philadelphia'. When the successor to that congress met in 1787 to frame the Constitution, an aged Benjamin Franklin (uncharacteristically) asked it to open each session with prayers. The delegates ignored his motion. As Franklin wrote, 'The Convention, except three or four persons, thought Prayers unnecessary.'

In the nineteenth century the example of the Founders informed not only the writing of politician-thinkers such as Daniel Webster and Henry Clay but more important works such as John C. Calhoun's *Disquisition on Government* (1849) and Abraham Lincoln's briefer but equally profound pronouncements on power and the state in the 1850s and 1860s. Absorbed by the political institutions of the United States, this tradition of thought has not been without critics. It often lacked an appreciation of revolutionary human interaction, easily forgetting its own origins and suggesting the moderate dimension of these origins. Some commentators have castigated the tradition as inherently conservative, constrained by the parameters of the political culture in which it was immersed and out of which it came. Although the tradition may not have been without merit, such commentators said, it had little perspective on itself and denigrated what was not of 'the real world'.

By the end of the nineteenth century and certainly by the twentieth, the nature of political leadership in America had changed, and politicians no longer contributed to political theory, although Woodrow Wilson (president from 1913 to 1921) still published on these topics. But the concern for political practice remained at the core of this genre, what I will call political or social theory. In the twentieth century, for example, Thorstein Veblen (a social scientist); Herbert Croly, Walter Lippmann, and Randolph Bourne (journalists); Walter Rauschenbusch (a social gospel minister); Vance Packard (a popular intellectual); C. Wright Mills (a sociologist); and Christopher Lasch (a historian) all conceived of the political (and social) as discrete areas of experience, and were interested witnesses to and critics of those experiences. Thus, political theory continued to rely on participation in *or* close observation of political life that accepted it as its own autonomous realm of human activity; contributors were generally *not* people who were abstract thinkers.

The Calvinist theology of Edwards surely had a social locus and was not without political overtones, but ratiocination in the library was primary. The ideas of the Founding Fathers paid heed to logic and were not unconnected to religious speculation, but political experience and the history of this experience were their guiding lights. Indeed, it was common at the end of the eighteenth century—though not universal—to view the ministry as uniquely unqualified for politics. As John Adams mused, no 'good effects' came from mixing 'the sacred character with that of the Statesman'. 'The clergy are universally too little acquainted with the World, and the Modes of Business, to engage in civil affairs with any Advantage.' Learned religious men had 'conversed with Books so much more than Men, as to be too much loaded with Vanity, to be good Politicians'.

In this context the people who followed Edwards and who have been designated 'philosophers' by historians of philosophy and scholars of American intellectual life have played a peculiar role. Edwards most of all had made the core intellectual problems ones of meditation. From such reflection immediately flowed religious and moral commitments, but they were frequently tangential to communal concern and not based in a connectedness to political life. By the nineteenth and twentieth centuries, tradition, training, and institutionalization had made philosophic understanding a different order of knowing from that pursued by the students of political theory.

Theologians and then philosophers occasionally tried their hands at politics, but their political philosophy tended to be almost different in kind from the genre defined from Paine onwards. Following what was implicit in Edwards's deliberations, philosophers developed a hierarchical notion of their field of expertise in which the priority became the exertion of a certain form of high mental energy to solve the most general problems of how one knew the world. Once these problems were answered, one might use the results at once to answer questions about moral and religious questions; philosophers believed issues social and political in character were further down on a list of 'applied' topics. The social and political were usually of secondary or even tertiary interest; they had little independent status; and substantive conclusions about political life, they believed, could be read off from the conclusions of what became the chief philosophic discipline—the theory of knowledge or epistemology.

Political philosophy in the United States existed but was not a central aspect of the philosophic enterprise. None the less, so long as the carriers of the enterprise remained religious, their deracinated ideas about the bases of civic order found an audience in a culture predisposed to welcome views on civics touched by Protestant Christianity. We find this development in the terrified response of Calvinist divines to Jefferson's ascension to the presidency in 1801; in the ahistoric and moralistic vision of American politics that can be seen in the Transcendentalists; in the reflections on government evident in the Scottish college philosophers; and in the individualist and religiously colored social theorizing common to pragmatists such as William James. When philosophers rejected religion in the twentieth century, they continued to locate the social and political in abstractions but found less of an audience in a culture still attuned to religion. Even in the political evaluations of those philosophers later guided by German organicism—the St Louis Hegelians, Josiah Royce, John Dewey, Herbert Marcuse, and Richard Rorty—the priorities of speculative reason were substantial, although this group had claims to be considered, in my usage, political theorists and not political philosophers.

Franklin, Edwards, and Philosophy

Back in the eighteenth century, Benjamin Franklin's foray into what he called 'metaphysics' cast an important light on the problems of this chapter. Franklin was a close student of Locke's *Essay*, and in 1724, in London, he assisted in the printing of William Wollaston's *Religion of Nature*. Wollaston was one of the liberal Christians of the time who, thirty years later, were subject to the withering critique of Edwards's *Freedom of the Will*. In 1725 the

19-year-old Franklin attacked Wollaston in a brief *Dissertation on Liberty and Necessity, Pleasure and Pain*.

In the first part of the *Dissertation* Franklin argued for the existence of an all-powerful, all-good, and all-wise creator of the universe. Franklin went on to claim that in this universe all events, including human actions, must be causally analysed. He denied the will's freedom if that meant the liberty of indifference. Human actions had only the same sort of freedom as did that of a heavy body that fell to the ground: both were free if they behaved according to their nature, and if there was no 'intervening event or obstacle' to hinder the normal causal sequence itself determined by past events. Human beings were free if an external event did not constrain them when they acted, although all their behavior was caused. Since God was all-good, it also followed that humans could not really do evil, or suffer. This did not mean in common-sense terms that pain and suffering did not exist, but rather that they 'are not in Reality Evils, Ills, or Defects in the order of the Universe'. Indeed, Franklin had an ingenious bit of reasoning to back up this claim. Human beings were defective in gauging the consequences of alternative courses of action. Had they the liberty of indifference, they might be expected to stumble around in their decision-making, corrupting the scheme of the divine ordainer, with perhaps only one in ten thousand decisions being the best one to make. But because we knew that the world was perfect, it was more likely that God had causally necessitated everything that took place, that the propensity for individuals to get things wrong was an illusion.

In the second part of his *Dissertation*, Franklin analysed human motivation solely in terms of the organism's ability to avoid pain and achieve pleasure. Every desire, he wrote, was fulfilled for every pain did end, if only at death. Thus, the amount of pleasure human beings experienced always equaled the amount of pain they endured, so that in respect to the net balance, all individuals were equal. Franklin's conclusion in this half of the *Dissertation* was a consequence of his view that God had created a perfect universe, but Franklin discerned its perfection in this life; he rejected the need for an afterlife that was justified because God, in a future life, had to adjust the balance of pleasure or pain that was unjustly distributed in this world. On Franklin's account, there was no 'Occasion for a future Adjustment'. The soul was 'incapable of Destruction itself', but after death 'necessarily cease[d] to think or act'. We could not assume it retained consciousness or a sense of personal identity after death.

The *Dissertation* was remarkable not because of the similarity it bore in the structure of its argumentation to Edwards's *Freedom of the Will*; nor because Franklin had adumbrated in such short compass claims about the will and its relation to providence that were taken up in far greater detail by the philosophical theologians who wrote in the style of Edwards in the second half of the eighteenth century and through much of the nineteenth. Rather, it is worth calling to mind that very soon after its publication Franklin not only repudiated his substantive conclusions but then repudiated the entire project of philosophic exposition.

In the late 1720s and early 1730s Franklin continued to ponder these issues of religion and morality, and wrote even briefer pieces rejecting the arguments of the *Dissertation* and reversing his position. In his famous *Autobiography* (1754) he recalled that his doctrines did not give him much solace about the treatment he had received from the many people who he felt had mistreated him during his growing-up years. '[T]his doctrine [of determinism] tho' it might be true, was not very useful.' As many commentators have pointed out, Franklin may have written that virtue and vice were 'empty distinctions', but without them he early concluded that social intercourse was impossible, and that conclusion was sufficient for Franklin to abandon his burgeoning career as a philosopher. 'My London Pamphlet', wrote Franklin, 'appear'd not so clever a Performance as I once thought it; and I doubted whether some Error had not insinuated itself unperceiv'd into my Argument, so as to infect all that follow'd, as is common in metaphysical Reasonings.' Even later, in 1779, he wrote that 'the Great Uncertainty I found in Metaphysical Reasonings disgusted me, and I quitted that kind of Reading & Study for others more satisfactory'. He told one correspondent, 'Mr. J. H.', who asked for comment on a deistical tract similar to what Franklin had written earlier, to burn the effort.

When considering questions of human pleasure and pain, the mature Franklin looked to the culture in which he was embedded as a human person. Philosophical discourse became subordinate to social practice as a way of understanding the human predicament. He also went on to a career in politics, although his actual writing on political theory was even more fragmented than his earlier efforts in metaphysics. But Franklin's sense of the distinction between the two styles of thinking about the world marked an important disjunction in the history of philosophy in America.

3   *Theological Dispute, 1750–1858*

The New England Theology

When Jonathan Edwards died, he left a corpus of writing that attracted the labors of gifted thinkers for the next century and a quarter. The committed interpretation of this writing has been called the New England Theology. Its adherents, usually proponents of denominational Protestantism in New England and the Middle Atlantic States, adapted Edwards's teachings to a changing society and intellectual climate, and also resolved problems they believed he had handled inadequately. Although these men, like Edwards, usually expounded ideas already prominent in Western Christianity, a peculiar system emerged, a chapter in the history of theology. In American speculative thought, the New England Theology forms a tradition comparable to later American pragmatism.

The first and most important group of followers had begun refining Edwards's ideas even when he was alive. Opponents called them men of the New Divinity, because, it was claimed, they introduced novel doctrines into Calvinism, more indebted to modern philosophy than to religion. Joseph Bellamy, Samuel Hopkins, Nathaniel Emmons, Jonathan Edwards the Younger, and Timothy Dwight were its leading lights.

The New Divinity was succeeded by the New Haven Theology, focused around the stunning thought of Nathaniel William Taylor and his colleagues at Yale. Later, Henry Boynton Smith and the New School Presbyterianism of Union Seminary in New York picked up Edwardsean themes, and the philosophy of religion formulated at the Andover Seminary in Andover, Massachusetts, from the time of Leonard Woods and Moses Stuart to that of Edwards Amasa Park also reflected Edwards's impact. Although Andover was more conservative than innovative, more tenacious than expansive, the tradition ended only with Park's retirement in 1881.

The New England Theology molded other thinking. The New Divinity influenced liberal religious thought in Boston, which overthrew Calvinism at Harvard in the early 1800s. Many of the creatively religious of the mid-century were indebted to Germany. But these men—James Marsh, Horace

Bushnell, and John Williamson Nevin—owed Taylor an equal debt. Of these other movements, the one considered in this chapter, Princeton Seminary's Old School Presbyterianism, resisted theological New England, but Princeton seminarians defined themselves by what they were not, displaying their connection to the New England Theology in attending to its writings. Moreover, Princeton was not above associating itself with Edwards. His name was so great that, undistorted by his followers, he was often worthy of Princeton approbation, especially because he had briefly been president of the College of New Jersey.

Edwards and the New England Theologians assumed a great divide between God and humanity, and between the realms of nature and grace. Both distinctions were paramount in the persistent argument over human responsibility for sin and God's arbitrary gift of grace. Accountability uneasily comported with omnipotence, especially when grace was so clearly supernatural. The issues of sovereignty, responsibility, grace, and depravity all found their critical locus in the question of the will's freedom, the most important recurring theme in the literature. To render their beliefs consistent the theologians again and again displayed an interest in an idealistic metaphysics that joined the realms of finite and infinite by demonstrating the former to be a limited aspect of the latter. Finally, Edwards's legacy included a revivalistic heritage. The New England Theology was committed to evangelicalism, a living affectional creed, and believed in a synthesis of 'logic and tears'.

The Social Context

The leadership of New England always desired an educated clergy, establishing Harvard College in 1636. During the early eighteenth century Harvard and Yale, and later Princeton, emerged as the leading clerical training schools, preparing students who could step immediately into pastoral roles. Sometimes graduates with intellectual tastes stayed on at their colleges and received additional theological instruction. The Great Awakening shifted attention to an apprenticeship system, and it also kindled interest in systematic theology in provincial cultures more capable of supporting specialization in trades and professions than they had been earlier in the eighteenth century. The interest was most pronounced among prospective divines lured to complicated metaphysics. After attending college, aspiring clergymen regularly resided with theoretically inclined ministers to learn both the intricacies of Calvinism and the practical business of ministering to a congregation. Young men eager to absorb the religious life and to learn the secrets of the Great Awakening wanted to sit at the feet of the great revivalist theologians. Joseph Bellamy and Samuel Hopkins, two of the leaders of the New Divinity movement, had studied with Edwards. After Bellamy's summation of Edwards's Calvinism, *True Religion Delineated*, appeared in 1750, his house became a small theological boarding school. Bellamy was not unique. The New Divinity men were known as trainers of clergymen, and Nathaniel Emmons, the most outstanding, had close to one hundred students. But Calvinists of all opinions attracted devotees. As the collegiate course of study embraced more subjects, the established ministry backed the parsonage seminaries in inculcating the fine points of divine science.

The student mastered a relatively small number of Calvinist tracts, covering standard topics. He wrote papers for his mentor and discussed his writing. As an apprentice, a young man delivered occasional sermons, participated in the round of clerical activities, and attended conferences and prayer meetings. Ideally, a cleric licensed to preach and called to a church would be equipped to handle his new responsibilities; he would have combined systematic knowledge of the gospels with a grasp of daily duties. The 'Schools of the Prophets' joined speculative divinity and practical piety; the examination of doctrine accompanied the cultivation of a life in service. Knowledge of the Bible and its system of truth enhanced religious experience and so the success of the calling. The religious leadership thus educated a generation of pastors.

The New Divinity men were originally almost all from Yale. Although its administration was frequently suspicious of their efforts, the association with New Divinity made Yale the institutional center of speculative thought in America. Suspicious of urban and more cosmopolitan Harvard, the Yale group also set itself against the less Calvinist orientation and smaller appetite for European philosophy that characterized Cambridge. Yale thinkers would not relinquish their intellectual leadership till the end of the nineteenth century.

The novel theological movement arose in the aftermath of the Awakening, as American Calvinism factionalized. Liberals in Boston and Cambridge drifted away from Calvinism, and their ideas eventually flowered into Unitarianism and generated a major controversy. But the main opposition to the New Divinity came not from the liberals but from the Old Calvinists, who saw themselves as promoting the ancient Puritan covenant theology and, indeed, gave the name of New Divinity to the followers of Edwards. The Old Calvinists were known for their comparative lack of interest in doctrine. They believed that the philosophy of religion could little serve the spiritual life. Less troubled by speculative worries, this group had negotiated the acclimatization of Calvinism to the political order that had characterized the Puritan past in America. These divines underestimated the commitment of systematic theologians to building a community of virtue and castigated what they saw as the New Divinity's elevation of theory over a strong orthodox community. The Old Calvinists did recognize that New Divinity emphasized epistemology as the necessary precedent to a religious ethics, but their own unwillingness to defend their position enabled the New Divinity men victoriously to attack them. By the end of the century Edwards's position—or the position of centrist New Divinity men—became conventional in many circles. The movement achieved its great success in the forefront of the Second Great Awakening, the religious revival that occurred at the beginning of the new century.

Contours of the New Divinity

The Lockian ideas at work in Edwards framed New Divinity, as its advocates continued to import into Calvinism the views of thinkers inclined to idealism. The New Divinity believed that the cosmos symbolized the divine, but the symbol was incompletely decipherable. The natural world was not a sure transcript of what existed, although the moral and religious world of man exhibited itself through the natural. The created world was God's will in action. But finite comprehension could only dimly grasp God. His perspective and the human one differed in kind. The New Divinity thus simultaneously preserved God's sovereignty and human responsibility. Hopkins wrote that all activity embodied 'two different agents, and two very different kinds of agency, as distinct and different from each other as if there were no connection between them, and the one did not imply the other'. Emmons urged that people were both dependent and free. These facts were plain, but the 'manner of their existence or production' was 'mysterious'. Reason told us conclusively of our dependence, common sense equally conclusively of our freedom.

As in Edwards, two sorts of causal analysis existed. God's will was the sole efficacious cause. Causes in the finite world, both natural and moral, only occasioned their effects. Particular sorts of effects were associated with particular sorts of preceding events. Although this coincidence was certain, it was not necessary. The moral or metaphysical certainty involved was a function of knowing that an effect of one type would follow a cause of another type. Efficient causality never lay in events themselves. In Emmons, especially, these principles meant that a central Calvinist teaching was perhaps relinquished. Critics claimed he had no doctrine of the supernatural. For example, God gave special grace—something extraordinary happened. But the ordinary and extraordinary each occurred because

God's will constantly preserved the entire system. In Emmons, natural and supernatural events were both caused by God's moment-by-moment conservative power.

The New Divinity men stressed that humanity was not coequal in reality with God and equated God not merely with the moral history of the cosmos but with the cosmos itself. For this reason their opponents accused them of pantheism, a view that equated God and the world, and that had a long history of negative connotations in American thought. Bellamy argued that 'the physical and moral evil in the world' contained 'nothing positive . . . only a shadow fleeing before the light'. Such evil was the 'inevitable result of the term of life imposed upon all things which are not God', existing 'for the harmony of the whole which God created'. The only real existent for the New Divinity, critics concluded, was a great (materialistic) All. One tenet of the New Divinity implied something different.

God did not act arbitrarily and conformed to the nature of things; or rather the nature of things mirrored his will just as his will mirrored the nature of things. For example, Hopkins said that God could not empower unregenerate understanding to discern beauty. The divine was not impeached, Hopkins went on, because it could not accomplish that 'which in itself, implies a contradiction'. Emmons held that moral distinctions existed independently of God's will. To set God above rectitude was debasing, said Emmons. God's glory consisted in always choosing to do what was fit. For God to change the essence of morality was an impossibility, as if he should will two plus two not to equal four or a circle to be equivalent to a square.

Within New Divinity, Samuel Hopkins and Nathaniel Emmons were the most creative intellects. Hopkinsianism, the derogatory label for the ideas of Hopkins, eventually became a term of respect for the main New Divinity concepts. Emmons, a generation younger than Hopkins, also purveyed a set of distinctive ideas—Emmonsism—that attracted a following.

Hopkins's fame as a controversialist and extreme proponent of Edwards stemmed from a debate in the late 1760s and 1770s on the means of regeneration, and later from the views of the first modern treatise on systematic theology published in the United States, his two-volume *System of Doctrines* (1793). Hopkins developed Edwards's notion that a chasm separated the unregenerate, motivated by self-love, and the regenerate, whose psyches grace had transformed. In expounding these ideas Hopkins became known as a gifted polemicist. Unregenerate doings, he argued, could never be meritorious. In fact, sinners could never be so evil as when they became most conscious of their evil ways through using the means of grace—meditation and perusal of the Bible—and yet still neglected to repent. The ministry improperly advocated such unregenerate acts as the means of grace; any hint that God would reward them was wrong. It followed that the unrepentant were as well off murdering their parents as dutifully reading the Bible and searching their hearts—and so ultimately they were. But Hopkins wanted to stress that the minister must exhort his audience immediately to convert. To accept anything less allowed the unrepentant to wallow in sin.

Hopkins believed that using the means implied that goodness could reside in an unregenerate person's scheming to repent. His opponents contended that the cleavage between regenerate and unregenerate was not as strict as Hopkins said, that the psychology of grace was more complex. The activities of natural humanity were tied, Old Calvinists wrote, to the supernatural. But New Divinity made Edwards's rigid dichotomy between nature and grace acceptable in a new era. Hopkins told sinners to repent at once. Old Calvinism implied that they could go through the motions of conscientious church membership and wait on God to save them because they were externally worthy or respectable.

Hopkins was best known for his definition of holiness as disinterested benevolence. Edwards had argued that true human virtue consisted in benevolence to being in general. The New Divinity theologians modified this idea. They held that the glory of God equaled the greatest good in the universe, but this good sought the happiness of intelligent creatures. Universal being for Hopkins mainly included God and his intelligent creatures, so that true virtue (or holiness) comprised friendly affection to all intelligent beings. The glory of God centered more on humanity and human happiness.

All individuals were interested in their own happiness. This self-regarding impulse was part of what it was to be a living being and was neither moral nor immoral. In all but the regenerate, however, this interest became selfishness. Individuals promoted their interests above others equally worthy. On the contrary, virtuous behavior relinquished the interest in happiness to the extent that this interest was inconsistent with the interests of all beings. Benevolence was love to every being in proportion to that being's worth in the cosmic scheme. The single interest was always part of this scheme and could not be nil. Hopkins even allowed that it was consistent with disinterested benevolence that an individual show the greatest concern for the community nearer in space and time. Intimating his views about a virtuous and harmonious society, Hopkins conceived the moral universe as a system of the interests of intelligent beings. An uncorrupted being would perceive the harmony, but unavoidably from its own perspective. Consequently, the interests in its proximity would rightly be more significant than they would for a being viewing the system differently. But disinterested benevolence of this sort was distinct from the selfish behavior of the unregenerate, who sacrificed other interests to their own or inappropriately elevated the interests around them. The natural world of Newton, Hopkins said, bore a 'conspicuous analogy' to the system of holiness:

the general law of attraction, the common bond of union in our material system, by which all bodies are mutually attracted, and ebb, tend to one centre; every part, which it attracts, being also attracted by the whole, is fixed in its station and extends its influence to all; so that each particle has, in a sense, a regard to the whole, and contributes to the general good.

The New Divinity contended that sin was necessary to the greatest good. Infinitely benevolent, God created a universe expressing this good. Some practitioners said evil was the way finite creatures interpreted aspects of a perfect world. More New Divinity men implied that evil was a necessary means to God's perfection. Sin was evil *per se*—it always tended to bad consequences. But God's order insured that every evil occasioned a greater good. Sin was necessary and sufficient to the greatest good, although the greater good that evil brought might be forever invisible, and the explanation of the good unintelligible. But New Divinity authors also showed how various evils 'caused' greater goods. Characteristically the good to which the greatest, most terrible, and most incomprehensible sins answered was the display of God's glory. Some evils were so dreadful that their meaning for humanity could not justify them. They were so ghastly that only God's glory appeared of greater moment, and so their purpose must be to manifest it. The theologians were sure that the universe did not center on human beings, that humanity must show piety in the face of mystery. They consequently urged, too, that the worst horrors gave us the most compelling reason to be worshipful.

Was God, then, the author of sin? No New Divinity man would say so explicitly. They all agreed that God chose that wickedness should exist. As Joseph Bellamy stated, God did not hinder the occurrence of evil. Although he hated it, he permitted sin. Hopkins went further. God 'determined to permit' sin. Emmons typically carried the idea to its just and logical conclusion. Sin existed because of 'the immediate interposition of the Deity'. If God were an all-powerful creator, if he made evil a means to good, then he caused evil. He was its cause, however, only in the infinite order where he caused everything. In the temporal world, individuals were responsible.

This insistence on the distinct worlds of God and of humanity enabled the New Divinity vigorously to elaborate Edwards's teaching on the will. The distinction between natural and moral ability and inability was pertinent to the human world. God created intelligent creatures with all the powers that made them free. Acting on wants was what freedom meant. A person indisposed to change a wicked temper was accountable precisely for that reason. In some way, God may have created the temperament, but that did not remove responsibility. For creating temperaments and dispositions was exactly how God made free individuals. Opponents of the New Divinity attacked this position as making God responsible for sin: he would not be if people truly had free will. God then also held people guilty for crimes over which they had no control: God determined them to act the way they had. The followers of Edwards gradually developed two successive sets of arguments, the 'taste' and 'exercise' positions, to meet this critique.

Emmons on Exercise

Although less circumspect than Edwards, the 'tasters' followed him closely. They argued that individuals had a taste, relish, or disposition to sin that caused sin; this mental property provided the ground or reason for evil-doing. This taste was unlike the color of one's eyes: such a physical characteristic would relieve the wicked of responsibility. Yet the taste was like a physical characteristic in that its presence meant that sins were not spontaneous outbursts: the taste was like physical strength enabling one to lift heavy objects, yet was also innate in humankind. The taste accounted for depravity without requiring that God be the author of iniquity. The taste belonged to people, and so the sins. Emmons pointed out that the tasters could not distinguish this taste from a physical characteristic and so save responsibility. Additionally, Emmons said, on this account God created the sin because he had created the taste. If he had not, the taste for depravity was a spontaneous power. This inference led Emmons to disparage tasters as disguised Arminians, if they did not make God the author of sin.

The leader of the 'Consistent Calvinists', Emmons put forth his ideas in philosophically rigorous sermons. In them he worked out a conception of the will that avoided the problems of the tasters. By an 'exercise' Emmons meant a creature's affections, desires, intentions, or volitions meriting praise or blame. An exercise was paradigmatically the mind's moral impulse, its choice, and not the overt act associated with the exercise when individuals acted without constraint. The heart or will consisted in these exercises. In the widest sense willing was intent. No cause or ground of a sinful nature existed beneath the exercises. Only the exercises existed, and in natural individuals they were sinful. Asked what made up sin, Emmons replied, 'Sinning'. A sinful taste did not cause sin, but this did not mean that corruption was uncaused. Rather, Emmons believed, like Edwards, that if a taste for sin caused sin, then the cause of sin would not have been illumi-nated. The reasoning would be circular, explaining sin by sin itself. For Emmons, Edwards's argument against the will's self-determination repudi-ated the view of taste of his supposed successors.

Exercisers stated both our absolute responsibility and God's sovereignty. Emmons happily conceded that God efficiently caused the exercises. But discovering the cause of sin had no bearing on individual responsibility. Individuals were responsible for wickedness because it was rightly attrib-uted to their wills. People chose to sin. If they were not physically com-pelled, they effectuated their wills by doing what they wanted; they had the power of agency unfettered by any taste or relish for sin. Emmons's views were encapsulated in a single proposition: 'the divine influence upon the heart, in producing volitions, does not imply compulsion on the part of God, nor destroy liberty on the part of man.'

Emmons contrasted sovereignty in God's world and accountability in the creature's. But some of his bold assertions may have obscured a greater subtlety in his sermons. Timothy Dwight, Edwards's grandson, implied that Emmons was a Calvinist Hume, reducing man to a 'chain of [phenom-enal] exercises'. Emmons did take seriously Edwards's (sometime) denial of a substantial soul, and closely studied Berkeley. In Emmons's work a version of British empiricism emerged, distinct from Continental rationalism, as the context of speculation. Historians of philosophy have argued that Hume took Berkeley's results to their conclusion and discredited Berkeley's notion of minds just as Berkeley disclaimed Locke's material substance. There is much to the view that Emmons belittled Berkeley's notions of finite minds but left an absolute divine power as the cause of all the finite instants called human hearts. But there was more to Emmons, who did not distinguish an evil taste and evil acts. Some philosophers conceived the same connection between a substance and its effects. A substance did not exist apart from its effects, but neither did they exist apart from the sub-stance. They were effects because they were bound up with a substance. Substance was such because certain effects were displayed. The human soul for Emmons was not a chain of exercises; rather, the soul was a certain struc-ture of exercises.

In at least one of his sermons, Emmons said that people had powers prior to agency that they did not exercise. Here he hinted that a power, taste, or disposition antecedent to all exercise was appropriately understood as the structure of actual volitions. Tastes were not any collection of exercises but codified an order or organization in the world, the systematic connection of possible internal impulses and external actions. Tastes might exist and never be actualized. If someone were to will a good act, in some instances something good would occur. And individuals were able to will so if they wanted to. But this fact only implied that a benign taste was just the way God had structured possible exercises and doings; the taste did not entail benign exercises.

New Divinity at Princeton

Jonathan Edwards had gone to the College of New Jersey in 1758 to stabilize this struggling school founded to prosper revival theology. The Presbyterians who had called it into existence were theoretically more committed to church hierarchy than the Congregational founders of Yale and Harvard. But Princeton believed that the leadership at both Yale and Harvard was unsympathetic to revivalism, and determined to carry forward both Presbyterianism and heartfelt religion. Yet the College too soon fought over revivalism. In the aftermath of the Awakening, Harvard had become Arminian and liberal, declining from Calvinism. Yale's commitment to Calvinist evangelicalism existed, as its production of New Divinity men exhibited, but Yale's leaders into the 1790s were ambivalent if not downright hostile to the disorder that revivalist religion might cause the social and intellectual establishment in Connecticut. A similar rift occurred at Princeton.

After Edwards died, the New Divinity influenced the College of New Jersey. Joseph Bellamy, the political leader of the Edwardseans, corresponded with ministers active at Princeton. In the mid-1760s revivalist Presbyterians almost had Samuel Hopkins named to a divinity professorship. Although they failed, New Divinity tutors ran the college from 1766 to 1768. Joseph Periam gained the most notoriety, but Jonathan Edwards the Younger, who had studied with both Bellamy and Hopkins, was probably more prominent. Periam expounded Bishop Berkeley, and until the early 1770s, at least, students were reading Bellamy's *True Religion Delineated*. Then, in 1768, the Scottish churchman John Witherspoon became president and led the College, and later its Seminary, to oppose metaphysical Calvinism and most forms of revival. The leader of a counter-revolution, Witherspoon turned the college irrevocably away from Edwards's use of the Lockian tradition in modern philosophy.

When eighteenth-century thinkers wrote of idealism, they usually referred to the representative theory of perception that Locke exemplified. Physical objects existed outside the mind but were known only as mediated by ideas. Locke was an idea-ist. From early in his career Witherspoon believed that objects were directly known in consciousness and so countered Locke. As Stanhope Smith, another Princetonian opposed to philosophical divinity, later tellingly wrote, the object itself was discovered in sensation, not its idea. Ideas were conceptions of the fancy or reminiscences of objects, and when objects were perceived, ideas were unknown and unperceived. Princeton's chief philosophical conception was a belief in direct perception, a presentational and not a representational theory of knowledge.

Presentationalism *per se*, however, was consistent with Berkeley. He too dismissed Lockian ideas mediating objects. Instead, Berkeley held, individuals knew objects of knowledge directly. But these objects were themselves ideal. For Berkeley, no objects lurked behind the ideas. Both Berkeley and Witherspoon believed in direct perception. But Berkeley held that the objects of perception were ideas, Witherspoon that they were physical things.

In the eighteenth century Berkeley was known as an immaterialist, and Witherspoon inveighed against him as well as Locke. But Witherspoon meant by Berkeleyanism that objects were merely subjective ideas, that is, ideas 'in our head'. But this was not Berkeley's position. The ideas constituting the world were not those of individuals; they were God's and imposed with such order and regularity that they had all the characteristics of the external world. Berkeley distinguished between ideas of individuals—conceptions of the fancy or reminiscences of objects, for example—and God's ideas, which Witherspoon considered independently existing objects.

Witherspoon repudiated 'Berkeleyanism' through ridicule. Students could not believe, could they, that Nassau Hall was a figment of their imagination? Berkeley would not have said this, however, and although his philosophy and Princeton's differed, the difference was not so clear as Witherspoon made out. Witherspoon and his followers feared that Berkeley would lead to skepticism. It was dangerous, especially for adolescents, to question ordinary beliefs as Berkeley had done. In associating its theology with the tradition of Lockian empiricism, New Divinity ran the risk of acclimatizing students to non-Christian ideas. Edwards and his followers, Princeton thinkers believed, were playing with fire in attempting to reconstruct Calvinism using modern philosophy. Protestant principles must be defended in a way that was not itself dangerous to faith. Princeton replaced the ruminations of Edwards and New Divinity with a position borrowed from Scotland, first from Francis Hutcheson and then Thomas Reid and Dugald Stewart, who opposed Locke's 'way of ideas'.

The Scottish position developed in Aberdeen, Glasgow, and Edinburgh was the first competent British attempt to refute Hume. Fearing first that doubt about ethical and religious imperatives might flow from the Lockian tradition, Princeton emphasized Hutcheson's view that in consciousness people grasped absolute sentiments of obligation. In addition to this moral sense intuitionism, Princeton argued, with Reid and Stewart, that the primary data of experience were not the discrete ideas of British empiricism; the mind contacted physical objects immediately. This was the 'direct', 'natural', 'common sense', or 'Scottish' realism that Witherspoon contrasted to immaterialism and that, in simplified form, he promulgated in New Jersey. By the 1830s Princeton typified the way in which the United States domesticated these Scottish Enlightenment thinkers. More to the point, the Scots provided the intellectual context in which, in the first third of the nineteenth century, the focus on Locke, Berkeley, and Hume that we have seen in Edwards and Emmons was compromised. The Scots provided in America a new basis for philosophizing about religion.

Individuals directly knew right principles of benevolence *and* the basic substances, mind and matter. To deny such principles of common sense— that self-consciousness and the senses were trustworthy and conveyed what humanity thought they conveyed—was self-destructive, for such principles grounded all reasoning. Doubts about the immediate apprehension of the self and of the external world undercut doubt itself. Locke had disastrously erred. By interposing ideas between selves and the objects of knowledge he undermined belief, and the result, through Berkeley, was Hume's skepticism. For Hume, only an inexplicable collection of ideas existed. Not only was there no external world, but no inner world. Reality was a momentary phenomenon, and knowledge impossible. But merely recalling the principles of common sense refuted Hume. He relied on the very principles he discounted. In assuming he could show the impossibility of knowledge, Hume presupposed the reasoning he ruled out.

None the less, Princeton realism did not simply reject Locke and Berkeley. Princeton got closer to the external world than Lockian representationalism but hedged its supposition that individuals immediately grasped external reality. Although what was external to people was not merely an idea of Berkeley's God, it was not clearly an idea-less object. Princeton wavered between Locke and Berkeley, but never developed its ideas enough to say exactly where it stood. The school had primarily developed an epistemology to support its Hutchesonian concern for undeniable springs of virtue, suggesting the logical primacy of the theory of knowledge over practical philosophy.

Amateurs to Professionals

The New Divinity home-seminaries not only legitimated advanced training in divinity, but also further heightened tensions within American

Protestantism. Moderate churchmen were threatened, and more liberal Protestants felt justified in their falling away from orthodoxy, as both groups saw in New Divinity instruction a rabid movement. In 1803, David Tappan, an Old Calvinist and professor of divinity at Harvard, died. In the late eighteenth century Harvard conciliated competing factions, but Tappan's death touched off a struggle over his replacement. Initially Harvard was divided, but soon religious leadership passed into the hands of those who disbelieved in original sin and who thought human beings capable of benign impulses. By the second decade of the new century these Harvard Arminians took the label of 'Unitarians', a designation that showed they thought there was one God but, to their opponents' dismay, not much more. Specifically, the Unitarians held that while Jesus was God's divinely appointed messenger, he was not the Son of God. While the Unitarians emphasized Jesus and his miraculous powers, they read the Bible more freely. The book was consciously interpreted and made to conform to what cultured Bostonians of the early nineteenth century might find acceptable.

Although Unitarianism remained a local phenomenon for many years, it shocked and outraged Calvinists. They recognized that Harvard would no longer be suitable for ministerial training, and Old Calvinists and more radical followers of Edwards put aside a half-century-long quarrel in the face of a single powerful enemy. After much negotiating, more conventional Edwardseans and an unyielding New Divinity coterie around Nathaniel Emmons founded a higher school of theology in 1808—the Andover Theological Seminary would carry forward the work of centrist New Divinity ministers in a novel institutional setting. Theological instruction at Andover came under the purview of Leonard Woods, an able if timid Edwardsean who served with distinction from 1808 to 1846. In 1810 he was joined by Moses Stuart, who became the first professional biblical scholar in America, and a defender, against Harvard, of a conservative interpretation of the Bible. The two men were central to theology in the nineteenth century. Andover claimed the earlier New England Theology as its inheritance, and continued this tradition in the writing of Woods's successor, Edwards Amasa Park.

Andover's founding in 1808 put the orthodox ahead, but Harvard soon responded. When John Kirkland became president in 1810, he gave prospective ministers systematic guidance. By 1815 he singled out and specially instructed students of the Bible, and a year later organized a Society for the Promotion of Theological Education in Harvard University. By 1819 a faculty of theology competed with Andover's.

The larger context in which this battle was waged is important to remember. At the time law and medical schools were growing quickly. The college presidents who oversaw such developments acknowledged practical pressures, but as clergymen and theologians they thought that the most practical advance would be professional schools of theology. Moses Stuart conceived Andover as a 'sacred West Point'. When the Andover founders justified their school, they wrote: 'What is the value of property, health, or life compared with that of immortal souls?' Yale's president, Timothy Dwight, agreeably gave his blessing to Andover. But Dwight also planned a department of theology at Yale for the same reason. Divinity was more important than law and medicine, and Yale did not want to fall behind schools that might be its competitors.

At Princeton, Stanhope Smith, whose moderate Calvinism had been acceptable in the late eighteenth century, was forced to resign as president in 1812. But this change was not enough for Smith's opponents. That same year the Princeton Theological Seminary initiated instruction to prospective clerics. Presbyterian leaders believed that only such a move would enable Princeton to fight not just New Divinity but the liberalism emanating from Harvard. Distinct from the College of New Jersey, Princeton Seminary first shared the grounds of the College and the support of the church, and dominated the College for the next fifty years.

Thus, in the first two decades of the nineteenth century, New Divinity spurred a new institutional organization. The New Divinity made systematic theology a science with a student constituency. Westward expansion convinced divines of an enlarging market for a learned ministry. The finely drawn controversies gave a rationale for sectarian splintering and caused aggressive theologians to push for divinity schools for their doctrines. Fourteen seminaries opened between 1808 and 1836.

The professionalization of divinity had significant consequences. When theology withdrew from the center of the college to a professional school at the margin of the academic community, the tiny but growing American university began to lose its continuity with the past and the tradition of classical learning. In the ancient universities theology had been responsible for animating schools of higher learning with a sense of their comprehensive calling. Professionalization was thus an early and potent symbol of the fragmentation of knowledge and culture. The seminaries enunciated a training method that made the apprentice system defunct. More scholastic and abstract, the new schooling did not familiarize ministerial candidates with pastoral work. By the middle of the nineteenth century the faculty of divinity schools knew little of daily clerical responsibilities. The seminaries did promote mastery of theology and assured uniformity in denominations, but they stamped entire ministries with the doctrinal peculiarities of a few men.

The Calvinism of Charles Hodge

In 1822 the Princeton Theological Seminary appointed a young cleric, Charles Hodge, a cautious if intelligent theologian, deliberative but belligerent in controversy. A comprehensive thinker, he became one of the leading American divines of the nineteenth century, and presided over the growth of his seminary. In over sixty years, until his death in 1878, three thousand students heard his version of Protestant thought. His *Systematic Theology* (1872–3) which drew on material dating from the middle of the century, became the standard text in Presbyterianism.

Hodge found Leonard Woods of the Andover Seminary and Bennet Tyler of the Hartford Seminary the most congenial among his colleagues. These men, like Hodge, used Edwards prudently to block theological innovation. But Hodge was not satisfied with all of Edwards. Princeton Seminary thought that the New Divinity of Edwards's followers bordered on heresy, and on the critical issue of the will Hodge parted company from Edwards.

The mind for Edwards was not so much an entity as a function, and there were two reciprocally related functions—cognition and volition. Following the Scots, Hodge found comfort in a different conception of mind that divided mental substance into a series of separate powers. For those opposing Edwards (and Hume) the mind had three functions, not two, and they were more clearly separated into entities—thus the phrase 'faculty psychology'. The understanding was not so much an activity as a substance that did the cognizing. The affections were capable of emotion, and the will, another substance, had the capacity for choice. Thus, in human behavior the reason (or understanding or cognition) set out goals; the affections provided the motives; and the will made action possible.

As a separate faculty the will, for Hodge, chose freely. To be effective, however, it had to act in accord with the reason and the feelings, and Hodge's tripartite system was so constituted that human beings were unable to do what they ought. Hodge accepted the notion of a taste for sin, as did Edwards and his less bold followers. With the Edwardseans, too, Hodge said the question was the nature of human character, not its cause or origin. But Hodge did not mean simply that people *would* not do what was holy, but that they *could* not. The controlling states, moral characters, or sinful natures of agents were not under the power of their wills. Individuals could not control their disposition or tendency to evil, yet were blameworthy. When self-determined, said Hodge along with Edwards, people were free, but this freedom did not imply that an individual could shape basic character traits. Inability, said Hodge, comported with responsibility. People ought to will better than they could; they were bound to do what was beyond their power. People were not able to do as they ought even though they were responsible.

Hodge admitted that this position had difficulties. But he thought it best accorded with the Bible and dismissed arguments that made speculative reasoning a measure of what to accept. He warned against Edwards's 'metaphysical' attempt to make the Bible consistent with current ideas of what was appropriate. Readers might find Hodge's scriptural view of responsibility unfair, but God's purpose was not to have a plan they liked or understood.

The New Haven Theology

Hodge's fear of the consequences of Edwards's 'Yankee Metaphysics' was borne out, for him, by developments at the Yale Divinity School, which Hodge saw as a disturbing evolution of New Divinity. But the New Divinity also disavowed the novel ideas coming from Yale. In New Haven, under the direction of its leading figure, Nathaniel William Taylor, the Divinity School was formulating an innovative philosophy of religion that would challenge basic notions of Edwards himself.

Taylor had gone to Yale, graduating in 1806, and had long been recognized there as an impressive thinker and a powerful pulpit orator at his Center Church. When Yale founded its theological department in 1822, Taylor was named its first professor of theology. In 1828, in the annual sermon of public advice to the clergy, 'Concio ad Clerum', Taylor publicized ideas that he and his colleagues had been brooding upon. They were soon known as expounding 'Taylorism', or, more formally, the New Haven Theology. His posthumous lectures of 1858, *The Moral Government of God*, codified work of high ability somewhere between the clever and the brilliant.

Taylor's notoriety derived from what his opponents charged was an illegitimate emphasis on philosophical reasoning. Like his peers, Taylor was conversant with Scottish thought and adhered to its faculty psychology. Theological analysis also began for Taylor by exploring the concepts depicting the world. Making definitions, said Taylor, was 'the severest labor of the human mind'. He looked at meanings and the implications derived from them. Because meanings really existed, when he discovered identity of meaning or self-contradiction, he knew something about the universe's order. Conceptualization uncovered necessary truth about the world's structure because language adumbrated this structure. While the bounds of reason were limited, thinkers who simplistically resorted to mystery to solve problems, who claimed to believe what they did not understand, 'must expect to be charged with holding contradictions and must, I think, be aware of the justice of the charge'. None the less, Taylor said, theologians often could not define concepts adequately or be guaranteed that their examination was wholly correct.

According to Taylor, the chief problem of the Edwardsean tradition was that it could not explain how an agent could be free, yet simultaneously have motives determine behavior. How could free will exist if, given certain motives, behavior could inevitably be predicted? Edwards was content to show that agency did not consist in the self-determination of the will. Yet by not showing how freedom was consistent with motives that led to the certainty of sin, said Taylor, Edwards left the way open to Emmons. For Emmons, motives were the free and sinful volitional exercises of individuals. But God caused these exercises. Emmons left room for agency only by unjustifiably distinguishing between God's activity in creating and preserving the world and this same activity defined as human action. And Emmons, like the other New Divinity men, then explained sin by saying it was God's means to the greatest good. Evil constrained God in the achievement of his purposes.

Taylor had as little regard for the more conventional theory of taste. It made sin the product of a sinful nature, a relish or taste for sin that Taylor believed was analogous to a physical trait. Nor did the tasters have an acceptable understanding of freedom. In their view individuals were as much responsible for sin as for the color of their eyes. Taylor wanted to do even more than show the compatibility of natural depravity and freedom. Failing to make them consistent made the God of orthodoxy malign: he brought evil into the universe and caused persons to sin, and then sentenced them to death. Taylor wanted to show how God could truly be a *moral* governor.

God's moral government was a theocratic polity peopled by moral agents. This idea came to us 'in the very nature and structure of the mind— it is given to us in actual cognitions of the inner man, in the knowledge of ourselves; and therefore in a manner not less distinct nor less impressive than were it sent in thunder from . . . [God's] throne'. But being a moral agent meant having free will. If human beings were to participate in God's kingdom, they must freely choose to worship him. So far this was good Edwardsean doctrine, but by 'free will' Taylor had in mind the inner freedom, a 'power to the contrary', that Edwards found unintelligible. For Taylor, people had the ability to act contrary to the way they had acted, be their circumstances and their character the same. Moral agency, Taylor continued, could 'no more exist without this [spontaneous] power than matter can exist without solidity and a triangle without sides and angles'. God's moral polity was characterized by the liberty of indifference, his government circumscribed by the 'self-determining' aspects of the governed. When Edwards argued for freedom while denying this power to the will, Taylor observed, he might as well have said that a part was equal to the whole. Edwards's notion of freedom missed the essentials of the true definition.

New Haven explicated *Freedom of the Will* in a way that was not true to Edwards but did creatively develop philosophical theology. Edwards contrasted natural and moral determinism, but the contrast involved more the terms connected—physical cause and physical effect, on the one hand, and volition and action, on the other—than the nature of the connection. Edwards was ambiguous about this connection. From God's perspective it was efficient causation. From the human perspective one event was the occasion of another. The antecedent inevitably occurred in conjunction with the consequent, and the appearance of the antecedent guaranteed the prediction that the consequent would occur. In any case, said New Haven, moral determinism for Edwards involved only the certainty that two things were connected. Thus, Edwards maintained that although free, people were morally unable to do good. New Haven read Edwards as saying only that individuals would surely sin, and he need not believe that they could not have done otherwise. Many New Divinity followers of Edwards, Yale theologians suggested, held him to a position he never asserted when they made him deny the will's power to the contrary. Moreover, Edwards wanted to place all sinning in acts of will, distinct from any prior cause determining these acts. For New Haven, Edwards's argument against the self-determination of the will attacked the idea of taste. Self-determination was a physical characteristic causing willing, and Edwards showed this to be self-contradictory.

Edwards's psychology assimilated affections and will, motive and choice. The will (choice) was as the greatest apparent good (motive). Motive was choice or volition. Action followed choice, in appropriate circumstances, because God was the efficient cause, although human motive or volition might occasion action. Taylor's Scottish psychology differed. For him, motives were distinct from choice or volition, and volition caused action. Taylor's psychology was tripartite, consisting of the affections, will, and understanding; Edwards's was dual, consisting of the affections (emotions and will) and understanding. For Edwards these were functions of the mind; for Taylor they were more like different spiritual entities. But as Taylor read Edwards, the issue was not distinguishing the affections from the will; the issue was the will's self-determination. Taylor said he agreed with Edwards. The will did not determine itself or have the liberty of indifference. But, contended Taylor, Edwards neglected the connection between motive and act. Edwards merely argued that, given the motives, sinful acts followed. Taylor analysed this occurrence. But, unlike Edwards, he inserted the will between motive and act, and used Edwards's notions of efficient and occasional causality in a novel way. For Taylor, efficient causation did not connect motive and act. Motives occasioned will and act, and were the ground and reason of the will's activity. Given the motive, willing an action would certainly follow.The motive, however, did not necessitate the will. Rather, the will had its own efficacious power.

Initiated by nothing but itself, the human will efficiently caused acts. This was not, Taylor thought, a position Edwards had stigmatized. Taylor made his ideas compatible with *Freedom of the Will* by noting Edwards's inference from the Arminians Edwards himself had cited. These divines had argued that the will was determined only by itself. Then, according to Edwards's famous argument, there was a volition before the first volition. A previous act of will determined the initial will. This might have been fairly inferred, but no one defended such a position. Arminians did believe that the stronger motive induced the will and that individuals acted freely, or not, in spite of all motives. Yet no one said that the will acted in the absence of motives. Taylor argued that the will always acted with motives, but had the power to act however it wished whatever the motives. He concurred with Edwards that the will was never self-determined. But Taylor's reason for this agreement was that motives always accompanied willing, not that the will lacked a spontaneous power. In truth Edwards's earlier opponents limited the spontaneous power of the will in the same way as Taylor did. The will had a competency to attend or not to attend to a presented motive and to act or not to act as it pleased. But Taylor used this notion of freedom to defend orthodox ideals.

Taylor argued that people always sinned. He said they sinned 'by nature', meaning that at all times and in all circumstances they did and would sin. They also had a power to the contrary, a power not to sin. The identical people could have chosen differently in an identical situation. The physical or constitutional properties that belonged to individuals in the circumstances of their existence were the context of depravity. The motive for depravity lay in their nature—their physical and constitutional properties—and not circumstance, because individuals continued to sin in whatever circumstances they were placed. Like Edwards, Taylor thought people depraved by nature, but their acts were still subject to their spontaneous powers of moral agency. They were the efficient cause of their sin; their nature was sin's occasion, the *causa sine qua non*. Human nature was just the typical motives that accompanied sin.

Everyone, said Taylor, had the inner liberty to adopt the Christian faith. The want of grace did not prevent the repentance of sinners. But people did not or would not repent on their own, and God's grace interposed an influence that converted the elect. Human beings could not comprehend the workings of grace. Although not miraculous, grace was supernatural; it overcame human nature. Just as the unrepentant could choose to repent, though none did, those who received grace could choose to sin, though none did. For Taylor irresistible grace was simply an appeal that was never resisted, and never would be. God intended to secure the perfect holiness and happiness of each and all, consistently with securing the perfect holiness of the greatest number. God wanted to save as many as possible. But individuals had spontaneous wills and could rebel. If the number receiving grace changed, no one could know that the overall result might not be worse than the present one. It was conceivable that people would resist grace, and perhaps if even a single additional person received it, a sinful revolution among all those receiving grace might occur. Who could judge, said Taylor, that God had not secured the best possible moral government by limiting grace?

God was omniscient and created the best possible system, but agency limited his power. The extent of salvation hinged on possibilities finite creatures could not foresee. Taylor had a dual perspective. From God's viewpoint grace was necessarily and sufficiently efficacious. He knew those to whom he gave it would not resist, and he achieved his righteous end in election. But from the human viewpoint regeneration depended on every individual's faith and moral choices. Individuals did not know whom God had elected. Because all had the power to sin or not to sin, salvation was each individual's responsibility.

4   *Collegiate Philosophy, 1800–1868*

Background

In the eighteenth century, philosophy as we know it did not exist in America as an independent pursuit. As we have seen, clergymen and theologians incorporated its modes of reasoning into their work in varying degrees. As a study in its own right, philosophy got its start as the Princeton divines struggled to free themselves from New Divinity, and examined epistemology as means to support their ideas of religious virtue. By the early nineteenth century a growing number of colleges in the United States—paralleling the proliferation of seminaries—afforded a venue in which thinkers might pursue speculative topics in relative independence from religion. The old colleges in the east remained dominant but schools in the South and Midwest joined their ranks, and a professoriate emerged to deliver instruction in an array of subjects. The philosophers at these colleges provided their pupils with a moral sense of their place in the world. The endeavor was socially justified but intellectually thin because the first responsibility of academics was not understanding the cosmos but coaching schoolboys in small provincial academies. Philosophy was written not for the learned but for students, and the standard production was the student textbook.

On the contrary, the theologians disdained writing textbooks. The closest they came to this genre were treatises of systematic theology. If these efforts were in a measure directed at aspiring ministers, in larger measure they innovatively contributed to the science of the deity. More frequently, the theologians engaged in original polemic. Theologians and not philosophers waged the pamphlet wars in both the eighteenth and nineteenth centuries. Divines and not metaphysicians wrote the scholarly monographic literature of the nineteenth century. The work of the philosophers remained at an intellectual level below that of the theologians. At the same time, unlike the theologians, whose intricate dialogue and indigenous tradition made them less concerned with what happened overseas, the philosophers depended on European thought. They were bound up with developments in Britain, and later Germany. The college philosophers only slowly drew on German ideas, but the divinity school felt even less of a need to go beyond local resources.

The professionalism of American theology stunted divines. From the heyday of Edwards's disciples in the 1780s on, critics complained of the technicality of orthodox thought. By the 1830s, after the first flush of enthusiasm for the New Haven Theology, theological debate in New England had relinquished none of its rigor but much of its appeal. Theological thinkers did not lose the sanction of their legitimating communities but did lose their interest. In the first American ivory towers, the divines catered more and more to advanced ministerial students and said little to people outside graduate classrooms. Often contemptuous of changes in European thought and unmoved by the need to diversify their ranks, theologians lost vigor.

On the other side, philosophy was a recognizably modern enterprise, committed to the century of Hegel and John Stuart Mill and not that of Calvin, even though practiced didactically and without much creativity. The collegiate philosophers began to assume the esteemed public role of guarantor of middle-class values that was also that of the active clergy. The philosophers themselves were ministers, but their work centered more on the moral and less on the religious. As colleges gradually claimed the guardianship of the character of upper-class youth, seminaries became more elevated above, and thus isolated from, ordinary life. The college philosophers, frequently also the presidents of their institutions, gained recognition as intellectual spokesmen in their communities. These men inculcated into pupils the dominant values of the various local collegiate cultures. Motivated by established moral and religious conventions, teachers fortified the standards of the educated classes.

Scottish Philosophy in America

The growth of textbooks marked the progress of the independent role of philosophy. Princeton president John Witherspoon wrote the earliest of the major American texts. Circulated in manuscript before his death, *Lectures on Moral Philosophy* was published posthumously in 1800. Even major works of later date—such as *The Human Intellect* (1868), written by Yale's president Noah Porter—were didactically designed and, like Porter's, often abridged for the pre-college level. The texts usually summarized European ideas, and were often modeled after foreign tracts. Throughout the nineteenth century, texts regularly appeared, and vied with student editions of favored European authors. American professors abbreviated for their classrooms Thomas Reid's *Essays on the Intellectual . . . and Active*

Powers, and Dugald Stewart's *Philosophy of the Human Mind* and *The Active and Moral Powers*. Authors divided philosophy into two branches mirroring the faculty psychology that came to dominate the study of the mind, as speculators ruminated on ways to refute Edwards on the will. Intellectual or mental philosophy included roughly logic, metaphysics, and epistemology. Moral philosophy included ethics and the social sciences viewed as explicitly normative, and dealt with the two 'active' faculties, the emotions and the will. Americans drilled students with the works of foreigners but also drew up their own textbooks in two volumes, the first on the mind's cognitive powers, the second on the moral.

Reid and Stewart contended that the data of experience were not the ideas of classical empiricism but judgements accompanying sensations. In such 'sense perception' the mind contacted the external world. Sensation implied the qualities of objects; perception of the world accompanied sensory experience. In the phrase 'common sense' Reid referred to the principles reflecting this peculiar constitution of the mind and asserting the mutual connection of sensation and perception. Similarly for Stewart, these principles were part of human nature, primary elements of reason, fundamental conceptions without which understanding was inconceivable and impossible. They guaranteed presentational knowledge of the external world.

American philosophers wedded Scottish views to a belief in Locke's greatness and the poverty of 'metaphysical' speculation. They gave Locke high marks for his empiricism, use of the inductive method, reliance on sensory evidence, and belief in an external world. But Locke went astray, they thought, in his representational realism. He erred in having ideas mediate objects. Once Locke restricted himself to his own consciousness, the immaterialism of Berkeley and the skepticism of Hume followed. American philosophers read Locke as someone meaning to espouse presentationalism and only confusedly adopting representationalism, and pointed to ambiguities in the *Essay* on these issues. The Scottish tradition clarified Locke and carried on the approved aspects of British empiricism.

At Princeton Witherspoon said that the sensations of color, taste, and so on—secondary qualities—did not exist in matter, but the quality corresponding to them did—a capacity to produce sensation. His Princeton lectures stated that sensations brought with them the inescapable supposition that an external object produced them. Substance was not separable from its sensible qualities. Whiteness did not exist without a white object. Sensible qualities implied their objects. Witherspoon's student and successor, Stanhope Smith, elaborated this realism. When external objects were presented, they produced impressions followed by corresponding sensations. The sensations were co-ordinate with a perception of the existence and qualities of the object on which the mind was concentrated. Cognition synthesized both sensation and perception. There was feeling by the appropriate senses (sensation) and the revelation of the object (perception). One *tasted* the sweetness of *sugar*.

At Harvard Levi Frisbie was a presence before his death in 1822 and lectured on Scottish realism. The first professor of philosophy was Levi Hedge, who taught in Cambridge from 1792 until 1832. In his later years he used his own *Elements of Logick* (1816) and his edition of the 1820 *Treatise on the Philosophy of the Human Mind* by the Scot Thomas Brown. Hedge's successor in philosophy was James Walker. Later president of Harvard, Walker abridged Dugald Stewart's three-volume *Philosophy of the Human Mind* (1792, 1814, 1827) for students.

Francis Bowen, Walker's replacement and the premier nineteenth-century philosopher at Harvard, also edited an edition of Stewart for students. A ground had to be found for urging that the external world existed, that experience replicated the way things were, that the world was as it appeared in consciousness. Scottish realism did this, said Bowen, by proving the legitimacy of intuitive principles. Certain propositions inwrought in the mind were seen to be immediately true and true about the world as it was. Their truth was patent because they were necessary to experience and their contradiction inconceivable. Some such propositions assured that the world of everyday experience really existed as presented. The mind furnished concepts through which thought about the world occurred, but these concepts merely duplicated things as they were in themselves. Intuitive knowledge guaranteed this correspondence between the world and the way it appeared to us via concepts.

The Scot James McCosh became president of Princeton in 1868 and had written his major work in 1860. *Intuitions of the Mind* made realism more subtle. The intuitions were singular and discovered by observing them in action. Implied in the acquisition of experience, these agents or instruments taught what the external and the internal worlds were like. There were certain primitive intuitions or cognitions including sense perception of the individual's body and self-consciousness of the mind. In addition to guaranteeing access to the external world, intuitions assured access to the self. Self-consciousness and sense perception together told a person directly not only of the physical body but also, with at least the senses of touch and sight, of outer objects as they affected the body. The individual knew something as it affected the organism. But intuition also warranted knowledge of objects as existing separately from and independently of the body. Objects were known as they impinged on the body and through it the mind, and were known to exist out of relation to the self. Finally, knowledge of bodies—one's own and others—also involved knowledge of self. All knowledge implied intuitive self-consciousness.

In addition to a presentational theory of knowledge and a psychology that affirmed various faculties having quasi-substantial status, American philosophers also had a well-defined theory of science. Edwards's speculation had allowed theorizing to dominate science. Nature might then be subservient to what (unregenerate) scientists wanted to find in it. On the contrary, the conceptions about science promoted by the early-modern thinker Francis Bacon became conventional in the nineteenth century. Based on a strict and limited empiricism, Scottish or Baconian science learned about the world from careful observation. The five senses conveyed the way the world was. After systematic accumulation of facts, natural scientists induced laws of nature. But these laws did not go beyond the observed. Judiciously collecting data, the scientist found uniformities in nature and, on the basis of the uniformities, extrapolated the principles governing regularities. These 'laws' perspicaciously digested the facts, and although the induction was never spelled out, it was not at odds with the taxonomic naturalism that defined much of the science of the day. A descriptive endeavor, the discovery of scientific law correlated various sorts of phenomena. Science codified ordinary experience, and more clearly revealed what nature presented to the senses. In inducing generalizations the mind was active, but the principles organizing sense perception were simply a shorthand for expressing the way things interacted. Finally, Bacon's empiricism supplied the chief argument for God, the argument from design. Science exhibited a harmonious universe, governed by a pleasing order and regularity that implied a benign creator. Baconian philosophers believed that science led toward religious understanding. Indeed, in 'doxological science' one assembled biblical facts and induced from them the understanding of scripture. Princeton in particular used this procedure in theology's various branches, accepting Bible stories as given, and inferring from them spiritual truth.

German Philosophy

In the nineteenth century the tradition of British empiricism from Locke to Berkeley to Hume was agreed to have culminated in skepticism. It was also agreed that Immanuel Kant had designed the *Critique of Pure Reason* (1781) to refute Hume. Kant settled competing claims about knowledge: he intended to secure knowledge in the world of experience but simultaneously to avoid dogmatism about any supra-experiential realm. Kant required two elements for knowledge: the active powers of mind and the raw data of sense. The mind imposed order on data, producing the 'experience' of the world of objects. Mind dynamically structured what was known so that we could say we knew it at all.

Kant studied the principles expressed in such statements as 'Every effect has a cause'. Philosophy investigated these synthetic a priori propositions whose truth assured the possibility of a world of experience. The propositions were necessarily and universally true of experience and true independent of experiential corroboration. They were thus a priori, yet they were synthetic, in the sense of somehow adding to our knowledge. They displayed the organizing and structural formulas—forms and categories— by which the mind made experience. The material of sense presented itself through the forms of space and time. The categories of the understanding, in conjunction with the forms, organized the sense data and made the world. Human beings must be justified in applying the categories because in their absence experience would not be possible. Thus, according to the common understanding, Kant refuted Hume.

Kant called his philosophy 'transcendental', and considered the only legitimate metaphysics to be his examination of the conditions of possible experience and the justification of knowledge. Transcendent metaphysics went beyond the limits of experience in answering ultimate questions and was illegitimate. For Kant knowledge was of the 'phenomenal' world that sense and mental activity generated. The 'noumenal' world of things in themselves irrespective of the mind's activity was closed. Human beings could never know the thing in itself, the *Ding an sich*; such knowledge was contradictory, for the noumenal was beyond knowledge, the organizing processes defining mind. When the mind attempted to surpass these bounds and comprehend beyond its realm, Kant said the mind exercised its capacity of reason. Although his followers frequently ignored the point, reason had almost a pejorative connotation. The *Critique of Pure Reason* demonstrated how the pretensions of reason must fail, how attempts to grasp the noumenal could never succeed.

Kant did allow that whereas categories of the understanding *constituted* knowledge, principles of reason *regulated*, within experience, the ineradicable tendency to master the noumenal. The ideas of God, freedom, and immortality were such regulative concepts. Although people could not have knowledge of God, for example, reason in a limited fashion could warrant faith, a rationale for activity.

The key to the 'constructionalist' position—that existence did not transcend consciousness (and vice versa)—was Cartesian and Lockian realism. Confronted only by ideas, people believed that what appeared in consciousness corresponded to what really was. How could such a belief be legitimated? Individuals never got outside their ideas to see if the ideas were caused by the objects people thought caused them or to see if the ideas were related as the objects were, and so skepticism could not be avoided. Kant argued that our ways of understanding the world were justified since a world existed only because the modes of understanding were as they were. Realism became incoherent. To speak of objects exterior to mind was meaningless, and skepticism was dissolved.

Kant and the Scots had much in common. They both circumvented the nihilism to which Hume brought philosophy. Hume's conclusions followed from his premiss that only direct awareness of phenomena was possible. He then argued that the phenomena never revealed causal connections. In reply, Kant maintained that Hume's notions of phenomena and causality were incorrect. Causality was the mind's necessary category. Although nothing of the noumena, of things in themselves, could be known, relations in the phenomenal world could be sure. The latter world was the product of the activity of mind on the data of sense. In refuting Hume, the Scots denied that direct awareness applied only to the contents of consciousness. In rejecting representational realism, Reid and Stewart contended that objects were perceived as they were in themselves and, therefore, as they really interacted.

For the Americans, Locke, as emended by the Scots, had anticipated what was correct in Kant. Locke urged that knowledge came through experience. But while maintaining experience as the source of knowledge, Locke did not believe that knowledge came only from experience; he was not skeptical like Hume. For Locke and the Scots, said the Americans, the mind was the vehicle or avenue of knowledge. Its active nature shaped experience to furnish knowledge. Kant rightly stated that although knowledge began with experience, knowledge did not derive solely from experience. But Locke said it first. Kant then wrongly assumed that the human conceptual apparatus applied only to the phenomenal. The Scots showed that this apparatus afforded knowledge of the world as it was.

By the 1830s German ideas were making inroads at the American colleges. Many Germans immigrating to the United States had read German philosophy directly. Additionally, a trickle of American students returned from Germany with Kantian theories, and translations of German work were periodically published. Most important was the philosophy, in English, of Sir William Hamilton.

Although Kant and the Scots had a single enemy in Hume, they still disagreed. Was the noumenal world, that of things in themselves, known? Kant said no, the Scots yes. In the middle of the nineteenth century

Hamilton adjudicated this quarrel. An erudite Scottish thinker, Hamilton made German thought relevant to British debate. On the East Coast of the United States his reputation lay in joining the German and Scottish positions. But in welcoming Hamilton the Americans took the first step in transforming collegiate philosophy.

For Hamilton knowledge was relative to the mental faculties. He called the knowable phenomenon an effect, and the cause or ground of its reality the noumenon. The noumenon must remain unknown. The relativity of knowledge implied that known and unknown coexisted. This distinction between phenomenal and noumenal did not coincide with that between ego and non-ego. The relativity of knowledge did not mean that the objects of knowledge depended on consciousness. Knowledge consisted of the effects of noumena, said Hamilton, but it did not follow that these were effects on human beings. The 'secondary qualities' of objects (for example, color) were effects of the noumenal world on human beings. These qualities were essentially connected to consciousness. But the 'primary qualities' (for example, extension) were simply effects of the noumena. Objects external to consciousness were immediately cognized, although there was no knowledge of things as they are in themselves. Only their effects were known. Hamilton's realism contested that direct knowledge existed of what was exterior to mind. Knowledge of the non-ego (primary qualities) was as immediate as knowledge of individual sensations (secondary qualities), and only through phenomena of both sorts were the noumenal (non-ego and ego) known at all. Matter and mind in themselves were not known except as the two real causes or necessary substrata of the phenomena. This union of Kant and Locke was Hamilton's pivotal contribution in the United States.

From Locke to Hamilton

The power of non-Scottish ideas differed in different places. The provincial colleges represented a variety of local usages, some more open to the outside world than others, some disdainful of the Continent. The absorption of ideas depended on the vitality of individuals, on either their rejection of Continental thinking or their willingness to examine it. The style of philosophizing in various sections of the country can also be partly attributed to the availability of certain books. Finally, philosophy was the common ground for the diverse denominational theologies. Philosophy and theology moved along similar but distinct courses, the former vaguely but stubbornly thought to undergird the latter. For some time all the creeds presupposed Scottish realism. But as different theological schools were variously threatened, the philosophers in associated colleges adopted different positions. Some variants of Scottish thought were more congenial to some theological details than others. In general, however, the college philosophers moved away from Scottish realism, as they adapted to various currents from Germany.

This contamination of realism was noticeable everywhere. Witherspoon and Stanhope Smith had vindicated common sense at the College of New Jersey, and after their presidencies leadership passed from the college to the school of theology. There Charles Hodge and his colleagues made realism crucial to Presbyterian Calvinism, and Princeton a bastion of Scottish views. But the College was revitalized when McCosh arrived in 1868. The influence of Hamilton can be seen in *Intuitions of the Mind*, and in the twenty years of his tenure at Princeton McCosh turned even more to German ideas. At Harvard the comparative lack of interest in theology at the Divinity School led the college to a relatively independent philosophical tradition, indebted to the Scots. But by mid-century Bowen turned away from Reid and Stewart. He edited Hamilton for his students and conceded much to German ideas. At Yale, Scottish ideas never gained the same hold. Nathaniel Taylor's theology was rooted in realism, but philosophy grew independent of theology when Taylor's son-in-law, Noah Porter, became professor of philosophy in 1846. President of Yale from 1871 to 1886, Porter often identified with the Scottish tradition. But he had studied in Germany, and *The Human Intellect* also revised common sense.

Continental speculation influenced other Northeastern collegians who wrote on intellectual philosophy. Laurens Perseus Hickok of Union College was indebted to Kant. Caleb Sprague Henry of New York University obtained a hearing for Victor Cousin's French version of German ideas. Thomas C. Upham of Bowdoin and Asa Mahan of Oberlin and Adrian College (Michigan) blended Scottish ideas with a variety of other sources. Even Brown's Francis Wayland, whose *Elements of Moral Science* (1835) expounded realist notions paradigmatically, delivered Hamiltonian lectures at Brown by the mid-1840s.

The currents that carried Americans away from Reid and Stewart were most apparent in Yale's Porter. Porter allowed direct entrée to the ego in consciousness. In sense perception both the ego, and the non-ego in the form of the body, were known directly. But the non-ego that was not the body was an object of acquired perception. Using the data of one sense as a sign of another, human beings learned that some aspects of the non-ego were not their bodies. The sense perception involved in touching a table or seeing a tree immediately informed individuals of themselves—an ego—and a non-ego. In grasping how the distinctive aspects of the five senses were integrated, this non-ego was distinguished into the body and what was not the body. Direct knowledge of individual sense organs existed, but only indirect knowledge of objects in space and time. Porter did not delineate how sense perceptions were sorted out, but German thought, especially Kant's view of mental operations, had influenced him. Sense perception was active, the product of the excitement furnished by material nature and the mind's own energy. The mind united sense perceptions in two steps. First, under a whole in space and time, then under the relation of substance and attributive quality. On the one hand, Porter affirmed his realism when he wrote that sense perception could not make what in reality had no existence. On the other hand, he argued that the mind created no more than it perceived and perceived no more than it created.

Knowledge of primary and secondary qualities was of substance and its attributes. This knowledge, Porter said, was not of reality, but of the nature of existing things as they were and as they affected human beings. Adapting Hamiltonian language, he wrote that these things existed only in relation to objects or to people. The productive or sustaining force of all other beings in the universe caused the character of things. Speaking strictly, Porter would not say that things existed independently, that they were real. In Porter the grip on the external world was less sure than in McCosh.

Harvard's Bowen also grew uncertain of the world's independent existence. Mind was immediately revealed, known directly, as a datum of consciousness, a resisting force, a power outside ourselves. Was this resisting force the material world? In the 1860s and 1870s Bowen could only infer this world. He postulated it as an unknown force. But such a postulate was technically illegitimate. The finite intellect could not fathom the nature of the external force, wrote Bowen; and could not ascertain the character of the external universe as noumenon. But Bowen did believe that the sole reality could not be the physical universe independent of thought. Immediately conscious of an external non-ego, individuals were presented with externally existing objects. This was, said Bowen, Hamiltonian presentational realism. On this account the question was not whether the phenomena existed independently, but the mode or manner in which they presented themselves. According to Hamilton, said Bowen, external objects were known immediately as presented but might not exist 'absolutely'.

The most original modification of these ideas among eastern academics appeared in the work of Laurens Hickok. After graduating from Union College, Hickok ministered in Connecticut before going to Western Reserve and Auburn Seminaries as a professor of theology. He wrote his major work, *Rational Psychology* (1849), at Auburn but was later president of Union College and spent a vigorous old age at Amherst.

Hickok used the techniques of the *Critique* to achieve the ends of Scottish realism (as well as orthodox Calvinism). *Rational Psychology* sought the conditions of knowledge, the necessary and universal principles that possible experience presupposed, the a priori requirements that made experience intelligible. Hickok thus examined the three intellectual faculties of the mind—the connections of sense, the constructions of the understanding, and the comprehension of reason. He first uncovered what must be true of such a faculty if it existed; then showed that the actual faculty had these characteristics; and, finally, warranted the belief that the concept of such a faculty corresponded to the actuality. For Hickok, truth lay in ascertaining the correspondence of idea to object. For example, the idea of a connection of sense and its referent was first learned; then how sense material validly connected with a referent.

The argument was not entirely clear, but Hickok took the Kantian notion of philosophical proof for his model. He also went beyond Kant. Discriminating sense and understanding steered between idealism and materialism. While sense and understanding together secured the a priori grounds of knowledge of a world of objects, the objects themselves were independently real. Secondary qualities such as color, analyzed in the connection of sense, were mental. Primary qualities such as substance and cause, examined in the understanding, were 'out there'. The understanding could not connect substances, wrote Hickok, unless they were already connected. Substances would be known by any intelligence that knew things directly in their essence, without any organs of sensibility (to provide secondary qualities). Hickok took a Lockian view of the real existence of objects, but argued that the mind's a priori structures permitted direct rather than inferential knowledge of the primary qualities. The world of objects was not phenomenal, as Kant supposed. It was, Kantian reasoning demonstrated, in Hickok's word, notional. The object world was as a pure intelligence would know it.

Hickok condemned confusions between the phenomenal world of sense and the notional world of objects of understanding. If the phenomenal were elevated to the notional, atheism and materialism resulted. We mistook the world of sense qualities for the real. If, conversely, philosophers mistook the notional world of understanding for the phenomenal, they assumed that sensation itself possessed constructive aspects. This confusion reduced the divine to nature; deity was degraded to the phenomenal. God, said Hickok, was above the phenomenal and notional, in the supersensual or supernatural realm. For Hickok, unlike Kant, this realm did not just regulate conduct. He explored the third faculty of the mind, reason, through comprehension and reached constitutive conclusions about it as about the other faculties. Hickok's system posited knowledge of God, freedom, and immortality. *Rational Psychology* ended by showing that Calvinism was congruent with the findings of comprehensive reason. Indeed, Hickok later claimed to deduce the Gospel view of sin and redemption, a priori, along Kantian lines.

Beyond Hamilton

Kant's transcendental idealism gave rise to varieties of transcendent metaphysics that he had ruled out. German, English, and American thinkers claimed to adopt his methods but rejected his constraints. For Kant, I must conceive the phenomena that I do not now sense as linked in some definable unity connecting them with present experience. For what is now happening to me merely instanced an experience including all physical facts. The experiences of everyone else must be unified with my present experience. These other experiences were all possible experiences of mine and therefore possessed a unity correlating with the unity of my own self. For Kant, thinking a world of objects involved postulating this fact. All human experience belonged to a single system of possible experience. Kant called this 'virtual unity' of the consciousness of a single self the Transcendental Unity of Apperception. For him knowledge formally presupposed it. For the post-Kantians, his successors, it became a knowable entity, an absolute self, and as the *Ding an sich* vanished, this self defined the world.

These systems culminated with G. W. F. Hegel, for whom the absolute self was revealed in time, the progressive stages of history bringing the human mind somehow ever 'closer' to the world-defining mind. In temporal experience national cultures grew, expressing higher, richer, and more complex aspects of consciousness. These developments occurred through Hegel's dialectic, the inherent rhythm of experience. According to the conventional interpretation, an antithesis was formed in response to a thesis, and both were reconciled and overcome in a synthesis that would continue the process by itself becoming a thesis. In the popular example pointing to Hegel's own ethnocentrism, Greek individualism contrasted to Roman legalism, both of which were subsumed by Prussian freedom under law, the highest stage yet reached by the spirit of humanity. Belief or knowledge was not in being, but in becoming. Change for Hegel did not depart from or recover a given truth; it essentially exemplified truth and interpretation.

American philosophers accommodated German ideas, primarily because they had no tradition of their own. Deriving their ideas from Europe, they were inevitably subject to its authority. When British (and French) thinkers looked to Germany, so did the Americans. Academic philosophy, moreover, served religious and moral convention. Popular because of its modesty, the sort of realism adopted by Reid and Stewart endowed the mind with intuitive spiritual powers and did not result in skepticism. By the 1840s, as various German doctrines acquired a public, collegiate thinkers were required not merely to disparage Hume's empiricism but also to fight post-Kantianism, which was often stigmatized as pantheism, the position that God was the universe. A way had to be found between this extreme, which falsely identified the material world with the deity, and skepticism. Hamilton became even more appealing as a mediator because some expositors were connecting Locke with Hume's skeptical empiricism. Hamilton was cautious: if knowledge of the noumenal was impossible, knowledge of the phenomenal world of primary and secondary qualities was unassailable. Embracing Kant and hesitating about the character of the noumenal was now more appealing to Americans. In limiting the power of reason, thinkers could deny the pantheism of full-fledged idealists. In insisting on the cloudy nature of the noumenal, they suggested God's transcendence and the need for scriptural revelation.

Scottish realism disclosed how knowing was possible. Against Locke it argued that knowledge of things was unmediated. Against Berkeley and Hume it argued that the things known were not ideas. The Scottish realists were not in the first instance concerned with the ultimate nature of known objects. It was unclear if the world existed independent of mind. Scottish realism, that is, was not certainly metaphysical realism. We have already noted this ambiguity in discussing Witherspoon's renunciation of Berkeley. Witherspoon repudiated Locke's representational theory, along with the belief Witherspoon attributed to Berkeley that physical objects were ideas in the minds of individuals. As I have indicated, this position left many of Berkeley's (and Edwards's) assumptions untouched. Although Witherspoon rebutted his version of Berkeley, he as well as other Scottish realists did not speak to the arguments of the less subjective idealism that animated much of the New England Theology.

The character of realism grew even more ambiguous in the nineteenth century, and was illustrated in the professors' grasp of space and time. Were they contingent on the deity? How did God relate to space and its objects? Newton had answered these questions by conjecturing that infinitely extended space was the sensorium of the deity. In some obscure passages Witherspoon irresolutely addressed the same issues. Taylor at Yale later denigrated the importance of the questions because both mind and matter were contingent on God. But even Taylor allowed that it was 'impossible for us to determine either from the nature of mind or matter, whether the world if once created and left alone, would continue or not'. Other

Calvinists took similar paths. Henry Boynton Smith of Union Seminary in New York had studied in Germany and mildly criticized Scottish thought. He argued that the 'divine fullness' manifested itself in so far as this was possible in the forms of space and time. Even Charles Hodge proclaimed that imperfect understanding of the connection of God and nature generated the mystery of spirit's relation to space.

The primary responsibility of the theologians was not to investigate these conundrums. After Hamilton became important, collegiate philosophers asked the questions and, in time, answered idealistically. Hamilton's notes to Reid's *Collected Writings* distinguished presentationalism and representationalism in epistemology. Representationalists were like Locke and Descartes. Within presentationalism Hamilton then distinguished between absolute idealists and realists or dualists. The first group, for Hamilton, consisted of philosophers who believed there was a direct perception of reality, but that the only reality was mind. The second group, for Hamilton, was composed of Scottish realists like himself. His direct perception of reality included perception of a mental world and a distinct material world. But American thinkers would not leap at the implication that such a cleavage made matter independent of God. That left them with Hamilton's first form of presentationalism, absolute idealism.

McCosh's *Intuitions of the Mind* accepted Newton's view that God 'constituted' space and time. This notion insinuated that McCosh may have agreed with Hamilton that objects were known in themselves immediately but not necessarily absolutely. The real world was known, but knowledge need not guarantee that this world existed out of relation to everything else.

Harvard's Bowen had said that Scottish realism made some forms of metaphysical idealism implausible but by the late 1860s wrote that realism conflicted sharply only with subjective idealism, an extreme Berkeleyan view. One could be an idealist and natural realist. Bowen defined the self as the exercise of will displayed in the manifestation of force. In such a manifestation the self directly knew the not-self or material. But, said Bowen, the not-self similarly manifested force; and Berkeley called the not-self spiritual. That is, for Berkeley and perhaps for Bowen, matter was essentially the resistance directly confronted and identified with the self's exertion of force. Matter was the way other mind presented itself to the ego, to one's self.

The Americans were not extravagantly metaphysical. Scottish realism protected them from skepticism and allowed them to enter the world of spirit. As the century wore on and materialistic challenges intensified, the Americans turned from realism. Hamilton's dualism might indeed put matter beyond deity, and the Americans would not defend it. At the same time they were not prepared to embrace another metaphysics. Porter ended his *Human Intellect* by discussing space and time and pointed, like his peers, to the topic's mysteries. But Porter had studied in Berlin and sympathized with German thought. He concluded that the universe was the single thought of an individual thinker, fraught with design and including the origination of forces (matter) and their laws. Porter stumbled into absolute idealism, and pressed Scottish thought to its limits. Although he wrote at the end of the period of collegiate philosophizing, even then his view was uncommon. None the less, Porter typified the growing discomfort among academic philosophers with the ability of realism to reconcile science and theology.

At the end of the eighteenth century Scottish thought supported religion. By the 1830s the initial turn toward Germany was motivated by a belief that even Locke's and Reid's moderate empiricism would not sustain some creeds. Theologians trained in Scottish philosophy resisted German thought for thirty years, but by the 1850s and 1860s college philosophers and theologians feared anti-religious empiricism as much as German pantheism.

Moral Philosophy

In studying the undoing of Scottish realism, we have examined epistemological problems, usually addressed in textbooks on 'the cognitive powers' involved in knowledge of the mental and the material. In the second of the pair of textbooks eastern academics commonly wrote, they turned to the motive powers, and elaborated on what I have called Scottish psychology, a theory of how the mind operated. The professors acknowledged the tripartite division that Hodge and Taylor, along with other critics of Edwards, had made conventional. When they inspected the cognitive powers, the philosophers focused on the understanding. In scrutinizing the motive powers, they concentrated on the affections and the will. Although the study of cognition was a necessary preliminary to the study of the motive powers, the latter was practically more important. It concerned morality and duty, and would often include analyses of conscience, which had both intellectual and motive dimensions, enabling individuals to contemplate the character of acts obligating action.

The college philosophers were mechanistic. The soul responded to objects with emotions, feelings, sensibility, or affections. Human beings had desires and were motivated to fulfill them. Achieving appropriate goals satisfied desires. But the motives prompting action only occasionally or proximately caused acts. The efficient causality was the human will that 'penetrated and energized' the affections. Self-caused, the will gave moral character to the realization of desire. Here conscience came into play as an intuitive cognitive power revealing what ought to be done, what desires ought to be fulfilled. But conscience could not dictate to a perverted will. At the same time, although directly perceiving duty, conscience could be trained and educated. Its enlightenment intimated that cognition might influence the will.

The leading intellectual philosophers—Porter, McCosh, and Hickok—all wrote moral philosophy. But the leading ethical theorists were a more varied group, generally known by their successful texts. The two most notable were Mark Hopkins of Williams, whose *Lectures on Moral Science* (1862) augmented his fame as a teacher; and Francis Wayland of Brown, whose *Elements of Moral Science* (1835) was popular for over fifty years. Only a third of the *Elements* treated the scheme of the active powers theoretically. More important were the practical aspects of moral science, the final two-thirds of the book.

Many of the academic speculators were also the college presidents who taught the traditional senior course in moral philosophy. Custodian of the truths essential to civilization, the philosopher-president conveyed them to young men who would assume leadership on the East Coast. The culmination of collegiate education, the class in moral philosophy followed the major texts. It rationalized human duties and exhorted the students to carry them out. Individuals had obligations to themselves and to others. Nature made the satisfaction of individual wants consistent with benevolence to others. The social duties owed to the family, and the universally acknowledged necessities of human nature, eventuated in the state. Thus, the moral theorists outlined the obligations to political authority. The framework of deferential patterns culminated in duties to God, and so in the religious ground of obligation. But duties to oneself stemmed from appreciating the will of God. Personal morality expressed humanity's highest end. The supernatural sanctions for practical ethics were displayed at the logical beginning and end of the enquiry. The moralists assumed that their version of the precepts of Jesus was the best law of individual conduct. Collegians elucidated human obligations through introspection, and extrapolated from the mind's powers appropriate rules for ordering social life and political economy. The ground of morals and politics was the same, individuals and nations under the same God.

The principles ingrained in every human heart still had to be cultivated. In properly trained people, understanding ruled the emotions, and the hierarchies in civilization clarified life's duties. In educating character philosophers made virtue and self-control possible. The civil law culturally manifested them, but the deity always measured their reality.

As one critic has noted, the flat metallic taste of facile moralism and unacknowledged self-aggrandizement that is so unfortunately characteristic of antebellum America filled the professoriate's theorizing. But however jejune their perspective on the moral and political, the collegians actively attended to public affairs. Believing informed discussion essential to the Republic's health, and sanctioned as spokesmen for the upper-middle class in the Northeast, they debated the great issues of the day. Although not perspicacious, the philosophers were not removed from the world. They distinguished between politics and public affairs and offered learned comment on the world without being of it. Their textbook analyses dissociated political morality from political life, or rather mirrored knowledge of only a narrow, restricted, and genteel life.

5   *Innovative Amateurs, 1829–1867*

The prospect for creative thought that would preserve nineteenth-century speculation lay with people at the periphery of the educational system. Although their influence was often curtailed, they energetically responded to challenges and did not fear that Germany would undermine cultural verities. This chapter surveys five innovative strategies, in both philosophy and religion, to outline a vision of the world less constricted than that of American academic divines and philosophers. James Marsh, president of the University of Vermont in the 1820s and 1830s, struggled to make it a viable institution, and used Kantian ideas in what might be called the philosophy of religion to push the New England Theology into a less intellectualist direction. The more well-known Ralph Waldo Emerson rejected this theology, and in eastern Massachusetts made German idealism prominent in a new religion—Transcendentalism. Emerson had Harvard connections but was not an academic and gave up a pulpit; he became an exemplary man of letters, lacking any institutional affiliation. In Connecticut, the minister Horace Bushnell took German ideas and moved in the direction of Hegel. In Mercersburg, a small isolated German Reformed Seminary in western Pennsylvania, John Williamson Nevin did appropriate Hegel to revivify Protestantism. Further west, a group of philosophers outside any college applied Hegel in a secular manner to interpret the civic life of American culture. William Torrey Harris led these 'St Louis Hegelians'.

Kant in Vermont

James Marsh, who was born in Hartford, Vermont, in 1794, graduated from nearby Dartmouth College in 1817. His later education, which included influences from the Andover, Harvard, and Princeton seminaries, left him disenchanted with the individualism of American theology, and he brought to his presidency at Vermont a different orientation. His main achievement was making idealist philosophy available in the United States by publishing in 1829 an American edition of Samuel Taylor Coleridge's work, *Aids to Reflection* (1825).

Coleridge was renowned as an English Romantic but hardly philoso-phized systematically. *Aids to Reflection* was an English impression of Kant's *Critique of Pure Reason* and reduced its complexities to demarcating the functions of understanding and reason. Moreover, commentators such as Coleridge overlooked Kant's strictures on reason. For Coleridge under-standing yielded truths about the natural world. Reason provided timeless insight about the realm beyond nature, grounding morality and religion in the spirit.

In his introduction Marsh set the *Aids* in an American context. His impact on future developments was twofold. First, he highlighted Coleridge's sense of the importance of language. Marsh believed that the structure of language reflected the nature of mind and the world. Language pertaining to the moral world of the mind was figurative. Language origi-nally describing objects of sense was metaphorically applied to the moral. 'The external world which is visible is made to shadow for the speculations of the mind which are invisible.' Marsh did not elaborate this idea but con-tributed to a major trend among the amateurs for which only Emerson was widely known—that language cannot be straightforwardly understood in a literal, referential, fashion.

Marsh's second significant concern was the division between nature and spirit and the connected one between understanding and reason. The understanding gave knowledge of nature, of the sensuous. Marsh used 'reason' ambiguously. Speculative reason provided intuitive truths about nature, operating through the understanding. Practical reason or con-science informed individuals of duties and the meaning of life in the spir-itual, and correlated with the will, the faculty defining accountable creatures and the condition of responsibility. For Marsh the will was a supernatural power and enabled people to act without regard to nature. But without grace, the will limited itself to the sensual; in bondage to nature, the spiritual was subject to the worldly. Sin, our love of self, left us part of the causal relations of the physical world. An ultimate fact, sin was also a 'deep mystery'. Only grace could redeem the depraved will from nature and restore its true relationship to spirit. The prima–facie cleavage between speculative and practical reason vanished when grace was invoked. The redeemed will transformed the world. Practical reason ter-minated in action, actualizing the spiritual potential found in speculative reason.

Marsh held that his analysis uncovered 'the great constituent principles of our own permanent being and proper humanity'. Coleridge was an anti-dote to the mechanistic and individualistic ideas Marsh found in Scottish realism and mainstream American theology. For in examining reason, said

Marsh, one came to acknowledge faith. In exploring the self, one confronted Christianity's essence—a fallen will, bondage to sin, and realization that
one had to rely on the mercy of God. Marsh expressed this insight in testi-
fying that the discovery of reason was living the Christian faith.

This explication stretches Marsh as a philosopher. Christianity for him
was most of all a form of being and not a species of knowledge. Leonard
Woods, the leading mid-century theologian at Andover Seminary, conveyed this notion to Marsh himself when the latter overstressed correct reasoning. 'The philosophy of religion is, after all, worth but little. What can it
do towards saving the world? What can it do for a Christian, when death
draws near?' As Marsh wrote, the heart had to grasp 'spiritual maladies and
perishing wants'. Speculation would not suffice.

We bring our spiritual powers in the sphere of a finite nature, and then seek to
make it the instrument for satiating our infinite desires. We strive with capricious
folly and madness to stimulate and task the powers of corporeal and perishable
nature, and to accumulate the means of sensual enjoyment, till they shall satisfy
the infinite and endless cravings of that which only the infinite God and the
absolute good can ever fill.

Absolute Idealism in Concord

By 1800 Harvard had turned its back on Calvinism and embraced a version
of Arminian Christianity that was soon transformed into Unitarianism,
which postulated a theistic deity and looked to the life of Jesus and the New
Testament for moral inspiration, but refused to consider Jesus the Son of
God. The apostasy of Cambridge was, according to its enemies, a horrific
example of where the declension from Calvinism could lead and instru-
mental to founding the Andover Seminary, but thinkers in Boston spent
comparatively little effort on theology and developed instead cosmopolitan literary interests. Cambridge and Boston became the home to
America's first 'intellectuals' and, assisted by inherited wealth, an associated genteel literary society.

In the 1830s, disaffected Unitarians began to search for a religion that,
they thought, would avoid the British ideas that sapped theology. The spir-
itual essence in preaching had been lost. In the fall of 1836, a group of
Unitarian ministers and ex-ministers formed the Transcendental Club,
which gathered irregularly for three or four years. Members included
Emerson (who had left the Unitarian ministry in 1832) and Henry David
Thoreau, who later gathered with others of like mind in Concord,
Massachusetts, near Cambridge. The name 'Transcendentalism' implied

that the new basis for religion derived from Kant and his distinction between reason and understanding, but commentators have pointed out that the Transcendentalists were, in Kantian terminology, Transcendentists, and took only what they wanted from Kant. Moreover, German philosophy was only the ultimate source of Transcendentalism; more important was the version of Kant that reached America via Marsh.

Despite his orthodoxy, Marsh elaborated ideas primary for Transcendentalism: a disdain for a British foundation for religion; concern for a theology of the heart; belief in the centrality of the dichotomies between reason and understanding, and between spirit and nature; and acceptance of the static quality of these categories. For Transcendentalism religion did not depend, as for the Unitarians, on facts, or on tradition or authority for that matter, but on an unerring witness in the soul. Religion rose above empirical observations. The Scottish moral sense served Emerson's belief in a higher intuition of religious truth, but his faculty of reason had little to do with ratiocinative processes or science as understood by the Scots.

Although the Transcendentalists sought alternatives to the dominant American philosophy of religion, they were not primarily expository thinkers, and Emerson's brief *Nature*, published in 1836, the same year the club got under way, was the most sustained vindication of Transcendentalism. But despite its short compass *Nature* laid out a systematic position. Emerson turned away from the disputes in the New England Theology and from a religion based on inessentials:

Our age is retrospective. It builds the sepulchers of the fathers . . . The foregoing generations beheld God and nature face to face; we, through their eyes. Why should not we also enjoy an original relation to the universe? Why should not we have a poetry and philosophy of insight and not of tradition, and a religion by revelation to us, and not the history of others?

Nature found the 'original relation' in a version of Kantian idealism.

Emerson defined nature as everything, the entire cosmos, except the individual soul. Friendly to man, nature somehow wore 'the colors of the spirit'. He asked, then, the purpose or function of nature. Initially, it was practically useful, the locus of work and provider of goods necessary to survival. But a nobler purpose of nature afforded aesthetic enjoyment. It satisfied the soul's desire for beauty. Moreover, said Emerson, nature grounded communication. Here he relied on the linguistic theories suggesting, first, that language was not a transparent medium; and, second, that the language of mind depended on the language of the physical. Emerson urged that language had two branches, one to discuss nature, the other spirit.

Words signified natural facts but were then used metaphorically to pick out spiritual facts. 'Right' meant 'straight', referring to a 'material appearance'. The word later described a moral, or non-material, characteristic. For Emerson, nature as a whole typified, or symbolized, spirit. The analogies between the natural and the spiritual were not arbitrary, but evidenced that nature was the human mind writ large. A further purpose of nature enabled individuals, through language, to reach other spirits. Finally, nature furnished a discipline. The properties of nature demanded explanation, a theory of nature embodied in physical science.

If one of nature's purposes generated science, might it not be that nature existed 'absolutely', and that spirit came to know it? Emerson said no to this lifeless dualism. The material world was phenomenal, as Berkeley had written. But for Emerson this sort of idealism was merely a step to a more comprehensive philosophy. Berkeleyan idealism only analysed what matter was; it did not convey matter's purpose. Having sketched higher and more comprehensive purposes, Emerson argued for a more absolute idealism. Individual spirits were fragments or parts of a greater Spirit, God. Nature was an 'expositor' of the divine, God incarnate, the way Spirit appeared to fragments of itself. Nature's purpose, to these fragmentary souls, was to reveal God as their greater self.

Nature modified Emerson's notable individualism and 'naturalism'. Although he pleaded with his audiences to be self-reliant, he joined these exhortations with his belief in the result of self-realization. Self-development would progressively expose one's partial identity with Spirit. True individuality for him, as for the tradition of Edwards, never displayed selfishness. The saved person was rather part of a corporate whole. 'Mean egotism', Emerson said, would vanish. The currents of the 'Universal Being' would circulate through people: 'I am part or parcel of God.' Unable to see spiritual beauty in nature, human beings were selfish. In talking about salvation, Emerson asked individuals to envision themselves as aspects of a greater self. The problem was human perception. 'The axis of vision is not coincident with the axis of things, and so they appear not transparent but opaque.'

How could human beings look at the world with new eyes? Emerson was unclear. Commentators have stressed his naturalism, his belief that the individual need only draw on inner resources, on an inner spirit, to attain unity with the divine. Emerson also said people were to be restored 'by the redemption of the soul'. This 'instantaneous instreaming causing power' did not exist in time or space. Examples of the exercise of such power included the tradition of miracles, the history of Jesus Christ, the achievement of principle in religious and political revolution, the miracles of enthusiasm, and the obscure and contested facts then conceptualized as instances of animal magnetism. Salvation for Emerson might have been available to all people if they only called on what they truly were. But his belief did not entail the Arminianism that the followers of Edwards associated with the respectable churchgoing practices of Unitarians. Rather, for Emerson, regeneration tapped a source that Unitarians considered above nature. Although this source might be in everyone, people rarely drew on it successfully, and it was at hand for Emerson only because German idealism altered the conception of nature paramount in Unitarianism. God did not *create* nature to accomplish his work and to evidence himself. Nature *was* God as he appeared to parts of himself.

While *Nature* displayed theoretical impulses, systematic theology hardly concerned Emerson, who was convinced that the philosophy of religion had reached a dead end. Unlike Marsh, for example, who reconstructed theology using German thought, Emerson wanted to overcome theology. Its role in Transcendentalist thought aside, *Nature* was obscurely and idiosyncratically written for a limited readership. But in 1838, after Emerson delivered a notorious speech at the Harvard Divinity School, Transcendentalism became a local scandal. 'The Divinity School Address' stated directly that intuition revealed God incarnate in everyone. Unitarianism had been mistakenly centered on Jesus and his miracles. But, Emerson said, the whole of life was miraculous; the miracles were 'one with the blowing clover and the falling rain'. Jesus's spirituality and not his supposed supernatural powers were crucial.

For the American followers of the Scots, empirical evidence and intuitions worked simultaneously to justify common-sense beliefs. The Scots had long since asserted that intuitions existed but were meaningful only when integrated with sensation. Just as empirical evidence was necessary to legitimate ordinary beliefs, so it was necessary for belief in Christianity. The moral sense responded to the uplifting doctrines of the Bible, but did so in conjunction with directly given facts. Emerson argued on the contrary for experiential knowledge that was immediate, not discursive.

By the early 1840s Theodore Parker, an eloquent and learned polemicist and another ex-Unitarian minister, clearly stated the Emersonian view. 'A Discourse of the Transient and Permanent in Christianity' (1841) urged that religion's abiding elements were the divine life in the soul and love to God and man, notions communicated ephemerally and imperfectly in all theologies. The greatness of Jesus was his perfect exhibition of mutual love and the divinity of God. These truths, not Christ's personal authority or the Scriptures, sanctioned Christianity; and the oracle God placed in every breast, not historical facts, tested these truths. Yet Parker affirmed his

Christianity: Jesus was the only person in history who discerned and taught religious truth.

Radical Unitarians might have given birth to non-Christian, vaguely theistic theologies, but this impact was peripheral to the purpose of Emerson and Parker. The reinvigoration of religiosity through preaching was central. The Transcendentalists thought that the philosophy of religion in America was sterile; the minister rather had to save souls by moving the heart of his congregation. Transcendentalism was not infidelity; it saw its alternatives as a debilitating professionalism; or as skepticism, materialism, and atheism. The belligerence of Emerson's 1838 address resulted from his frustration with theology; the address itself spoke of 'the great and perpetual' office of the clergy. Emerson's early Transcendentalism was designed for the minister to convince audiences of a religion of feeling. Despite the fact that Unitarians closed their pulpits to Parker, he had the largest parish in Boston by the late 1840s. Magnificently popular, he was known as 'the Great American preacher'.

Unitarianism and Transcendentalism were rooted in the same milieu. The Unitarians downplayed theology, preferring to embrace religion as an elegant and refined moral sense. Their achievements were in such avocations essay-writing, literary criticism, poetry, and other non-religious intellectual pursuits. The Unitarians produced meritorious newspapers and periodicals, the *North American Review* chief among them, and the contributors were a good index to the flowering of nineteenth-century life. The Transcendentalists extended this tradition. Their peculiarity lay in adjusting to the changing urban world. New England had traditionally countenanced the ministry as the calling for men of altruistic and literary impulses. But by mid-century the minister's status as the community's most learned man was being eroded, and conventional spirituality was lifeless. Moreover, a range of non-ministerial outlets for these genteel impulses emerged. Temperance, anti-slavery, and other reform activities; the lyceum or new lecture forum; and the religious press undermined the church's unique function and created alternative yet vaguely defined vocations. The Transcendentalists saw themselves as self-reliant poet-priests, a nebulous image that none the less accurately portrayed their half-religious ambition and the lack of an institutionalized role to fulfill it.

The lyceum in which the Transcendentalists displayed their chief talent, oratory akin to preaching, was, Emerson wrote, 'the new pulpit'. The characteristic Transcendentalist expression, the essay, partook of both oral and written tradition. Often originally a lecture, the essay arose from experience of the preacher and resembled the sermonic style that the Transcendentalists had mastered. As a literary exercise, the essay was also indebted to the conversation clubs of fashionable nineteenth-century Boston. The Unitarian sermon broadened the range of pulpit subjects, and the Transcendentalists began where the Unitarians stopped. Transcendentalist writing distrusted both orthodox doctrine and profane fiction. The writing aesthetically expressed noble truths. Transcendentalism combined literary taste and the theocentric framework of New England discourse. The Transcendentalists' social role coincided with their part in advancing *belles-lettres*.

Biblical study also had an influence. The tradition embodied by Parker argued that scriptural 'myths' were allegories, declaring in pre-rational form what scholars could now state more accurately. But myths could also be symbolic, imperfectly voicing higher truths. Thinkers such as the Transcendentalists believed that history was associated with the understanding. Imaginative writing associated with intuitive reason might be closer to the truth. In this case, the Bible mythically affirmed otherwise inaccessible truths. Literature could best pronounce spiritual verities.

Marsh applied German speculation to American theology. Emerson and his followers concentrated on the distinction between nature and spirit and the symbolic aspect of spiritual language. This focus, along with Emerson's disdain for systematic thought, led him, unlike Marsh, to chart a new career as an American man of letters. For Emerson, the lecture supplanted the sermon as the public forum. Issues of divinity were confronted through aesthetics. When values were discussed, people had to be persuaded rather than reasoned with. These developments cannot be separated from the inability of traditional theology to convince some well-educated groups in the Northeast, a failure that lessened Marsh's impact. Transcendentalism's subsequent dominance of academic literary life demonstrated that its idiosyncratic perspective—between metaphysics and metaphor—had an enduring and compelling attraction. From the perspective of the philosophy of religion, Transcendentalism contributed to a new, avant-garde culture in which religion was a matter of symbol and feeling. Over the next forty years, however, these ideas had trouble penetrating institutionalized philosophical and theological discussion.

Horace Bushnell

Bushnell's life illustrated typical currents in the careers of successful mid-nineteenth-century men of letters and culture. As a young man in the 1820s and 1830s, he vacillated among law, journalism, and the ministry before entering the Yale seminary, where he studied with Nathaniel William Taylor and received his degree in 1833 at the age of 31. Minister to the North

Congregational Church in Hartford, Connecticut, Bushnell earned a reputation for oratorical eloquence and effective, if controversial, pastoral leadership. He later remembered hoping for a professorship of moral
philosophy, which he regarded as a more satisfactory and higher calling
than that of a preacher. But although he coveted a professorship at Harvard
in the 1830s, Bushnell turned down the presidency of Middlebury College
in 1840 and, much later, in 1861, the presidency of the new University of
California.

Bushnell's success as a pulpit lecturer and author overcame the pull he
felt toward a major post in the academy. In this era, popularizing the philosophy of religion through speaking talent won wide audiences. Some
commentators have lamented the romantic and unsystematic theology of
the period and the sentimental religion that Bushnell promoted. But the
desire for fame that he satisfied also liberated him from conventions.
Emphasizing pulpit eloquence meshed with a radical theory of language
indebted to Kant and post-Kantian idealism.

Bushnell's thought came to public attention in *Discourses on Christian
Nurture* (1847). In his early years in Hartford he had failed at revivals. The
orthodox had suggested that 'parental fondness' might promote self-
indulgence as the soul's 'master principle' long before a child was aware of
the duties or rights of others. On becoming a moral agent, the child would
already be disposed to sin, to gratify the self. Bushnell reversed this argument.
By the same reasoning, grace might be imperceptibly imparted. Contrary to
the early nineteenth-century model, children, especially in Christian homes,
might simply grow up regenerate. Bushnell noted that no human method
could achieve such gracious nurture. The holy principles involved were not
natural, and a Christian education did not draw out the good in children.
Nonetheless, having Christian parents changed the children's presumptive
relation to God. Redeemed parents might be the means of grace for their
offspring because their holy spirits blended with the child's will.

Taylor's theories had fit adult revivalism, Bushnell's answered to genteel
domesticity. Both stressed the will's autonomy. Taylor, however, argued that
adult decisions were critical. In contrast, Bushnell claimed that institutions
communicated their spirit to the person they embraced. Virtue was not an
act; it was a state for which people were responsible, but for which others
might prepare the way. The holy will of parents, for example, mingled with a
child's 'incipient and half-formed exercises'. Bushnell opposed this organicism to the prevailing 'fictitious and mischievous individualism'.

Princeton's Charles Hodge sympathized with Bushnell's dislike of revivalism, but perceptively argued that the preacher could not justify supernatural
grace. Hodge accepted a central traditional conundrum: that sin was not

God's act, but that grace was; human beings were responsible for their salvation, though a holy will was God's gift. Hodge claimed that Bushnell could not distinguish between natural sinfulness and supernatural grace. For Bushnell, God's providential agency in originating the laws of nature was inseparable from his gracious regeneration of depraved souls. Hodge devastatingly quoted Bushnell as saying that depravity and grace must be brought under the same organic laws. Whereas Bushnell might accordingly argue that nature was inherently gracious, Hodge said men were not then naturally depraved. The supernatural had no status other than what nature could explain. Bushnell might write that he was a supernaturalist because he believed God was in nature, but sacralizing nature could only end in naturalizing the sacred. Bushnell, Hodge concluded, was nothing more or less than a German philosopher of immanence, close to pantheism.

Bushnell considered himself orthodox and agonized over the dispute. After months of turmoil, he had a transforming experience in the late 1840s. The presumptions to which he came shaped the rest of his life. Bushnell was stung into articulating a connected set of ideas. There was, he believed, a cleavage between nature and spirit, roughly between the world of objects existing in space and time and the world constituted by their meaning and value. Although this distinction existed, spirit also conditioned and informed nature. Interrogating nature revealed the spirit logically prior to it; the invisible was grasped via the visible.

A lecture delivered in various places in 1847, 'Life, Or the Lives', argued that lives were immaterial powers organizing and conserving the bodies they inhabited. The entire cosmos was 'ensouled'. Edwards had reduced the will to nature and destroyed religion. Although it was not possible to conceive the will under the laws of causation applicable to matter, in altered language Bushnell still emphasized some of Edwards's ideas. Christianity essentially 'incorporated' Jesus in the life of the believer, and grace overwhelmed one sort of formative impulse by another. Christ became the form of the soul. This theme reappeared in a late essay, 'Science and Religion' (1868). Science was possible only because purpose and spirit enclosed nature and postulated that an all-present mind informed law in the world. A lawful universe was contingent on the meaningful but uncaused and supernatural activity of mind. At the same time, increasing scientific knowledge furnished clues for deciphering the divine plan at nature's heart. Constrained by their finitude human beings lived in the world of nature. God then displayed himself in an imperfect medium. Finite boundaries impeded the infinite purpose, and human beings fathomed its significance from hints personified in nature. God could not adequately express himself in a finite mode, and, therefore, we could not completely understand him.

For Bushnell, this meant that religion was not literally but figuratively true. Calvinist theology purported to explain the biblical narrative of the Creation, the Fall, the Coming of Christ, and the Crucifixion, all of which were events in nature, but as a thing of the spirit, meaning was only imperfectly displayed in the physical world or explained by science. 'It is', Bushnell wrote, 'a great trouble with us that we cannot put a whole scheme of redemption, which God could execute only by the volume of expression contained in the life and death of his incarnate son, into a theologic formula or article of ten words.' Theologians could not 'decoct the whole mass of symbol'.

The fullest expression of Bushnell's ideas was his 'Preliminary Dissertation on Language' in a book of 1849 called *God in Christ*, perhaps the most significant nineteenth-century exploration of language and the heart of Bushnell's attempt to rehabilitate Calvinism. Marsh had written on the issue, and Emerson had taken it up in *Nature*, but Bushnell made language central.

Although Taylor's theology influenced him, Bushnell had also studied with Josiah Willard Gibbs, the biblical critic of the Yale Divinity School. Gibbs's mentor was Moses Stuart, the Andover opponent of Harvard's liberal construal of the Bible. Gibbs continued in New Haven the perusal of sacred texts pioneered by Stuart. Inordinately cautious, Gibbs still accepted that biblical language could be metaphorical. When describing the mind, physical-object language functioned analogically. The resulting passages in the Bible might consequently call for non-literal interpretation if the intent were to be grasped. This insight motivated Bushnell's 'Preliminary Dissertation'.

There were two departments of language, said the dissertation. Referential in import, literal language was about the physical, about objects in the world. Language pertaining to the mental, spiritual, or human world was figurative. It derived from the physical but necessarily proceeded from analogy. Propositions might depict literal truths about the material, but also served as 'natural figures' when spiritual truth was in question. Theology could thus never be scientific as geology was, and religious statements could never be identical to statements of geology. Systematic theology predicated on literal language must fail. Yet we had to search out the most adequate symbolic or figurative rendition of religious truth.

Bushnell was not hostile to science. Nature typified spirit because a divine 'Logos' in the outer world answered to the human 'logos', our capacity for language. If nature were understood more fully, religious language would become more adequate. The pursuit of science was thus a religious duty. Indeed, since the Logos initially informed the physical world,

Bushnell could not definitively distinguish figurative from non-figurative language. Truths about geology were not, finally, literally true. The outer world was really a vast 'menstruum' of thought or intelligence. Religion was not, finally, figurative. A perfect science would mean a truer religion because some analogies were better than others. Arbitrary figures did not convey religious sentiment.

Earlier, in the controversy over *Christian Nurture*, Bushnell had said that in nurturance the infant's mind was as 'passive as the wax to the seal'. In *God in Christ* this metaphor from British epistemology vanished. Instead he used the images of German idealism. Creatures 'under time and succession' could know God only through 'finite molds of action'. Because human life was incapable of dealing with the infinite, religious knowledge was incomplete.

Christ was God's last metaphor, communicating his real union with humanity. But the divine–human incarnation remained mysterious. The incarnation was a historic fact valuable for what it divulged of God, not for the riddle it offered metaphysics. Bushnell constructed a double view of the meaning of Jesus's murder and rebirth. The objective aspect was an outward form—roughly the report of the suffering and death of Christ. The facts, for Bushnell, were that Jesus was crucified, dead, and buried, and on the third day arose from the dead. This objective aspect signified the subjective; the physical carried the truth only inferentially. The subjective seemed to be the symbol of what had occurred in nature. The subjective atonement displayed Christ as manifesting eternal life, as a power that quickened or regenerated human character.

Bushnell emphasized the temporal. History was a figure that had its value not in facts but in what they portended. In the creation God outwardly exemplified himself. In Christ God became more fully part of humanity. He grafted himself onto individuals. Christ incorporated the divine into humanity and gave humanity history, a story with an overriding purpose. The church, Bushnell said, was not 'a body of men holding certain dogmas, or maintaining, as men, certain theologic wars for God; but it is the Society of the Life, the Embodied Word'.

Bushnell's theory rationalized pulpit eloquence and attacked the whole idea of systematic theology. He was sarcastic about the history of American divinity and called theologians 'male spinsters of logic'. Arrayed before him, he saw:

the multitudes of leaders and schools and theologic wars of only the century past,—the Supralapsarians, and Sublapsarians; the Arminianizers, and the true Calvinists; the Pelagians, and Augustinians; the Tasters, and the Exercisers; Exercisers by Divine Efficiency, and by Self-Efficiency; the love-to-being-in-general virtue, the willing-to-be-damned virtue, and the love-to-one's-greatest-happiness virtue; no ability, all ability, and moral and natural ability distinguished; disciples by the new-creating act of Omnipotence, and by change of the governing purpose; atonement by punishment, and by expression; limited, and general; by imputation, and without imputation; trinitarians of a threefold distinction, of three psychologic persons, or of three sets of attributes; under a unity of oneness, or of necessary agreement, or of society and deliberative council;— nothing I think would more certainly disenchant us of our confidence in systematic orthodoxy, and the possibility, in human language, of an exact theologic science, than an exposition so practical and serious and withal so indisputably mournful,—so mournfully indisputable.

He told an Andover audience that seminaries produced 'pernicious results':

They are such, in great part, as result from the assembling of a large body of young men in a society of their own, where they mingle, exhibit their powers one to another, debate opinions, criticise performances, measure capacities, applaud demonstrations of genius, talk of places filled by others, and conjecture, of course, not seldom, what places they may be called to fill themselves. They are thus prepared to exhibit Christ scholastically, rhetorically, dogmatically—too often ambitiously, too seldom as spirit and life. Perhaps it is only by sore mortification and the stern discipline of defeat or diminishing repute, that they will, at last, be humbled into the true knowledge of Christ, and prepared to bear his cross.

In another sense Bushnell was theologically ambitious, for *God in Christ* tried to convert New England to his views. He was using eloquence to win divines to his thinking, but by emphasizing that religious language was metaphorical, he was also claiming that he had not been previously understood. If his theory of language exemplified how conventional philosophy of religion might be overthrown, his theology would demonstrate the untrustworthiness of theology itself.

God in Christ defended a transcendent God who insufficiently disclosed himself in a finite medium. Christianity and its symbols were his imperfect unfolding. The phenomenal was a defective vehicle of the noumenal, and the Bible a metaphorical expression. Bushnell consequently asked the religious to play down biblical literalism, but his theology also made it possible to view Christianity invidiously as poetry. Bushnell himself, however, stated that religion was not merely symbolic. In *Nature and the Supernatural As Together Constituting the One System of God* (1858) he made his greatest effort to clarify his supernaturalism.

In a set of striking images, Bushnell argued that nature never fully embosomed God's beauty and his mind's eternal order. Nature must be 'to some wide extent, a realm of deformity and abortion, groaning with the discords of sin'. The travails of pain in the creation resulted from the 'grand assault' of our supernatural sinful agency on the world. Sin was to the natural world what a grain of sand was to the eye: 'it is [still] an organ of sight; only it sees through tears'. Bushnell thus did not believe in the adequacy of nature but could not elaborate his supernaturalism. Christianity—God's gift of Jesus—creatively repaired the damage caused by the sinful will. Grace transformed sinners and so, finally, the world. This was Christ's meaning in history. Bushnell's later refusal to accept evolutionary biology, despite his stress on organicism and history, also testified to his anti-naturalism. Souls were supernatural entities, and only special creation could account for them. The natural world could never, in itself, harbor them. But Bushnell could not think his way out of the naturalism that he had been accused of earlier in his career. God operated supernaturally in nature just as people did. The giving of grace was no different from a person's intentionally raising an arm. Nor could Bushnell show how God could alter human volition without infringing on human freedom. Although Bushnell denounced the Transcendentalist notion that self-development was saving and emphasized the divinity of Christ, he could not distinguish our will from God's. In reviewing *Nature and the Supernatural,* Noah Porter, a moderate supporter of Bushnell's, pointed out that Bushnell did not effectively merge orthodoxy and naturalism. His theology was too traditional and his naturalism too distinct to be melded without more subtle and systematic thinking than Bushnell exhibited.

Organicism in Mercersburg

In 1825 the German Reformed Church in the United States established a seminary in York, Pennsylvania, a rural center 100 miles west of Philadelphia. In 1832 the church's synod hired Frederich Augustus Rauch as a second member of the faculty and principal of the seminary's Classical School to train seminarians in the classics. With a doctorate from Marburg, Rauch was eager to publish in classical literature and philology. Despite his youth—he was only in his mid-twenties—his German career had been blemished when he migrated to the United States. But whatever his problems in Germany, Rauch succeeded in Pennsylvania. A few years later the seminary at York moved further west to Mercersburg, and Rauch became president of both it and Marshall College, the new name for the Classical School, which had received an independent charter.

Marshall College and the Mercersburg Seminary were not important enterprises. Ever on the edge of bankruptcy, they educated a trickle of adolescents and struggled to keep even a minimally qualified faculty. But in

Rauch the Reformed Church secured an able scholar. In 1840 he published *Psychology; or a view of the Human Soul; including Anthropology*, the first statement in English of Hegelian principles of mind. The same year John Williamson Nevin joined him on the seminary faculty. Educated at Union College and Princeton Seminary, and indebted to Charles Hodge, Nevin had transferred to the German Reformed Church. He discovered German thought by reading Marsh's edition of *Aids to Reflection* but went on to the Hegelian ideas common among German theologians. At Mercersburg Rauch reinforced Nevin's interest in idealist theology. In 1841, shortly after Nevin's arrival, Rauch died at the age of 34. In 1844 the synod replaced him with Philip Schaff, a 25-year-old Swiss instructor at Berlin. Schaff had studied under the most distinguished German theologians and historians at three universities: at Tübingen with Ferdinand Christian Baur and Isaac Dorner; at Halle with Julius Mueller and Frederick Tholuck; at Berlin (where he received his doctorate) with August Neander, Karl Ritter, Leopold von Ranke, and Ernst Hengstenberg. In 1841 he heard Friedrich Schelling's lectures at Berlin and sat in the same audience with Søren Kierkegaard, Michael Bakunin, and Friedrich Engels.

When Schaff arrived in the Pennsylvania wilderness 3,000 miles from Berlin, he found in Nevin a congenial colleague acquainted with contemporary German ideas. Nevin himself welcomed someone who could enrich his theology. In the next ten years they expounded a distinctive Christian vision, known as the Mercersburg Theology, and their mountain village was recognized throughout the Western world as a center of disputation.

Nevin and Schaff brought together individualism and churchly hierarchy. Individualism without the church, they held, was as little to be trusted as ecclesiasticism without personal experience. They immediately conflicted with American religious ideas: in addition to rejecting the emphasis on the solitary believer, the German Reformed thinkers also argued that Christianity was not a supernatural science or a system of doctrine that could be proved; it was a form of life. Faith was less an assent to propositions than an appreciation of divine reality, analogous to sense experience. An organic growth, the church incorporated the work of Christ. It evolved, like an Aristotelian telos, into what it was destined to become. Christianity, wrote Nevin was 'a perpetual fact, that starts in the incarnation of the Son of God, and reaches forward as a continuous supernatural reality to the end of time'. The Bible was neither the principle of Christianity nor the rock on which the church was built. Rather the actual living revelation of Jesus was the foundation. The human race was not an aggregate of people, but the power of a single life, inwardly bound together. The redeemed were mystically unified in this life and drawn to its center in Christ. The traditions of the church, its institutions, patterns of worship, and creeds organically and temporally expressed Christianity.

Ecclesiastical formalism missed the essence of Christianity. But Nevin and Schaff also affirmed that the individual's experience of Christ occurred in the community of the faithful tracing its roots to the ancient church. In 1844 Nevin delivered the keynote sermon, 'Catholic Unity', before the convention of the German and Dutch Reformed Churches. It was published ten months later with a translation of the expanded version of Schaff's inaugural address, *The Principle of Protestantism*. Nevin's sermon spoke of the great evil of sectarianism and said that church unity would not occur through one sect's attacks on others. Protestants must repent of denominationalism. Ecumenical unity would be a gracious gift manifesting the inner life of the Church: 'Our Protestant Christianity cannot continue to stand in its present form.' *The Principle of Protestantism* reiterated these themes. Expressing a positive attitude toward the Middle Ages, Schaff added that the Reformation sprang from medieval Catholicism. The reformers were reformed Catholics, representing the better tendencies of the Roman Church. Christianity developed dialectically. Catholicism was not a great evil, nor was orthodox Protestantism the final and fixed religion. The unity of Christendom would synthesize Romanism and Protestantism.

When Schaff wrote, he was unaware of the anti-Catholic feeling in the United States and had unwittingly suggested inherited continuities to be indispensable for understanding Scripture. But American Protestants knew that the Bible interpreted itself. Views such as Schaff's, organized around communitarian traditionalism, were at least suspicious. Indeed, they resulted in cries of heresy against the Mercersburg professors. Their perspective was distinctive in America, but in England, Oxford Anglo-Catholicism mooted the same themes, as did High Church Lutherans in Germany. Indeed, the orientation of Nevin and Schaff was common in Germany by the 1840s. But in the context of New England Protestantism, wedded to the single believer, Mercersburg was idiosyncratic. Essentially, however, the Mercersburg thinkers were orthodox Protestants. They believed in depravity and the need for supernatural grace. Natural humanity, unaided by faith, could never save itself. Jesus' death resulted in a new life for the community. Yet these views were formulated within a framework that contrasted with the ahistoric individualism of New England. Nevin and Schaff believed that the spiritual and moral life had no meaning aside from history. Only the society of the elect, the institutions of the church extended in time, could comprehend spiritual truth. Emerson shared with Mercersburg an idealist organicism, but with New England

Protestantism he shared a static individualism. Mercersburg emphasized a historical community, going further along this path than Bushnell.

Hegel in St Louis

In 1858 William Torrey Harris and Henry C. Brokmeyer met at a philosophical discussion in St Louis. In 1866, after the Civil War, they started the St Louis Philosophical Society, the most important Western attempt at philosophical (in contrast to theological) speculation. Harris, Brokmeyer, and their associates became famous as the St Louis Hegelians. The leadership of Harris and Brokmeyer was consistent with the joint heritage of the group. Harris was a transplanted Easterner teaching shorthand in St Louis in the late 1850s. But he had independent philosophical interests stirred by the Transcendentalists. A convert to their idealism, he had read German philosophy before he went west. Brokmeyer was a German jack-of-all-trades who had come to the United States in 1844 and had direct access to German thought. By the time he met Harris he was devoted to Hegel's *Larger Logic*, having begun a translation project that would continue for nearly half a century.

The priority of Brokmeyer and Harris rested in Hegel and history. Many groups on the frontier duplicated these concerns. From the 1830s on, Americans with a pensive bent took their Emerson with them when they moved to Ohio, Indiana, Illinois, and Missouri. The Transcendentalists were unconcerned with systematic thought and contemptuous of institutionalized speculation. None the less, they popularized spirituality among literate Americans with an interest in the life of the mind. Collegiate philosophers and theologians appeared formal and scholastic; Emerson and his circle were a breath of fresh air. Some of the migrants, however, soon discarded the static idealism of Emerson when they met émigré German intellectuals and consequently learned of Hegel. German communities existed not just in Pennsylvania villages but also in Cincinnati, Chicago, Milwaukee, and St Louis, and contributed to a connected group of speculative societies. The St Louis Hegelians were only *primus inter pares* among Western philosophers.

The St Louis group adopted more dynamic and historical ideas than Concord. The Hegelians defined the individual as a dialectic of self and other necessarily involving society. As pure being individuals were nothing. But in temporal existence, they acquired identity in relation to other individuals and events. Defining themselves through past experiences and future expectations, none of which was present, individuals came to selfhood through social context and historical connection. Reaching out for self-definition in ever-widening social and institutional bonds, the self confronted reality as an endless unfolding, with the 'me' and the 'not me' resulting in a 'larger and more complete me'. The larger and more complete the self, the greater the self-knowledge and freedom. For Emerson, the self's link to the world had only to be discovered. The Hegelians constructed it. For each, the world functioned to define the individual. But for the earlier thinkers, the definition was given. For the later ones, temporal interaction with 'the other' created the individual.

St Louis differed from Concord in its dynamic conception of the self and the self's connection to the other. Moreover, St Louis denigrated the individual, however defined. For the Hegelians, the bearers of spirit were not individuals but institutions, cultures, stages of history, and civilizations. Following Hegel, the St Louis thinkers saw the mind of God emerging in dialectical social progress. God endlessly but always more fully exposed himself in communal experience. As in Emerson, the individual self was a part or particle of God, but it was God in his becoming, not in his being. History necessarily advanced as the divine nature of the finite gradually exhibited itself, or rather developed into what it was.

Accordingly, for St Louis, ever larger groups and participation in them were supremely important: the family, the circle of friends, the work organization, the church, the school, the city, the political party, and the state. Every cultural association could achieve progress. Individuals became free only in institutions where they significantly related to others.

The western idealists mainly regarded themselves as citizens. The legitimate ends of the state bounded social action. For St Louis, Hegel's dialectic made progress inevitable but also restricted what it could accomplish. St Louis transcended the self-culture essential to other western philosophers and to Concord, but its wider cultural interest did not transgress the legally sanctioned. Harris became the American Commissioner of Education; Brokmeyer Lieutenant Governor of Missouri; others participated in civic, judicial, and educational institutions.

As much exponents of social programs as interpreters of universal history, the Hegelians comprehended events as episodes in the eternal flowering of an all-embracing plan that rose above conflict. The American Civil War (1861–5) crystalized ideas in St Louis. The Southern cause represented abstract right, for the plantation owners literally had property at stake, even though slavery was an evil. Committed to equality and freedom for all people, the North represented abstract morality. Yet for the North, the state was no more than collected individuals, and for the Hegelians government was neither a contract, nor a system of checks and balances, nor a summary of group interests. The United States as conceived by the Founding Fathers was inadequate. The state rather institutionalized the national consciousness in a political document and a tradition. Abraham Lincoln believed in just this notion of the Constitution and the Union, said the Hegelians. The constitutional issue on which he based the war made him the hero of St Louis. The Transcendentalists supported the war on anti-slavery grounds, but anti-slavery was secondary. The purpose of the war was that of Lincoln—to establish an 'ethical state', a living regime welding law and morality.

The office of the Hegelians, they thought, was not merely to show how the war might transform North and South. From their perch in the 'future great city of the world', they could reflect on the social order. In the progressive West they would synthesize Union and Confederate ideals, industrialism and agriculture, liberalism and reaction.

In 1881, Harris moved to Massachusetts at the behest of the remaining Transcendentalists. Emerson wanted this man of speculative strength as a counterpoint to the 'debility of scholars in Massachusetts'. Harris was to reinvigorate higher thought. Since the 1840s Emerson and others had desired a permanent school for philosophical lectures and discussion. The Transcendentalists recognized that their own ideas were still antagonistic to prevailing religious philosophy and needed their own center. Their idea for an institute was realized in 1879 and 1880. The Concord School of Philosophy convened for ten summers thereafter, affiliating many distinguished lecturers and college instructors and students. The latter paid modest fees to audit courses on literary and philosophical topics.

The most notable of such arrangement in the 1870s, 1880s, and 1890s, the Concord School informally institutionalized the work of people of letters and of various marginal thinkers. Although implicitly aware that they might not transmit their achievement unless they organized, these people were unsure how to organize. Their attempts to position themselves in the emerging university system also suggested this organizational concern. At the same time, the Eastern migration showed that the ideas of historical and organic idealism were coming to New England. The consequences of this movement for the American speculative tradition were far-reaching.

Harris's most significant act of institution-building occurred in 1867, when he brought into being the *Journal of Speculative Philosophy*, the first English-language philosophical periodical, and during most of its existence the only one in the United States. The journal helped to professionalize philosophy in a way that the growth of journals of theology had assisted in professionalizing that discipline in the first half of the century. Few would remember Brokmeyer, Harris, or the magazine. But commentators would almost exclusively focus on those thinkers to whom the magazine gave a voice: Charles Peirce, William James, Josiah Royce, and John Dewey, whose first essays appeared in it.

The Impact of the Amateurs

In the middle third of the nineteenth century, the thought of the amateurs slowly impressed thinkers in the colleges and seminaries. In philosophy, German notions gained credibility in many circles after the Civil War. In the same post-war period, professional theology paid heed to German ideas that might advance the study of divinity—idealism, an organicist interest in history, and theories of symbolic language. Exemplary here was the work of Henry Boynton Smith of the Union Theological Seminary in New York; and Edwards Amasa Park of Andover Seminary. Smith was a Presbyterian influenced by Taylor, but a thinker concerned with historical faith more than individual sinners; Park was, as it turned out, the last in the line of the New England Theologians and, although a disciple of Edwards, a man who acknowledged the metaphorical nature of religious language.

The amateurs successfully carved out careers outside the major Eastern colleges and divinity schools. They credited belief in a vigorous public culture in which men of ability might convey important thought to an educated public without merely being considered popularizers. But these triumphs were short-lived. In the aftermath of the Civil War intellectual and social developments swept the amateurs from the scene.

PART II

The Age of Pragmatism, 1859–1934

The work of Charles Darwin dealt a body blow to the religious orientation of American speculative endeavor in the last third of the nineteenth century. The primacy of divinity schools in the scholarly world ended, and the explicit Christian thought that governed intellectual life all but disappeared. At the same time, in the space of thirty years, many colleges were transformed into larger, internationally recognized centers of learning, while new public and private universities commanded national attention. Students who a generation earlier would have sought 'graduate' training in Europe, especially Germany, or in an American seminary, would by 1900 attend a post-baccalaureate program in an American university to obtain the Ph.D., the doctoral degree. Many of these students now found in philosophy what previously had been sought in the ministry or theological education. The amateurs who had been a creative force in the nineteenth century vanished as professional philosophers took their place.

Among the first generation of university thinkers from 1865 to 1895, philosophical idealism was consensual. At the end of the nineteenth century, one form of idealism—pragmatism—came to dominate the discourse of these thinkers. Pragmatism won out not only because its proponents were competent and well placed but also because they showed the philosophy's compatibility with the natural and social sciences and with human effort in the modern, secular world. A rich and ambiguous set of commitments—thirteen according to one famous commentator—pragmatism associated mind with action, and investigated the problems of knowledge through the practices of enquiry, tinting the physical world with intelligence and a modest teleology.

There were two main variants of pragmatism. One was associated with Harvard and a tradition that eventually extended to the end of the twentieth century. It included Charles Peirce, William James, and Josiah Royce; and later C. I. Lewis, Nelson Goodman, W. V. Quine, Thomas Kuhn, and Hilary Putnam. The second variant was called 'instrumentalism' by its leading light, John Dewey. Dewey's vision inspired a school of thinkers at the

University of Chicago, where he taught in the 1890s, and shaped the intellectual life of New York City and its universities—NYU, CCNY, the New School for Social Research, and Columbia—after Dewey moved to Columbia in 1904. What is called the Golden Age, which ended with Dewey's retirement in 1929, gave philosophy in America its greatest influence and public import.

6 The Shape of Revolution

In the years after the Civil War five sets of events—three in the intellectual world, two in the social world—influenced philosophers in the United States. This chapter surveys how these changes transformed the speculative tradition.

Mill and Hamilton

In 1865 the Englishman John Stuart Mill published his *Examination of Sir William Hamilton's Philosophy.* At his intellectual zenith, Mill was a talented thinker with wide tastes who defended Hume's outlook, distanced himself from religion, and emphasized the world of science. Along with some others Mill became known as a 'positivist' and champion of skeptical empiricism. The *Examination* was a masterly polemic that buried the reputation of Hamilton, who had been dead for almost ten years. The book lacked sympathy and even justice in discussing the Scottish reply to Hume and Hamilton's realism, but Mill did expose their shortcomings and evasions. He did not grasp Hamilton's distinction between knowledge of the primary and of the secondary qualities, of the effects of the noumena and the effects of the noumena on people. The scattered and unsystematic quality of Hamilton's writing and the frequent vagueness and even contradictions in his thought played into Mill's hands. The misapprehension allowed Mill to ridicule a major failing in Hamilton's exposition. Mill asked if knowledge was relative to phenomena, how could Hamilton defend realism, a claim to direct awareness of noumena? On Mill's analysis Hamilton's relativism was inconsistent with his realism.

Instead of realism Mill reinstated a Humean empiricism. We had before us phenomena that scientists were best equipped, for practical purposes, to observe and measure. Mill also introduced *nominalism* into American debate. We had to relinquish knowledge of universal truths and a presumption to see real connections in the world. Instead all we could be certain of were fleeting, individual impressions. When it was convenient, we gave the same names to constellations of these impressions in the interests of everyday life. Nominalism was the doctrine that things had in common only a name; insight into their true nature was beyond us. Mill's book had a major impact on American thought, but it is hard to define this impact precisely. Hamilton's followers might have been able to ward off Mill's assault had it been all that they had to contend with. But at the same time intellectuals in America were acquainting themselves with Charles Darwin's *Origin of Species*, published in 1859, which made its presence felt after the Civil War.

The Impact of Darwin

To account for life on earth Darwin formulated two principles in his *Origin of Species* and his later *Descent of Man* (1871). According to the principle of fortuitous variation, offspring varied slightly from their parents. Because these variations were inheritable, an endless proliferation of forms diverged from the original ancestors, and the present diversity of species resulted. To explain the contours of this evolution, Darwin introduced different means of selection, chief among them a second principle. Organisms reproduced at a rate exceeding the increase of their food supply and other necessities. Consequently, a struggle for existence ensued for the available necessities. In the struggle some of the inherited variations paid off, others did not. Nature acted as a historical force by 'selecting' for survival those organisms whose variations were adapted to their environment. They lived and reproduced their kind; the others were eliminated. Darwin was not the first to hold this sort of view, nor was his work free from ambiguities and problems that successive editions of the *Origin* tried to sort out. The time span he required was embarrassingly great, and his explanation of the transmission of traits equivocal. Yet the hypothesis accounting for the origin and growth of species was persuasive and cogently reasoned, and an array of evidence backed it. The scientific community fought over Darwin's theory but rapidly accepted some of its chief tenets.

Or rather, the scientific and speculative community quickly agreed that some form of evolution—often embracing teleology—had occurred and could best explain the present diversity of life forms and their ordering from higher to lower. In the United States this vision propelled into prominence theorists of benign biological and social progress such as the Englishman Herbert Spencer. At the same time American intellectuals feared those aspects of Darwin's theory that could easily be construed to rule out purpose in creation. Spencer's faddish 'evolutionism' was at odds with the purposelessness that many could see in the *Origin of Species*. Darwin's less teleological views were often linked to the sort of empiricism that Mill espoused. Together the two could make a potent argument for religious skepticism and scientific materialism. Behind Mill's phenomena might be a world of matter that had produced a variety of organisms that arose and perished aimlessly.

Skeptical Darwinists were a small minority, but what easily triumphed in America was still an analysis of the most ancient past that conflicted with the Bible. The story of creation that the Protestant establishment took from Genesis no longer passed scrutiny among the learned. Indeed, by the turn of the century, invoking the Bible story signaled backwardness. Popular evolutionism left much room for religious thinking, and its commitments remained in command in higher education. But Darwin mortally wounded a robust biblically oriented Protestantism.

Darwin destroyed revealed theology. According to evolution, the Bible tale of the creation was false. Darwin proffered another story, on many accounts substituting chance for the divine fiat of Genesis. The miracles of Christ no longer reflected God's purpose and the suspension of natural laws. Rather, the continuous action of these laws had produced human beings from primeval slime. Theologians had previously reasoned from an ever more orderly and law-governed universe to a majestic deity. Instead, Darwin postulated waste and extinction. In place of a world in which all creation conspired to produce a natural harmony, Darwin's world was a slaughterhouse where salvation occurred only by chance adaptation.

In a sense, Darwin downgraded the role of empirical evidence: the mind made an immense constructive leap in accepting his hypothesis. The believer had to admit the workings of natural processes in the past far beyond the historical record; and had to allow that these same workings, at some time in the past, produced a world very different from the contemporary world, but one that changed into it. And the believer had to accept these ideas, even though the transmission of traits and the temporal span were questionable. Evolution left only a peripheral place for the presently verifiable and previously given truths that its devotees accepted; some empirical evidence was inconsistent with it. In short, in addition to presenting difficult problems for traditional Christianity, evolution could easily be seen to clash with a common-sense empiricism—of both the Scots *and* Mill—that relied on what people observed in everyday experience. Darwin required an alteration of both religious and scientific views, especially if the latter were based on a simple empiricism. Religion was defended after Darwin, but Scottish realism and the view of science it shared with Mill were no longer equal to the task; nor would the optimistic pronouncements of Spencer remain unchallenged.

The New University System

From the Civil War to World War I American higher education changed rapidly. The Morrill Act of 1862 aided agricultural and technical training in colleges, and by 1900 the core of a distinguished group of state universities in the Midwest—pre-eminently Michigan, Minnesota, and Wisconsin—joined California (Berkeley) in the West. Moreover, after the Civil War, Northern entrepreneurs who had become rich as the United States industrialized used some of their money to support private higher education. Although a few 'liberal arts' colleges, such as Williams, Amherst, and Carleton, remained important, Yale, Harvard, Princeton, Pennsylvania, and Columbia were transformed from small and provincial academies into universities of international note with highly regarded faculties, training thousands of students and attracting scholars from abroad. Simultaneously, new private universities, including Cornell, Johns Hopkins, Clark, Chicago, and Stanford, sprang up to challenge the leadership of the older schools.

These institutions and many others routinely offered training beyond the undergraduate degree. Research in various fields became a desideratum, and students were admitted to assist with research, to carry on the policy of advanced scholarship, and eventually to staff the growing system.

The ministry had controlled education since the seventeenth century, but now lost this control to a different breed of administrator. Like their predecessors, the new managers believed that higher education served the nation, but their vision of the nation's future was different. Post-Civil War America would be a business culture requiring many kinds of skilled men. The universities would train these men and serve as a repository for the knowledge an advancing and complex society would need. The new academic leadership were businessmen-savants, worldly-wise enough to see that money meant scholarly pre-eminence for a school and astute enough to obtain funds from both public and private sources. The old-time clerical presidents had not been without guile, but their temporal wisdom was suited to a different sort of society from that inhabited by the captains of education led by Harvard's enterprising president, Charles William Eliot.

These administrators conceived the modern university as a group of associated schools where scholars of diverse interests would prepare students for success in American life. Leadership believed that social usefulness and truth-seeking were compatible and asked the public not to look for immediate returns from universities. But the erudite were convinced that institutions engaged in liberal studies would produce public-spirited men engaged in productive careers. Modern education would foster open minds and broad sympathies, not detached scholarship. Although the university would not be practical in a shallow sense, it would be scientific in the sense of wedding theory and practice.

Many in the new leadership imbibed an ideal of research from Germany, and at older (Protestant) colleges and at new institutions this ideal often altered the role of religion in higher education. From a later perspective the rule of this American group of bureaucrats was an important moment in the secularization of the academy. Yet the administrators also believed in divine truth. They did not want religion to intrude into the expert work of the university in any controversial, untoward way; they did want religiously safe researchers who upheld Judaeo-Christian convictions. Even at the anomalous if pre-eminent Harvard (always on the American Protestant 'left'), professors imparted Protestant cultural values if not a devotion to the religion of Christ. The new university presidents were thus not areligious men, but professional divinity was tangential to their vision. They supported theology's practical aspects, or social ethics, but not its systematics. Although their view of philosophy was not unambiguous, in general it fit well into the vision of the new leadership. Hopkins's president Daniel Gilman was suspicious of philosophy's abstract nature in contrast to the sciences. Harvard's Eliot supported its anti-authoritarian reputation for stimulating free enquiry. Philosophy benefited whenever it could sustain conventional values or fortify the new vision of the university.

The university did not only disseminate results of applied natural science, for during this period the human sciences as distinct from older forms of moral and political philosophy were invented. In previous generations young men with contemplative bents had one option for advanced schooling—the seminary. Now they might take a doctorate in an American university in philosophy, or in one of the many reformist-inclined social sciences. Indeed, many of the early graduate students in these emerging disciplines had had some training in divinity, or had passed through a spiritual crisis, or had even been ministers. In an earlier era, they might have made lives as theologians or as active clergymen. Now the university opened up for them influential and rewarding callings permeated with a sense of service. The discipline of history expanded: the study of government and politics became a separate area of enquiry and modern history a legitimate area of research. Economics was another offshoot of history. Perhaps most striking was the creation of the field of sociology, the contemporary study of the social order. Finally, claiming to offer an empirical analysis of mind, psychology broke from philosophy. These disciplines all proclaimed their scientific status, fit the university ideal of gaining useful knowledge, and mirrored the social order's novel respect for the reasoned and measured control of affairs. In this order philosophy gained a place of honor. It generated a rationale for the new scientific enterprises and for the human connection to them. In making intelligible our place in the new universe, the philosophers had an otherworldly task. Another job, however, was construing the underpinnings of human work in the world in a way that was spiritual but resolutely this-worldly.

Biblical Criticism

Another potent scholarly approach, if silent and less noted, reached its high point after the Civil War. Jonathan Edwards and his followers had given a set of peculiar interpretations to the Bible but defended it as a compelling guide to the moral and natural world. The Edwardseans additionally thought of the Bible as a master text for grasping human history. By the beginning of the nineteenth century even orthodox Protestants had reduced the book's importance. Traditionalists argued against liberal readers of the Bible (located only in and around Harvard) but generally declined to elaborate how the text might explain specific events in the present or predict the future. By the middle of the nineteenth century various Protestant thinkers—some, like Horace Bushnell, who considered themselves orthodox—were expounding symbolic views of language that allowed them freely to construe the Bible and to make it mean what, for many, the book plainly did not say.

Scholars such as Moses Stuart had once been content to examine biblical texts and sources with philological expertise to discover what they said, practicing what was called 'the lower criticism'. But in 1835–6 the German D. F. Strauss gave 'the higher criticism' notoriety. His *Leben Jesu* was translated into English and available in the United States in the 1840s and called into question the miracles of Christ and so the divinity of Jesus and the crux of Christianity. Strauss examined the New Testament stories suggesting Jesus' divinity in light of Strauss's own best knowledge of the way the world was. Multitudes could not be fed with a few bits of food, nor did people rise from the dead. Scholars must reinterpret a history that asserted such occurrences in order to uncover what ancient authors were about. Perhaps they really had meant something else, or perhaps their beliefs had to be translated in the way an anthropologically inclined European would, with sympathy, explain the rain dance of a primitive tribe.

Strauss was so radical, and biblicism still so entrenched in the United States that his work, which could also be subject to technical critique, did not make the impact it otherwise might have. But a crucial test came in the 1870s and 1880s when Americans encountered the work of another

German, Julius Wellhausen. His magnum opus, *Prolegomena to the History of Israel*, was ready in English in 1878. Wellhausen challenged Moses' authorship of the Pentateuch, the first five books of the Bible, showing that they were composed from four other sources. With impeccable scholarship Wellhausen argued that Moses himself might never have existed. Overall, the books of the Old Testament almost all came from compilers rather than a single author. The Old Testament had begun as a body of oral traditions and brief documents handed down from generation to generation. At certain periods scribes collected them and put them into a single account. Evidence for different traditions behind the Old Testament stories could be detected through variations and duplications in the biblical books themselves. For example, in Genesis two tales of the creation appeared. Genesis 2: 4–3: 24 told the well-known story of Adam and Eve, but Genesis 1–2: 4 told another story probably of later vintage. As was true throughout much of the nineteenth century, intellectual progress depended on the willingness of the learned to accept the legitimacy of hypotheses in their investigations. Wellhausen said the Pentateuch derived from documents that no one had read, just as Darwin had inferred from present mineral deposits called 'fossils' the existence of certain antique life forms that no one had ever seen. Both scholars in libraries and naturalists had similarly postulated texts, languages, cultures, or species that existed before the rise of present civilized humanity.

Wellhausen brought the higher criticism to fruition and additionally subjected the texts to 'literary' analysis. He wanted to know how they got to us in their present state, and so presumed that repetitions and different styles mingled in a single existing document indicated the compound nature of biblical writing. He was not so radical as Strauss, but both students of the Old and New Testaments reasoned similarly. Scholars would treat the Bible as they did any other book and subject its arrangement and factual claims to scrutiny identical to that which any history written in the nineteenth century would undergo. Wellhausen concentrated on grasping the true history of the composition of the Old Testament, rather than the religious truth of what the documents said. Whereas Darwin's work demanded that Christian scholars confront a narrative of creation *substantively* different from what they had previously believed, the higher criticism compelled scholars to revise their ideas of the permissible *logic* of their arguments, what reasoning was acceptable in understanding the past. By the late nineteenth century the influence of Strauss, Wellhausen, and comparable figures meant that present authority—one's own experiences of how the world worked, the prized truths of contemporary investigation—was the background to one's analysis of the past. If scholars would not believe something could be true in 1890, they could not warrant it to be true for AD 33. In the higher criticism was the coming to clear consciousness of the way the human mind reasoned: it presupposed that what one credited about the past must conform to current canons of rationality; the past was brought to the bar of present conceptions of believability. Darwin's findings damaged the historical trustworthiness of the Bible and, undermining the Scottish ideas that Americans had defended for three generations, Mill rejuvenated a skeptical empiricism that would corroborate some interpretations of Darwin. The principles behind the higher criticism were just as disquieting, for Wellhausen prohibited any recourse to the supernatural. On the one hand, the Germans claimed that investigation of the human past could not include the supernatural; on the other hand, religious truth had to be experienced in temporal terms. Thinkers could barely suppress this tension when they fretted over the higher criticism, which presented a seeming insoluble problem for believers.

Industrialism and the Social Question

Struggle and violence permeated the social and political history of America from the end of the Civil War to the 1890s. The influx of foreigners accelerated urban growth after the war. In the later period especially, immigrants alien in dress, mores, and religion altered the size and structure of American cities. The boss system of politics flowered as city governments coped with demographic changes. Old immigrants took charge of new, as wealthier classes fled. The Irish ruled Italians, Poles, Austro-Hungarians, and Eastern European Jews. The cities deteriorated physically. Housing and municipal services decayed. Crime, violence, and disorder grew. Cities became known for their tenements, opium dens, all-night dives, saloons, pool rooms, low theaters, brothels, and sweatshops. Vice, drunkenness, and sordid activities of all kinds were thought to have their home in urban centers.

Brought this information by the better newspapers and journals of opinion, educated Americans were uneasy. The unease became almost hysteria when disorder expressed itself as labor unrest. The first portent came in the summer of 1877, during a business depression. A wildcat railway strike led to confrontation and deaths in Pittsburgh, Chicago, and many other rail centers. Discontent accelerated in the 1880s and reached its height in 1886. That year strikes, armed encounters, and more bloodshed occurred in cities across the country. In May 1886, in an anarchist rally in Chicago's Haymarket Square, a bomb injured seventy policemen and killed one. Four demonstrators were killed and many wounded when the police retaliated with gun and club.

Class warfare, alien radicalism, and mass disturbance had coalesced in the Haymarket, but the following decade brought no relief. The depression of the 1890s was the most severe up to that time in American history, and little was done to alleviate its effects. Jobless men thronged urban streets, exacerbating tensions. In 1892 striking steelworkers clashed with Andrew Carnegie's Pinkerton agents at his Homestead works near Pittsburgh. In 1894 the American Railway Union struck to oppose wage cuts and high rents in the company town of railroad-car manufacturer George M. Pullman. Bloody disputes followed throughout railroad centers. In Chicago, again, the situation was worst. At least thirteen people were killed and substantial property destroyed while 14,000 federal troops, deputies, and police patrolled troubled areas.

The uglier consequences of industrialism in the United States—the problems of masses of ill-housed and ill-fed people in the cities, often immigrant, often non-Protestant—were now apparent to the upper-middle class. For the more traditionally cultured, an assault on older values and strikes and labor upheaval sullied the 1870s, 1880s, and 1890s. Critics agreed that the prolonged crisis involved irrational forces embodied in a lower *class*. Views dramatically differed, however, on what should be done. Some advocated government repression. Other witnesses to the turmoil of the cities and the apparently senseless conduct of their inhabitants argued that the masses were driven to desperate behavior. The miserable conditions of employment, a sordid and shameful environment, as well as different, European cultural values promoted riotous and destructive acts. In light of what upper-middlebrow magazines categorized as the 'social question', the masses were not responsible for their behavior. The more popular writing of religious thinkers warned of social disintegration and demanded that the élite display a sense of obligation to the new class, if only to preserve for the well-to-do their own respected place in society. Some scholars found it less interesting to ask how every individual was responsible, and more interesting to formulate how they could be responsible for the many who were not. These ideas were discussed in the first two decades of the twentieth century during what historians call the Progressive Era and later during the New Deal of Franklin Roosevelt in the 1930s.

Changes in Thought

This constellation of cultural and intellectual developments undermined speculative assumptions while the social structure of speculative knowledge shifted. The informal balance among theologians, philosophers, and amateurs prevalent for the preceding 100 years was upset. The last one-third of the century saw the rise of professional philosophy at the expense of professional theology; but the large, internationally situated university and not the small and local college or seminary became the setting of thought; and the oratory of the man of letters gave way to the popular lecturing of scholarly philosophical professors.

The primary and devastating effect was on theology. Scholarship has made it conventional that evolutionary and empirical modes of thinking confronted the many believers in biblical literalism with hard questions concerning Christianity's story of creation. In limiting the sort of historical reasoning that was acceptable, biblical criticism further restricted the options theologians had in responding to the life sciences. But troubles for professional divinity ran even deeper.

The new social climate changed the way thinkers explored the freedom of the will. Instead of stressing individual morality, some academics stressed the social explanation of behavior. They believed with greater or lesser certainty that people acted irresponsibly because of forces beyond their control. Inadequate housing, schooling, working conditions, and recreation, as well as the negative force of such institutions as the saloon and the brothel, made it impossible for workers to conduct themselves with propriety. The growth of the social sciences in the university reinforced this explanatory shift. Even when psychology, the science of individual consciousness, was added to the repertoire of the social scientists, the new discipline often postulated that the determinants of behavior were factors not subject to individual governance. Christian proponents of the new Social Gospel, reinforced by social scientists, rightly inferred from these premises that manipulating the environment would alter conduct. They reasoned that if they applied the appropriate social knowledge, they could produce better human beings. Appraising the causes of urban evil would lead, through technical expertise, to eliminating the evil. Scholars of social phenomena naturally inclined to the view that practitioners of the human sciences were obliged not merely to observe but to respond morally. Intellectual trends diluted the theoreticians' older concern with the solitary duty of every soul. Traditional Protestant ideas did not die, but the intellectual climate became less attuned to individualism. In this context, the supreme question of personal salvation became less urgent than it previously had been. Philosophers were more inclined to talk about collectivities, communities, and wholes.

Perhaps even more important for the demise of theology was the institutional environment of knowledge. The intellectual space that high religious thinking occupied in academic life shrank. Whereas schools of divinity previously had had no competition for 'graduate' students, they now had to share students with more up-to-date (and more secular) programs in philosophy and the social sciences that offered a life in many ways vocationally equivalent to that of the ministry but one that afforded greater status in the emerging industrial society. Departments of philosophy attracted money, support, and human talent. In brief, with the rise of the great universities and of scientific creeds, philosophy rather than theology came to command the respect of educated communities inside and outside universities.

As events transpired, theological progressives won victories over Calvinism at some American seminaries. But these victories paled in comparison to the triumph of professional philosophy over professional theology. Liberals defeated the orthodox at Andover Seminary, for example, in the 1880s, but by the turn of the century Andover itself declined radically, and was removed to Harvard in 1908. The size and influence of other divinity schools melted away. Meanwhile, Johns Hopkins president Gilman built a faculty of scientific philosophy, and got into a losing battle with Harvard for primacy in the field: Eliot in Cambridge created a philosophy department with internationally respected figures that was the envy of his fellow university presidents. And with its graduates Harvard constructed a secondary center for its ideas at California, Berkeley. Other schools were not quiescent. At Princeton James McCosh asserted the primacy of the college and of philosophy after a half-century of theological domination, and at new universities such as Clark in Massachusetts and Cornell in New York philosophy emerged as the modern equivalent to theology but fashionably antithetic to it. Even Yale, which permanently lost its position of speculative primacy, created a philosophy department that overshadowed its Divinity School. A number of Midwestern universities—not only the previously mentioned Minnesota, Wisconsin, and Michigan, but also Illinois and Indiana—constructed distinguished departments of philosophy. The most successful was the University of Chicago in the 1890s, where a coterie of like-minded thinkers established themselves under the leadership of John Dewey.

The amateur men of letters who were a force to be reckoned with in the middle of the nineteenth century suffered about as much as professional theologians. As the university grew in importance, the pulpit and the lyceum declined as public forums. Many men with spiritual concerns tried to obtain teaching positions and saw their influence wane if they could not. The sort of career open to Emerson and those of his generation nearly vanished as the professoriate came to dominate a new genteel learned life. 'Intellectuals' without university affiliation continued to exist but the university almost always sustained them through its journals of opinion, visiting fellowships, professional societies, financial resources, or, eventually, institutes of the humanities that the universities sponsored.

At the same time the amateurs left their mark on the professionalizing philosophers. By the early part of the new century, philosophers had developed a division of labor whereby they separated their work into the rigorous and tightly reasoned (for their peers) and the popular (for their wider public). From the late nineteenth century through the first three decades of the twentieth century philosophers, often ostentatiously, took up the popularizing role that the amateurs had had in the nineteenth century. Much philosophic reasoning in the new order became looser and more accessible. Philosophers were now the chief interpreters of human perplexity to the literate public; the most influential additionally spoke out on politics. But these men espoused their philosophies of religion and civic affairs from departments of philosophy and had not received their training from divinity schools. Their platform was not the pulpit but the university lecture hall. The philosophers developed tendencies first at work in Unitarianism and Transcendentalism, and carried on the democratization of high thought that had been part of the oratory of men such as Emerson, Bushnell, and Parker. And while the philosophers wrote for their own learned journals, they also contributed to the leading non-religious journals of opinion, magazines such as *The Nation* and *The New Republic*. Through the first third of the twentieth century, philosophy rationalized the work of the new social sciences, the disciplines that promised solutions to the problems of life for which religion had previously offered only consolation. Public speaking went from ministerial exhortation to normative social-science reformism. This mix of the popular and the professorial gave philosophy in America its greatest successes.

The amateurs influenced the university philosophers in another way. The philosophers all expounded doctrines about humanity and science. But unlike their predecessors who had stumbled and hesitated in coming to terms with idealism, the new philosophers eagerly appropriated the interest of the amateurs in Germany. The post-Civil War thinkers seized on German idealism to interpret Darwin in a way that had positive religious implications, although theology was often neglected. For a time they easily fitted evolutionary ideas—Darwinism—into an idealistic, quasi-Hegelian religious framework.

Other religious writers were more far-seeing. Dismissed by later commentators because they rejected evolutionary modes of thought and thus a major advance in the biological sciences, these men usually held Scottish realist views. They shrewdly sensed that the alliance between idealism and Darwin, between religion and science, was temporary. They believed that

Darwin's thought was incompatible with all religion and pointed to the agnosticism or atheism of followers who dismissed any ultimate meaning to life. This was the view of Charles Hodge's *What is Darwinism?* (1874). Hodge answered the question that was the title of his book by saying: 'It is atheism.' In any event, biology now conflicted with the sort of Christianity associated with the static views of Scottish realism. Varieties of German idealism, in the novel social setting, would prolong the ascendancy of theistic ideas of the universe, but not of traditional Protestantism.

German thought also promised a way out of the problems that Darwin set for the theory of science. The fascination with Mill's view of science proved, during this period, short-lived. His phenomenalistic empiricism was believed to be as inadequate as that of the Scots, and joined to them in its limited view of hypothetical reasoning. In Kant, as we have seen, another approach had emerged. Mind constructed the world from the raw data of sense. The a priori powers of the understanding were crucial; the postulated as important as the given. It was not accidental that German overwhelmed Scottish thought in Northeastern philosophical circles soon after Darwin published. Germany provided a basis for the rebuilding of religion but also aided the new biology.

The most vigorous form of idealism was called pragmatism, which developed by denying the conventional theses of Scottish Realism. Overall, the Scottish epistemology was static: the mind knew an externally existing universe. The mind itself was substantive—Scottish psychology studied a sort of thing that had certain features or characteristics. And Scottish philosophy of science was founded on a recipe: to obtain scientific knowledge, the natural philosopher followed certain rules, more or less mechanically.

In contrast, pragmatic epistemology was dynamic and interactive. Knowledge of the world was ascertainable, but the pragmatists did not define it as the intuitive grasp of a pre-existing external object. Knowledge was rather our ability to secure satisfactory adjustment in an only semi-hospitable environment. Beliefs were modes of action and true if they survived; experience competitively tested them. The pragmatists used Darwinian concepts in the service of philosophy. None the less, at another level, pragmatism's use of Darwin permitted the reinstatement, in a chastened fashion, of beliefs that were religious if not Protestant. Pragmatists emphasized the way that ideas actually established themselves in communities of investigators and what their acceptance meant. If beliefs about the spiritual prospered, they were also true. In part, the world was what human beings collectively made of it; when most influential, pragmatism was a form of communitarian idealism.

Consciousness was not a thing for pragmatists; it was a function.

Pragmatic psychology stressed not what the psyche was but what behavior defined the mental. The mind did not have being, but was a form of doing. As psychology emerged as a separate empirical discipline in the new university system, the Edwardsean functional view again gained credibility, although now its activity was found to be self-generated and not a product of God's power. That is, by the end of the nineteenth century, a different voluntaristic psychology arose.

New scientific practices in the late nineteenth century were not limited to psychology. As we have seen, innovation was key to biologists whose taxonomic undertaking became more theoretical. Indeed, in the period after the Civil War the entire structure of knowledge was changing, and the activities of men (and later women) of mind were altering. In the social sciences a dialogue arose that examined the factors that, over time, gave rise to differences in the world's cultures. The pragmatist theory of science did not emphasize rules, but the practice of scientists. The linguistic turn that theology had taken in its era of declining public influence vanished. Hopeful about the impact philosophy would make on the world, pragmatists did not worry about language but looked at what varied groups of scientists did.

7 The Consensus on Idealism, 1870–1900

From the Civil War until almost World War I idealism dominated the emerging profession of philosophy. As the old generation of college thinkers more or less committed to Scottish thought passed from the scene, younger men, whose loyalties were German, took their places.

The occupants of the first philosophical positions in a university setting were diverse. The influence and ability of nine men epitomized professional speculation in this period: Borden Parker Bowne taught at Boston University; Jacob Gould Schurman and J. E. Creighton at Cornell; G. S. Fullerton at Pennsylvania and Columbia; George Holmes Howison at California, Berkeley; George Ladd at Yale; and G. S. Morris at Michigan. A Scot, James Seth, was at Brown only from 1892 till 1898 but wrote his most important book, *A Study of Ethical Principles* (1894) while in the United States; and Elisha Mulford held no academic position until the end of his career, when he taught at the Episcopal Theological School in Massachusetts from 1881 to 1885.

Five of them—Fullerton, Howison, Ladd, Morris, and Mulford—had advanced training in theological seminaries where their mentors were renegades from orthodox Calvinism. Five studied in Germany—Bowne, Howison, Morris, Schurman, and Mulford. Three wrote book-length essays attacking the empiricist tradition in Britain and modifying it with idealist insights. Morris's *British Thought and Thinkers* appeared in 1880, and Seth's *English Philosophers and Schools of Philosophy* in 1912. In 1887 Ladd wrote the first text in what was known as the 'new' psychology, *Elements of Physiological Psychology*. It rejected the British tradition, which consisted in introspection of the mind's powers or faculties; instead Ladd combined experimentalism and Hegelianism in a mixture that was for a time conventional. Mind was construed as an activity, immanent spirituality that could be studied by examining how the human organism behaved.

Only one—Creighton, a student of Schurman's at Cornell—had an advanced degree in philosophy. Yet many were part of the professionalizing mode in the university. Schurman founded the Sage School of Philosophy at Cornell, and started the *Philosophical Review*, counted after the short-lived *Journal of Speculative Philosophy*, the first modern scholarly journal in the United States devoted to philosophy. Ladd organized the American Psychological Association in 1892 and was its second president. Creighton helped to create the premier professional group, the American Philosophical Association; served as the first president of what became its Eastern Division in 1902–3; and was the American editor of the prestigious German magazine, *Kant-Studien*. Morris at Michigan, Schurman at Cornell, and Howison at Berkeley established their schools as philosophical centers. After Fullerton spent twenty years in an endowed chair of philosophy at Pennsylvania, Columbia attracted him as a research professor who would teach only half-time; Bowne refused offers from other institutions; Seth was 'called' from Brown to Cornell to a named professorship before returning to his native Scotland. China and Japan recognized Bowne and Ladd as important American thinkers. Bowne, Creighton, and Fullerton were named deans of their respective graduate faculties, while Schurman became president of Cornell. These thinkers also began graduate programs at their universities.

All nine formulated varieties of idealism indebted to Kant and Hegel. This chapter surveys their work and the speculative climate in the last thirty years of the century, and concludes with longer analyses of the writing of two even younger idealists, early students in the American doctoral system, Josiah Royce and John Dewey.

Varieties of Idealism

The initial generation of university-inhabiting philosophers also first delved deeply into the history of philosophy. Kant was mainly targeted, but Spinoza too was scrutinized, while Morris's *British Thought and Thinkers* proposed a Teutonic, post-Kantian fruition to the various failed empiricisms of Hobbes, Locke, Hume, and Mill—'the English philosophical mind'. As a group the Americans also promoted the critical teaching of the history of philosophy as a way of investigating contemporary problems, and here too they focused on the *Critique of Pure Reason*. Fullerton exhibited a certain self-conscious style of philosophizing, discriminating various speculative meanings and positions, and allowing his own view to emerge elliptically. A series of philosophers who speculated in this manner, among them Arthur O. Lovejoy and Roderick Chisholm, followed Fullerton in the twentieth century.

Idealism itself was not so much argued for but assumed. In a famous symposium held at Berkeley in 1895, 'The Great Philosophical Discussion', Howison proclaimed a 'profound agreement' among the four professorial disputants despite their differences. They agreed on 'the entire foundation of philosophy itself' and 'the great tenet that evidently underlies . . . [our] whole way of thinking. Our common philosophy is Idealism—that explanation of the world which maintains that the only thing absolutely real is mind; that all material and all temporal existences take their being from mind . . .'

Kant's results were assumed to be so conclusive and enduring that of these men perhaps Bowne was the only one to offer an *argument* in behalf of idealism. Knowledge was impossible, Bowne said, if one were a realist: if objects were independent of mind, no way could be found of warranting that our beliefs about objects were justified. But skepticism was self-refuting, and more important we could not rid ourselves of the view that we possessed knowledge. Thus, a theory of knowledge, by process of elimination, must be idealistic—the known was known because it conformed to the laws of mind.

The Americans were not, however, comfortable with objective idealism. Only Schurman and his student Creighton would commit to absolutism outright, and were more Kantian in their tone than Hegelian. For both of them the absolute was the unity-in-difference of individual selves *and* the not-self or physical world. This larger mind was the function that realized for itself the significance and relations of a world of persons and things. There was no object outside this mind but also no 'mind in itself' standing apart and in abstraction from things. To have a mind—finite or infinite— was just to stand in self-conscious relation to the objects. Thus, for Schurman and Creighton the infinite mind was immanent in the finite, and the absolute manifested itself in evolution; spirit inhered in the physical. For many idealists who would elaborate these ideas in a field that would later be called developmental psychology, the coming to consciousness of individual selves was a social process in which the world of objects in space and time emerged from a primordial consciousness: to a plurality of finite selves the infinite mind appeared as the material world. Those idealists, such as Ladd and Bowne, interested in morality promoted 'self-realization ethics'—the moral being developed a communal sense of harmony with the greater self, and in time the best human selves would mimic the growth of the world-defining soul. The spiritual, wrote Bowne, was 'the natural itself, rising toward its ideal form through the free activity of the moral person'. Mulford applied this insight to political philosophy, an idiosyncratic area of endeavor. Following Hegel, Mulford believed that the nation-state, an organic growth infused with religious feeling, was the basic entity in which human life and moral flowering occurred. With the St Louis Hegelians, Mulford applied these ideas to the United States, which was realizing an immanent Christian God.

But Schurman, Creighton, and Mulford were a minority. Most of the idealists thought that absolute idealism could not be distinguished from pantheism. Human experience, wrote Howison, had to 'change its meaning *in kind*' when the same experience was considered as part of the absolute or else it could not function as anything other than our experience of a world of objects. But how could personal experience then be part of the absolute experience? The absolute idealists positively named the world as it was 'the universal consciousness', and hoped that such semantic maneuvering would satisfy religious needs. This was indeed just the critique of Spinoza that Fullerton promoted. Spinoza, who identified the world with God, according to Fullerton, could not extract from this identification any object of worship other than the world. The absolutist conception of 'human immortality' was equally a bit of linguistic legerdemain: eternal life was only what the phenomenal processes that defined the world achieved, since this whole cosmos was synonymous with the absolute. (And this line of reasoning led Fullerton to renounce idealism itself at the end of his career.) Finally, human freedom could not be defended if individual minds were merely fragments of a greater mind. Objective idealism, for these critics, came close to atheism. Bowne's views echoed those of the critics of Edwards and his followers: 'The difference between materialism and absolute idealism is only one of words.'

The later critics, however, had difficulty in stating their own alternatives. Morris and Howison failed to advance positive doctrines. Howison held that to preserve freedom and immortality creatures and creator had to be equally real but not identical so that the finite had duties and rights. Morris construed all existence as personal, and the greater consciousness— a theistic God—could not be defined as all-embracing.

Only Bowne defended a more individualistic idealism, 'personalism', but did so cautiously and hesitantly. Kant correctly argued that an absolute intelligence was necessary to construct the object world. But we had to go beyond Kant and show that although we lived through this intelligence, it was theistic, and the 'logical subordination' of individual to absolute did not have 'fatal ontological implication'. Yet Bowne could not lay out the theism in which creator and created finite beings were each somehow free; the nature of a non-absolutistic God was mysterious and beyond our ken. Bowne toyed with urging that the finite minds were endowed with an inner life à la Leibniz, the philosopher who had postulated individual 'monads' that were not entirely subordinate to anything outside themselves, but that operated in a pre-established harmony with other monads. More usually, Bowne tried to synthesize Kant and Berkeley—he called his position a Kantianized Berkeleianism. The world for Kant was ultimately subjective, defined by the transcendental unity of apperception, but our *individual* knowledge of it was also subjective. The world for Bowne rather had to be understood as a 'universal object . . . common to all' and not 'a private dream . . . confined to the individual', whether infinite or finite. Somehow Berkeley's idealism could be used in this program and preserve human individuality, but Bowne never clarified these murky views.

Josiah Royce

Born in 1855 and raised a provincial Californian, Royce—by force of intellect—successively obtained an undergraduate degree from Berkeley, studied philosophy in Germany for a long year where his interest in Kant matured, and then went on to an early doctorate in philosophy from Johns Hopkins in 1878. With no jobs in philosophy, Royce returned to Berkeley to teach English, but hated his work. In 1882 he jumped at the chance to teach at Harvard for a year, and stretched the temporary appointment for another two years. In the meantime, he was preparing a book on idealist metaphysics, *The Religious Aspect of Philosophy*, published in 1885. The book culminated writing that Royce had begun even before his Hopkins dissertation.

Royce struggled with Kant's problems and elaborated a voluntaristic idealism. He analyzed the purpose of thought—to learn the laws of phenomena and to predict experience. Experience, however, had a dual nature. First, something was given, 'something that I passively receive and cannot at this time alter. . . . I cannot resist the force that puts it into my consciousness.' The finite knower was not aware of a physical object but of the momentarily present. We could best, if inadequately, speak about what was immediately before the mind using such locutions as, 'This appears black to me', or 'It seems as if there is a black cow in front of me', or perhaps even 'black spot, here, now'. Second, we contributed something to experience. Every judgement expressing truths about phenomena exceeded the given. The notions of past and future were necessary to such judgements. But the given never included the past and future. Royce conjectured that the past and future were constructs made up to reduce the given to coherence. We interpreted the given as a sign of something not given. For instance, we implied that some aspects of the given were memories, indicating that something not present was once present: 'To declare that there has been a past time at all, is to attribute to some element of the present a reality that does not belong to it as present.' This active construction defined mind.

What anticipation and completion added to the given determined knowledge. Like Kant, Royce said that in consciousness both a given and the spontaneous activity of thought existed. Unlike Kant, Royce did not divorce the two and then have thought organize the given; rather, thought constructed the not given from the given. The thinking activity did not infuse sense with form, but from present sense projected past and future.

A set of constructs and a form of acting, knowing expressed the interest we had in 'reality' and subserved practical inclinations. Why should we accept it? In what sense could we justify knowledge?

Royce answered these questions with a dialectical argument. Consider the sentence, 'There is no future'. Acceptance implies denial. To conceive a condition in which time has ceased introduced a temporal element into the assumed condition, that is, a future time. Thinking of a non-future was thinking of something that was after the present and, therefore, in the future. Royce had a conception (the assumption of a future) that he said was absolutely true. He argued analogously for the absoluteness of the past. To put the position in another way, the momentarily present given necessarily involved the past and future. These constructs exhibited the essence of thought itself. Time, Royce contended, was not some independent thing-in-itself but indicated that constructs determined the nature of experience: we could not conceive that the basic forms of experience could be other than they were.

The argument that some postulates were logically and practically justified had a weakness. However much they might be necessary aspects of thought itself, the future and the past were our constructions. We meant by past and future what we conceived as past and future, and, for example, fiat solved the problem of induction: the future resembled the past because we determined it to be so. Royce's logic had done too much. To doubt anything was impossible, for what we posited to be true must be true.

Royce handled this difficulty inadequately. We meant by error, he claimed, that an expectation was disappointed when we found a present content of experience contrasting with the expectation conceived as past: error depended on remembering that a past expectation now disappointed us. But Royce defined the reality of the past as our present consciousness of the past, and for error to disappear we need only suppose an appropriately bad memory. As Royce admitted, error became the consciousness of error. For a conveniently forgetful person, error would not exist. But without an adequate explanation of error, his theory of truth was unsatisfactory. If he could not distinguish error from truth, Royce had failed to set out the purpose of thought as learning the laws of phenomena: prediction exempt from error was not prediction at all.

Before we can understand how Royce resolved this problem, we must grasp another aspect of his work, the postulational basis of knowledge. He could not explain why the assumptions of thought were satisfactory; although experience verified them, we could not enquire why it did. It was inexplicable that 'our sensations do occur with such a degree of regularity that the activity of thought has the power of making enough valid hypotheses for practical use'. The 'critical doctrine' rested with this analysis, and Royce stated that if mind were removed from the universe, 'the order of inanimate Nature' might still exist, although there would be no knowledge of it, no truth or error. In his dissertation written a year later he went further, proclaiming that his philosophy was idealistic. This did not mean that consciousness constituted existence; rather, existence was not external or foreign to 'Consciousness'. Then Royce declared that although human selves 'are transient in Consciousness . . . Existence remains'. But if existence did not transcend consciousness, how could existence remain when human consciousness passed? For Royce this was another unanswerable question: 'We cannot in the least determine why and how various kinds of consciousness may exist.'

Two essays published in 1880 and 1881, 'The Nature of Voluntary Progress' and 'Doubting and Working', made explicit the tension between individual consciousness and 'Consciousness'. For any person, Royce wrote, beliefs always satisfied individual wants. The one whose intellectual wants a belief satisfied applied to it the adjective 'true' at the time of satisfaction. But this did not mean that what we found acceptable was true. 'My needs are narrow and changing. It is humanity in its highest development to which the truth will be acceptable.' An adequate view of truth must substitute the broader view of mankind for the personal view: there must be some measure of truth outside any individual's ideas.

By 1882 Royce had convinced himself that some truths were necessary as well as practically demanded, and he examined the relation between this theory and his two kinds of consciousness. If ideas were true, we could not create reality; it must be independent of our ideas; we could justify them only if they corresponded to it. But this reality simultaneously had to be related to our consciousness.

Some past, present, and future experiences were not experienced; yet we required them to make sense of the world. We wanted to say that the cows in the field existed when no one of us was experiencing them. Moreover, this possible experience could not be 'empty' or 'merely' possible. When no one was about, black cows were in the field; green ones were not. I could imagine green cows in the field, but the possible experiences defining the external world had a different status; they were 'valid' possibilities.

Reasoning led, Royce surmised, to the conception of one uniform experience. A consistent idealist who postulated an actual absolute experience must claim that this was experience for some consciousness, or consciousness itself. Moreover, the consciousness involved could not simply be an individual consciousness, for example, mine. Royce met this problem by postulating a 'hypothetical subject', whose existence was not a necessary result of the postulate of an external reality, that is, of an absolute experience. One could form other hypotheses, for example, panpsychism—the position that every individual thing had a spiritual element—but his hypothesis had the advantage of being simple and adequate.

Ideas existed in order to fulfill our needs, but because they had to refer beyond us if they were true, Royce supposed an 'impersonal experience' to which true ideas corresponded. To explain the special status of this reality-defining experience, he postulated a hypothetical subject for it; yet he maintained that he could not prove this subject's existence. So far, epistemology depended on a suppositional metaphysics. We could not expect to have an 'an absolute vision of truth, free from all taint of postulate'. Finally, human beings still could not err about the reality that the hypothetical subject defined beyond them.

The Religious Aspect of Philosophy made the hypothetical subject actual. Chapter 11, 'The Possibility of Error', set forth the most significant argument of Royce's career, the 'steadfast rock' on which he would build an untainted metaphysics. This world consisted of contents of consciousness or, equivalently, of actual and possible experience: his cardinal principle was that experiences were ideas, internal data, and that these ideas made up the world. It was some sort of arrangement, combination, or synthesis of ideas. It went beyond any we had or could be aware of at any time, but we must account for the world in ideal terms, that is, in ways that ruled out external existents. Ideas or perceptions—the present content of consciousness—were true or false of their object in a real, although still ideal, world beyond them. If I saw that some cows in the field were black, I might say that the cows were black and my statement would be correct if experience verified the belief. I might also believe, sitting in my study, that the cows were black. Then the statement, 'The cows are black', would be true if the cows were black, that is, if my belief were true. Because Royce believed that whatever was before the mind was an idea, he treated both these cases as equivalent, as ones of the thinker having true or false ideas, assimilating states of belief, and so on, to perceptual states or experiences.

What was the 'correspondence' between the real world and my ideas—Royce's hypothetical absolute consciousness and my immediate experience? According to Royce, Berkeley argued that it was their cause. On the one hand, Royce sometimes felt that this theory implied polytheism: if the external consciousness caused ideas, it and my consciousness must be distinct, each an independent center of consciousness. On the other hand, this analysis might construe causality as a relation independent of thought; or, to put the analysis another way, the external consciousness would not be a consciousness but a 'power', a cause. Against both positions, Royce contended that the external world could not cause our ideas (perceptions) about it; the correspondence relation must be different.

Royce argued that the belief that the external world caused our ideas necessitated something prior to the principle of causation: our thought demanded that our idea of causality and our idea of the specific causal relation involved corresponded to the truth of things. We could not conceive of a cause of our ideas except by postulating that our conception of the cause was similar to the cause itself. Suppose we defined the real object as the cause of present ideas, experience. Royce must still ask what causation meant: it was a relation between facts, and we must have some idea of this relation before attributing it to the outer object, which we never experienced. Therefore, we must first believe in the objective truth about the relation between the real object and the ideas:

there is here at least *one* external truth, and so one object (viz.:-the external fact of the causation itself), which I believe in, not because it is itself the cause of my idea of the causation, but because I trust that my idea of causation is valid, and corresponds to the truth. And it is only by *first* believing in this objective truth, viz., the causation, that I come to believe in *x* the cause. Hence it follows that even in case of immediate sense-perception, my belief in the external object is always primarily not so much a belief that my experiences need causes, as an assurance that certain inner beliefs of mine are as such, valid, i.e., that they correspond with that which is beyond them.

The Religious Aspect of Philosophy concluded that the reality entailed by the search for causes was subordinate to another conception—that ideas had something beyond them and like them.

Royce must answer three questions. The first: What was the nature of the correspondence between our ideas and the real world? The second was left over from his earlier ruminations: What was the status of the hypothetical external consciousness that served as the real world? The third, which he believed he had dissolved earlier, now took primacy: How was error possible? To answer these questions Royce went to 'the very heart of skepticism itself'. Extreme skepticism would bring him to absolute truth.

What guarantee did we have that ideas, experiences, in any way corresponded to the real world? What basis did we have for saying that what we took to be true was in fact so? The skeptic urged that everything was doubtful and that we might always be mistaken. Even this skepticism implied that error existed. Was there any way to avoid this assumption? Suppose we argued that the truth was true for us, that two assertions met on no common ground, so that neither was 'really true' or 'really false'. This position went further than skepticism and declared the belief in error itself to be erroneous. Royce called this view that of the total relativity of truth, and he argued against it. If the statement 'There is error' is true, there is error; if it is false, then there is, *ipso facto*, error. He could only conclude that error existed; to deny its existence was contradictory. The dialectical argument Royce discovered five years before rescued him from relativism. At least he had one truth—that there was error—and he asked, how was error possible, what conditions allowed us to err?

Error was commonly defined as a judgement that did not agree with its object. An erroneous judgement combined subject and predicate in a way that the corresponding elements in the world were not combined. Royce was again investigating thought's 'correspondence' to the real world. The statement that the cows were black was not true because the cows caused my perceptions (ideas) of the animals; rather the statement would be true if my perceptions corresponded to the real world in some non-causal sense of 'correspond'. What was this sense? Royce said his account explicated the common-sense view. Although he felt it correct, it allowed little room for error and pushed him towards absolute idealism. In order to think about an object—even if falsely, even in error—I did more than have an idea resembling the object. I meant my idea to resemble the object. To make the point in another way, I aimed at the object, picked it out; that is, I possessed the object enough to identify it as what I meant. Suppose I burned my fingers; I experienced (that is, had an idea of) burned fingers. Another person might also have burned fingers; my idea would then be like his idea, his experience. But I would not be thinking of his fingers when I said 'This thumb is burned'. To think of an object I did not merely have an idea that resembled the object, but meant to have the idea resemble just that object.

The intention of the speaker, Royce noted, picked out the object, and that was paradoxical. If, in judging, I meant or intended the object to which the judgement would refer, to which a perception might correspond, then I knew the object. But if I knew the object, how could I err about it? If I said falsely that the cows were black, I knowingly referred to some aspect of the situation about which I made the judgement. For example, black horses or white cows were in the field, and I somehow intended to refer to this fact. If I had no knowledge like this, my judgement might just as well refer to the black cows in another field, and then my judgement would be true and not false. But given that I knew all this, how could I err?

Error was possible if an object, on the one hand, was not wholly present to mind and, on the other, was yet partially present. But however difficult it was to account for error on this 'common-sense' analysis of correspondence and reference, it proved impossible to account for specific erroneous judgements.

Royce's fame as a dialectician derived from his skill in urging that errors about the mental states of others were inexplicable. If two people, John and Thomas, were talking together we must really consider four people: the real John, the real Thomas, John as Thomas conceives him, and Thomas as John conceives him. When John made judgements about Thomas, of whom did John judge? Plainly of his Thomas, for nothing else could be an object of John's judgements. But could he err about his Thomas? It would seem not, for his Thomas was not outside his thoughts; John's conception of Thomas was John's conception, and what he asserted it to be, that for him it must be. Moreover, John could not err about the real Thomas, because as far as John was concerned the real Thomas was unknown.

To resolve these dilemmas required regarding the matter from the perspective of a third person. Suppose John made a judgement about Thomas. If I were familiar with the judgement, 'saw' the real Thomas that John could not see, and 'saw' that John's conception was unlike the real Thomas in some critical respect, I could say that John's assertion was in error. Of course, in this case I would have present to my consciousness what normally would be thought of as an external object—the real Thomas—as well as John's consciousness. But since, like John, I was locked in my own consciousness, this recourse to a third person would not do the job. Moreover, the mere perception of the disagreement of thought with an object would not make a thought erroneous. The judgement must disagree with the object to which the judger meant the judgement to refer. If John never had the real Thomas 'in mind' how could John even begin to choose the real Thomas as his object? The third-person hypothesis again appeared to solve this puzzle. Suppose that a being existed for whom the real Thomas and John's conception of him were both directly present. This being could tell if John's conception of Thomas meant the real Thomas. This being could compare the one to the other. If John's conception of Thomas agreed with the real Thomas, then we could declare John's ideas true; otherwise, erroneous.

Although it solved the problem, we might reject this suggestion because it contradicted the presupposition that John and Thomas were separate beings, external to any person's consciousness. But we could account for error on no other supposition, and it was necessary that we did so. Suppose then, Royce declared, 'we drop the natural presupposition, and say that John and Thomas are both actually present to and included in a third and higher thought . . . and declare time once for all present in all its moments to an universal all inclusive thought'.

Royce defined an error as an 'incomplete thought'. A higher thought that included the erroneous judgement and its intended object knew the judgement to have failed in the purpose it more or less clearly had. His doctrine made intelligible the common-sense view that even an erroneous judgement partially intended its object: the idea prompting the judgement and the intended object were fragments of a more inclusive thought that compared the idea to its intended object. If I remembered a forgotten name, I was sure that I meant just one particular name and no other. In remembering, I recognized it as the name I meant all along: in its hunt my present self presupposed that the 'deeper self' of which the name was a part already possessed what was sought. The search for truth demanded what I already had, and my deepest doubts and profoundest ignorance entailed the larger self. Even in error I could not mean an object, Royce said, unless 'my larger self', 'my complete consciousness', had it 'already present in essence'. The absolute was the only real or complete self; I and all finite creatures were fragments of the absolute. Consider, Royce said elsewhere, what it meant to be either the self of 'this moment' or a being who thought about 'this world of objects'. We must be organically related to an infinite person implied by our finite consciousness: only one existent person was possible, namely, the one complete self.

Evolution was the form in which finite creatures, constrained to time and space, must perceive the world-self. The developmental world-view hinted at how the temporal constantly yearned to overreach itself: with the ever-increasing growth of consciousness it strove for the eternal.

Royce went on to a career at Harvard in which his prolific writings and a rush of words would often overwhelm adversaries. But early in his scholarly life he had laid out a set of arguments that would dominate epistemology for well over a century.

John Dewey

Born in Burlington, Vermont, in 1859, Dewey attended the University there, coming under the influences of those who had taken the then idiosyncratic path of James Marsh. Like Royce, Dewey went to Johns Hopkins, where he received a Ph.D. in philosophy in 1884, studying with George Sylvester Morris, whom he followed to Michigan. Whereas Kant brought

Royce to idealism, the British thinkers Thomas Hill Green and Edward Caird that Morris had taught to Dewey steeped him in neo-Hegelianism. Unlike Royce, who sought a 'proof' for absolute idealism, Dewey more or less assumed the absolute consciousness, but tried to make this assumption more plausible to common sense. As a Hegelian, Dewey, more than the Kantian Royce, emphasized not the individual consciousness but the society of knowers.

Dewey's early work conventionally mixed evolution and idealism and gave philosophy the role of justifying a religious orientation to the universe. The inherence of the psychical in the physical, spirit in nature, he wrote, would define future enquiry. Mind presented itself in the entire body in the fundamental mode of nervous, adjusting, or teleological activity. Darwinism established this principle in the universe. 'The structure of nature itself is such that it gives rise to . . . purposive action.' The physical world for Dewey wanted to be the spiritual. Intelligence was latent in matter. Evolution told how this happened. He read physical causes as part of a rational design. Evolution was transforming the natural world into the moral: 'this whole structure of the physical is only the garment with which the ethical has clothed itself . . . the germ shall finally flower in the splendor of the moral life . . . the garment shall finally manifest the living form within . . .' In evolution, Dewey said, God embodied himself in matter, just as the body incarnated the individual soul. Dewey's idealism was less absolute than Hegel's but his teleology more pronounced than Darwin's. Here Dewey followed his mentor Morris, whose *Philosophy and Christianity* had appeared in 1883.

Dewey strove for a more genuine philosophy of immanence than philosophers or theologians had worked out. Contending that the mental invested the material and the infinite the finite, he distrusted the Kantian dualisms of mental form and material content and of noumena and phenomena (spirit and nature); and the Hegelian dualism of infinite form and finite content (God and individual). To come to a more acceptable idealism, Dewey criticized British idealism, which had revived Kant and Hegel, but which, Dewey believed, was 'formalistic'.

In the mid- to late 1880s Dewey turned to an innovative science of psychology to find a position that would not distinguish the absolute and the relative. For much of the nineteenth century psychology was, roughly, the science of the soul and the introspective examination of consciousness. Now, at the end of the century, Americans were embracing the methods of the Germans and creating a new discipline that used experimental techniques to measure mental phenomena. The psychologist combined introspection with empirical observations of the way, for example, people accomplished certain tasks; and could thereafter infer the structure of the mind from different ways of behaving. The publication of Dewey's first book, *Psychology*, in 1887, and two subsequent editions of 1889 and 1891 demonstrated his interest in these developments. This text was also conventional in its blend of experimentalism with older notions that psychology was additionally a philosophical—and to some extent a priori— exploration of consciousness. In Dewey's case this exploration related the individual to absolute consciousness.

Dewey's 'New Psychology' would use experimentation to analyse mental phenomena. Moreover, biology, anthropology, and most of all 'those vast and as yet undefined topics of inquiry which may be vaguely designated as the social and historical sciences—the science of the origins and development of the various spheres of man's activity'—would help the New Psychology. The social sciences gave Dewey 'the method of experiments' and 'the method of objective observation'. His indefinite but enriched psychology synthesized physiology and social science. Yet it would additionally construe mind as an evolving teleological unity disclosing the divine. Defining this area of novel enquiry, Dewey contrasted his view with that of the dualistic British idealists.

Green claimed with Dewey that psychology was the science of the individual soul. But philosophy or metaphysics was the science of the absolute soul, and the tool for understanding it was Hegelian logic. Green denied that the techniques of mere natural science suited metaphysics, but Dewey argued that because mankind comprehended the absolute only in so far as consciousness developed temporally, the methods of psychology and philosophy (or metaphysics) were not distinct. Somehow the tools of physiology and the social sciences could grasp the absolute. The New Psychology could study how it exhibited itself in time. Thus his enlarged psychology became 'the method' of philosophy. Philosophy would replace the abstractions of Hegelian logic with the experiments and observation of Dewey's psychology. With psychology as its method, philosophy would not be metaphysical in a bad sense, but scientific. Indeed, using the social sciences, Dewey said in *Psychology*, the scientist could examine the way actual selves might realize their true selves 'with the wider and more permanent conditions of well-being' that were found in the universal self.

With the British idealists, Dewey believed that philosophy terminated in knowledge of the absolute. Philosophers could examine this consciousness either as the process of its coming to self-realization, that is, as the development of individual consciousnesses; or as the end result or the product, that is, as the consciousness of the process, as the absolute. Yet the British method of delineating this dichotomy troubled Dewey. The realization of the universe in individuals (psychology) could not be divorced from the significance of the universe as a whole (metaphysics). The being of things, he said, was to be experienced. Although only the absolute experienced the world, the absolute existed 'only so far as it has manifested itself in his [human] conscious experience'. The absolute could be treated 'only so far as it has become in a being like man'. More, the individual and universal orders were 'built out of a common stock', and defined reciprocally. Individuality was composed of the finite experience of the world; the world comprised individual experiences. Individuals realized content, and the content realized individuals. The New Psychology studied the self scientifically, divulging the immanence of God in the human, the eternal's constitution of the relative.

Dewey put his criticism of formalist absolutism into a wider context. Two dense essays of 1890, 'On Some Current Conceptions of the Term "Self"' and a review of Edward Caird's *Critical Philosophy of Immanuel Kant*, outlined Green's views. Green, Dewey said here and elsewhere, had built on the more dualist Kantian position, not the less dualist Hegelian one. Although indebted to Hegel, Green had advanced Kant's work after eliminating from it the *Ding an sich*, which idealist thinkers believed to be a cancer on the critical philosophy. Green located the ground of experience, of this world, in a self known only in so far as it effloresced in experience. Experience intrinsically unified thought and sense, and this self made the unity possible. Because experience depended on the self, experience could not exhaust it. That is, the self could not be this world. Moreover, philosophers could not understand the activity of the self in experience—this self's self-consciousness—through any human categories. Here Dewey and Green contemplated Hegel's revision of the Kantian categories and Hegel's view that the highest category was self-consciousness. Bringing the self's activity, its self-consciousness, under finite categories could not explain it. Rather the self's activity made using these categories possible.

For Dewey, Green's extension of Kant brought to the fore this question: how was one to describe the absolute self and its activity—its self-consciousness? Green had lamely answered that the self was just that: a blank, abiding self. Its activity was communicating itself in the world, constituting single selves, making organisms the vehicle of its temporal emergence. According to Dewey, Green held that we could not comprehend the self that grounded the world. We knew it only as a perfectly realized being, existing as a bare form that finite consciousnesses filled. The progression of human minds realized in time what already existed.

Green had a genuine problem, and Dewey sympathized with his difficulties. The obvious answers to Green's questions would not do. In the schematic self he did not merely posit an abstraction. The self was not the world because it conditioned the world. The world did not exhaust the self. Moreover, we could not understand the self's activity as human self-consciousness because knowledge of the world conditioned this self-consciousness.

In reviewing the work of Edward Caird, another leading British idealist, Dewey wrote later in 1890 that one's opinion of the book would depend on one's own philosophy, and then acclaimed it 'the best account of philosophy itself in the English language'. According to Dewey, Caird's magnum opus carried forward the reconstruction of Kant past Green. Caird's work, Dewey believed, permitted 'a solution of the most contemporary problem'. Caird had demonstrated the reality of the absolute. Dewey called this self God and the world its phenomenal manifestation. Its activity was a movement in which the lower figured in the spiritual growth of the higher. Apparently, interpreting absolute self-consciousness as an evolutionary procreation avoided the problems of construing it via the physical relations among objects in space and time. If the infinite was appropriately understood only as embosomed in the finite, its temporal activity was to overcome the dualism of mind and matter. Caird's work prompted Dewey to throw out both distinctions between form and content compromising idealism: the distinctions between absolute form and finite content (God and man) and between mental form and material content (spirit and nature).

Dewey later wrote that Green's formalism suited speculation in a static era. More dynamic explications comported with the growth of knowledge. Philosophers now recognized that the known was organically connected to what was becoming known, 'the thought of a continuous unit embodied in all natural process'. Such an organizing principle was apparent only because it was concretely manifested, 'only because, indeed, it has secured such embodiment as to appear as the directing principle or method of life'.

This interpretation of idealism gave Dewey a rationale for his own thought. Green's trouble was his Kantianism. He divorced the conceptual and the empirical, the infinite form and the finite content. Philosophic progress for Dewey consisted not, as it did for Royce, in the 'return to Kant', but in stressing the dynamic and concrete in Hegel. Even formalists like Green did not believe that a great spirit hovered over the world. Rather, for him and for Dewey, the trick was to formulate a belief about the self and its activity and to prove that this meant (roughly) that intelligibility continuously manifested itself in things. 'Self' was not a mere name, and the problem was to state the name's designation.

This self was not the known world, but the knowable world; the self's activity was not reproducing itself in time, but human organisms knowing and transforming the world. The possibilities of meaning were the self. Increased knowledge of these possibilities and the transformation of the natural into the spiritual were this self's activity, its self-consciousness. Dewey replaced Green's static and abstract concepts with dynamic ones. Meaning was continuously actualized as people learned more and experienced the world's spirituality.

The world of experience, for Dewey, was the absolute as finitely grasped. He became most comfortable not talking of the absolute but indicating how it was displayed. Idealism, he said, viewed form (or meaning) as immanent in content. Dewey's statements varied. Content was informed; at any point experience was meaningful; sense material was pregnant with the potential of its transformation into more enriched or integrated experience; it was intelligible or knowable; it would ever make sense; it was amenable to the use to be made of it. Dewey redefined Green's blank self at the basis of the world as the ground of meaning. Dewey said the harmonious growth of experience achieved in unfolding latent meaning realized this self. The philosopher understood the activity of the self by acknowledging the spirituality of things and connecting the physical to the spiritual.

A summary of this program finally requires mention of how Dewey reconceived the method that would enhance Caird's insights. Dewey had urged the compatibility of science (psychology) and religion (absolutist metaphysics). The method of the young science was also the tool of legitimate metaphysics. Psychological conclusions about the self interpreted the absolute as conveyed to us. But Dewey's psychology was an Ur-science, or super-science, minimally including physiology and the systematic studies of humanity. Dewey emphasized that the findings of these sciences would describe the absolute's flowering in time. The appropriate organon for philosophy would be scientific method. The earlier essays were recast so that the method of Science, writ large, became philosophic method, still opposed to 'formalist' logic. The scientific method uncovered how at any time individual consciousnesses depicted the self's realization. Philosophy studied the synergistic emergence of content and form.

Dewey called this investigation 'experimental idealism' and labeled it 'neo-Hegelian'. His philosophy of immanence unified selves and absolute self, and nature and spirit. The possibility of science meant having the self at the basis of the world. The self's temporal realization was scientific progress demonstrating that spirit inhered in nature. But, said Dewey, Hegel had to be made practical. The task was to use the method of science in ethics and to uncover how moral experience—the experience of the actualizing selves—arose out of nature, how the natural had the moral implicit in it.

8 Pragmatism in Cambridge, 1867–1923

Pragmatic idealism had a unique and pronounced identity in the United States. Although its links to the idealism of the personalists can easily be seen, pragmatism also had absolutistic variants and, most significantly, communitarian ones. More important, it was a philosophical position that, at least in theory, attended closely to the practice of the physical sciences and the new social sciences; and that, professionally, the younger generation of philosophy doctorates trained in the United States adopted. Pragmatism got its start, however, among amateurs in Cambridge, Massachusetts, in the 1870s. In the 1890s Harvard institutionalized their ideas under the primary aegis of one of their number, the celebrated William James. This chapter takes up the ideas of the amateurs, chief among them the eccentric luminary Charles Peirce, and traces the growth of the reasoning that finally led to the triumph of Harvard over Yale as the premier center of thought in the United States.

The Metaphysical Club

As we have noted, speculative societies of various kinds sprang up all over New England after the Civil War. These Eastern clubs were part of a disorganized and inchoate national group bent on revitalizing American intellectual life in quasi-institutional forms. The one that proved to be most influential was located in Cambridge. This self-styled Metaphysical Club was flourishing in the early 1870s, and its members later made a mark. The core of the club consisted of six men: William James, who went on to a striking philosophical career at Harvard; Oliver Wendell Holmes, future Supreme Court justice; philosopher Chauncey Wright; scientist and theorist Charles Peirce; and lawyers Nicholas St John Green and Joseph Bangs Warner.

There were three sources of the members' opinions: Green's appraisal of the work of the British psychologist Alexander Bain, the legal analyses of Green and Holmes, and the evolutionary theorizing of Wright.

Green urged that the membership look to 'the practical significance of every proposition', and that 'every form of words that means anything indicates some sensible fact on the existence of which its truth depends'. Green appeared to have derived this view from Bain's definition of belief— 'of that upon which a man is prepared to act'. Wright lectured on Bain in a Harvard psychology course but, Peirce recalled, Green pushed this definition. Bain came alive for Peirce and the others as Green and then Holmes saw that Bain's ideas articulated the viewpoint of practicing lawyers. In an erudite article in the 1870 *American Law Review*, 'Proximate and Remote Cause', Green traced the genesis and history of that phrase and its shifts in meaning from the legal principle 'In Jure non remota Causa, sed Proxima, Spectatur'. Analyzing the meaning of the word 'cause', Green concluded that the principle was ambiguous: talking about proximate and remote causes did not clarify our reasoning when we meant 'only the degree of certainty or uncertainty with which the connection between cause and effect might have been anticipated'. When discussing whether an individual was 'legally responsible' for certain acts, lawyers did not discuss the 'remoteness' of an individual's behavior from its effects; rather they considered if they could predict the effects from the behavior. The activities that concerned the law defined legal concepts.

Other scattered hints of these ideas exist in Green's writings, but Holmes spelled out the implicit beliefs. In 1871–2 he was propounding 'the prediction theory of law' in his Harvard lectures:

What . . . is a statute; and in what other sense law, than that we believe that the motive which we think that it offers to the judges will prevail, and will induce them to decide a certain case in a certain way, and so shape our conduct on that anticipation? . . . The only question for the lawyer is, how will the judges act?

In *The Common Law* (1881) and *The Path of the Law* (1897) Holmes stated his position at greater length: to understand the law on a certain subject, we viewed it as would unscrupulous people who would do anything to avoid punishment. The object of study was predicting the incidence of the use of public force through the courts. What the courts did in fact constituted the meaning of the law; the lawyer's job was to assess for clients what would happen as a consequence of acting or not acting in conformity to certain statutes.

The legal reasoning of Green and Holmes was put in the context of biological science. The *Common Law* emphasized the similarities between legal and evolutionary thinking: 'The law embodies the story of a nation's development through many centuries and it cannot be dealt with as if it contained only the axioms and corollaries of a book of mathematics. In order to know what it is we must know what it has been, and what it tends to become.' A philosopher of evolution, Wright had adhered to these notions earlier. His 1873 'The Evolution of Self-Consciousness' declared:

The judge cannot rightfully change the laws that govern his judgements; and the just judge does not consciously do so. Nevertheless, legal usages change from age to age. Laws, in their practical effects, are ameliorated by courts as well as by legislatures. No new principles are consciously introduced; but interpretations of old ones (and combinations, under more precise and qualified statements) are made, which disregard old decisions, seemingly by new and better definitions of that which in its nature is unalterable, but really, in their practical effects, by alterations at least in the proximate grounds of decision.

In addition to finding evolutionary ideas implicit in legal beliefs, Wright saw that adopting Bain's psychology would buttress Darwin. Suppose beliefs were tendencies to act and not mysterious 'intellectual phases of the mind', as some thinkers said. We could then examine changes in the structure of beliefs by examining changes in behavior. Beliefs might then be said to evolve, argued Wright, the most mature and rational resulting 'from the survival of the fittest among our original and spontaneous beliefs'. Bain's analysis would allow us to confirm this hypothesis empirically; we would investigate any supposed shift in beliefs by perusing changes in action. In linking Bain's doctrine to evolution, Wright supplied the Darwinian context in which the Metaphysical Club formulated its lasting contribution, the principle of pragmatism.

One controversial aspect of Darwinian theory was its applicability to human evolution, and the controversy concerned not so much the links between the human organism and those of the lower animals but rather between reason and animal instinct. The pragmatic idea came to fruition in naturalizing the mind and was one dimension of a defense of Darwin's theory as applied to human evolution. Construing beliefs as habits of action, Wright married intelligence and reason to instinct by analyzing changes in behavior and identifying certain changes as evidence of mind. These were the ideas that William James popularized a few years later:

The organism of thought . . . is teleological through and through. . . . Far from being vouched for by the past these [our hypotheses and beliefs] are verified only by the future. The survivors constitute the right way of thinking.

The theory of evolution is beginning to do very good service by its reduction of all mentality to the type of reflex action. Cognition, in this view, is but a fleeting moment, a cross-section at a certain point, of what in its totality is a motor phenomenon.

The new conceptions, emotions, and active tendencies which evolve are originally produced in the shape of random images, fancies, accidental out-births of spontaneous variation in the functional activity of the excessively instable human brain, which the outer environment simply confirms or refutes, adopts or rejects, preserves or destroys,—selects in short just as it selects morphological and social variations due to molecular accidents of an analogous sort.

Within this common framework Peirce formulated 'the pragmatic maxim'. Rightfully credited as its father, he drew up a paper lest the club be dissolved without a 'material Souvenir'. He probably read it, a version of a paper entitled 'How to Make Our Ideas Clear', in November 1872, but did not publish it until some six years later, and then in altered form, in the *Popular Science Monthly* as part of a series, 'Illustrations of the Logic of Science'.

Mill's *Examination of Hamilton* had been a polemical success everywhere, and by the early 1870s Hamilton's reputation as a philosopher had already declined. Mill's book shocked Peirce, who had been taught the Scottish position as an undergraduate. The Metaphysical Club proposed sidestepping skepticism by focusing on the practical consequences of activity and on how professionals behaved. Peirce was doing extended scientific work on stellar photometry, metrology, and geodesy, and as a careful and talented experimentalist he would come to believe that the meaning of every scientific statement was that if a given prescription for an experiment was carried out, then an experience of a given description would result. Instead of fretting about doubt in an armchair, philosophers might study the substance of enquiry.

So far as we can recapture discussion, Peirce set down what all his fellows agreed on: practice must define belief; a belief was not a mental entity but a habit of action to be interrogated by examining behavior. For the club, pragmatism was a maxim for investigating the nature of belief consistent with the theory of evolution. Individuals believed what they would be ready to act on and risk much upon, and scientists could investigate the growth and change of these beliefs empirically. The group concluded that the meaning of a belief consisted (ambiguously) in its sensible effects, or the rule, habit, or law from which investigators might derive these effects given the occurrence of appropriate antecedent conditions.

The name given to this doctrine—pragmatism—was Kantian and probably originated with Peirce, although James first put the term into print years later in his 1898 address, 'Philosophical Conceptions and Practical Results'. In the *Critique of Pure Reason* Kant wrote:

The physician must do something in the case of a patient who is in danger, even if he is not sure of the disease. He looks out for symptoms and judges, according to his best knowledge . . . His belief is even in his own judgement only a contingent one; someone else might perhaps judge better. I call such contingent belief . . . pragmatic . . . The . . . test of . . . firm belief is the bet. . . . A bet makes one stop short. . . . If in our thoughts we imagine the happiness of our whole life at stake, our triumphant judgement disappears, we tremble lest our belief has gone too far. Thus pragmatic belief has degrees of strength varying in proportion to the magnitude of the diverse interests involved.

The Kantian word *pragmatisch* stood for the means–ends relation expressed in hypothetical imperatives—for example, counsels of prudence. For the Metaphysical Club a connection to definite human purposes and conceivable empirical consequences guided all reasoning. Meaningful beliefs were inseparably linked to practical activity. Whatever the substantive relations between the Americans and Kant, his *pragmatisch* became the English pragmatic and did so as an extension of Darwinian ideas.

Charles Peirce

Holmes's passion for philosophy waned as he threw himself into the law, and he soon dropped out of the club. Wright died in 1875, Green a year later—both in their mid-forties. For the better part of both these years Peirce was in Europe, employed by the United States Coast and Geodetic Survey, and thereafter ceased even nominally to reside in Cambridge, and James had a budding career at Harvard. Philosophical societies continued in Cambridge, but Peirce was on his own and turned his efforts to producing a number of papers in the 1870s that would refine pragmatism and place the doctrine within a complex system.

Peirce was the second son of Benjamin Peirce, professor of mathematics and astronomy at Harvard and the most famous mathematician of his generation. Benjamin recognized his son's genius early and exercised the boy's aptitude for abstract thought in various ways. After receiving a Harvard BA, Charles entered the new Lawrence Scientific School in 1862, and there demanding work resulted in a BS in chemistry, summa cum laude. Benjamin also indulged his favorite by using his position at Harvard to secure Charles's advance, a strategy guaranteed to make enemies. The son gained the reputation of being spoiled, hostile, and neurotic, though scholars have argued that a painful neurological disease accounted for his use of drugs and consequent aberrant behavior. His unconventional sexual conduct—he once lived with a woman not his wife—also made him suspect. None the less, Peirce led a successful scholarly and scientific life. His father supervised the Coast Survey in which Charles was employed, and he continued to work for it after being hired as an assistant to the director of the

Harvard Observatory, another job made possible by his father, but one in which the son's original grasp of photometrics justified the position. On the basis of Charles's philosophical research, President Daniel Coit Gilman of Johns Hopkins appointed him part-time lecturer in logic in 1879. For four more years Gilman reappointed Peirce, and he looked forward to a professorship at the end of that time.

Peirce had primarily come to philosophy by reading the *Critique of Pure Reason*—three hours a day for two years, if we take his recollections seriously. For Kant knowledge consisted of the mind's synthesis of the data of sense by means of a fundamental set of categories, a priori true of all possible experience. Peirce believed that the clue to refining Kant's position lay in the examination of these categories, which for Peirce began with how subjects were related to predicates in assertions. This investigation led to a broader concern. The connection between a statement's subject and predicate was a variant of what Peirce called the sign relation. Subjects were signs of predicates. To advance on Kant's understanding of the categories, of the basic ways in which we structured the world, Peirce explored signhood; he asked how one thing could stand for another, how representation was possible and in what it consisted. His answers to these questions appeared in a group of articles published in 1867 and 1868 in the *Proceedings of the American Academy of Arts and Sciences* and the *Journal of Speculative Philosophy*, the central one being 'On a New List of Categories'.

Peirce dissected the sign relation as assertions exhibited it. In 'The cow is black', one affirmed the predicate 'black' of the object, a cow, for which the subject, the word 'cow' stood: one connected the quality (blackness) and object (the cow) by affirming the predicate ('black') of the subject ('cow') by the copula 'is'; and affirmed that the subject and predicate referred to the same object. Peirce defined a sign as that which stood for something to someone in some respect, and believed that a sign relation connected subject and predicate. If one asserted that the cow was black, the predicate 'black' stood for the cow in respect to blackness. This complex was the irreducible relation of signification.

Signhood was triadic—it embraced what Peirce called the ground (blackness), the correlate (the object that was black), and the interpreting representation (the predicate 'black'). These three conceptions were central to his new list of categories, the chief a priori modes that gave us knowledge of the world.

Kant argued that the categories arose to unify sense data. These data did not refer, they simply were, and in order to refer, the mind must attend to and recognize them as something, as It. Peirce claimed this operation already displayed rudimentary conceptualization. To speak of 'It', of 'the present in general', used the broadest 'perhaps most vague' concept, but it was none the less a concept. We must assume sense data, but no data were immediately known, and so Peirce directed his animus against the British empiricist doctrine that we could begin with impressions of sense that were given. Neural stimuli might precede our conceptualizations, but it was impossible to distinguish the given from the interpreted: all 'phenomena' were interpretations of the data and so were to some degree conceptual. We could pursue these cognitions, as Peirce called them, as far back as we wanted and never reach a first impression or intuition: we would always find that prior cognitions of the same object had determined any cognition. Moreover, every cognition might call forth a further cognition, and Peirce concluded that our series of cognitions, or interpretations of the data of sense, formed an infinite series without beginning or end. Because the categories involved in the sign relation were fundamental to all conceptualization, to all cognitions, Peirce stated that the sign series was also infinite. Every sign needed a further sign to interpret it. Death or other factors might interrupt the series of signs, but it would of itself go on forever. Thus, thinking was an endless interpretative process.

Being for Peirce must have a conceptual dimension, and 'the incognizable', what was not cognized, could not exist. 'Over against any cognition, there is an unknown but knowable reality; but over against all possible cognition, there is only the self-contradictory. In short, cognizability (in its widest sense) and being are not merely metaphysically the same, but are synonymous terms.' Existence did not transcend conceptualization, interpretation, the mental—Peirce was an idealist.

If we had no intuitions, we could not have them of ourselves, and so there was no direct introspection or immediate knowledge of ourselves as self-conscious. Sensations, volitions, and thoughts first occurred as a response to external stimuli; we became aware of them afterward by abstraction and inference from experience of the rest of the world. Individual self-consciousness arose to explain error and ignorance.

Peirce saw himself as attacking the premises of early modern philosophy. In stressing that an individual could doubt everything and overcome this doubt as an individual, Descartes trivialized doubt and overlooked the importance of co-operative thinking on a problem. The reliance on solitary ratiocination came at the expense of scientific experimentation dependent on a community of investigators. More important, Peirce suspected Descartes's conclusion that a metaphysical substance, independent of consciousness, caused cognitions. This presupposition must eventuate in Hume's skepticism, the outcome of modern philosophy. Yet Peirce had also built his theories on cognitions, the momentary syntheses of data and concept. In a measure, this admission allied him to Descartes, Berkeley, and the skepticism and nominalism of Hume and Mill. Indeed, Peirce's theory of knowledge and his notion of signs had much in common with Berkeley, and Peirce's concern was to wed some form of phenomenalism, his reliance on the building blocks of cognition, to what he thought was Kant's anti-nominalistic position. He took this step in 1871 in a long review of a new edition of Berkeley's works. The review showed that the scientific onslaught on the spiritual disturbed Peirce, who initiated a reconstruction of science based on a form of absolute idealism.

The practice of science, Peirce believed, was more and more identified with the nominalism Mill had made prominent. Science appeared to be based on a simple positivism: scientists explored a series of discrete phenomena, the interaction of individual entities, and correlated the behavior of groups of phenomena to produce that body of knowledge and those laws identified with science. Scientists observed individual phenomena closely and calculated the relations among them carefully. In examining the underpinnings of science, Peirce found the situation more complex. Establishing laws and predicting on their basis, he said, were central to the laboratory, where experimentalists assumed that certain groups of objects had similar structures, enabling the scientists to move from what was true of one (examined) object to other (non-examined) similar objects; scientists assumed that a warrant existed for their belief that the future resembled the past, that induction was justified. For example, scientists identified properties of a piece of copper—its atomic weight and structure—allowing them to predict that an untested piece of copper would behave similarly to previously tested pieces.

Suppose one discovered in a field a black cow, twig, beetle, and tractor, and called them by the name *tows*, because they were in the field. A bad scientist might conclude, on the basis of existing evidence, that all tows were black and go on to predict that should something be put in the field—that is, if something should be a tow—it would be black. The procedure was ludicrous because science did not investigate generalizations based on just any common properties: that four objects had the property of being in the field did not warrant the generalization that anything else placed in the field would also have some further property they happened to possess. Rather, scientists distinguished lawlike, justifiable, generalizations from accidental ones, and this attempt committed them to a search for real similarities, such as the atomic weight and structure of a piece of copper. If they could justify their generalizations, that is, if the problem of induction were solvable and they could warrant reasoning from past to future, they had to admit that the search for real similarities was legitimate.

Peirce contended that if nominalism were the basis for science, scientists could not distinguish the two sorts of generalizations above, or legitimate the search for real similarities. For the nominalist only individuals were real, and predicates merely named individuals grouped together. There was no common quality whose existence justified the predictions made about copper and whose lack made dealing with tows foolish. Science could only circumvent Hume's problem of induction on other grounds.

Peirce described one view of the metaphysical question concerning the nature of existents:

We have, it is true, nothing immediately present to us but thoughts. Those thoughts, however, have been caused by sensations, and those sensations are constrained by something out of the mind. This thing out of the mind, which directly influences sensation, and through sensation thought, because it is out of the mind, is independent of how we think it, and is, in short, the real. Here is one view of reality, a very familiar one.

This view, metaphysical realism of the Cartesian or Lockian kind, the belief that objects existed independently of mind, entailed nominalism. On this view, to say that two things were both men was 'only to say that the one mental term or thought-sign "man" stands indifferently for either of the sensible objects caused by the two external realities; so that not even the two sensations have in themselves anything in common, and far less is it to be inferred that the external realities have'. Metaphysical realism made nominalism imperative and dictated that only individuals were real.

Alternatively, the view of 'epistemological realism' argued that predicates referred to qualities that individuals 'really have in common, independent of our thought'. 'Universals' were 'independent of your mind or mine or that of any number of persons'. On this view, Peirce went on, 'all human thought and opinion contains [*sic*] an arbitrary accidental element, dependent on the limitations in circumstances, power, and bent of the individual; an element of error, in short'. In the long run, however, 'human opinion universally tends . . . to definite form, which is the truth. Let any human being have enough information and exert enough thought on any question, and the result will be that he will arrive at a certain conclusion, which is the same that any other mind will reach under sufficiently favorable circumstances'. For epistemological realists, Peirce said, what was believed in 'this final opinion' truly existed; they concluded that the metaphysically ultimate was independent 'not indeed of thought in general, but of all that is arbitrary and individual in thought; is quite independent of how you, I, or any number of men think'. Metaphysical realism implied nominalism, but epistemological realism implied a metaphysical idealism—the real was the non-arbitrary in thought but did not exist independently of thought. In the final opinion some qualities would characterize individual things and those qualities would be *ipso facto* real.

Peirce said his idealism was 'instantly fatal' to a thing in itself existing independent of mind, the unknowable cause of sensations—instantly fatal to metaphysical realism. But his position would encourage us to regard sense appearance as signs of the ultimately real. Akin to universals, real objects would be intellectual constructs, Peirce said, devised to give structure and coherence to sensations; the real objects would be 'noumena, or intelligible conceptions which are the last products of the mental action which is set in motion by sensation . . . the unmoving form to which . . . [human thought] is flowing'.

This theory involves a phenomenalism. But it is the phenomenalism of Kant, and not that of Hume. Indeed, what Kant called his Copernican step was precisely the passage from the nominalistic to the [epistemologically] realistic view of reality. It was the essence of his philosophy to regard the real object as determined by the mind. That was nothing else than to consider every conception and intuition which enters necessarily into the experience of an object, and which is not transitory and accidental, as having objective validity. In short, it was to regard the reality as the normal product of mental action, and not as the incognizable cause of it.

Descartes was wrong; Kant, correctly understood, right.

The same object did not invariably produce an identical effect upon us, for 'our sensations are as various as our relations to the external things'. But Peirce took into account differing relations to the object and argued that if the object existed, there would be a series of 'if . . . then' statements asserting that under certain conditions of sensation, the object would have certain effects on us: if I went into the field, I would see the black cow; if I approached it, it would move away from me; if I took it to a stockyard, I could sell it; and so on. By postulating the object, Peirce gave experience coherence. We could verify that we had the experience under the specified condition; he justified the postulate because it explained how we verified the series of hypotheticals. To say that a universal (quality) existed meant just that there would be a regularity in the future behavior of certain objects and that speaking of the universal explained the regularity.

Peirce was committed to epistemological realism in order to justify science, and this commitment led him to an idealism that defined the real as the object believed in the final opinion:

The real . . . is that which, sooner or later, information and reasoning would finally result in, and which is therefore independent of the vagaries of me and you. Thus, the very origin of the conception of reality shows that this conception essentially involves the notion of COMMUNITY without definite limits, and capable of a definite increase of knowledge.

The investigations of a temporally extended community defined the real; such investigations constantly weeded out error and false opinion, always approaching more closely to the truth.

Peirce's paradigmatic community was the scientific one, but he had previously analysed individual self-consciousness as an idea that arose to explain ignorance and error: 'Ignorance and error are all that distinguish our private selves from the absolute ego of pure apperception.' As the scientific community struggled to reach agreement and eliminate error, it also approached a unity that absorbed individual egos into an absolute self. Like other nineteenth-century idealists, Peirce believed that Kant's notion of a connected order of experience affirmed a single experience of which human experience was a part. For Peirce, Kant's transcendental unity of apperception appeared as an infinite community, a system of consistent signs. For Kant the transcendental unity of apperception grounded all knowledge of objects. For Peirce the agreement of the community yielded the objectively real, but these real objects were also ideas in the mind of God. The ongoing activity of the community manifested this universal mind. That this mind knew itself meant that the community had a further interpretation, a subsequent community of signs. Since all cognitions required further cognitions, this series was infinite, the community of signs temporally unlimited.

Religious in import, the scientific vocation aimed at oneness with the divine. But to argue that we could ground science, solve the problem of induction, within a philosophy embracing idealism and epistemological realism did not solve the problem, 'the lock upon the door of philosophy'. Peirce had to offer a solution, and his argument was simple: a world in which induction would fail as often as lead to truth was impossible. In such a world one could not associate any two characters significantly, that is, one could not predict any character from the appearance of any other. But this situation could occur only if every possible combination of characters occurred the same number of times, and that would not reflect disorder, but the simplest order; the world would not be unintelligible but, on the contrary, everything conceivable would be found in it with equal frequency. The notion of a universe in which probable arguments would fail as often as hold true was absurd. 'We can suppose it in general terms, but we cannot specify how it should be other than self-contradictory.' Since we could not conceive of a world in which induction was not justifiable, and since the inconceivable was non-existent, induction was justifiable. Could the nominalist show that induction was justifiable in his world? Peirce said no: the nominalist's world postulated incognizable realities, *Dinge an sich*, and since they could not exist, the nominalists world was contradictory, no world at all.

By the late 1860s Peirce was reconstructing science on a basis congenial to religion. As long as scientists mistakenly based their views on nominalism, he said, 'doctrines of a debasing moral tendency' would accompany science—'those daughters of nominalism—sensationalism, phenomenalism, individualism, and materialism'. Peirce apparently identified materialism with all forms of metaphysical realism. Grant this position, Peirce believed, and the mental became epiphenomenal, a subtle form of matter (the general name given to the independently existing objects). 'A man who enters into the scientific thought of the day and has not materialistic tendencies', he wrote, 'is getting to be an impossibility.' Yet science had no affinity with these views and was antagonistic to nominalism. Moreover, science based on epistemological realism led to a communitarian idealism and a defensible religion

though the question of realism and nominalism has its roots in the technicalities of logic, its branches reach about our life. The question whether the genus homo has any existence except as individuals, is the question whether there is anything of any more dignity, worth, and importance than individual happiness, individual aspiration, and individual life. Whether men really have anything in common, so that the *community* is to be considered as an end in itself, and if so, what the relative value of the two factors is, is the most fundamental practical question in regard to every public institution the constitution of which we have it in our power to influence.

Peirce based his theory of the 'New List' of categories on the primacy of subject–predicate logic, but soon saw the importance of the new 'logic of relatives', which analyzed assertions in terms of relations. If relations were as abstract and as fundamental as the qualities of subject–predicate logic, the meaning of our concept of an object might lie in its relations to other objects or in the relations among its states at various times. The relations in which a thing stood to other things might determine its 'essential nature' (quality) rather than this nature determining its relations to other things. Consequently, the meaning of our conception of objects might depend on the law governing its relations to other objects and not on the quality it embodied. Peirce had already nearly said this: his view that sensation varied with the relation to the object defined an object's qualities by the relations of operations on the object to perceived effects; that is, the definition involved a law.

When he enunciated the principle of pragmatism to the Metaphysical Club in 1872, Peirce elucidated the meaning of a concept in a way that would take advantage of his logical advance. The problem was that within his larger system, the maxim caused difficulties. These became clear when Peirce published a second series of articles, 'Illustrations of the Logic of Science', in the *Popular Science Monthly* in 1877–8; he designed them to carry forward a scientific philosophy congruent with idealism.

The articles defended Alexander Bain's theories as the Metaphysical Club had accepted them. A state of belief was satisfied and indicated the formation of some habit that determined actions. Believing conditioned us to behave in a certain way when an appropriate occasion arose. On the other side, doubt was an irritation, a stimulus to action and a struggle to reach the reposeful state of belief; this struggle Peirce called enquiry. He had previously stated that truth was what a community obtained in the final opinion, and he now asserted that the end of enquiry was the settlement of opinion. If this fixing of opinion occurred, we had truth, and the question became: what was the best means, the best method, to fix opinion and, therefore, reach the truth?

The *Popular Science Monthly* series intimated that evolutionary modes of thinking had attracted Peirce, and he wedded them to Bain's work and his own ideas of the previous decade. The first article, 'The Fixation of Belief', held that logical thinking was 'the most useful quality an animal can possess, and might, therefore, result from the action of natural selection'. The evolution of human culture produced the scientific method, a description of the psychological structure of modern reasoning. Peirce considered four methods of fixing belief: (1) tenacity—believing what one wanted to believe; (2) authority—allowing the state to control belief; (3) the a priori method—coming to conclusions via reason's natural light; and (4) the method of science. In a rough way he charted the evolution of rational thinking or 'philosophizing'; we had gone from pre-philosophic ideas, to the speculation of the Middle Ages, to Continental rationalism typified by Descartes, to contemporary scientific theorizing exemplified by Peirce. In any event, he rejected the first three methods because they did not work. They did not 'fix' belief and, accordingly, could not lead to truth. The scientific method won his praise—one could not gainsay its achievements in settling opinion—and Peirce made an eloquent appeal for accepting it.

There were tensions in 'The Fixation of Belief'. If the final opinion defined the real and the determination of this opinion was the end of enquiry, Peirce had no good reason to defend science. Authority might better settle opinion, and the best bet might be to support it. To avoid this sort of rejoinder Peirce emphasized existents exterior to our thought. These existents were only constructs accounting for peculiarities of experience, but the defense of science stressed their independence: we would reach truth only if we took account of them, and we could take account of them only if we used the method of science. But if objects existed independently of thought, Peirce had contradicted himself.

The dilemma became plainer when Peirce examined the scientific method in 'How to Make Our Ideas Clear', the essay analysing the meaning of ideas, beliefs, or conceptions. His model of meaningfulness came from the laboratory. A conception had meaning if it produced experienced effects under controlled conditions; and he defined a conception's meaning by the consequences produced by operating with it. Peirce had already argued that any belief's essence was the creation of a habit. It followed that the different 'modes of action' to which beliefs gave rise distinguished different beliefs:

If beliefs do not differ in this respect, if they appease the same doubt by producing the same rule of action, then no mere differences in the manner of consciousness of them can make them different beliefs, any more than playing a tune in different keys is playing different tunes. Imaginary distinctions are often drawn between beliefs which differ only in their mode of expression. Such false distinctions do as much harm as the confusion of beliefs [that are really different.]

This definition of belief was congruent with the presuppositions of laboratory experimentation, and Peirce concluded that we explicated the meaning of a belief by examining the habits it entailed:

To develop its [thought's] meaning, we have, therefore, simply to determine what habits it produces, for what a thing means is simply what habits it involves. Now, the identity of a habit depends on how it might lead us to act, not merely under such circumstances as are likely to arise, but under such as might possibly occur, no matter how improbable they may be. What the habit is depends on when and how it causes us to act. As for the when, every stimulus to action is derived from perception; as for the how, every purpose of action is to produce some sensible result. Thus, we come down to what is tangible and practical as the root of every real distinction of thought, no matter how subtle it may be; and there is no distinction of meaning so fine as to consist in anything but a possible difference of practice.

To call a thing black was to say how it would appear when contrasted with other colors. The conception of this quality lay in the conception of the effects that would occur were we to act on the basis of our understanding of the quality: Peirce reduced qualities to relations. In this context he stated his contribution to the Metaphysical Club, the pragmatic theory of meaning: 'Consider what effects, which might conceivably have practical bearings, we conceive the object of our conception to have. Then, our conception of these effects is the whole of our conception of the object.' As the maxim was written, the conception of an idea's conceivable effects, the possible consequences of acting on it, defined the idea's meaning. Elsewhere in 'How to Make Our Ideas Clear' and in his other writings of this period, Peirce equated an idea's meaning with the habits of action it involved. The consequences of acting on an idea did not determine its meaning, but rather the set of statements relating consequences to the conditions under which they occurred. An idea's meaning was exhibited by the set of hypothetical statements, 'if . . . then' statements, relating operations on the object of the concept to experienced effects.

Peirce's explication of the meaning of meaning undermined his attempt to bring together science and religion. He had previously defined the real object as a construct that gave coherence to experience. The object was necessary to understanding the relation of experience to conditions of cognition: the existence of the postulated object implied certain experience under certain conditions. Now Peirce made the object definitionally equivalent to the relation of the conditions of cognition to experience. The object was nothing but our ways of operating on experiences.

The commitment to science as the only workable method of settling opinion in 'The Fixation of Belief' drove Peirce close to metaphysical realism. 'How to Make Our Ideas Clear' appeared to demonstrate that we could base our conception of objects on nominalism. The analysis of meaning rested only on a study of phenomena and their relation to us: we needed no additional 'intelligible construct'. But Peirce linked this position, phenomenalism, with nominalism, that individual entities alone existed. Thus, 'The Fixation of Belief' came near to asserting an independently existing object causing the phenomena: nominalism followed from metaphysical realism.

Everything for Peirce was actual or would become actual. The cognizable was cognized at some time; and since only the cognizable was real, everything was cognized. Peirce came to see that this idea entailed the reduction of the real to a set of phenomena, and this view left him open to the charge of nominalism. He thought that the infinite future saved his position: the future transformed possibility into actuality without compromising either the inexhaustibility of the possible or the limitations of the actual. The real was both a permanent and inexhaustible possibility of sensation and wholly cognized. Peirce rendered this notion consistent by postulating an infinite future that realized those possibilities of sensation. But one could not know that enquiry would go on forever. Consequently, that enquiry would go on forever was incognizable, and so for Peirce infinite enquiry did not exist. Even if enquiry did go on forever (and did converge), Peirce had to deny that there were real possibilities of sensation at any time that no one was cognizing them. The infinite future could not exist on Peirce's premisses and even if it did, it could not solve his problems.

Another instance of this dilemma was the two different statements of the pragmatic maxim—that meaning was an object's effects or the set of habits the object involved. Peirce did not distinguish a law from the set of its actual instances, and he did not do so because making the distinction would have required admitting possible instances that were never actualized. Similarly, Peirce identified the universal mind containing those ideas toward which the community gravitated with the infinite community that could contain only actual instances of these ideas. All these troubles stemmed from combining a version of phenomenalism with epistemological realism and idealism.

It is a minor irony in the history of philosophy that more recent 'operationalists' and positivists hailed these articles as seminal works in the tradition of twentieth-century scientific philosophy; Peirce conceived them as part of an argument against these modernist doctrines and rejected the nominalistic aspects of his philosophy as soon as he realized they were leading him to scientific and religious skepticism.

Later Life and Work

In January 1884, Gilman abruptly dismissed Peirce from Hopkins. The reasons were unclear. His first marriage had ended in a divorce, and a few months later, in 1883, he had married a still mysterious Frenchwoman, Madame Juliette Pourtalai. Throughout this time Peirce had been personally difficult in managing his affairs and in carrying out some of his academic duties, but despite this troublesome behavior and his marital straits, through the end of 1883 he had satisfied Gilman with his teaching and publication record. After 1884 he never held another scholarly post, and being fired from Hopkins did much to destroy his chances in the American academy.

Peirce's life and philosophizing did not immediately disintegrate. He still had his job with the Coast Survey, and although the death of his father in 1880 had left him without a patron, he stayed on, collecting a salary, until asked to resign in 1891. Meanwhile, he had received his family inheritance on the death of his mother in 1887, and moved to Milford, Pennsylvania, a resort town on the Delaware River, with his second wife. He added to the moneys that came to him a small annuity of Juliette's, and they speculated in real estate and built a country home. Peirce named it

Arisbe, after the colony of Miletus, the home of the first Greek philosophers. The Peirces coped until the depression of 1893 bankrupted them. In debt for the rest of his life, Peirce sold off his land, and after 1905 depended on charity. From 1907, William James put together a fund to provide Peirce, then 68, with minimal money to carry on.

Through the teaching of James and Josiah Royce, who had also, like James, gone on to fame at Harvard, Peirce became a legendary figure among Harvard graduate students. In the academic years 1897–8, 1902–3, and 1903–4 he lectured in Cambridge. Despite the philosophers' efforts and the status of his brother—for a time chairman of the mathematics department and dean of the faculty—Charles could get no appointment at Harvard. As James put it, Peirce had 'dished himself' there and at every other university. The Baltimore scandal followed him to his grave.

Without Peirce at Hopkins, the pre-eminence of the Harvard philosophers was guaranteed. Peirce and Hopkins were perhaps the one combination that could have challenged Cambridge. But after Gilman fired Peirce, philosophy in Baltimore declined. More promoter than thinker, psychologist G. Stanley Hall got the chair Gilman had to offer, and the idealist George Sylvester Morris and his protégé John Dewey, who were also in Baltimore, left soon after Peirce. A few years later Hall went to Clark University, thereby depriving Gilman of the man he had picked, however unwisely. Hopkins did not rebuild until 1910, when Arthur Lovejoy took a job there, but by then its leadership had been lost.

Peirce suffered more than Hopkins. Even his early writing was so oblique that he probably would never have acquired the public repute of James or Royce. But, as the profession of philosophy grew, he could have expected academic fame and a circle of students. There was only one way, he wrote to James, that his work 'could find its way to people's brains': 'if I could meet a class of young men for an hour thrice or even twice a week for the bulk of the academical year, even for a single year, that . . . would spread the truth'. This was not to be, and Peirce's growing isolation led him to abandon any concern for fluency and good style perhaps as a defensive measure. He consequently expounded his ideas in a way that made it almost impossible even for thinkers like James and Royce to follow him— Peirce himself admitted to being 'a very snarl of twine'. Turned away from the academy, he also lost the minimal regularity of a scholarly schedule. Aside from a few series of articles in the journals—when large books were the style—he did not publish in the thirty years after he left Hopkins; everything remained in manuscript. None the less, his influence was greater even during his lifetime than one might have predicted, although students inevitably emphasized his writing of the 1860s and 1870s.

Peirce left Hopkins at roughly the same time that he altered his philosophic views to avoid skepticism. During the years of his isolation he built on advances in logic and the foundations of mathematics, which we have seen undermined the ideas based on a subject–predicate logic. He tried, moreover, to solve the difficulties presented in his analysis of possible experience by arguing that some unexperienced possibilities were real. He also saw that the doubt–belief theory based the scientific method on a description of those procedures identified with science and made it relative to a particular psychological organization that might alter in evolution. To avoid this consequence Peirce's later work elaborated a normative theory of scientific method. He also revised his commitment to the convergence of enquiry as grounding his epistemology. In his early work the mind's categories could not fail to correspond to reality since reality was only mind's construction in the final opinion; in the later work he argued, hypothetically, that the character of experience was explicable if an absolute mind existed with categories identical to our own. In both systems the human mind was commensurate with reality and scientific investigation converged to a final opinion if enquiry went on forever, because the real was knowable and the processes of the absolute mind were identical to those of the human mind. But in the later work enquiry was not a matter of escaping doubt but of realizing a universal harmony. The scientific method was the correct means to reach this goal and not merely a psychological description of behavior. Pragmatism—or what Peirce in his own version renamed 'pragmaticism'—defined the contribution to that goal a concept made and the difference applying the concept would have in fulfilling the world purpose. Pragmaticism was not just a tool for exploring the meaning of concepts but told us something of the purpose we had in formulating them. Perhaps most important, Peirce cast his views in a new language that took him away from 'the way of ideas' associated with Locke and Descartes, and thus from the easy designation of himself as 'idealist'.

Peirce called his theory of signs 'semiotic', and as he elaborated it, he concentrated on the difference between an 'idea' and a 'sign'. An idea occurred, in Descartes's terminology, 'clearly and distinctly'. Because the idea was perceived introspectively in the mind, its meaning was intuited, or immediately known. A sign, as Peirce employed the term, was also a thought, but it differed from an idea in that its meaning was not self-evident. A sign received its meaning by being interpreted by a subsequent thought or action. A stop sign at a street corner, for example, was first perceived as an octagonal shape bearing the letters S-T-O-P. It was only in relation to a subsequent thought—the Peircean interpretant—that the sign attained meaning. The meaning lay not in the perception but in the interpretation of the perception as a signal to stop or, better still, as the act of stopping. Peirce held that, like the perception of the stop sign, every thought was a sign without meaning until interpreted by a subsequent thought, an interpretant. Thus a triadic relation, an interpretation of the thought as a sign of a determining object, established the meaning of every thought. Thought was not immediate perception or undeniable experience of ideas within a self but occurred in signs that acquired meaning in a variant of Peirce's triadic relation of interpretation of the 1860s and 1870s: object sign interpretant.

Peirce's later work has been more recently described as 'semiotic realism', based on a common-sense acceptance of the world as apprehended. Peirce held that the world was accurately represented to us because the very thoughts or signs by which we conceived the world shared a substantial identity with it. Thinking, in Peirce's view, was not something somehow to be related to behavior: thinking was behavior. For him unjustifiable methodological biases were, at bottom, derived from either materialist or conventional idealist rebellions against Cartesian dualism. Peirce's semiotic offered a middle ground, a rejection of dualism that nevertheless avoided materialism and a standard idealism. Even though he designated matter as thought, thought did not occur as ideas immediately perceived 'in' a self.

Peirce in American Thought

Early in the spring of 1914, a strange recluse, Peirce died in a dark, unheated room of Arisbe. Harvard's relation to him was as ambivalent after his death as it had been in his life. Royce arranged for Peirce's widow to give his library and papers to the institution. In December of 1914, one of Royce's students, Victor Lenzen, took the first shipment by horse-sled from Arisbe to Port Jervis, New York, in the initial stage of the trip to Cambridge. There another student, Fergus Kernan, catalogued the manuscripts with Royce. The books were soon scattered in various Harvard libraries, and elsewhere. The manuscripts—thousands of pages in Peirce's handwriting—began their own career stacked on chairs, table, and floor in Royce's crowded office at Harvard. After Royce died in 1916, plans for quickly publishing an edited collection of Peirce's writings faded. Kernan stored the papers in filing cabinets, but then left Cambridge to join the war against Germany in 1917.

Over the next several years Harvard tried to get various hands authoritatively to examine the manuscripts. Lenzen made another preliminary catalogue (which indicated eighty-three boxes of material), and then English philosopher Bertrand Russell; young instructor Henry Sheffer; former

Harvard professor George Santayana; and a Berkeley philosopher, C. I. Lewis, were invited to work on the papers. Lewis spent two years with them in the early 1920s, as part of an arrangement that obtained him a Harvard assistant professorship, but declined to do any editing. Finally Morris Cohen, who had done a Ph.D. in philosophy at Harvard in 1906 and had gone on to a distinguished career in New York at City College, examined the collection. Although he too refused to be responsible for a full-scale edition, Cohen published, in 1923, the first posthumous edition of Peirce's writings, *Chance, Love, and Logic: Philosophical Essays by the Late Charles S. Peirce, the Founder of Pragmatism*. Cohen's edition was a remarkable *tour de force*. Although a far cry from what philosophers or historians might wish, the introduction gave an unusually competent overview of Peirce as a philosopher and made a selection of his writing widely available. Students used the book for many years, and as 'pragmatism' became a distinctive American philosophical position, the volume effectively promoted Peirce as its inventor.

Meanwhile, the manuscripts themselves were now in disarray, picked over by numerous hands. 'Persistent rumors', as one scholar has put it, have attested that in the 1920s and even much later, manuscripts were thrown away out of ignorance; relocated to other more appropriate collections; destroyed to protect reputations; or taken as souvenirs. In the late 1920s two new graduate students, Charles Hartshorne and Paul Weiss, at last published six volumes from 1931 to 1935, *Collected Papers of Charles Sanders Peirce*, which together with two more volumes published in 1958, for a long time were the standard source on Peirce.

Hartshorne's and Weiss's project was an enormous achievement, but it came at great cost. They decided on a thematic edition, and disregarded chronological and textual considerations. They printed continuous pieces of writing in separate volumes, and printed side by side excerpts from work written more than thirty years apart. The disorganization of the manuscripts continued as Hartshorne and Weiss even cut single pages in two, and put them in different piles.

By the early 1960s systematic reordering of the papers began, but a new, chronological edition of the papers was not under way until the 1980s, and publication of it promised to go far into the twenty-first century. At the same time the sorry history of the Peirce papers had certain positive consequences for his growing repute after his death. Cohen's book secured Peirce's worth as a significant American philosopher. But the continued disorder of his œuvre and the various failed efforts properly to house it set the stage for aspiring philosophers to dramatize the narrative of Peirce's life. Moreover, the Harvard Department of Philosophy had clumsily restricted access to some of the papers because Peirce's immoral lifestyle had to be factored into his value as a thinker. This institutional bias only allowed the greater philosophical community to embroider the stories of what was in the manuscripts. Peirce became honored as a genius not recognized by professionals at Harvard. His life and work were both a warning to those who might follow him, and a balm for those unappreciated and not at Harvard. Who knew what untold treasures still lay in the Peirce archives? Founded at mid-century, the Charles S. Peirce Society promulgated the study of the man, and began to issue a journal in 1965. By that time dissertations and books were regularly appearing, first by Americans and then by European scholars. 'Peirce studies' became one of the more significant philosophic industries in the United States, and Arisbe was named a national historical site.

9 Pragmatism at Harvard, 1878–1913

William James was born in New York City in 1842, the oldest son of Henry James, a literary and religious writer of independent means. The elder James reigned over an exuberant family life but was also eccentric and overbearing. William became one of America's most famous philosophers, and his younger brother Henry James, Jr., one of the country's most famous novelists. But three other children had difficult and unhappy lives, and William himself, unable to please his father, went through a long period of aimless insecurity. As a teenager, he studied painting. Later he attended classes in science at Harvard and received a medical degree from there in 1869, but he was unable to establish himself. Part of the cause of what today might be diagnosed as clinical depression was his intellectual puzzlement over evolution. Cogitating over the atheistic interpretation of Darwin, James feared that evolution might rule out any spiritual interpretation of human life and reduce people to organisms determined by forces beyond their control. The popular philosophic answer of absolute idealism did not attract him, since for James it too entailed determinism and precluded genuine freedom. If either speculative system were true, work in the world was useless.

In the late 1860s and early 1870s James lived as a semi-invalid, and indeed for the rest of his life, commentators have argued, he was subject to recurring periods of depression. But in 1872 he was appointed instructor in anatomy and physiology at Harvard, and over the next ten years moved from teaching the biological sciences, to psychology, to philosophy. Getting a job may not have cured James, but with a secure profession, he began to write regularly. By the 1880s his gifted observations about our conscious intellectual and emotional life, which he studied as a psychologist, had made him a thinker of note.

Charles William Eliot, who had been named president of Harvard in 1869 and who would become the most able academic administrator in the United States, had hired James. When Eliot retired forty years later in 1909, he had turned Harvard into an internationally famous institution, easily the most influential in America. Eliot's appointments in philosophy—of which James was an early one—built a department in the subject that has long been recognized as the most formidable to have existed in the United States. The two senior people were James and idealist moral philosopher George Herbert Palmer; somewhat younger were Royce, who had come from California and gained a permanent position in the mid-1880s, and the German philosopher and psychologist Hugo Münsterberg; finally three men who had received philosophy doctorates at Harvard joined its faculty in this era—George Santayana; Ralph Barton Perry; and Edwin Bissell Holt.

Together these men came close to defining philosophy in the United States from 1885 to 1910, and the tradition of thought that emerged in that department dominated American philosophy through the twentieth century. When linked to the work of James's old friend Charles Peirce and such people as Chauncey Wright, these views have been called 'Cambridge Pragmatism', and at Harvard they initially centered on the joint ideas of James and Royce. For those trained in Cambridge there was an architectonic vision of philosophy with epistemology and metaphysics as the core areas of study; Harvard Pragmatism found in Kant its most significant progenitor. Although maintaining his idealistic preconceptions, Harvard adapted him to an era when change and evolution triumphed over static categories. Finally, in trying to understand knowledge, Harvard Pragmatism emphasized practical attitudes, the human will, social practices, and especially—at least in theory—the work of logicians and scientists.

James as Psychologist

In the 1870s and 1880s James moved from physiology to philosophy; interested himself in what might later have been called philosophical psychology; and developed the rudiments of a modest idealistic philosophy. He adhered to the 'fundamental and well established' 'reflex theory of mind'. The structural unit of the nervous system was a triad: of sensation or perception, conveying what was given; of reflection, conception, thinking, or awareness, displaying consciousness; and of the propensity to action, willing, or what James regularly called the 'fiat', indicating mind. None of these three existed independently.

Mind was identified with the spontaneous activity of selecting, of willing. James usually defined the 'middle department' of conceiving as consciousness, the locus or forum for investigating how mind worked on 'outward existence', the given. The senses made this given known to us. The contents of consciousness, James wrote, were empirical, and the function of mind was selective attention: it accentuated and emphasized certain items and did the reverse with others. This contrast was between the empirical (empirical contents of the mind) and a priori (the selective attention definitive of mind). Indeed, the given in consciousness came with the emphases defining mind. Outward existence and mind were constructs needed to explain certain features of consciousness; the content of consciousness was actually a product of two elements, the spontaneous activity of selection (mind) and the given (outward existence); together they yielded the world as we knew it. The content of consciousness was mind's sustenance of certain elements of the given in a place of transit. Consciousness was a stream, and there really was no given, but an instant redolent of the past and smelling of the future. James contended that 'we are led to a curious view of the relations between the inner and the outer worlds':

The ideas [consciousness] . . . seem set up midway between them [the mind and the given] to form a sort of atmosphere in which Reality floats and plays. The mind can take any one of these ideas and make it its reality—sustain it, adopt it, adhere to it. But the mind's state will be Error, unless the outer force 'backs' the same idea. If it backs it, the mind is cognitive of Truth; but whether in error, or in truth, the mind's espousal of the idea is called Belief. The ideas backed by both parties are the Reality; those backed by neither, or by the mind alone, form a . . . sort of limbo.

The mind constructed the world of objects that we knew by allowing certain present elements of our awareness to stand for other selected nonactual elements (of possible awareness). The present functioned as a sign of what was not present, and the representing elements and the elements they represented constituted the real world. Selectivity produced the real from sensation.

Was the will, mind, or fiat free? James's theory was consistent with the notion that the fiat accompanied every struggle of ideas but that the victorious ideas determined it—the fiat might be 'a simple resultant of the victory which was a foregone conclusion decided by the intrinsic strength of the conflicting ideas alone'. James's central argument for the will's freedom occurred in two articles of the late 1870s, 'Remarks on Spencer's Definition of Mind as Correspondence' and 'Are We Automata?' Evolutionary science taught that if an organ had a use, it was unlikely to be supernumerary: it would contribute to the organism's survival. Consequently, James asked if the mind was useful to human beings. The brain, he said, had an indeterminate nervous system: stimuli could give birth to any number of responses. Mind determined, in light of human needs and interests, to which stimuli we attended. Without a mind's selective activity, an animal with an indeterminate nervous system could hardly survive and would succumb in the struggle for existence, unable to act appropriately in its environment. Mind was efficacious and added something to the strife of representations in awareness; it partially created the real. Moreover, continued James, only if we adopted this position could we meet the strongest criticism made against Darwin. The problem was that the time required for natural selection to lead to human beings was far longer than much of late nineteenth-century science could justify. In a defense of Darwin and free will, James urged that only if mind contributed to the race's survival, could scientists shorten the time necessary for evolution, otherwise dependent on fortuitous variation.

the knower is not simply a mirror floating with no foot-hold anywhere, and passively reflecting an order that he comes upon and finds simply existing. The knower is an actor, and coefficient of the truth on one side, whilst on the other he registers the truth which he helps to create. Mental interests, hypotheses, postulates, so far as they are bases for human action—action which to a great extent transforms the world—help to make the truth which they declare. In other words, there belongs to mind, from its birth upward, a spontaneity, a vote. It is in the game, and not a mere looker-on.

James also interpreted this 'mighty metaphysical problem' of the will's freedom as part of the conflict between metaphysical realism and idealism. If a world independent of knowledge existed, and if we were to know it, then in the context of James's argument mind would be passive. In arguing that mind was not passive, however, James accepted a variety of idealism: the will in part created the world, and no world existed independently of it. Mind was inherently teleological; it acted according to our interests and propensities, and the world was partly what we took it to be and must partly conform to our deepest needs.

James acknowledged that his arguments were inconclusive, and that his view and that of the determinist and scientific materialist were both defensible; the latter might be true, and mind might be determined. One of James's trademarks was his repeated declaration that people assented to philosophic beliefs, definitions of the universe and conceptions of the world, because of subjective, temperamental factors. The great philosophic positions had equal logical merit and only the satisfaction of certain aesthetic demands made us defenders of any one of them. Would we ever learn which was true? James indicated two different criteria for answering this question: the first was that we must slowly and painfully find out what position worked better, the survivor constituting the right way of thinking; the second was his opponents' 'objective' criterion, that reality coerced thought in the long run. James rebutted that we must then wait to see what was coercive. In either case, truth was 'the fate of thought', and we would only learn this fate in the future. We would achieve the truth *ambulando*, where our commitments helped to determine the truth. This doctrine gave James a reputation for philosophic tolerance, but he also defined the limits within which acceptable beliefs would fall. Deserving of human aesthetic preference were the beliefs congenial to the articulate public of nineteenth-century New England, and James often tried to show that because of our practical nature and desire for moral action, a theistic God was the only rational and possible object for us to conceive as lying at the root of the universe.

In 1885, James read Royce's *The Religious Aspect of Philosophy*, and converted unhappily and half-heartedly to absolute idealism. The book, whose argument convinced James on an intellectual level, proclaimed that the world of life was 'an organic total'; individual selves were 'drops in this ocean of the absolute truth'. The world was no 'mass of separate facts', but everything was 'fully present in the unity of one eternal moment'. The finite individual was in the 'all-pervading thought'. This conception was not, prima facie, one in which there was room for freedom or individuality. Moreover, Royce was indifferent 'whether anybody calls all this Theism or Pantheism'. He deprecated those who enunciated a doctrine of 'Universal Thought' and tried to foist it on plain people as 'the God of our Fathers'. He did not care if his notion of God agreed with anyone else's and acknowledged that his was not that of much traditional theology.

James's response was to give up for the time the more individualistic and voluntaristic idealism he was constructing and to retreat to the viewpoint of the psychologist that had occasionally defined his writing and that carried over into the 1890s.

Psychology studied mental life, and took for granted the world of objects that caused the content of consciousness—or consciousness itself—to appear. For James, that is, psychology ostensibly depended on the premisses of representative realism that were presumed to underwrite all empirical science. But as a psychologist, James chose to bracket these premisses because they involved the scientific researcher in contested metaphysical disputes about the nature of the real. For James the realism that was bracketed might well be materialistic and deterministic. On the other hand bracketing was still useful if Royce were correct—his arguments also led in a deterministic direction. Indeed for James a dynamic relation existed between the revival of English materialistic empiricism and German monism. James disliked German thought. Its language invited grotesque and unlimited expatiation; the Germans had an 'overweening tendency to theorize'; Hegel was a poseur who promulgated nonsense. These prejudices would have made absolute idealism difficult for James to treat sympathetically under any circumstances, but its inability to find a place for free will sealed the matter for him. For some British thinkers the consequences of empiricism led to the same conclusions as German idealism. In denying individual initiative as a force, the evolutionary materialism of many of Darwin's followers, James maintained, lapsed into fatalism, a metaphysical mood of contemplative pantheism that an activist religious thinker must avoid.

As a psychologist, however, James could distance himself from these metaphysical perplexities. He later cited his 1884 paper, 'The Function of Cognition', as an early account of pragmatism, and many scholars have stressed that his work at this time contained the main premises of his later doctrines. But there was a difference, traceable to James's wary respect for Royce. Cognition, said James, was a function of consciousness. We affirmed states of consciousness cognizant of—true of—an external reality if the practical consequences of operating on these states were acceptable to other observers. Ideas were plans of action: we assumed ideas knew their objects if acting on the ideas satisfied others whom we supposed confronted the same objects. Knowing the real world commonsensically meant that the consequences of acting on ideas worked. So far, this is James's pragmatism. But James couched his discussion in terms of Royce's analysis of how thought referred to an external object and admitted that Royce's argument was effective against James's own position, conceived as philosophy. James took refuge in a 'practical and psychological point of view'; he would 'stick to practical psychology, and ignore metaphysical difficulties'; his essay was 'a chapter in descriptive psychology, hardly anything more'. He did not ask how thought's self-transcendence was possible: Royce's answer was probably correct, and it was possible only if the absolute existed. Rather, James assumed thought's self-transcendence and engaged in what he took to be a psychological task. He explored conscious life as it came to us, and looked for the criteria used by common sense to distinguish beliefs thought to be true from others. James's writings into the 1890s renounced philosophic import and excluded any attempt to justify these criteria.

In 1890 James published his great two-volume text, *The Principles of Psychology*. This large, amorphous book summarized the work in this new field of scholarship and extended its range and depth by James's own theories about pertinent disputes. In particular, because of his bracketing of philosophical issues, he took the discipline away from its Hegelian presuppositions that, for example, can be seen in Dewey's *Psychology*. James worried that metaphysics 'leak[ed] in' to his *Principles* but overall contented himself with his role as a subtle observer of intellectual *cum* emotional life.

James's Pragmatism

In 1897 James published a collection of previously written essays. *The Will to Believe*—the name of the lead article—expressed a viewpoint that, if not a philosophical system, at least spoke to the hopes of a large public audience. By publishing these essays together and subtitling his book '*Essays in Popular Philosophy*', James intimated by the mid-1890s that his older ideas might again do service as philosophy. What had previously been scientific observation was now construed as having a deeper significance. A more famous statement was an 1898 address at Howison's Philosophical Union at Berkeley, 'Philosophical Conceptions and Practical Results'. James resurrected some of the ideas of the Cambridge Metaphysical Club, and his alternative to Royce reshaped the course of American philosophy.

James explicated the principle of practicalism or pragmatism that, he said, Peirce had put forward in Cambridge over twenty years before. Peirce's 'maxim' analysed meaning as a set of consequences, although his more careful analyses used the notion of a set of hypotheticals. James stressed Peirce's definition in setting forth the maxim. So, said James: 'To attain perfect clearness in our thoughts of an object, then, we need only consider what effects of a conceivably practical kind the object may involve—what sensations we are to expect from it and what reactions we must prepare. Our conception of these effects, then, is for us the whole of our conception of the object . . .'

In time James diverged so radically from Peirce that the latter renounced the child that James had nurtured. In writing about the set of hypotheticals, Peirce had in mind scientific concepts. A concept was clear if we ascertained and verified the effects that followed when we stipulated the conditions for investigating the object of conception; we usually carried out this sort of procedure in the laboratory. Peirce did not write, as James often did, of an individual's psychology, of the immediately felt effects of pleasure or pain, or of the satisfaction or dissatisfaction associated with entertaining ideas. But by emphasizing consequences James included in a concept's meaning not only experimental effects but also the experiential consequences that might follow from belief in the concept, the particular strategic effects this belief might have in benefiting a person's psyche. The principle of pragmatism ought to 'be expressed more broadly than Mr. Peirce expresses it':

The ultimate test for us of what a truth means is indeed the conduct it dictates or inspires. But it inspires that conduct because it first foretells some particular turn to our experience which shall call forth just that conduct from us. And I should prefer . . . to express Peirce's principle by saying that the effective meaning of any philosophic proposition can always be brought down to some particular consequence, in our future practical experience.

James used the pragmatic principle as a statement of method, as a means of clarifying philosophic problems. He subjected statements of various philosophical positions to this pragmatic test. If opposing formulations implied no difference in the future detail of experience or conduct, the opposition was trivial and idle.

His 1904 'Humanism and Truth' and the 1906 Lowell Lectures published as *Pragmatism*, radically declared that the description of how we sought truth spoke directly to epistemology. The pragmatic notion of meaning might be used to define 'truth', explicitly transforming James's psychological position into philosophy. Ideas and beliefs were plans of action expressed in statements. True ideas or beliefs were then those that led us satisfactorily and expeditiously through experience. Truth was what it was 'known-as'—a class name for all sorts of working values in experience. Truth meant what James had previously declared to be an analysis of how human beings arrived at what they accepted as truth. To give such an exact description answered the philosophic question of truth.

Did James confuse psychology and logic, our ways of attaining belief with what it meant for a statement to be true, with justifying truth claims? When he was most subtle, James's argument was clear. There was no distinction between the psychological and the logical:

A favorite way of opposing the more abstract to the more concrete account is to accuse those who favor the latter of 'confounding psychology with logic'. Our critics say that when we are asked what truth *means*, we reply by telling only how it is *arrived at* . . . the logical relation stands to the psychological relation between idea and object only as saltatory abstractness stands to ambulatory concreteness . . . the 'logical' one is simply the 'psychological' one disemboweled of its fulness, and reduced to a bare abstractional scheme.

Carefully describing how we arrived at the most impressive of our claims to truth did not differ from justifying these claims. The matrix of circumstance 'surrounding' ideas and allowing them to lead to successful action constituted truth.

Royce had argued that we required the absolute as that objective thing external to our consciousnesses, to our ideas, to which our ideas could correspond: they would be true only if they agreed with the absolute consciousness, where agreement was a teleological notion. Royce erred, James believed, in isolating a thought and then asking how it referred to a thing outside it. Following his analysis of the stream of consciousness, James said that the present thought overreached itself. This 'elementary drag' in the passing moment yielded the basic notion of what knowing was, of one thing leading to another. In this process James found the self-transcendence of thought that constituted knowing.

For Royce, it did not matter if an idea worked or if future experience verified it. Workings did not warrant or ground an idea's truthfulness. They only allowed us to act on the idea successfully; they in no way guaranteed that the idea had any relation to anything beyond our consciousness. James replied that even absolutists could point to nothing other than this guiding process in discussing truth; they took 'the mere name and nature of a fact' and clapped it 'behind the fact as a duplicate entity to make it possible'. 'Definitely experienceable workings' warranted truths just as well as the absolute's intentions, and these workings were verifiable. Knowing fell within experience, and the analysis of knowledge presupposed nothing beyond human experience.

The absolutists, said James, mistakenly assumed that their logic ensured the possibility of possessing truth. But this sort of logical warranting was impossible. We could never be certain that beliefs were true, that truth was 'objectively' obtainable, that ideas corresponded to something external to them. James could give the 'nominal essence' of truth, its definition. The question of justification was fruitless; no way of answering it existed. To distinguish description from justification either made a distinction without a difference or set a problem that had no solution. Properly understood, the two notions fell together. The issue for Royce, on the contrary, was not so much whether we possessed truth but whether we could coherently conceive it without a referent beyond our consciousnesses. James adopted a Peircean solution: the pragmatist maintained his ideas to be absolutely true but meant only that everyone would adopt the pragmatist position in the long run. James admitted the notion of absolute truth as an 'inevitable regulative postulate'—the forever satisfying for all. With Peirce, James wrote, 'The maximal conceivable truth in an idea would . . . lead to an actual merging of ourselves with the object, to an utter mutual confluence and identification. *Total conflux of the mind with the reality* would be the absolute limit of truth, there could be no better or more satisfying knowledge than that.'

What did a careful description of how we arrived at truth look like? James spoke of true beliefs satisfactorily leading us in experience, but his view was more complex. Satisfactoriness concretely felt at that time made a belief true for any individual at any moment. A belief, idea, or hypothesis (belief for short) was true just to the extent that it was useful. But James measured such prima-facie truths against what was satisfactory for all of us in the long run. He thus allowed for the accumulation of new truths in the future and preserved the common-sense notion that certainty escaped us.

What did the broad term 'satisfying', or its Jamesean equivalents, 'useful', 'expedient', and 'workable', mean? First, a belief was an instrument of action, and its truth consisted in its verification, in having the experiences that the belief predicted we would have. A simple and fully verified 'leading' typified the truth process. 'Experience offers indeed other forms of truth-process, but they are all conceivable as being primary verifications arrested, multiplied or substituted one for another.' Indirect verifications, James added, passed muster thereafter:

For one truth-process completed there are a million in our lives that function in this state of nascency. They turn us towards direct verification; lead us into the surroundings of the objects they envisage; and then, if everything runs on harmoniously, we are so sure that verification is possible that we omit it, and are usually justified by all that happens.

Moreover, he allowed the verifications of others: 'You accept my verification of one thing, I yours of another. We trade on each other's truth. But beliefs verified concretely by somebody are the posts of the whole superstructure.'

Additionally, a belief 'must mediate between all previous truths and certain new experiences. It must derange common sense and previous belief as little as possible.' A truth was 'pent in' between the coercions of the world of sense and 'the whole body of funded truths'. The role of 'older truths' was controlling. Workability or usefulness meant not just that a truth was verifiable but also consistent with previous truth, congruent with our residual beliefs. Finally, there was a last criterion, a subjective one of elegance. When alternative theoretic formulas were equally compatible with all the truths we knew, we choose between them for subjective reasons. 'We choose the kind of theory to which we are already partial; we follow "elegance" or "economy" . . . it would be "poor scientific taste" to choose the more complicated of two equally well-evidenced conceptions . . .' Scientific truth gave us 'the maximum possible sum of satisfactions, taste included, but consistency both with previous truth and with novel fact is always the most important claimant'.

James also looked at the historical development of our conceptual apparatus:

our fundamental ways of thinking about things are discoveries of exceedingly remote ancestors, which have been able to preserve themselves throughout the experience of all subsequent time. They form one great stage of equilibrium in the human mind's development, the stage of *common sense*. Other stages have grafted themselves upon this stage, but have never succeeded in displacing it.

Our nouns and adjectives are all humanized heirlooms, and in the theories we build them into, the inner order and arrangement is wholly dictated by human considerations, intellectual consistency being one of them. . . . We plunge forward into the field of fresh experience with the beliefs our ancestors and we have made already; these determine what we notice; what we notice determines what we do; what we do determines what we experience; so from one thing to another, although the stubborn fact remains that there is a sensible flux, what is *true of it* seems from first to last to be largely a matter of our own creation.

Was James, then, a believer in Kantian categories?

Superficially this sounds like Kant's view; but between categories fulminated before nature began, and categories gradually forming themselves in nature's presence, the whole chasm between rationalism and empiricism yawns.

There is much to be said for James's denial. The whole of the nineteenth century's emphasis on change and development and the impact of Darwin mediated between him and Kant. But equally certain was James's debt to German idealism.

Royce accepted the Kantian and post-Kantian view that an epistemology—an account of how thought connected to its object—was necessary to meet Hume's skepticism. At times James neared a revolutionary denial of the need for any theory of knowledge. But just as often he assented to a primitive Kantianism. How could truth consist of satisfactory leadings, critics asked, when we always assumed that beliefs were true of something? If James did not shift his position in answering this query, he accentuated its Kantian dimensions. 'Reality' was what truths had to take account of, and its significant aspects were the sensations and relations given in the stream of consciousness. Reality acted as something independent, as a thing found in experience. We had, however, a certain freedom in dealing with this reality: we attended to what we wanted in the flux. The 'that' of sensations was indisputable; we determined its 'what'. James wrote elsewhere that there was 'an imperfect plasticity of them [realities] to our conceptual manipulations'.

In any functioning body of truth, said James, it was impossible to weed out the 'subjective' and 'objective' factors. But a new truth's development showed, by comparison, that subjective factors must always have been active; they were thus potent and in some degree creative. If our beliefs were annihilated, the reality would still be there, though it might be lacking whatever belief supplied. That reality was independent meant that something in experience escaped our control. This something might be independent of all possible experience, a *Ding an sich*, but James was interested only in the determinations that asserted themselves within experience where the sanctions of truth, the only guarantee against licentious thinking, occurred.

James walked a tightrope. When he allied the description of the modes of attaining beliefs with their justification, he talked of satisfactions. But his tack changed when he responded to the retort that he could not then account for our feeling that beliefs were true *of* something. Of course, said James, belief was about something in experience. To mention a belief's content, however, immediately raised the question of justification aside from description. If 'reality' had to exist if we were to have truths, whatever our satisfactions, James had somehow to warrant that beliefs could get at this reality. Describing the peculiar characteristics of true beliefs was inadequate as an account of truth once he admitted that they could be true only if they led to the object.

Royce's Pragmatism

Both James and Royce easily equated the possible with the actual. For Royce there was actual experience that none of us experienced—valid possible experiences, the experiences of the absolute. James ruled out these possible experiences—the possible did not transcend the actual experiences of finite beings. He dismissed experience unverifiable for us. Whatever Royce said of possible experience (defined in the absolute) transcending actual experience (of finite beings), James found the sole value of this transcendence in finite experience: transcendence could only be 'known as' certain actual experiences for us. Royce said that to justify claims to truth we required possible experience beyond what we experienced and different from human experience. On the contrary, James said, we defined truth by the structure of actual experience to which acting on ideas led us.

To meet James, Royce must show that the pragmatist account of truth failed when stated in this way, and the period 1905–15 culminated changes in Royce's ideas that had been building from the time James had first confronted him in the 1890s. In his earliest work Royce had put forward ideas of practice and voluntarism that scholars have associated with pragmatism. His early 'world of postulates' was only practically justified (and, thus, in *The Religious Aspect of Philosophy* found to be unacceptable). Even in this first book, judgements picked out or intended their objects. But just as individuality was repressed in Royce's system, so was his early voluntarism. In what many regarded as his masterwork, the two-volume *World and the Individual* (1899, 1901), Royce reintroduced the voluntaristic element as the unique loving choice made by the Absolute in determining which individuals would exist. Royce hoped that this shift away from an intellectualist position would protect him from the charge that he had compromised individualism and freedom; and the same sorts of alterations, he believed, made him more of a theistic thinker.

Now, after James delivered his lectures on pragmatism in 1906, Royce went further and claimed that he too was a pragmatist—but an absolute one. Royce said he largely agreed with James. The assertion of truth was a deed, 'a practical attitude, an active acknowledgement . . . [T]he effort to verify this acknowledgement by one's own personal experience and the attempt to find truth in the form of practical congruity between our assertions and our attained empirical results, is an effort which in our individual lives inevitably accompanies and sustains our every undertaking in the cause of truth seeking.' Royce declared that 'all search for truth is a practical activity, with an ethical purpose . . . a purely theoretical truth, such as should guide no significant active process, is a barren absurdity'.

A true idea was practically successful, but we could not define success in James's terms. What is it that people rationally meant to do when they intended to tell the truth? They were not predicting the consequences that they expected to result from what they said. Nor would the truth of a statement be equivalent to the expediency or success of the consequences—either to themselves or others—that might follow the statement; nor did their belief in the statements or its congruence with their present memories define truth. Asserting that something was true, Royce said, meant something different. If 'true' meant 'expedient' then it was redundant to ask 'That's expedient but is it true?' But this question was not redundant; designating a belief as expedient gave 'a scrap of your personal biography'. To define 'truth' in this way defined what we all alike regarded as the attitude of one who chose not to tell the truth. The contrast between James's doctrine and an adequate theory was 'not between intellectualism and pragmatism. It is the contrast between two well-known attitudes of will—the will that is loyal to truth as an universal ideal—and the will that is concerned with its own passing caprices.'

Yet James stressed that true statements were not merely verified by an individual. They were statements that others had verified or would verify. Some statements were true because they would be verified 'in the long run', although they were not verified now. Royce's most formidable analysis attacked this formulation of Jamesean pragmatism. What did we do with statements whose truth depended on the experiences of others? James said that we accepted the verifications of others. Did the totality of experience then exist? If so, how, on Jamesean grounds, could we claim that statement as true? Would 'the long run' then verify a statement? If so, how, on Jamesean grounds, were we able to claim the statement true? If James were correct, these statements must be true, but on Jamesean grounds we could never ascertain their truth.

Suppose the assertion 'The testing of ideas by the course of experience as pragmatism presupposes actually takes place' were true; if pragmatism were justifiable, the statement should be verified or verifiable. Yet it was logically impossible for any individual or group of individuals to verify the statement or for it to be verifiable for human individuals or groups of them—it was inconceivable that anyone could verify it. James dealt with experience that no human knower could have. No one could experience anyone else's experiences; nor could someone now verify that something had been verified in the past or would be verified in the future. But such unverifiable statements had to be true if pragmatism were true. We could be pragmatists only 'by constantly presupposing certain assertions about experience, about the order of the interrelations, the significance, and the unity of empirical facts, to be true, although their truth is never verified and could not be verified in James's sense of an empirical test, at any moment of our experience'. Royce concluded that James's pragmatism accounted for how human beings sought truth, but demanded other truths for which it could not account.

Although we never experienced the unity of experience James's ideas required, Royce interpreted this fact not as a 'defect in the truth, but as a defect in our present state of knowledge, a limitation due to our present type of individuality'. Truth necessitated a whole of experience to which James also inevitably appealed. Royce accepted James's pragmatism to the extent that he did because its outcome was 'Absolute Pragmatism'.

Public Philosophy

The 'Battle of the Absolute' was reflected not only in Royce and James's technical but also their popular philosophy. Throughout the first decade of the century each developed his moral and religious view and applied it to practical problems, communicating the results to audiences outside the academy. Not only theorizing but also using theory to understand our place in the world could win converts to the alternative forms of pragmatic idealism; in any event the philosopher had a public duty to speculate on real-life problems. In fact, the illumination that technical expertise shed on less arcane matters justified philosophy for James and Royce, and measured the worth of the technical.

The most substantial attempt in such a popular vein was James's 1902 *Varieties of Religious Experience*. Commentators have long recognized it as a pioneering work in the psychology of religion but, more significantly, it defended religious conviction on Jamesean grounds. To be religious, James declared, was to believe in a potent unseen order and to be willing to put ourselves at the mercy of this force greater than ourselves because our supreme good lay in adjustment to it. The book then outlined various kinds of experience that grounded religious belief for individuals, and examined the forms of religious consciousness to which the experiences gave rise. James's interest was not merely typological. The essence of religion lay not in theological formulation, but in the promise of the richer and more satis-fying lives we lived because we were assured that a force greater than our-selves also fought our moral battles.

Religion as a hypothesis, James said, was true in so far as it worked and gave value to existence. But belief also essentially referred to existing high-er powers. Consequently, a religious creed was true if the higher power made demands that created a real effect when we fulfilled them. For the deity to exist was only for us to behave differently on earth because of this existence; if we behaved differently we had evidence for this belief. A prag-matic argument on such a scale, James concluded, characterized a perspec-tive on the universe, an 'overbelief'. He provided a more vital religion than Royce offered. Monistic religion encouraged passivity; James's religion was activist, a creed compatible with the moral life. He defended a 'meliorist' religious position: to believe in God entailed faith in a spiritual force greater than ourselves. Allied with this force, we would secure some vaguely defined benefits to all mankind and assure some deep meaning to life. For James, to believe in God went a long way toward making the belief true. If we acted on the belief, the world would probably become better, and this evidence corroborated our belief. We secured the necessary human push to triumph over evil.

James conceded that absolutism had fruitful consequences for human experience and could give us a romantic sense of cosmic well-being: 'What do believers in the Absolute mean by saying that their belief affords them comfort? They mean that . . . we have a right ever and anon to take a moral holiday, to let the world wag in its own way . . . [T]hat is part . . . of what the Absolute is 'known-as', that is . . . his cash-value when he is pragmatically interpreted.' James continued, however, that a belief had to survive the gauntlet of our other beliefs, and this notion permitted him to reject Royce's monism:

it clashes with other truths of mine whose benefits I hate to give up on its account. It happens to be associated with a kind of logic of which I am the enemy, I find that it entangles me in metaphysical paradoxes that are unacceptable . . . But as I have enough trouble in life already without adding the trouble of carrying these intellectual inconsistencies, I personally just give up the Absolute. I just take my moral holidays; or else as a professional philosopher, I try to justify them by some other principle.

James was most persuasive in discussing the absolutist view of evil, which became more and more a sticking point for him. Evil was explicable but necessary for Royce. The absolute guaranteed the triumph of goodness in the universe, but Royce consequently defined goodness as the over-whelming of evil, sometimes in our finite experience, always in the absolute. James found it repugnant that Royce comprehended the unspeakable horrors of human existence—the suffering and death that surrounded us—in a few pages of dialectic logic. James charged that absolute idealism solved the problem of evil grotesquely and, moreover, might sanction passivity in the face of evil—allowing too many moral holidays.

Royce's response to James's climaxed with his work of 1908, *The Philosophy of Loyalty*, which gave his idealism an active, practical cast. Conduct was right or wrong, Royce said, and 'the general doctrine of values' formulated this distinction. An evaluation was an act of will, and a first principle of ethics was that, as facts in the world, these acts all had the same kind of value. In a hypothetical debate with a head-hunter over the goodness of taking his life, Royce said that as far as they both had a 'rational consciousness' of human values, he and the head-hunter recognized each other's valuations as facts. Could we harmonize these conflicting wills? Suppose we adopted some plan that might change the lives of two moral opponents but would enable them to carry out their 'essential will'. This situation 'possesses more objective value' than the former: the co-operation of wills was better than their conflict. This was a second principle. In his debate Royce might alter the head-hunter's behavior in the direction of customs prevalent 'in a well-regulated company of civilized gentlemen'. The head-hunter might remain Royce's enemy but obtain the prestige he achieved through head-hunting by victory in philosophical debate or quest for political office. The alteration might satisfy the head-hunter, and Royce would retain his head. Believing as did many in his culture that historical change was progress, Royce argued that a Hegelian vision of history offered us examples of the increased harmony of human wills. The evolution from barbarism to civilization had been morally good. In the twentieth century people carried out their purposes with less conflict than savages. War had given way to commerce, and people gained prestige in peace rather than war.

Royce's two principles were essential for achieving harmony. We might apply the principles to bring tranquility to the self. Admitting our present and future valuations as equally worthy of regard, we would plan to bring them all into concert. That plan would be the best way to live, considering the individual alone, and such an ideal defined the finite self as a moral creature. This self was a dynamic conscious life.

Such a self, said Royce, was loyal—willingly, practically, and thoroughly devoted to a cause. The devotion of a patriot to country, a martyr to religion, and a robber to the band, exemplified loyalty, but Royce stressed that more common situations also illustrated loyalty—the mother's love for her family, the businessperson's allegiance to a firm. In fact, Royce packed into his definition of cause all he needed to make the loyal personality an adequate ideal. To the loyal person the cause was objective, serving more than individual self-interest. But the cause was not impersonal; the interests beyond one's own were social. Finally, the causes of the loyal self did not just collect the interests of separate individuals. The causes involved a unity and bound many individuals into one service. 'Where there is an object of loyalty', Royce wrote, 'there is . . . [a] union of various selves into one life.' The loyal achieved tranquility by ordering their desires as loyalty to a cause demanded. The cause preserved morality's social aspect without compromising individuality. Our 'divided being', he declared, 'demands reconciliation with itself'; it had 'one long struggle for unity'. The inner self and outer social realms naturally warred, and only loyalty reconciled them.

The Philosophy of Loyalty asserted Royce's principle of 'loyalty to loyalty' as the criterion for determining choices among conflicting causes. We should increase loyalty in the world and prevent its destruction. Although any loyalty was good, causes competed, and the principle of loyalty to loyalty resolved disputes. But Royce reckoned that we must judge the loyalty of others circumspectly. We best applied his 'general guiding maxim for conduct' to conflicts of personal loyalties, and even there it offered only a general guide, and could not prescribe specific courses of action. He also introduced loyalty to loyalty to explain how an individual chose 'insofar as he considers not merely his own supreme good, but that of mankind'.

Consider the truth seeker in this context. Whoever spoke of truth— Royce often had in mind the natural scientist—presupposed a spiritually unified world whose consciousness was higher than that of individual minds. The scientist's work implied the union of individual experiences with those of the scientific community, serving a cause that provided a greater-than-individual loyalty. 'Truth seeking and loyalty', Royce concluded, were 'essentially the same process of life'. This view of truth, Royce maintained, met at once an ethical and a logical need.

Although public philosophizing was ultimately important, James and Royce were not social and political thinkers of any stature. Some scholars have argued that classic pragmatism had a peculiar relation to social and political theorizing—those speculative concerns that define the understanding of the collective effort of Plato, Hobbes, Locke, Rousseau, Mill, and Marx—and embodied the rationale behind American political liberalism. The writings of the Chicago and Columbia instrumentalists—including John Dewey, George Herbert Mead, Jane Addams, and Sidney Hook—may give this argument plausibility. The argument, however, does not apply to Cambridge.

Charles Peirce had high hopes for a rejuvenated religious and political life based on the acceptance of his anti-nominalist, communtarian ideas, but his public program was a fantasy, and Peirce himself was an asocial and apolitical thinker. With Royce, James, and their epigoni at Harvard the situation was more complex. They were eminent at a time when the professor lecturing on speculative topics occupied a role requiring him to perform in an almost ministerial fashion. The educated élite expected 'the philosopher'—still conceived in the style of Emerson—to reassure it about the worth of human existence and traditional institutions and to join mild exhortation with a defense of fundamental verities. Because of this demand and because of their own proclivities, both Royce and James popularized their moral and religious ideas. In effect they buttressed the more critical convictions of literate, upper-middle class America. In a more secular era they carried forward the joint role previously occupied by college philosophers, divinity-school theologians, and independent people of letters. Philosophy for them enlightened humanity about the impenetrable universe that had given it birth.

George Santayana put it well, if acerbically, when he said that the Cambridge philosophers had an acute sense of duty 'because they were conscientiously teaching and guiding the community, as if they had been clergymen without a church . . . at once genuine philosophers and popular professors'. Harvard philosophy, he went on, represented faithfully the complex inspiration of the place and the hour. James and Royce were 'men of intense feeling, religious and romantic, but attentive to the facts of nature and the currents of worldly opinion; and each of them felt himself bound by two different responsibilities, that of describing things as they are, and that of finding them propitious to certain preconceived human desires'.

Whatever their concern for ethics and religion, James and Royce gave little time to social and political philosophizing. Their output in these areas was slight, their analyses lacked intellectual substance, and their applications were conventional and often trivial.

Despite Royce's concern for the cultural life of the individual, the corpus of his work in this sphere did not equal that in more recondite areas of philosophy. Moreover, this work represented a small investment of time. He rapidly composed the disparate essays on these topics for diverse public occasions, and they contained no sustained discussion. Finally, his ideas do not withstand examination. *The Philosophy of Loyalty* contained a chapter titled 'Some American Problems in Their Relation to Loyalty'. This chapter and a 1908 collection of essays, *Race Questions, Provincialism, and Other American Problems*, constituted the major part of Royce's contribution to social thought. Royce wrote these explicitly non-technical works 'for those who love[d] . . . their country' in a confused time. Lecturing in the Progressive period, Royce worried about the breakdown of community in America and the upsurge, on the one hand, of a vicious individualism and, on the other, of anomic masses. Royce pressed into service his principle of loyalty to loyalty as a nostrum for social ills. For example, we could transform selfish individualism if labor unions and captains of industry considered larger goods beyond their own immediate interests. If they were loyal to loyalty, their sense of self would enlarge, and by participating in American politics they would contribute to a better life for all and to a healthy individualism.

Royce's discussion was uncritical: he discerned no problem in deciding which loyalties were rational, constructive, and healthy, and which irrational, destructive, and diseased. He took refuge in clichés about the nature of alienation that have been the currency of thinkers since Plato. Royce's ideas were not false, but rather trivially true. There was no analysis of the roots of social problems, no examination of the distribution of power that determined the structure of the economy, no concern with the patterns of interest represented by politics, and no grasp of the history of the American political economy. Royce derived his views from what he picked up in the press and popular literature and interpreted them in the light of his metaphysics. The result was comforting but trite, and the time he spent on it and the bulk it occupied in his corpus measured its importance for Royce himself.

If we look to James as a pragmatist concerned with American life, our expectations also go unfulfilled. To be sure, he was passionately interested in individuals. Underpinning his pragmatism was a commitment to creating the widest possible area of freedom in which people could operate. A major priority was defending a religious attitude that individuals could live by. James identified this attitude with an activist ethic but never developed an account of moral argument, and his social and political philosophy was negligible. In briefly treating the 'labor question', he did mention that the distribution of wealth must slowly change, and he was doubtless a sensitive, humane person. But the unhealthiness of the conflict between rich and poor, he said, consisted solely in the fact that 'one-half of our fellow-countrymen remain entirely blind to the internal significance of the lives of the other half'. The historian might find it remarkable that James thought half the population rich, but the crux of his theorizing was simply that the route to social amelioration was to grasp sincerely the inwardness of other individuals. 'If the poor and the rich could look at each other in this way, *sub specie aeternitatis*', James concluded, 'how gentle would grow their disputes! What tolerance and good humor, what willingness to live and let live, would come into the world!' This was strictly a sentiment for upper-class consumption.

'The Moral Equivalent of War', the famous essay he wrote near the end of his life, was noteworthy as James's longest statement on society. Although a brilliant critique of modern culture, it did not even sketch a social philosophy and only hinted at how James might have applied his theorizing to the polis.

The Philosophy of Loyalty repeatedly used the martial virtues as examples of constructive loyalty. Fealty to a cause and the duty, service, and discipline implied in this fealty were all tellingly illustrated in war. And more recent critics have noted that Royce's central virtue might justify the fanaticism associated with twentieth-century war. James was aware of this problem in 1910. Like Royce, he estimated courage and valor highly, and thought that war inspired some of their finest and most characteristic expressions. Apologists for war, said James, argued that its 'horrors' were a cheap price to pay for rescue from the only alternative supposed, 'of a world of clerks and teachers, of coeducation and zo-ophily, of "consumers' leagues" and associated charities, of industrialism unlimited, and feminism unabashed. No scorn, no hardness, no valor any more! Fie upon such a cattleyard of a planet!'':

Militarism is the great preserver of our ideals of hardihood, and human life with no use for hardihood would be contemptible. Without risks or prizes for the darer, history would be insipid indeed; and there is a type of military character which every one feels that the race should never cease to breed, for every one is sensitive to its superiority.

James suggested that we could achieve lasting peace and maintain admirable aspects of individuality only by sublimating the martial spirit, preserving some of its important elements:

A permanently successful peace-economy cannot be a simple pleasure-economy. In the more or less socialistic future towards which mankind seems drifting we must still subject ourselves collectively to those severities which answer to our real position upon this only partly hospitable globe. We must make new energies and hardihoods continue the manliness to which the military mind so faithfully clings. Martial virtues must be the enduring cement; intrepidity, contempt of softness, surrender of private interest, obedience to command, must still remain the rock upon which states are built.

James did not go further than this insight. His philosophy (and that of Royce) easily permitted inferences about social and political thought, and the success of pragmatism transformed the framework of intellectual debate in the United States and later made it possible for people such as Walter Lippmann and Herbert Croly to argue credibly for collective action of one kind or another. But this sort of thinking had a low priority for the Harvard philosophers themselves.

Why did James and Royce pledge their time and intelligence to justifying technical beliefs and not to applying them? Why were Karl Marx and Max Weber not read in Cambridge? The outlook of Royce and James derived from their place in the American religious traditions that had devalued history and politics as modes of knowing since the time of Edwards; this emphasis was passed on in the New England Theology, in Scottish Realism, and in the Transcendentalists. Harvard added to this heritage a respect for Kant's *Critique of Pure Reason* and the epistemological problems it generated. Moreover, Royce and James concentrated on the technical as the justification of the practical. The Cambridge Pragmatists had a hierarchical view of the branches of philosophy, making explicit what was implicit in American thought in the nineteenth century. Logic, epistemology, and metaphysics were logically prior, providing the rationale or basis for understanding the world. These technical areas of study grounded work in other areas—moral, religious, social, and political— although the technical was worthwhile because it legitimated applications. This vision resulted in the Cambridge Pragmatists occupying themselves with justifying their practical beliefs: this was the paradigm for philosophy. The exemplars of knowledge were mathematical proofs, deductive inferences, and the results of experimentation in such fields as chemistry and biology. Neither Royce nor James thought of *die Geisteswissenschaften*, so important in Germany, as constituting a fundamental branch of enquiry that might yield insights to philosophic scrutiny.

When James and Royce employed their ideas, they did so in a particular form. The Darwinian controversy focused on the capacity of individual minds to do more than reflect the order of nature. James and Royce successfully defended an active view of mind against the deterministic interpretation of Darwin. The conflict over Darwin and the Emersonian ideal of the philosopher made religious and ethical philosophy the areas of application. With greater or lesser success Cambridge professors joined their philosophic ideas to their personal moral and religious convictions and gave the product to the world. In so doing they followed the speculative tradition in America that centered not on our temporal concerns but on our eternal ones. Further down the list of applied topics was the study of society and politics, and the philosophers conceived it as an extension of the application of ethical and religious philosophy. To the extent they did political and social theory and applied it at all, it was anti-institutional and connected to the amelioration of personal troubles. Practical matters had no independent stature, and public social and political philosophy, like public moral and religious philosophy, dealt with individuals.

John Dewey, who came to philosophy *via* Hegel, had a different idea about the speculative hierarchy, the centrality of epistemology, and the independent significance of social and political life. While Dewey was a figure of great repute, within philosophical circles the Harvard model dominated.

Of equal importance in understanding the lack of Cambridge social and political philosophy is comprehending how Royce and James lived. They were late nineteenth-century members of the Harvard faculty. The lifestyle accompanying that position was not conducive to social and political theorizing. Royce and James were in the first generation of successful American academics, self-satisfied and uncritical of the social order. This same academic milieu also affected Dewey, although its influence was mitigated by the urban environments of Chicago and New York, which were surely less bland than Cambridge.

James's Metaphysics

Continuing the attack on Royce's absolute, James developed a metaphysics of 'radical empiricism'. A series of articles appearing in the 1904 and 1905 *Journal of Philosophy* set forth James's belief in 'a world of pure experience'. The first, 'Does 'Consciousness' Exist?', denied that the word 'consciousness' stood for an entity: there was no 'aboriginal stuff or quality of being' making up our thoughts that contrasted to the matter of physical objects. The world's 'stuff' was neither mental nor physical: 'there is only one primal stuff or material in the world, a stuff of which everything is composed . . . if we call that stuff "pure experience", then knowing can easily be explained as a particular sort of relation towards one another into which portions of pure experience may enter.'

When the neutral data were organized in one fashion, we called the various organized structures physical objects; when the data were organized in another fashion the result was (knowing) consciousnesses. Consciousness was a function: when certain portions of pure experience were appropriately related, we said consciousness existed. The function that defined consciousness was knowing, and functioning in the knowledge relation, the pure experiences were thoughts.

The possibility of overcoming mind–body dualism by analysing immediate perception fascinated James. When I looked at the desk in front of me, my 'content of consciousness' was my mind or consciousness at that moment, and at that moment the content was identical to the physical desk. Of course, this identity was only momentary. The career of the desk was that organization of pure experience determined by its occurrence in various tactile and visual fields of consciousness; my consciousness was that organization of pure experience determined by my perception of opening the desk drawer, the following perception of a checkbook, a thought of my money flowing from the bank, and so on. The bits of experience received their mental or physical character from the context in which they existed:

If at this moment I think of my hat which a while ago I left in the cloakroom, where is the dualism, the discontinuity between the hat of my thoughts and the real hat? My mind is thinking of a truly *absent hat*. I reckon with it practically as with a reality. If it were present on this table, the hat would occasion a movement of my hand: I would pick it up. In the same way, this hat as a concept, this idea-hat, will presently determine the direction of my steps. I will go retrieve it. The idea of it will last up to the sensible presence of the hat, and then will blend harmoniously with it. I conclude, then, that—although there be a practical dualism—inasmuch as representations are distinguished from objects, stand in their stead and lead us to them, there is no reason to attribute to them an essential difference of nature. Thought and actuality are made of one and the same stuff, the stuff of experience in general.

Pragmatism had a place within this metaphysics. James's theory of truth described human enquiry, that is, what truth amounted to in practice. This description detailed how some experiences—ideas—lead to certain other experiences—the object of the idea, the successful termination in percepts, direct experience—through a series of transitional experiences that the world supplied. Pragmatism explored that aspect of James's world of pure experience in which one mode of organization (the physical world) interacted with another (consciousness) when things were known.

The methodological postulate of radical empiricism was:

Nothing shall be admitted as fact . . . except what can be experienced at some definite time by some experient; and for every feature or fact ever so experienced, a definite place must be found somewhere in the final system of reality. In other words: Everything real must be experienceable somewhere, and every kind of thing experienced must somewhere be real.

Elsewhere he wrote:

The only fully complete concrete data are . . . the successive moments of our own several histories, taken with their subjective personal aspect, as well as with their 'objective' deliverance or 'content' . . . Radical empiricism thus leads to the assumption of a collectivism of personal lives (which may be of any grade of complication, and superhuman or infrahuman as well as human), variously cognitive of each other, variously conative and impulsive, genuinely evolving and changing by effort and trial, and by their interaction and cumulative achievements making up the world.

The world consisted of neutral stuff out of which mind and matter developed. But everything experienced must count as part of the stuff, and only what was experienced would so count. Because things were as they were known, James refused to admit anything outside experience as real: to do so would lead to a monism in which we allowed the absolutely unverifiable on grounds of logic. The alternative to his approach was the abstraction of the block universe.

What was the status of my desk in the library when neither I nor anyone else was experiencing it? James wanted to say the desk existed; it did not pass in and out of existence when we entered the library. James's methodological principle permitted him to say that the desk existed because it was actually experienced. But who experienced the desk when none of us was around? Not the absolute. James's way out lay in panpsychism, the view that mind was in all things. The desk existed when we were not in its vicinity because it was self-conscious, experiencing itself directly: 'it must be a thing in itself . . . that is . . . it must be an experience for itself whose relation to other things we translate into the action of molecules, etherwaves, or whatever else the physical symbols may be. This opens the chapter of the relations of radical empiricism to panpsychism.'

For James consciousness now constituted existence. Rejecting Royce's absolute, he was none the less attracted to the form of Royce's solution: 'the pure experiences of our philosophy are, in themselves considered, so many little absolutes, the philosophy of pure experience being only a more comminuted *Identitätsphilosophie*.' But in 1904 James was only *almost* committed to panpsychism. It seemed to imply that the desk's experience of itself differed from the direct experience the rest of us had of it: we experienced it as the action of molecules or ether waves, whereas it did not seem likely that the desk experienced itself that way. But if this were so, panpsychism did not solve James's problem: when we were not around, it was not the desk as we experienced it that existed, but something else:

The difficulty for me here is the same that I lay so much stress on in my criticism of Royce's Absolute, only it is inverted. If the whole is all that is experienced, how can the parts be experienced otherwise than as it experiences them? That is Royce's difficulty. My difficulty is the opposite: if the parts are all the experience there is, how can the whole be experienced otherwise than as any of them experiences it?

James could not resolve the issue; by 1907, in metaphysics, he was still only 'squinting' toward panpsychism, but of that, he said, 'I have no doubt'.

In his Hibbert Lectures delivered at Oxford in May 1908 and published the next year as *A Pluralistic Universe* James made his final declaration. If we were to get 'insight' into the 'flux' of concrete experience, we must, for James, abandon logic. We learned what existed from intuitive sympathy, from a live understanding of reality's movement. Using this understanding we recognized that every minimal pulse of experience was self-transcendent. In itself experience was compounded and continuous with other bits of experience. In sensational immediacy things were both one and many, flowing and coexisting. We knew from experience of self, for example, that our immediate selves were parts of a wider unconscious self. But to grasp these ideas required us to think without conceptualizing.

'Compenetration' showed James how panpsychism could succeed and answer the troubling questions over possibility. *A Pluralistic Universe* related, in an autobiographical section, James's attempts to circumvent problems that were entailed by accepting logic and science. By 'logic' he meant the theorizing by which Royce proved the absolute. 'Intellectualistic logic' and the 'logic of identity' were the villains. He had previously rejected the doctrine of absolute mind because he had accepted Roycean logic. On Royce's own grounds, James had held that each thing was self-identical; finite experience could not also be absolute experience. If we were fragments of the absolute experience, then that absolute experience only named all our experiences, and monism was a fraud. He accepted throughout much of his career, he said, that each stream of consciousness had no parts and that no other stream included it. Each stream was what it was and nothing else, and the compounding of consciousness was impossible. His god, James continued, had been theistic, another (larger) consciousness of which we were not parts; God did not consist of smaller minds.

Now that *A Pluralistic Universe* had rejected logic, the old arguments against absolutism, based on logic, no longer held. Although James still rejected monistic idealism, ironically he most clearly embraced a form of idealism when he finally gave up logic, idealism's most formidable weapon.

James's new disavowal of monism as a hypothesis rested in part on the old charge that it did not solve the problem of evil and was pragmatically unsatisfying. But to this charge James added another: if we empathically grasped the flux of experience, we saw that in sensational immediacy things were one and many, that conscious experiences freely compounded and separated themselves. James found it difficult to verbalize what he had in mind, appropriately enough if he was going beyond logic. If we did, however, we found 'a pluralistic panpsychic view of the universe'. Neutral experience was now not neutral, but throbbing, alive, constantly coalescing and recoalescing. This conscious experience was not unitary but contained ever-widening spans of consciousness within some of which human consciousness might exist:

The drift of all the evidence we have seems to me to sweep us very strongly toward the belief in some form of superhuman life with which we may, unknown to ourselves, be coconscious. We may be in the universe as dogs and cats are in our libraries, seeing the books and hearing the conversation, but having no inkling of the meaning of it all. The outlines of the superhuman consciousness thus made probable must remain, however, very vague.

James identified human 'substance' with the divine 'substance', but this divine substance need not be in the 'all' form, which might not exist: 'the substance of reality may never get totally collected . . . some of it may remain outside the largest combination of it ever made, and . . . a distributive form of reality, the each-form . . . [may be] as acceptable and empirically as probable as the all-form commonly acquiesced in as so obviously the self-evident thing.' James added that a reality in which various kinds of consciousness compounded, although spiritual, was not theistic, but pantheistic and pluralistic.

As James moved firmly to idealism at the end of his life, Royce moved to pluralism. Absolute Pragmatism proved a transitional step, for in his last major work, *The Problem of Christianity* (1913), Royce espoused a less absolutist idealism. As its title suggests, *The Problem of Christianity* was a volume that brought Royce into the camp of Christian theism, but not so clearly as a monist. Instead of considering the relation of the individual to the universal consciousness, Royce instead argued that human beings were members of progressively larger groups that came to fruition in the widest community of religion. Rather than being parts of a larger whole, they were members of a more inclusive body, their separateness more strongly preserved, their oneness with the body more complexly defined. In order to defend this new set of approaches, Royce—as had James—returned to Peirce's essays of the 1870s and Peirce's conception of the sign relation and his triadic notion of interpretation. For Royce in 1913, individuals formed an interpretative community through the work of a mediating element that engaged all of them with a larger spiritual entity, which itself demanded further interpretation. Royce was on his way to a communitarian idealism.

The convergence of Royce and James also demonstrated the slow pace of change in intellectual life and the crypto-dialectical path toward modernity and secularism, even in a period that I, with other commentators, have described as revolutionary. In his defense of individual free will and liberal religion James was not far removed from the Harvard religious liberals of the early nineteenth century. *The Problem of Christianity* defended Pauline notions of the Fall, grace, and redemption, bringing Royce's ideas close to that of the Edwardsean opponents of liberalism. The concerns of American theology in the eighteenth and nineteenth century still showed through Harvard pragmatism in its 'classic' period.

Royce's influence had been on the wane for several years and did not survive his death in 1916. Younger thinkers, most prominent among them James's student and famous biographer, Ralph Barton Perry, effectively portrayed Royce as outmoded and sentimental, ill equipped to serve American thought in the new century. World War I also diminished Royce's reputation. The war had begun in 1914, and intellectuals in the Northeast were almost immediately allied to Britain and France, a commitment formalized with the American declaration of war against Germany in 1917. German thought was stigmatized as promoting the militarist cause, and German idealism castigated; Royce suffered as idealism's most well-known proponent, despite his public hostility to the Germans.

An even more interesting transfiguration of reputations occurred in respect to James, once again assisted by Perry. Among younger thinkers he promoted a view of James as a utilitarian, humanist thinker who had rejected a romantic idealism. Perry's sleight of hand gained its widest credence later, but even in the first decade of the century it made an impact. After his death in 1910, James was championed, in contrast to Royce, as more contemporary, forward-looking, and typically American. This was the first step in the construction of a scientific pragmatism, with James as its center, as the essential philosophy of the United States. The next step, as we have already seen, was Harvard's contribution to making the mysterious Peirce the predecessor to James. It was not a bad story.

America's Gift to Philosophy

William James's guiding principles were implicit in all his writing. The penchant for popularizing manifested his need to convey to others his sense of the world; and his ability to speak to successive generations of readers suggests that the man communicated an attitude toward life expressing deep-felt needs. Darwinian science initially made him fear that a mechanistic universe produced humankind. Purposeful activity was illusory, and existence could have no meaning. In the face of death nothing justified James's flirtations with art, medicine, or the biological sciences. Having convinced himself, however, that the active nature of mind allowed the possibility of free will, James made his professional commitment a lifelong exploration and defense of the right to make commitments. For him, as for most of his generation who explored Darwin, a belief that spirituality was intrinsic to the universe was necessary to make life significant. Absolute idealism offered a means for reconciling the claims of religion with those of science, but James believed that monism vitiated any emotional strength that absolute idealism provided: rather than solving the problem of freedom, monism took one into even more perplexing difficulties. James consequently defended a pluralistic idealism and the reality of freedom. He also found the religious aspect of his idealism compatible with science. Empiricism and scientific investigation meant that we defined the world experientially, and if we believed in God, we justified this belief as we justified scientific beliefs, by finding that he made his presence known in our experience.

A Pluralistic Universe concluded, 'Let empiricism once become associated with religion, as hitherto, through some strange misunderstanding, it has been associated with irreligion, and I believe that a new era of religion as well as of philosophy will . . . begin.' James's God was a consciousness greater than ours but not necessarily all-embracing. His spiritual power was such that we would triumph over the evil in the universe and give meaning to human existence if our own powers for good were added to his. This perspective received confirmation within human experience—in the day-to-day vindications of our common humanity.

James's primary motive in writing was not professional advancement nor even a desire to contribute to knowledge, but a drive to understand the human predicament. At the heart of his vision was a world where personal striving mattered and human ideals might prevail. At the same time there was in James an awful loneliness. Surrounded by family and friends, in correspondence with an ever-widening circle of colleagues in Europe and America, he still felt that each of us was isolated, that only individual life counted, and that even its joys were fleeting. Much of his optimism was bravado. As he grew older he became more convinced that as the dark closed in on the spirit, it was left alone with its naked courage. Jamesean pragmatism was a form of fideism: 'I have no living sense of commerce with a God', he wrote in 1904, but 'I need it so that it "must" be true.' What one essentially finds in James is courage. 'The sanest and best of us', he said, 'are of one clay with lunatics and prison inmates, and death finally runs the robustest of us down'; 'the skull will grin in at the banquet'. He carried with him a sense of impending horror, of madness, illness, and suicide; his awareness of evil was intensely painful; and he wrote out of personal suffering. James believed that bitter dregs always remained at the bottom of the cup, yet he reached out to his audiences and heartened them to believe that we shall overcome.

10 *Instrumentalism in Chicago and New York, 1903–1934*

Philosophy in Chicago

After receiving his doctorate from Hopkins in 1884, Dewey spent the next ten years teaching almost entirely at the University of Michigan, becoming head of Philosophy after the early death of his mentor, G. S. Morris. In 1894 he left for a more prestigious position at the new University of Chicago. During his years at Chicago, his well-known instrumentalism emerged from his experimental idealism, as Dewey participated in the urban movements of the late nineteenth century.

He changed his practical focus from the religious to the political. His reformism of the 1890s first benefited from the ideas of the Social Gospel ministry that had influenced intellectual life at the end of the century. For the Social Gospelers, God was immanent in culture, and humanity was redeemable through social progress. Improved institutions would realize the Christian ideals of unity and brotherhood and usher in the Kingdom of God on earth. Teleological evolutionary change and not God's arbitrary will achieved salvation. Consequently, saving individual souls could not exhaust the work of the church. Instead, it should strive to reconstruct the social order, the conditions of spiritual and material growth. Politics and religion were inseparable for the Social Gospelers. Reform, which would result in a spiritually infused political life, had to galvanize the pulpit. The life of the spirit would be social, and culture religious.

The Social Gospel movement desired to preserve effective church institutions while the ethnic composition of cities was radically changing. Religion, prominent churchmen believed, had to attract the growing industrial class. Because American Protestantism could not influence immigrant Catholics and Jews, maintaining the allegiance of the non-immigrant workforce became even more crucial for the churches. To achieve this aim the ministry had to respond to socioeconomic problems of Protestant workers. Protestant thinkers, whether Social Gospelers or not, also believed that the common Protestant heritage allowed the church to mediate class disputes. Clergymen could become engaged in the social question without political partisanship.

Dewey had taken up these ideas as a young Hegelian, arguing that society produced individual character. God did not impart individual grace; rather, people realized the societal spirit. If the institutions of a culture embraced Christian virtues, the individual would be redeemed. As he moved toward instrumentalism, Dewey said that the democratic political system best promoted a religious commonwealth. On the one side, democratic polity was essentially classless. It broke down barriers among people and encouraged the social relations Jesus taught. Democracy would foster redemption. On the other side, genuine Christianity would express New Testament values in political life. With the added consideration of the peculiar religious nature of democracy, Dewey identified with the prudent Social Gospeler. But the role of the church in this milieu puzzled Dewey. Standard clerical practices, based on 'abstract' revelation, suited only other forms of government. The American pulpit had to address social issues, but in doing so, thought Dewey, it would restate religious doctrine and values in modern scientific, sociological terminology. For Dewey, this advance obscured the unique status of the church.

Shortly before he left Michigan in 1894, Dewey delivered a talk entitled 'Reconstruction', in which he articulated a diminished role for Protestantism in the United States. The church needed reconstruction, he asserted, because times had changed. Worshipers must respect other institutions as earthly vehicles of God's will. Christians must accept their principles as 'facts' 'revealed' in bodies other than religion. Political, domestic, and industrial institutions had become 'an organized Kingdom of God on Earth'. The church must dissolve into society: merging with various social institutions was its 'sacrifice'. It no longer exclusively furthered redemption, because other institutions functioned religiously. Democracy aided spirit's evolution into the apparently non-spiritual. That same year Dewey dropped his Protestant church affiliation. Having formerly believed in reformist religion, he now believed in a religiously informed culture. No longer committed to a socially aware spiritual life, he was committed to a spiritualized society.

Chicago epitomized urban problems, and Dewey arrived there in the summer of 1894, during the great Pullman strike. He experienced the social question in all its menace. A typhoid epidemic in which two thousand people died had opened the decade. When the depression of the 1890s struck three years later, the winter of 1893–4 found one-third of the working population unemployed. Chicagoans starved and slept in streets and public buildings. Even the economic recovery of the late 1890s left the city with poor sanitation, overcrowded housing, exploited child labor, sweatshops, and degrading, hazardous, and low-paid employment. Class conflict and industrial violence throve in Chicago. The Pullman strike vividly recalled the Haymarket bombing, which had occurred less than ten years before. Central and Eastern European immigrants, as well as native-born Americans, brought to the city labor militance and radical ideology. Chicago thus had its share of revolutionary socialist and anarchist politics.

Dewey now expounded his reformist impulses in a modern, secular way. In a social climate vastly different from Ann Arbor, Dewey had two notable new interests. In 1889, Jane Addams had founded Hull House, the most famous of the many social-settlement houses. Dewey served on its first board of trustees. During the same period he also became formally involved in education. By the end of the decade, Dewey headed the university's school of education and influenced public schooling in Chicago. Although his commitments to the social settlements and education were largely conceptual, he deserved his reputation as a reformer during the early Progressive era.

Dewey had a cautiously benign view of humanity. More radical political thinkers might also deny depravity and could explain that Chicago's troubles issued from capitalism, greed, and class conflict, but Dewey steered between those who thought progress impossible and those who thought dramatic progress immediately achievable by revolution. His evolutionary metaphysics made the present a fulcrum for modest and responsible change. Rational and moderate solutions to problems were ever-present possibilities. Chicago's conflicts, for Dewey, fruitfully exposed the deficiencies of conservatives and revolutionaries. Radicalism, as a future-oriented consciousness without mediation by the past and present, only rashly anticipated the world as it might be. Conservatism, on the contrary, unthinkingly imported the past into the present and future. According to Dewey, only the present, the meeting-place of past and future, could synthesize both political views into intelligent action. The genuine social reformer interpreted each of the extremes to the other. Joining the wisdom of the past to the vision of the future would resolve conflict in the present.

Dewey's technical and practical thought developed symbiotically. He replaced religion with a politically concerned sociology, as he went from theological concepts to self-consciously scientific ones. At the University he gathered around him a like-minded coterie. In 1903 these men produced a jointly authored volume, *Studies in Logical Theory*. Dewey wrote four of the essays, and in reviewing the volume William James, now a luminary, proclaimed Dewey the leader of 'a school of thought', 'the Chicago pragmatists'. In addition to him the group included George Herbert Mead, James R. Angell, Edward Scribner Ames, Addison Moore, and James H. Tufts.

The key notion in the book was the activity of the organism in its environment. The organism interacted more or less satisfactorily in problematic circumstances and struggled to obtain stability or greater harmony. The Chicago pragmatists called this behavioral interaction experience. The quality of this interaction in human experience displayed mind. Over the ages the species learned more successful techniques of coping. The leap forward was the development of systematic enquiry, the method of science. Human beings manipulated and exploited experience by carefully investigating the formation of phenomena. Experimental understanding then resulted in re-formed experience. Past and present controlled the future. With the scientific revolution the West had learned to manipulate the natural world and, through technology, to increase material wealth and to advance immeasureably human physical well-being.

A vision of evolution that displayed purpose grounded this position. Experience was *cognitive*; that is, one element in it signaled the occurrence of a following element. The experience became *cognized* when an organism recognized the signaling aspect of experience and shaped behavior on expectations of what would occur under certain conditions. Indeed, cognized experience was the criterion of the emergence of mind in nature; the intelligence that distinguished the progressive development of culture was just a pattern of activity that revealed the use of one experience to predict or control subsequent experiences.

Knowledge was never a static relation in which a disembodied mind knew the external world. Mind was only the name given to a peculiar active connection the organism had to its environment. When an organism behaved in an appropriate way (controlling its responses in terms of expected responses), we said mind existed. We were, in fact, better off talking of the mental—an adjective describing a way of behaving—than of mind—a noun. Truth was similarly a character of acting and thus adverbial and not substantive. We acted truly when we satisfactorily predicted or controlled future experience on the basis of understanding the connection of a present experience to a future experience. The Chicago theory of truth thus had limited respect for traditional accounts of objectivity, and instead urged that knowledge integrated present experience with guided activity that would deliver to us desired future experiences. Yet the Chicago school also presumed that experience contained within it the potential to be known.

Dewey's own step to instrumentalism consisted in part in finding more appropriate locutions in which to couch the ideas he had been expounding for many years. As a young man he had sought an anti-dualistic Hegelian idealism. As the scientific professional grew in importance, Hegel became less respectable, regarded as metaphysical in a bad sense. Adopting the language of instrumentalism, Dewey none the less maintained critical elements of his older position. He argued against the old dualisms in a different language although the ideas that had earlier defined his experimental idealism or neo-Hegelianism were still prominent. First, for instrumentalism experience was knowable, amenable to regulation and receptive to the attempt to extract connections from it. The connections were latent in the organism's interaction with the environment. Experience had inherent meaning. In his contributions to *Studies in Logical Theory* Dewey separated himself not from Green and Caird, his old British antagonists, but from their American equivalent, Josiah Royce, who had a Kantian view that individual experience contrasted with the absolute experience of the transcendental unity of apperception and who, wrote Dewey, was mistakenly called a neo-Hegelian. Both Dewey and Royce agreed that 'reflective thought grows organically out of an experience which is already organized, and that it functions within an organism'. Organized meaning, for both, was thought's work. But the misnamed neo-Hegelians such as Royce, wrote Dewey, postulated that a Constitutive Thought grounded human thinking. Rather, said Dewey, thinking arose from prior thinking. Actual reflection, consciously experienced thought-operations, constructed the world. A hypothetical experience was not needed.

A second idea essential to Dewey's earlier view also dominated instrumentalism. He carried forward his interest in psychology and, indeed, became a theoretician of the purpose and method of science itself. The meaning that science wrested from experience at any point permitted control of the present and allowed further advances. More complex integrations of individual and environment, more fully developed interactions, occurred. Dewey now added that control of experience would proceed from the natural to the moral. A scientific ethics would produce enriched experience that would encompass the understanding of the physical world but re-cognize it more completely.

Dewey's Darwinism also suggested how his instrumentalism was a new name for old ways of thinking. Late nineteenth-century thinkers who have remained minimally credible all adopted evolution. Darwin, however, did not always regard the procession of life on the planet as a happy affair. Traits in parents and offspring inexplicably varied. Random change helped offspring with peculiar variations to survive. Although Darwinian evolution was not free of teleology, chance was paramount. In contrast, intelligence and purpose informed Dewey's Darwinism. For Darwin, nature was tooth and claw. Naturalism for Dewey located knowing in a friendly environment: experience was persistently meaningful in the sense that value was intrinsic to the organism's interactions. Dewey's 1909 essay 'The Influence of Darwinism on Philosophy' made this point. Darwin contributed to philosophy the genetic method. For Dewey, value imbued experience, and ever greater integrations of value were realized. Darwin afforded philosophy a means to explore value and the conditions generating it. Philosophy after Darwin, said Dewey, rejected a single regulative principle or permanent end inhering in finite existence. Rather, philosophy could examine how change served specific purposes, how individual intelligences shaped things, how scientific administration might beget increments of justice and happiness. In short, Darwinism allowed Dewey to articulate a program that in the 1890s he had called neo-Hegelian.

Continuity and change in Dewey's doctrine must be noted. As a neo-Hegelian, he wanted to shore up a philosophy of immanence. He had argued against Constitutive Thought and formal logic, but for genetic logic, the intelligibility of the world, the immanence of mind in nature, the continuity of the physical and the moral, and the peculiar connection of science and philosophy. After the turn of the century, the same themes appeared when he argued that Royce and the other idealists were misnamed neo-Hegelians. Substantial elements of his thought remained the same. In the earlier period, however, Dewey spoke the language of Kant and Hegel. The meaning pervading existence evidenced the self. The evolution of the spiritual from the natural realized the self. In the later period Dewey formulated these beliefs in the vocabulary of science.

Yet instrumentalism was not only a new terminology, nor had Dewey merely made his career using rhetorical devices. Deploying the language of science revised the categories of discussion, shifted the debate, and altered the way problems were conceived and resolved. Commentators have regularly argued that Dewey's analyses were unclear. He wrote, they have claimed, at a general and abstract level—as my own interpretation has implied—and, less generous critics have added, his work lacked clarity. But Dewey's new language was almost deliberately ambiguous. 'The Influence of Darwinism on Philosophy' dismissed older philosophical problems of 'design versus chance, mind versus matter', and urged that through Darwin these problems could be 'outflanked'. Dewey's discursive apparatus self-consciously circumvented older dualisms. In speaking of the meaningfulness of experience, Dewey partly expressed God's immanence in human activity. But his instrumentalist idiom partly spoke to new issues. The meaningfulness of experience consisted both in its being 'of value' and 'susceptible to human understanding'. Critics have noted that Dewey could not distinguish process from progress. But in reformulating older views he rejected the cleavage between (random) natural process and (orderly) moral progress. Change and movement toward ends were not separated. The standard criticisms were weighty, but in and of themselves they missed the creative advance that equivocation permitted.

Dewey on Science and Value

In 1904, after a fight with the president of the University of Chicago, Dewey went to Columbia University in New York City, where he spent the rest of his career and an active retirement that ended only in 1952 when he died. Chicago continued to be a bastion of instrumentalism, and indeed made its greatest impact on the social sciences after Dewey left. Dewey himself remained a significant source of ideas for Chicago, but George Herbert Mead emerged as an independent leader among Chicago thinkers. His intellectual background roughly paralleled Dewey's: Mead came to Chicago in 1894 as a Hegelian who could translate idealist concern for society and the growth of culture into the language of naturalistic evolutionary thought. He remained at Chicago until his death in 1931 but during his time there could not put his ideas into a form that he found acceptable for publication, and the fragmentary writing curtailed his influence. After his death students and admirers published lecture notes and manuscripts, and his thought received attention, especially in the field of social psychology, where Mead's discussion of the social nature of personality proved to be of greater significance than Dewey's.

In New York Dewey himself quickly commanded the city's philosophical affairs, and achieved great authority as a philosopher at the height of the Progressive period, when Woodrow Wilson was president of the United States. Dewey's instrumentalism was regarded as a worthy successor to James's pragmatism, though oriented not to the trials of individual faith but to the amelioration of social problems; adapted to a modern industrializing democracy, this philosophy would lead us through the twentieth century in a more effective way than the Victorian idealism of a more old-fashioned thinker such as Royce. In his years at Columbia, Dewey vouchsafed this reputation by showing how the scientific method, which for him best exemplified the mind at work, applied to 'problems of men'. Like many American thinkers, Dewey believed that natural scientific thinking could be made sufficient for politics but also redefined the bases of natural science.

Dewey's interest in making political values scientific was a theme that ran from the early part of the twentieth century—most notably an essay of 1903, 'The Logical Conditions of a Scientific Treatment of Morality'—

through his great works of the 1920s, *Reconstruction in Philosophy* (1920), *Human Nature and Conduct* (1922), and *The Quest for Certainty* (1929).

Dewey viewed scientific truth as critical to securing control over experience and eloquently called for the 'method of intelligence' in human affairs. In separating the realm of ends and values from nature, previous philosophy (and theology) abdicated responsibility. 'Purely compensatory', philosophy consoled the intelligentsia 'for the actual and social impotency of the calling of thought to which they are devoted'. Philosophers sought 'a refuge of complacency in the notion that knowledge is something too sublime to be contaminated by contact with things of change and practice'. Philosophy made knowledge 'a morally irresponsible estheticism'. Again and again Dewey exclaimed that knowledge was 'active and operative'. If the ideal world existed, it existed as possibilities that experimentalism might realize. Only reorganizing the environment, scientifically removing specific troubles and perplexities, would secure human good. When met with skepticism about applying 'funded experience' and 'contriving intelligence' to social life, Dewey repeatedly contended that if instrumentalism were disallowed in the public arena, the sole options were 'routine, the force of some personality, strong leadership or . . . the pressure of momentary circumstances'.

Dewey defined the scientific method as a means of controlling the assertion of certain statements. To use the method was to assert a statement H as a conclusion that gained support from and was grounded by certain antecedents that had been established as H itself was being established; the consequences derived from H, in the manner in which H itself was derived, constituted the meaning of H. For Dewey we could apply this method to moral concerns. He urged that science rested on the commitment of the scientific community to judge truly. All scientists accepted this value or 'attitude'; hence, to assume that science dealt with facts and morality with attitudes was false, and would not distinguish science from ethics. Science presumed certain attitudes. None the less, Dewey acknowledged that scientific and moral judgements were *now* distinguished, even though the distinction did not lie in some easy cleavage between fact and attitude. The problem was that in scientific judgements the individual attitudes of the scientist were presupposed, were indifferent, or affected each judgement equally. Because every scientific researcher was, for example, committed to telling the truth, this attitude, although critical to the scientific enterprise, was not an issue in asserting any scientific proposition. When people made moral judgements, the situation differed. From Dewey's perspective the attitudes relevant to making warranted—that is scientific—ethical judgements were uncontrolled.

The trouble was that people were shortsighted and often confused about what they ought to do. They were unclear about the consequences of deciding in alternative ways. Moreover, they did not have a sense of whether they would like the consequences even if they had some idea of what they were. People made decisions not in malicious ways but in ignorant and unwitting ways; the result was conflict, the idiosyncrasies of personal moral choice, and interminable and unproductive argument about what course of action should be undertaken. The novel 'reflective morality' that Dewey called for had two initial requirements. First, it demanded a 'sociological' component: that people knew their options—the consequences that would ensue from different sorts of behavior. Second, it had a 'psychological' component: that people had knowledge of what they wanted, given that they knew what their options were. Dewey stressed that invoking sociology and psychology was 'the postulate of moral science' and exemplified 'the continuity of scientific judgement' in ethics. Dewey spelled out what was confusedly apparent to people when they made their usual misguided moral judgements. What people were after was a sense of what was likely to occur *and* what they individually wanted. As an analyst Dewey had to explicate what was involved in asserting these judgements and how they could be warranted.

The postulate here was not just that moral judgements were about the consequences of behavior that people desired. Dewey was also arguing that people could gauge the outcomes of certain kinds of behavior and attribute causality correctly and that in such rehearsals people would figure out what they wanted. Experience verified moral judgements, and the human sciences could make them more adequate. As *Human Nature and Conduct* stressed, no non-trivial ethical questions remained once the empirical enquiries were settled. Some of his significant critics argued that this analysis was off the mark. Assume people might know how to bring X into existence *and* want to bring X into existence; *and* will continue to want to have X. A sociological examination could explore the consequences of action and a psychological one could demonstrate that people desired one set of consequences and would continue to do so. But, critics added, it could still always be asked if people *ought* to have X. Such critics accepted that the sociological and psychological matters were determinate; but they said that agreement on the facts bore no relation to the question of morals. Critics might be right about this issue, but they had not seen that their understanding could make no sense to Dewey. Once the theorist worked out the consequences of alternative decisions and learned which ones people desired, Dewey believed moral dilemmas were solved. There was no further issue of whether something genuinely ought to be done. Dewey assumed there was no criterion of what ought to be desired beyond its experimentally validated tendency to lead people to consequences they in fact desired.

Dewey's ethical theory was in this sense rationalist. People were alike under the skin, and once the helpful instrumentality of science removed their intellectual confusions, their attitudes would come under control. That is, similar dispositions would guide moral judgements, just as such dispositions aided in justifying scientific ones. For Dewey, the world and the individual were transparent. Ambiguity, irony, and paradox were not part of his universe. He had no sense that people might not like what they wanted once they got it, if their wants were experimentally justified. Nor could he sense that people might not be able to spell out the consequences of alternative schemes of actions in any way that would distinguish what they desired from what they would not desire.

Chapter 10 of *The Quest for Certainty* expounded his ideas in a paradigmatic way. The difference between the predicates 'appears red' and 'is red' was for him the difference between a directly present quality, which was the foundation of knowledge, and a judgement about the relation of the presented quality that told us of its interactions with other such qualities. The qualities were something to be investigated, challenges to enquiry whose meaning was bound up with the qualities' connections to other qualities; the judgements that resulted were statements of knowledge that confidently expressed these connections. Empirical subject-matter 'given' prior to acts of experimental variation and redisposition differed from judgements that issued from such acts. In the same way the instrumentalist distinguished between the predicates 'is desired' and 'is desirable'—the latter meaning what was good and ought to be desired. The desired was an empirical liking; it became desirable when we judged the importance and need of bringing the desired into existence, or of sustaining it in existence. This was a matter of taste only if taste were 'the outcome of experience brought cumulatively to bear on the intelligent appreciation of the real worth of likings and enjoyments'. In the case of 'appears red' and 'is desired' the experimentalist was dealing with propositions *de facto*; in the case of 'is red' and 'is desirable' with *de jure* propositions that made claims. If we could elaborate and agree on the conditions that permitted us to judge that something was red, argued Dewey, we should be able to accomplish the same task with what was desirable.

Dewey and Political Life

The Progressive era ended with the entry of the United States into World War I and the American rejection of the League of Nations. The 1920s discredited many of the reformist inclinations for which Dewey spoke, and while his professional standing remained high, various creeds in addition to his clamored for attention in the philosophical world. By the early 1930s Dewey's instrumentalism competed with other academic systems of thought. The Great Depression and revolution within the international political system further eroded the optimistic belief that social science might save the world. Dewey, 70 in 1929, now devoted time to a political program. Among other volumes, he wrote *The Public and its Problems* in 1927, *Individualism Old and New* in 1930, *Liberalism and Social Action* in 1935, and *Freedom and Culture* in 1939. Each of these short efforts employed Dewey's well-known concepts in one area of social life and confirmed his thoughtful engagement with economic and political problems. Despite challenges to his philosophy and his civic commitments, he was the most influential intellectual spokesperson of the time, and anomalous among philosophers in giving political and social knowledge an independent authority.

The most important of these books, *The Public and its Problems,* partici-pated in a debate that raged in the 1920s and 1930s and evidenced a loss of innocence about the prospects for public culture in the United States. A number of thinkers who still claimed Dewey as an inspiration argued that democracy had to be reconstructed if not abandoned in an age of industri-al complexity. They pointed out that the notion of an educated public, able to make rational decisions, was nonsense. Instead American society need-ed an expert, administrative élite, which would act in the name of the pub-lic but with access to social knowledge located in the hands of a mandarin class. Journals of opinion such as *The New Republic*, the *Nation*, *Common Sense*, and *Plan Age*, promoted this view as did the writings of a host of 'managerial' intellectuals. For Dewey the most important was Walter Lippman, who had written *Public Opinion* (1922) and *The Phantom Public* (1925) to which *The Public and its Problems* responded.

These thinkers, who in part defined intellectual life outside philosophy in the middle of the twentieth century, were popularizing their own ethical precepts under the guise of being impartial experts. They claimed neutral-ity for a moralistic social science because they believed in an essentially good and orderly universe, and unconsciously assumed the validity of cer-tain values and could not imagine their rejection. That they embraced these values—for example, efficiency and administrative expertise—was not for them evidence of moralism but of rationality, communicated in loose and antiseptic phrases.

Managerial élitism looked to Dewey for support, and his ideas were occasionally so opaque that they could often buttress its prejudices. But

Dewey was clearly not on the side of the experts. *The Public and its Problems* argued that in order to use experimental, pragmatic social knowledge we *needed* an articulate public. Admitting that the United States did not have such a public, Dewey still insisted that experts were not a morally accept-able substitute. Rather, they could only avoid exuding their own class biases if an effective democratic polity made choices about social issues; without that polity, an élite was 'an oligarchy managed in the interests of the few'. A democratic civic culture was a precondition to effecting the sci-entific method in political life. The role of experts was to gain knowledge, but the public had to determine the problems to be investigated. 'The improvement of the methods and conditions of [public] debate, discus-sion, and persuasion' was mandatory. The technocratic class discovered and made known the facts and experimental knowledge on which policy depended. But framing and executing policy was the job of democratic debate. Dewey's public must 'have the ability to judge of the bearing of the knowledge supplied by others upon common concerns'. The problem in the United States was intelligently to articulate our joint will; this public interest would then direct the experts, who would become genuine man-agers but managers only.

Naturalism

Dewey was the most distinguished of the Columbia naturalists. This group included Dewey's peer, Frederick Woodbridge, one of the founders, in 1904, of a premier professional magazine, the *Journal of Philosophy*, which became an organ for views considered non-traditional, informally opposing the stance of the *Philosophical Review*; and several younger men—Irwin Edman, Herbert Schneider, John Herman Randall, and Ernest Nagel. Naturalism, however, was a much wider movement in New York, extending to New York University, which was dominated by Sidney Hook, a student of Dewey's and later his indefatigable defender; and to City College, where Morris Cohen sent generations of students to Columbia for graduate work. Finally, at the New School for Social Research, after its founding in 1919, naturalism influenced a more heterogeneous group of thinkers led by its director, Alvin Johnson.

Naturalism derived from Dewey's view that Darwin had allowed him to 'naturalize' Hegel: the growth of culture, previously associated with the march of an infinite thought, could now be socially located. But naturalism also drew on historical currents—the view that in ancient Greece Aristotle corrected Plato's ascent to an ideal world of Truth; and a new fashion for Spinoza, whom the American idealists of the 1890s had excoriated as a hidden atheist and materialist. And it also borrowed from George Santayana, an original thinker who had spent his early career at Harvard but who had permanently left the United States to promulgate an aloof and aesthetic vision of humankind's lonely existence in the universe.

Intelligence grew out of the 'natural', biological realm that yet provided an adequate locus for a moral and political life valuing humanism, social democracy, and internationalism. Naturalism was indeed more of a mood than a reasoned philosophy. One hostile critic noted that it was 'an unoriginal compound' of Santayana and Dewey, and the writings of the naturalists only murkily propounded concrete philosophical doctrines. At the same time, naturalism was an important episode in American philosophy, reflecting the heterogeneous, secular, and often Jewish intellectual life of New York City. Captained by Dewey, the New Yorkers and other allies were advancing an agenda at variance with the Protestant-encumbered idealism that was, in the eyes of the naturalists, still stubbornly entrenched. Such men as Wilbur Urban and Brand Blanshard of Yale, DeWitt Parker of Michigan, and William Ernest Hocking of Harvard still carried the banner of the spirit. Indeed, in 1924 they had been joined by Alfred North Whitehead, who had left England for Harvard, where he developed a speculative metaphysics. These men, although less powerful than idealists of the previous generation, were rooted in ecumenical Protestantism and imbued with the cultural commitment of Royce. Many of the younger New York naturalists were Jews who had witnessed the infuriatingly genteel anti-Semitism of Harvard, Yale, and Princeton—where careers had been stunted—and had established themselves only with difficulty in the system of higher education. Morris Cohen and Sidney Hook, for example, prized the diverse and combative scene in New York, and correctly saw that many of their philosophical adversaries stood for a bland conservatism in American life from which Jews were excluded. Naturalism defined itself in opposition to this continuing heritage of Protestantism in philosophy and its allegiance to a realm of the soul. At a time when the drive to professionalization was strong, naturalists also tried—with marginal success—to promote philosophy as part of a reform-oriented public dialogue.

Although Dewey led the naturalists, one of their problems was that he never established an effective tradition, either at Columbia or Chicago, that advanced his ideas; nor did he train outstanding students who would further his views, regardless of where they taught. Dewey was additionally a peculiar hero for the naturalists, since his instrumentalism, indeed, had grown out of his own version of protestant theology. Yet although he had come further than the anti-naturalists and was a real friend to the sometimes radical and always heterogeneous world of New York philosophy,

Dewey had not entirely left his heritage behind. *A Common Faith* (1934) distinguished Dewey from some of his disciples who had, in his eyes, gone too far in their naturalism. The book in part responded to Reinhold Niebuhr's *Moral Man and Immoral Society* of 1932. Niebuhr was the great figure in the rise of theological neo-orthodoxy. In the wake of World War I, the Depression, and the growth of totalitarianism in the 1930s, a diminished group of liberal theologians battled against a more pessimistic view that was barely represented in the philosophical profession. Niebuhr, who taught at Union Theological Seminary, was a successful theological counter-revolutionary. In an intellectual world that had marginalized divinity he defended the symbols of Calvinism and assumed a mysterious and transcendent God whose purposes were controlling but could not be identified with those of humanity. *Moral Man and Immoral Society* associated Dewey, not unreasonably, with the sentimentally optimistic belief that science could treat society's spiritual dilemmas. Noting that Dewey had not faced the conflicting interests generating social tensions, Niebuhr wrote that these conflicts were ineradicable. Individual human nature was corrupt, and society even more so, said Niebuhr. Dewey was oblivious to the social world's inherent resistance to management.

In answering Niebuhr, Dewey did not alter his commitments. He admitted that social knowledge was unsatisfactory, perhaps inevitably so; he conceded that domination by vested interests was the sticking point. But, Dewey asked, what other recourse did humanity have for its problems than science? Playing on Niebuhr's own reformism, Dewey implied that Niebuhr would not drift into unthinking and smug conservatism:

I will make no claim to knowing how far intelligence may and will develop in respect to social relations. But one thing I think I do know. The needed understanding will not develop unless we strive for it. The assumption that only supernatural agencies can give control is a sure method of retarding this effort. It is sure to be a hindering force now with respect to social intelligence, as the similar appeal was earlier an obstruction in the development of physical knowledge.

Niebuhr's progressive sympathies were in tension with his religious commitments. Although he never advocated reliance on the supernatural in day-to-day social practice, neo-orthodoxy had a difficult time defending liberal activism. Niebuhr sensed the limits of human control of the environment, but his critique of Dewey did not suggest theological alternatives that led to incremental reform. Unless one gave up the struggle for a humane social order, Dewey said, one had to choose. 'One alternative is dependence upon the supernatural; the other the use of natural agencies.'

A Common Faith additionally elaborated Dewey's view of religion. On the one side, wrote Dewey, were believers in a transcendent deity and a supernatural world. The other side believed that the supernatural but not the religious was discredited. Dewey allied himself with the latter group. While yielding the supernatural he would not surrender the religious. Religion with any cognitive content, said Dewey, was indefensible; religion was invested in beliefs about the world and had to be repudiated. But all experience might be religious, possessing a quality that arose from action in respect to an ideal, sustaining life and bringing security and peace. Religious experience was of the conditions of interaction with nature and with other people 'that support[ed] and deepen[ed] the sense of values which carry one through periods of darkness and despair'. Indeed, the experimental method secured religious feeling. Spiritual experience need not occur by chance. The scientist could investigate its origins, how to strengthen and nurture it.

Essentially, Dewey thought that science denied the supernatural and ended systems of religion. Religious qualities, however, were intrinsic to experience. Indeed, the decline of religion and the rise of science were of major significance to the existence of religious experience: experimentalism would foster this experience.

Many of Dewey's naturalist colleagues who shared his belief that science discredited the supernatural criticized his commitment to the religious. Eliminating the supernatural, they said, entailed dismissing religious qualities. Dewey acknowledged the partial justice of this assertion, and even wrote that his view might be 'an emotional hangover from childhood indoctrination'. He also suggested that many of the conflicts between himself and both his religious and anti-religious critics were semantic, including the connotations of terms such as 'God' and 'religion'. But Dewey insisted on dissociating religion and the religious. In attacking extreme naturalists, Dewey stated finally that anti-religious thinkers and 'traditional supernaturalism' shared a critical attitude. Each was occupied with the isolated person. The orthodox were obsessed with individual salvation, the areligious with the soul's lonely defiance in an indifferent and hostile world. Opposed to the 'lack of natural piety' in each of these views, Dewey's religious attitude conceived of humanity in a world that was the locus and support of its aspiration.

Dewey and his successors ruled out the supernatural, but only when they imported its values into the natural. These philosophers placed in the worldly a faith that had been formerly reserved for the otherworldly. How much change did this represent?

Many naturalist commentators on the roots of secular liberalism argued that in discounting religion the West differed dramatically from other societies. The combination of urbanization, a heterogeneous industrialized economy, and perhaps most important, the long scientific revolution extending from Newton to Darwin, had resulted in a new secular psychology. For most of these commentators, the change from a religious to a secular consciousness represented progress. Religion was a more primitive world-view. The West had to a degree discarded superstition. In order to achieve their ends modern civilizations turned to the systematic examination of phenomena in both the physical and social world. Although few analysts of secularization uncritically praised Western progress, they none the less stressed that scientific rationality, in opposition to religion, at least offered the possibility of progressive change.

Among other critics of Dewey, Niebuhr urged that the reliance on science was naïve; and Dewey *was* incautiously hopeful about the sciences of man. Yet the dominant tone of his lifelong appeal for the method of intelligence was sober and cautious. He tempered his confidence in instrumentalism by admitting that no one could predict how social science would be applied successfully to public affairs, when this would occur in significant ways, or what the results would be. Aware of the limitations of the human sciences, Dewey was still compelling in contending that science was better than its predecessor. If methodical intelligence were relinquished in human affairs, he reiterated, people would fall back on custom, habit, chance, or random choice. If social science was imperfect, he seemed to say, consider its alternatives.

On the other side of the issue, some commentators on twentieth-century culture rejected the claim that the psyche of Western industrialism was different from or better than that of more 'traditional' cultures. For these commentators, the scientific revolution had not caused deep change in consciousness. Religious attitudes were basic to the human mind and were present in all cultures. Some of these commentators, overtly committed to religion, asserted that it constituted whatever was of ultimate concern. Others affirmed that all belief systems must be accepted on faith, that all had mythological structures or fictional elements. For these critics, reason could never explain adherence to any belief system. Some even boldly theorized that science itself was religious. Fundamentally, all these commentators contested the notion that science had profoundly altered human understanding. The mind would ever have a place for religious sensibility.

Dewey lent support to these commentators as well as to their adversaries. His view in *A Common Faith* was that science stabilized the religious qualities of life. I believe, however, it is inappropriate to make Dewey a hidden carrier of religion among ostensibly secular intellectuals in the

United States. Although he talismanically invoked the method of intelligence by the 1920s, he lacked a sense of dogma even in his old age. Dewey struggled for twenty-five years—from the late 1870s to the early 1900s—to formulate his position. Certain themes abide in his work, but it also reinterpreted basic philosophical and theological categories. *A Common Faith* redefined the religious from Dewey's perspective. When Niebuhr argued with him, he adopted Dewey's language. Dewey was a poor choice as a secret bearer of the spiritual if only because, more than any other thinker in the United States, he changed intellectual debate, guiding it away from distinctively religious issues.

The second generation of Dewey's disciples was a better target of criticism. These thinkers, although not as influential in philosophy as the first generation, had critical links to the social sciences in the university system. They took instrumentalism not as a hard-won position but as a set of assumptions and transformed Dewey's position into 'an attitude and temper', 'the starting point of genuine philosophizing'. Dewey bore the scars of battles that his followers never had to fight and belabored points that they could afford to take for granted. 'The vanguard of the present generation', Dewey's follower Sidney Ratner wrote in 1951, 'has come to accept as commonplace many of the key ideas which were [Dewey's] revolutionary discoveries.' For these theoreticians in philosophy and the social sciences, Dewey's naturalism was something like a faith. Their attitude suggested that the supposed secularization of belief was doubtful.

This sort of naturalism pervasively influenced economists, sociologists, and political scientists both before and after World War II. The institutions of social science adopted experimentalism. The New School for Social Research came to stand for these ideas, as did Paul Lazarsfeld's Institute for Social Research at Columbia. These enterprises were in New York City, and Dewey affected them directly. In addition, the social science division of the government's National Science Foundation and other federal agencies funding research into human problems urged that Deweyite formulations would modestly transfigure culture. The Center for Advanced Study in the Behavioral Sciences, founded in the early 1950s on land owned by Stanford University, eventually became a pre-eminent institution in the United States for scientific investigation. One commentator has called it a physical monument to Dewey's views.

For the social scientists and the culture of expertise they nurtured (the social-work, counseling, and public-policy professionals), instrumentalist beliefs were home truths. Dewey's thought spoke brilliantly to this group's needs. At the same time the wider intellectual community had absorbed instrumentalist ideas, even as instrumentalism lost its pre-eminence with philosophers. This community was taught that the life of the mind—its vocation—was essential to daily life; that power in the modern world rightly belonged to the intellectuals; and that power could be exercised dispassionately, impartially, and objectively only if they had control. As one acute interpreter of Dewey has written, 'A more self-interested theory cannot be imagined.'

Intellectual life in the middle years of the twentieth century was charged with paradox and irony. Dewey's own growth made it difficult to associate him with any distinctive religious development. On the one hand, some of Dewey's epigoni in philosophy and the social sciences were usually less enamored of the religious than he was. Science had destroyed the credibility of religion and of religious experience. On the other hand, much in the belief system of the naturalists could lead a commentator to argue that they had their own religion. A Common Faith had argued that in their almost defiant attitude toward nature, the epigoni shared an attitude of orthodox Calvinism. Social science experts were often unrelenting in their view that the world would conform to human desire. As Dewey said, they lacked natural piety. Yet instrumentalist ideas also expressed a gritty realism. If we gave up the scientific method in human affairs, we left decisions to habit, authority, or chance. Unless we did nothing, what alternative did we have to the patient and systematic investigation of phenomena and the exploration of causes and consequences?

Dewey's Legacy

In bringing earlier pragmatist ideas to fruition, Dewey gave philosophy its greatest public standing. He elevated scientific knowing, but stressed not the abstract logic of scientific reasoning but the practice of people of knowledge and the application of science to the social realm—the continuity of facts and value. Truth was prized because it enabled us to lead fuller and more satisfying lives; and intelligence was a quality of the activities of the community.

Dewey came to maturity at a pregnant moment in American history. At the turn of the twentieth century, the modern university had grown up, intellectual life had become less dominated by the ministry, and politics had a more educated tone. In 1912 the three leading candidates for the presidency were graduates of Harvard, Yale, and Princeton—Theodore Roosevelt, William Howard Taft, and Woodrow Wilson—and the winner, Wilson, had been a professor of political science at Princeton. There were perhaps unique hopes that the irrational dimensions of the polity might be controlled. Dewey and some students of Royce and James influenced public debates in such periodicals as the *Nation* and *New Republic*. Even a professional magazine such as the *International Journal of Ethics*, which was most important in the first third of the century, combined theoretical and activist writing for professional philosophers and public intellectuals such as Jane Addams and W. E. B. DuBois. Many commentators have pointed to this era as linking admirable politics and a good epistemology, but pragmatism can be appreciated without adopting such a partisan stance if we simply note that pragmatism and instrumentalism made a critical contribution to twentieth-century intellectual life that went beyond the confines of Columbia and Harvard. James's work inspired literary modernists including Gertrude Stein, T. S. Eliot, Robert Frost, and Wallace Stevens, who found antecedents to James in Emerson. James, Royce, and Dewey provided a rationale (or a target) for cultural and political critics such as Herbert Croly, Walter Lippman, Randolph Bourne, Van Wyck Brooks, and Lewis Mumford. Later, in addition to his immense impact in the social sciences, Dewey influenced the sensibility of those historians creating the American past in the twentieth century: James Harvey Robinson, Charles Beard, Carl Becker, and Merle Curti all contributed to fashioning a 'usable past', oriented to an often benign but always reformist vision of America's work in the world. By the 1930s, largely because of Dewey's standing, pragmatism had become widely associated with the public philosophy of left-liberalism and Roosevelt's New Deal, struggling to achieve social democracy in the United States. Later, into the 1960s, such political intellectuals as Arthur Schlesinger, Jr., identified with this civic and speculative impulse.

Although the educated upper-middle class associated instrumentalist ideas with a self-consciously modern ethos that dominated industrial life, all the pragmatists had injected a sacred quality into their ruminations over science, and had intimated that a progressive, teleological impulse was intrinsic to the development of culture. When Dewey died in 1952, he was widely regarded as the twentieth century's foremost intellectual and the pre-eminent thinker in the United States—a worthy successor to Charles Peirce and William James, and the final member of the pragmatic triumvirate.

PART III

Professional Philosophy, 1912–2000

Although variants of pragmatism were never absent from discussion, in the second third of the century a number of vigorous professionals conducted a refined epistemological critique of the empirical bases of knowledge. Pragmatic assumptions were called into question as realistic doctrines made a comeback. C. I. Lewis's *Mind and the World-Order* (1929) was a critical text as were the essays of Wilfrid Sellars written mainly in the 1950s and 1960s. The intellectual migration from Europe, caused by the rise of totalitarianism in the 1930s, contributed to this argument when a uniquely stringent empiricism, logical positivism, made an impact on debate after World War II.

These developments gave American thought worldwide honor in professorial circles, but came at great cost to the public presence of philosophy and even to its audience in the academy. In contrast to what philosophy had been, both in and outside the university, during the period of James, Royce, and Dewey, philosophy after World War II had narrow concerns. The 1960s accentuated the new social role when the cultural radicalism and spirit of rebellion surrounding the Vietnam War further exacerbated the problems of professional speculation.

In the last quarter of the century a cacophony of voices competed for attention in the world of philosophy. The most influential movement still had a connection to Cambridge. Originating in the 'pragmatic analysis' developed after World War II by Nelson Goodman and Willard Quine and the ruminations of Sellars, this movement evolved from an extraordinary publication of 1962, *The Structure of Scientific Revolutions* by Thomas Kuhn. Although Kuhn's work was ambiguous, it soon justified an attack on the objectivity of science. The publications of Richard Rorty in the last twenty years of the century gave a deeper philosophical justification for these ideas.

The last part of this history traces these complicated developments. They took American philosophy from the high point of achievement and public influence of the classic pragmatists to a confused and less potent role at the end of the twentieth century.

11   *Professional Realism, 1912–1956*

At the turn of the century, a number of younger philosophers, identifying with the pragmatic emphasis on practice, called for co-operative endeavors to move philosophy away from an endless repetition of competing systems that led nowhere. This new generation hoped that scientific enquiry might become the model in philosophy and result in collaborative efforts and progress. The same impulse led many of these men, mainly but not exclusively associated with Harvard, to rebel against the pragmatic idealism that had been on offer in their graduate philosophy classes. In a series of joint publications, they argued for realistic philosophies that the sciences influenced and that went back to Descartes, Locke, and the Scots for inspiration. The younger philosophers who adopted realism were, like the Columbia naturalists, continuing an irregular walk away from religion. This chapter surveys the evolution of realism from the early stages of a revolt against Royce at the turn of the century to the professional concerns fifty years later.

Overall, the two generations of thinkers who formulated these views did not match their mentors in talent or creativity. In 1905 William James spoke of 'the gray-plaster temperament of our bald-headed young Ph.D'.s boring each other in seminaries, and writing those direful reports of the literature in the "Philosophical Review"'. James had one word for this 'dessicating and pedantifying process': 'Faugh!' 'The over technicality and consequent dreariness' of the young were appalling. The realists came of age in the new university order and exhibited the standard characteristics of individuals in that order: their philosophizing began with a set of problems that their mentors and graduate training had bequeathed. As James put it, they regurgitated 'what dusty-minded professors have written about what other previous professors have thought'. His students gained preferment by earning a Ph.D. and publishing about these problems. The professional system, with a set of professorial grades culminating in tenure and promotion to a full professorship, was established during this time. Professors not only moved up the ranks in a single institution, but also might move around the system, obtaining a coveted chaired professorship at a well known school. Finally, more complicated factors blocked or advanced the careers of these men—the perception of them as solid citizens or otherwise; their personalities; and calculations about the relation of their doctrines to their morals or politics. At the same time over the next half-century—in two succeeding generations—they worked out a sophisticated realist position that gave America much credit in the Western philosophical world.

New Realism, 1902–1914

In *The World and the Individual* Royce had denigrated realism. No 'first rate thinker' was a realist, Royce remarked, but he named none of its proponents. In suggesting the absolute independence of idea and object, Royce had only representational realism in mind. If realism meant that we were presented only with ideas and inferred objects as their cause or ground, he could easily claim their mutual independence: for how could the realist talk about relations between idea and object when limited to ideas alone?

In 1901 and 1902 two of his former students attacked their teacher in the learned journals. Harvard had recently placed William Pepperell Montague at Berkeley and Ralph Barton Perry at Smith College, and they seized on the polemical and abstract quality of Royce's analysis. Royce had never considered the view of the presentational realist, that we were directly presented with objects. Indeed, Montague reckoned, Royce's argument collapsed when the 'barriers [were] . . . removed so that the object can confront its idea in the bright light of immediate experience'. With an implicit view like this, Perry and Montague contended that no realist had to assert the absolute independence of idea and object; objects could be known as they were and yet not depend on knowing for their existence. But both men refused to state their critiques positively and simply pleaded for the 'lack of finality' of Royce's refutation. As Perry put it, 'the great critical epistemology of a priori idealism is as yet unanswered . . . at the same time I suggest that it is not unanswerable'.

In 1904, two years after these articles appeared, William James outlined his 'radical empiricism' in the *Journal of Philosophy*. Holding that neither consciousness nor its objects were substances, James said that both sorts of 'entities' organized pure experience, but differently. Just as a point occupied a position on two (or more) intersecting lines, James averred that in perception the stream of consciousness contained what, in an alternative organization, was the physical object. Perry and Montague had probably heard James say these things in the classroom but his publications impelled them to elaborate a full-fledged doctrine, New Realism or Neo-Realism.

Using James's insights, they argued that objects might be independent of ideas and yet enter into relations with them. Four others joined Perry and Montague and, of the six, Harvard had trained the three most important. Montague was by then at Columbia, and Perry had returned to Harvard. The third was Edwin Bissell Holt, another student of Royce and James, who had taught in a junior position at Harvard from the time he had received his degree in 1901. When the *Journal of Philosophy* agreed to become an 'organ' of neo-realism, 'to the extent of letting us thrash out any topic through its columns', the work of Royce and James had launched a new movement. In 1910 the six men (Royce called them 'the six little realists') published 'The Program and First Platform of Six Realists', which stressed their group inquiry and division of labor. In 1912 they produced a joint book of 500 pages, *The New Realism: Cooperative Studies in Philosophy*.

Although Holt was the most talented of the realists, Perry, their leader was the most influential. Perry was a favorite of William James, and his later biography of James evinced his sympathy for his subject. Perry was also a philosopher who believed that his discipline progressed and that its practitioners corrected old errors and solved new problems. He suggested that James was at heart a metaphysical realist; part of James's greatness lay in his 'anticipation' of Perry and the other neo-realists. This desire for a usable past emboldened Perry to feel that, properly interpreted, James's radical empiricism would liberate American philosophy from its bondage to Royce. In a remarkably astute and justly praised series of articles, Perry established himself as a controversialist to be reckoned with and as an energetic opponent of absolutism.

Perry's target was 'the cardinal principle of idealism': that knowledge was an originating or creative process, that it conditioned the nature of things. The chief argument for this principle—Perry named it 'the argument from the ego-centric predicament'— was that because all objects were known, knowing constituted objects. This argument proved only the unique difficulty of determining the modification of things in the knowing of them, for we could not construct a situation in which knowledge was not present without destroying the observational conditions. But to infer that objects depended on knowledge from the fact that all objects were known was an elementary example of the *post hoc ergo propter hoc* fallacy. At best, the idealist defended a tautology, that known objects were known objects, on the misapprehension that it was a self-evident synthetic truth.

We discovered objects as known, said Perry, but they moved in and out of the knowing relationship. To deny idealism we had only to realize that an idea was an office or relationship instead of a substance: a thing could occupy the office or assume the status of idea without being identified with it. When a citizen of the United States was elected president, the citizen and president were identical: there was no 'presidential' entity substituted for the citizen, no correspondence or representation. Similarly a thing might belong at once to nature and to mind.

Perry and the other neo-realists agreed with Royce that representational realism must lead either to solipsism or absolute idealism: we were trapped in the realm of our own ideas or, if we desired to escape the trap, we postulated an infinite idea that supplemented our fragmentary ideas. But this alternative was also solipsistic. It was absolute solipsism and, the neo-realists claimed, if we did not assume that knowing constituted the being of known objects, we avoided solipsism altogether. Perry and his cohorts espoused 'epistemological monism': 'when things are known, they are identical, element for element, with the idea, or content of the knowing state'. There was no division of the world into ideas and things that the philosopher must initially accept and then explain. There was rather the class of things; ideas were the subclass we knew. While knowledge did not condition the known thing, so far as the thing was known, it was identical with the knowledge of the thing. And Perry defined a person as an organization into which knowledge entered as an essential component.

Perry completed his case with a further observation. Nineteenth-century science had left faith and revelation unsupported in their demand that spirit subordinate nature. Absolute idealism arose, Perry said, to challenge science's alienation of humanity from the cosmos. God, 'the discarded hypothesis of science', was 'enthroned again as the masterknower of whom science itself is only the imperfect instrument'. Perry claimed, none the less, that absolutism subverted its own theological ends. In an argument that hearkened back to the critique of Spinoza as a religious thinker, Perry said that if the world were a universal consciousness, teleological through and through, then immortality consisted in existence in this whole. We would not consider such a conception religiously relevant had not philosophers expressed it in such phrases as 'the eternal life'. A scientific philosophy would avoid obfuscating issues by developing a more antiseptic vocabulary. Perry's work—an early variant of the popular naturalism we have discussed—had two effects. On one hand it demolished the claims of absolute idealism to prima-facie tenability; on the other it made a presentational variety of realism seem credible. Holt and Montague defended this realism.

Holt advocated a quasi-behaviorist theory of mind. The universe consisted of various sorts of entities that had being. Consciousness or mind was a smaller set of these entities, those selected by the body's nervous system. A principle independent of the principles organizing the entire class of entities defined mind, and entities classed in this way were called contents of consciousness:

The elements or parts of the universe selected, and thus included in the class mind, are all elements or parts to which the nervous system makes a specific response. It responds thus specifically if it brings the body to touch the object, to point toward it, to copy it, and so forth.

[If we look at a black cow] that color out there is the thing in consciousness selected for such inclusion by the nervous system's specific response.

Consciousness is, then, out there wherever the things specifically responded to are. Secondary qualities, Holt concluded, were as objective as primary qualities. The inclusion of either in the class of entities we designated a consciousness depended for both on the specific response of a nervous system.

The neo-realists said we could not infer that the object perceived was identical to the intra-organic means by which we perceived it, that because the means was internal the object was also. Arguing from perceptual physiology, Holt added that the nervous system complexly transmitted those aspects of the world defined by consciousness. But this view did not entail that consciousness was within the nervous system. Consciousness was not in the skull but 'out there' precisely where it appeared to be.

How did the neo-realists account for error? Holt urged that consciousness was 'out there'. But where did we locate the objects of illusion or delusion? Were the two desks I perceived when I pressed on my eyeballs both out there? Did Holt populate the universe with all the erroneous perceptions, fantasies, and hallucinations that had occurred? Representational realists argued that in limiting ideas to the subjective and postulating the objective, existence was rigidly controlled. Holt had not said that the entities composing the world existed, however; they had being or, as he put it, 'subsisted'. He contended, first, that perceived things need not be real: their reality hinged on classifying them with other subclasses of entities stipulated as real. He defined consciousness as that subclass of entities that the nervous system selected, and this definition did not imply the reality of every entity in that subclass. Second and more important, for any entity in the universe to have a spatio-temporal existence—and therefore reality of the physical sort—it must be systematically related to other elements. In cases of veridical perception, locating a content of consciousness out there acknowledged that what we saw was related to other entities. But a hallucinatory experience had no such relations, and Holt accordingly believed that this experience had no spatio-temporal location—either across the room or in my head—although it did have a position in my consciousness.

Montague disclaimed Holt's (and Perry's) behaviorist view of consciousness. For him it was 'a purely diaphanous medium which in no way supported or altered its objects'. If we analysed this medium as a 'specific response', it must then be a motion, simple or complex, of some or all of the material particles composing the organism. Any motion must be up or down, east or west, north or south, or in some intermediate spatial direction. How, asked Montague, could such a motion constitute what we experienced as the 'consciousness of' an object? The 'peculiar self-transcending thing called awareness puts an individual in relation to objects that are either in other places and times or not in space and time at all'. Montague's qualms over the Holt–Perry position reflected the uneasiness of many philosophers who thought consciousness either too complex or too spiritually fundamental for thinkers to reduce it to behavior.

Montague additionally objected to Holt's explanation of error, and other philosophers echoed this objection. In truth Holt was a fearless metaphysician who proposed to construct our universe from a system of neutral entities. He was a neo-realist, to be sure, but realism was only one aspect of a program whose audacity made it questionable, and Montague pointed out that Holt adumbrated only some of its consequences and that others were unreasonable.

For Holt, objects of perceptual illusion or other erroneous experiences did not have spatio-temporal existence either where they appeared to be or in our heads. What did we do with the various perceptions of objects that we had from different perspectives? From the rear platform of a train, I saw the tracks converging; in a place directly above you saw them as parallel. Appearances deceived neither of us—we each saw what we ought to see if we perceived veridically—but I saw something different from what you saw. We wanted to say, Montague contended, that the tracks existed out there, but we could not say that they existed as they appeared in my consciousness, for they did not converge. It was not clear how Holt handled this question, but Montague recalled Holt's believing in Relativistic Objectivism. According to this theory, all the objects appearing in space due to the effects of perspective existed. An object at each instant had no single position and shape but many positions and shapes, each one of which was relative to some observer. The convergent tracks were objectively in space just as the rails that were parallel, but in each case the objective existence was not absolute but relative. Holt apparently construed certain of these physical-existents-relative-to-an-observer as more convenient than others and as therefore defining the common physical object. But as Montague pointed out, to say that something existed in this way was close to saying that it was relative to or dependent on consciousness: the new realism degenerated into the solipsism or representational realism it had tried to avoid. Montague went on: if Holt 'selected', on the basis of convenience, certain physical-existents-relative-to-an-observer as defining the common object, he did not differ from Hume; objects became bundles of sense perceptions.

If Holt slipped into 'subjectivism', Montague did no better. He solved the problem of error by denying a locus of any kind to the non-existent things figuring in experience. Montague set up a dualism between perceptions that directly presented existing things and those identical only to subsisting entities without spatio-temporal position. If consciousness was 'a purely diaphanous medium', how was it possible that existing objects sometimes directly presented themselves while at other times subsisting entities appeared and led us into error? How did we tell when consciousness presented us with the real and when the unreal? Montague himself was on his way to representational realism in which the real objects themselves caused, as Montague said, 'a select aristocracy of appearances' distinct from the illusory perceptions.

The fratricidal arguments among the neo-realists and their pussyfooting with representational realism were not good omens. In fact, although *The New Realism* promised further 'cooperative investigations', no program developed, the concerted attack died out, and the group disintegrated. Although versions of presentational realism were defended later in the century, the doctrine never came near the influence it had in the teens. While Perry went on to a distinguished career at Harvard, his early exposition of neo-realism was his best work, and Holt, a gifted thinker, had little influence and left the academy.

Critical Realism, 1916–1930

George Santayana received his Ph.D. at Harvard in 1889, and struggled there for many years, an idiosyncratic philosopher whom Harvard tolerated as a tribute to its own liberalism. Although Santayana's imaginative genius escaped the technical categories common to many American academics of his era, William James also influenced him. His early writings were often described as pragmatic in spirit, and his five-volume *Life of Reason* (1905–6) concerned the interplay of realism, idealism, and pragmatism.

Santayana distinguished between appearance and reality: appearance was 'the flux'; its cause was reality, 'imputed being' existing whether or not we were there to experience the flux it caused. But Santayana took the tack of Perry and the neo-realists. We perceived, for example, a 9-inch candle as it was when observed; and later we perceived it as 7 inches long. When the candle was 8 inches long, it existed as an 8-inch candle although we did not observe it. Known things, Santayana implied, passed in and out of the knowing relation, but when known, were known as they were.

The upshot was that to account for unexperienced but experienceable possibilities (Royce's valid possibilities), we must postulate a material order that made them and actual experience possible. This scientific world was not relative to human thought but 'a real efficacious order discovered in the chaos of immediate experience'. With the neo-realists Santayana held that this order consisted 'bodily' of experienced elements and of others not experienced.

Neo-realism, however, was a passing phase for Santayana. Even the 'objective' aspect of the flux, he said, symbolized a natural world outside it. To explain the flux we hypothesized that ideal objects existed—the scientific world, which we never experienced beyond the flux, was the real. Scientific objects were intelligible entities adopted to account for and give coherence to appearance. The justification for these external things was 'the function and utility which a recognition of them may have in . . . life'. The external objects were the 'principles and sources of experience'; sensations were the 'effects of a permanent substance distributed in a permanent space'. This substance or matter differentiated essence and existence. Some things had being only in consciousness (essences) while others existed. As distinct from the possible, the actual was essence joined to matter; essences alone yielded the possible.

So conceived, consciousness was passive, an epiphenomenon, a characteristic associated with organisms of a certain level. Nature was the condition of mind, and bodily processes guided the mind. It was not active, nor did it enable the body to survive; rather, its survival indicated that the organism was agile in its environment. To the extent that this was the thrust of his book, 'the life of reason' was ironic. It appeared to survey the cultural achievements painfully fashioned from brute experience over the centuries. But it really analysed the play of ideas whose biological significance was nil: human action expressed irrational forces beyond us. Culture's value was making appearance congenial to a spectatorial mind.

Santayana did not fully develop his position until a second group of realistic philosophers, joined in another co-operative effort, agreed that neo-realism could not solve the problem of error. The critical realists banded together in 1916 and their book appeared in 1920, *Essays in Critical Realism*. Although Santayana was their leading light and their central idea was his, the other six critical realists were also distinguished and again a Harvard affiliation dominated. In addition to Santayana, James B. Pratt of Williams was a Harvard Ph.D. Neither C. A. Strong nor Arthur O. Lovejoy had doctorates, but both had studied at Harvard, as had Durant Drake of Vassar who was a Columbia Ph.D. Arthur Kenyon Rogers was a product of Chicago and taught at Yale before leaving the academy in 1920. Roy Wood Sellars had studied and then taught at Michigan.

Santayana gave the critical realists the crucial concept of essence. The given data in experience were 'character-complexes, essences, logical entities, which were irresistibly taken to be the characters of the existent perceived or otherwise known'. These data did not exist; we could not identify them with mental states; and they did not represent the external object. In perception we jumped to the conclusion that essences were the characters of objects, fusing 'the sense of the outer existence . . . with their appearance'. But the critical realists differentiated these two aspects of perception: essences immediately appeared; upon reflection we saw that the belief in the physical world was pragmatically justified. Moreover, we could not identify the appearing essences with consciousness; they appeared in consciousness; they were present to the mind. In perception there was an essence 'such and such a physical object', not the essence 'such and such a mental state'. Finally, when we knew an object, we were assigning an essence to some reality existing independently of knowledge. Truth was the identity of this essence with the actual character of the reality referred to, but the essence itself did not exist.

The critical realists claimed that their view of essences distinguished them not only from the neo-realists but also from the older representational realists (Descartes and Locke). Making this claim involved specifying the relation of essence to external object:

In the life-economy of the individual the quality-group [the essence] acts as a token of warning of experiences that may be expected and as a stimulus to certain forms of reaction. It *means, or immediately implies*, to him the presence and, to a considerable extent, the nature of some active entity of which it is well for him to be aware. It is, in short, the means of his perceiving the object. Here, then, the divergence of critical realism from the two other philosophical forms of realism plainly emerges. Locke and the neo-realists agree that the object of perception is the quality-group or some part of it, their disagreement arising upon the interpretation of these qualities. Critical realism differs from both in insisting that the quality-group which one finds in perception is not the object of perception but the means by which we perceive. By adopting this view the critical realist is able to avoid the difficulties about perception and error which . . . render neorealism altogether untenable, and at the same time escape from the falsely subjective Lockian view that we perceive only our perceptions and are thus imprisoned within our ideas.

The critical realists reckoned that the physical objects caused experience, that is, in some sense they caused essences to appear. But the realists rejected the Cartesian claim that perceptions (essences) were what we perceived: we perceived objects, essences appeared. Accepting the mistaken Cartesian view that we perceived appearances (essences), the neo-realists—in order to avoid Cartesian subjectivism—had to argue that what appeared was, literally, the object. The critical realist, however, said that appearance was the means of perceiving objects. 'What we perceive, conceive, and remember, think of, is the outer object itself.' Essence had 'a sort of revelatory identity with the object . . . it contains its structure, position, and changes'.

Critical realism introduced an object external to individual experience to warrant truth claims. It was only possible (pragmatically?) to validate knowledge if there were independent objects for judgements to be true of. The concern of the critical realists was the theory of knowledge, and they minimized the extent to which their realism implied anything positive about the nature of the objects postulated to make sense of knowledge claims. They wrote that some independent elements were necessarily involved in the knowledge relation but admitted to no metaphysical prejudices about the elements external to our consciousness. 'The question of the ultimate nature of these nonhuman entities . . . is much more obscure than that of their existence.' The nature of this reality might be neutral entities, experience, or panpsychical monads. 'The critical realist as such has no exhaustive theory upon the subject. For critical realism does not pretend to be metaphysics.'

Although the Critical Realists, like the New Realists, did not carry out their program of co-operative enquiry, they had a far greater impact on American thought. In addition to Santayana, two of them warrant further treatment.

Lovejoy and Sellars

Arthur O. Lovejoy was the finest critical mind in twentieth-century American philosophy, and his opponents feared and respected him. Born in 1873, Lovejoy received a Berkeley BA in 1895 and a Harvard MA in 1897—apparently at James's urging he did not take a Ph.D. After more postgraduate work in Paris, he taught at Stanford, Washington (in St Louis, Missouri), and from 1910 to 1938, at Johns Hopkins. One of the founders of the American Association of University Professors, Lovejoy zealously counseled co-operative enquiry that would root out error and progress toward truth and saw the united expertise of the professoriate as indispensable to civic health. About the time he went to Hopkins, he launched in the journals a devastating attack on neo-realism, particularly as Perry espoused it.

None the less, Lovejoy did not put forward his position until 1930, in his trenchant *The Revolt Against Dualism*. Even in this book, critics had mainly to infer Lovejoy's beliefs from his detailed and minute critique of his adversaries. *The Revolt Against Dualism* exposed the failures of pragmatism and neo-realism to escape the distinction between external realities and a mental content of which we were immediately aware. He devoted himself to vindicating the reality of ideas and images as entities in the mind, thereby pitting himself against Dewey and much of the tradition of philosophizing at Harvard. Lovejoy became known as a temporalistic realist, for he contended against pragmatism, absolute idealism, and new realism that we could never identify what appeared to us and what existed in the outside world. If we believed, as realists, in a spatially extended world, then it took *time* to apprehend something distant from us; this fact precluded equating the surface of the object with what appeared 'in our heads'.

Lovejoy's belief in the peculiar status of mental existents led him to intellectual history. His chief work in this area, in which his theory of knowledge was implicit, were his William James lectures of 1932–3, published in 1936 as *The Great Chain of Being*, a book that became the standard history of the 'unit ideas' that had defined thinking in the West until the nineteenth century. Indeed, the volume created the subfield of the history of ideas, which made Hopkins prominent.

Whereas Lovejoy only expounded his ideas indirectly, Roy Wood Sellars directly promoted critical realism and connected doctrines in a sustained manner for over sixty years. Sellars' first book of 1916—*Critical Realism*—antedated the group effort of the critical realists and provided the name for their position. In it and many succeeding volumes, Sellars set out a connected group of theses. Perhaps garrulous and vain in his conception of his significance, and with the disconcerting ability to state his views at length without arguing for them, he was yet a breath of fresh air on the philosophical scene. The one major thinker in the first half of the century without a connection to Harvard or Columbia, Sellars forsook the idealism that Michigan had taught him and originally developed his own thought. He spent his career in Ann Arbor, establishing the University as a center for philosophy after it had lost an early lead with the death of George Sylvester Morris and the departure of John Dewey at the end of the nineteenth century.

As a group, the critical realists refused to go beyond epistemology. On the contrary, Sellars had a synoptic view. Human beings were natural organisms produced, over the course of evolution, in a world of physical objects existing in space and time. Within these organisms mind, too, arose—the characteristic that permitted them to gain knowledge of the world of which they were a part. The philosopher's task was to give an account of this process, especially the question of how knowledge was possible. The critical realists had examined the relation between knowledge and our intuition of the given character complexes presented to us as the means by which we learned about the world. Slowly Sellars explicitly laid out his view that the objects of knowledge were physical realities; that mind had evolved naturally and was, finally, not to be distinguished from states of the brain; and that a metaphysics—materialism—had to be attached to the epistemology of critical realism. And as many like-minded thinkers of his era were prone to do, Sellars finally wished to show his materialism compatible with an activist and ethical perspective on life.

Sellars urged that there was a 'logical separation' of intuition from knowledge. 'The conditions of knowledge, physical, physiological, and psychological', he wrote, 'must not be put in the place of the nature and claim of knowledge as an act of the conscious organism.' It would not do to try to *construct* the physical world from these intuitions, for physical things were causally and logically prior to the intuitions. This was an ultimate categorical preconception: a causal connection existed between things and the character complexes that permitted us, at a later stage, to characterize things in light of the complexes. Sellars had a causal theory of the sense-appearances, which he distinguished from (an incorrect) causal theory of perceiving as a cognitive act. The appearances were data in standard cases correlated causally with the object of perception. The 'objective content' was intra-organic, and distinct from the physical existent in causal relation with it.

Thus, we did not apprehend the physical world, either directly or indirectly, or representatively; neither did we infer it. Rather we affirmed it through language in a framework of sentences; knowledge told us of an extra-mental reality but did not embrace this reality. It was linguistic and propositional, and warranted by perceptions—the means of knowledge.

We could not talk about the mind–matter distinction in the traditional way, for there was no motive for a copy-theory of knowledge. The propositions that were knowledge were not to be referred to percepts that were present in experience or to things *like* percepts outside experience. Our knowledge was of a realm distinct from consciousness, but was not an attempt to duplicate this realm—'facts are judgements and not objects apprehended'. Physical objects were not similar to what appeared in consciousness; we knew what they were by being taught about science. We should give up the attempt to picture the physical world, and recognize that knowledge was '*a structured system of contents and affirmations*'. Our 'most finished' knowledge, scientific knowledge, furnished us with exact measurements, mathematical formulations, and chains of deductions and predictions, but did not resemble things, nor permit us literally to grasp them.

Sellars himself grasped the nettle of materialism. Matter was the fundamental constituent of reality, but nature was such that different kinds of reality emerged from others—thus the biological from the chemical and physical—but it was not clear that the former could be reduced to the latter. The mind was identified with the brain, but not as two identical substances. Rather, the mind seemed to be a developed system of capacities or functions. Psychical contents were inseparable from cerebral states, consciousness a characteristic of 'the neural system in action'. Consciousness was, Sellars held, extended; the brain the organ of the mind. The human organism included consciousness and was the sole source of that differential behavior that distinguished it from bodies that were not conscious.

Sellars resisted, however, the designation of behaviorist, the hard psychological term that became popular in the early part of the century to describe those social scientists who, also like Dewey and Sellars, were engaged in a program that would correlate mind with what was externally observable. For Sellars the behaviorist was correct to rule out any spiritual notion of thought and to connect thought with bodily integration and adjustment; but the behaviorist went wrong in denying consciousness, and could not explain the linguistic habits that were the origin of knowledge.

In many respects Sellars systematically outlined the views that were cloudily apparent among the Columbia naturalists and their kinsmen in New York City, but also articulated by many other realists—Santayana, Perry, and Lovejoy, for example. Yet Sellars also reserved his hardest comments for the pragmatists. He wrote that if ever a movement had 'transition' labeled on it, it was instrumentalism. Dewey could not shed his idealism; he was 'half-reformed', and for Sellars it was time to admit that mind emerged out of a nature that clearly preceded it in existence and that gave it birth. In denying 'antecedent existence', Dewey's experientialism additionally turned its back on the common-sense view that personal consciousness was connected with cerebral activity. Why not simply accept the problems of what amounted to a sophisticated materialism? The mind had to be localized and naturalized, but since Dewey could not take thinghood and external reference seriously, he lost contact with a truly naturalistic perspective. In turning away from such obvious problems, Dewey had additionally attempted to give a bad name to epistemology—it was for Dewey, said Sellars, 'a vicious disease'. But what was needed, Sellars went on, was an adequate epistemology grounded in the realization that we were natural creatures who arose from a pre-existing world.

Human beings were the causal products of an evolutionary universe; they also came to know this universe. Sellars delineated the problem to which many philosophers would give priority for the rest of the twentieth century: to show that knowledge was not impossible in such a causally governed universe; or that if knowledge were possible, we could account for it without diluting scientific Darwinism with teleology or religion. Like Dewey, however, and like other naturalists of the first half of the century, Sellars felt he had to defend the religious sensibilities on new grounds, to 'naturalize the spiritual'. This he did in a series of popular, superficial books, most of which were written early in his career. Thus, the spiritual emerged when there was intelligence of a high order, and Sellars argued that religion was 'man's imaginative sense of life, a society's feeling for what is significant'. Once the true nature of religion was understood, churches would give up their creeds and become places of 'moral fellowship'. Mankind would gradually outgrow theism, and *'loyalty to the values of life'* would become the worship of the new age that would recognize that we lived 'within the bosom of the earth'. In politics Sellars looked toward the development of a humanistic, non-dogmatic liberal socialism.

C. I. Lewis

Clarence Irving Lewis—C. I. Lewis to the profession—was the most capable and influential American thinker of the inter-war period. Trained at Harvard under James and Royce, he taught at Berkeley from 1911 to 1920. By that time he had earned himself a reputation in the important new subfield of symbolic logic. Royce, who believed that the principles of the foundations of mathematics should ground philosophy, had awakened Lewis's interest. Royce weaned Lewis on the famous *Principia Mathematica* (1910–13) that Bertrand Russell and Alfred North Whitehead had co-authored. Their volumes had demonstrated that much of mathematics could be reduced to a few primitive operations of logic, and their clarity and reductionist program opened up new vistas to technically inclined thinkers. Embracing the methods of logic, philosophers might at last achieve the certitude of real scientists. With the American example of Royce in mind and with knowledge of the logical work of Peirce, Lewis had taken up some of these concerns in his *Survey of Symbolic Logic* (1918), and Harvard had invited him back with the hope that he would edit the Peirce papers, which contained much material on the foundations of logic. While Lewis's editorial efforts were inconsequential, work in the papers confirmed his interest in logic, epistemology, and his own version of pragmatism, and he also began to formalize the new role for logic in philosophy that Peirce and Royce had pioneered in America. Although philosophers made their logic subservient to their intuitions about the correct solutions to speculative problems, it became with Lewis an important new tool for professionals.

His neo-pragmatism was set forth in *Mind and the World-Order* (1929), the paradigmatic twentieth-century epistemological effort in the United States. First, Lewis developed his 'pragmatic a priori' from Royce. During the latter part of his life, Royce held that scientific progress depended upon 'leading ideas'. A leading idea in the natural sciences was a hypothesis, but a hypothesis different from those tested by observation and experience. Rather, scientists used leading ideas as guides—they were too general to test but determined the direction of research. Royce claimed that leading ideas, in Kant's language, were regulative principles.

The heir of Royce's leading ideas was Lewis's pragmatic a priori. The a priori for Lewis reflected our modes of classification, definitions, and logical categories with which we interpreted the given element of knowledge, the immediate data of sense. But the a priori did not compel the mind's acceptance. Its necessity prescribed nothing to the given and its application always permitted alternatives. Necessary truths explicated the way we chose to categorize.

[I]n all our knowledge—particularly in all science—there is an element of just such logical order which rises from our definitions. An initial definition . . . is always arbitrary in . . . that it cannot be false. In itself it does not tell us whether anything is true or not, or what the nature of existing objects is. It simply exhibits . . . a concept or meaning.

Definitions and their immediate consequence, analytic propositions generally, are necessarily true, true under all possible circumstances. Definition is legislative because it is in some sense arbitrary. Not only is the meaning assigned to a word more or less a matter of choice . . . but the manner in which the precise classifications which definition embodies shall be effected, is something not dictated by experience. If experience were other than it is, the definition and its corresponding classification might be inconvenient, fantastic, or useless, but it could not be false.

We developed and selected meanings because of their usefulness, and they were withdrawn, although not refuted, if they failed to help us. The a priori designated 'our categorical ways of acting' and formulated the definitive concepts or categorical tests that made investigation possible. Using such a conceptual framework implied characteristic ways of acting, and congruent behavior was our practical criterion of common meaning. A priori concepts were laws prescribing 'a certain uniformity of behavior to whatever is thus named'.

In addition to the a priori Lewis admitted a sensuous element confronting us independent of our wills, what we have already called 'the given', a name Lewis made famous: we must not overlook that a dimension of knowledge was beyond activity. Knowledge consisted in the 'intersection' of the a priori and given elements. Indeed, Lewis defined his epistemological position by adjudicating the claims of each and characteristically maintained a strict cleavage between the conceptual and the empirical. Exclusive emphasis on the latter—the given or immediate—characterized the mystic. Subordinating the empirical to the conceptual committed one to a metaphysics—a form of idealism in which existence did not transcend consciousness. His 'conceptual pragmatism' defended the independence of each element, stressed the interpretative act bringing them together, and avoided a commitment to either realism or idealism.

Lewis's analysis of the interpretative act had two parts: the first involved the content of knowledge and required him to refine Peirce's views; the second involved justifying knowledge. *Mind and the World-Order* argued that knowledge arose in applying categorical frameworks to the given:

the whole body of our conceptual interpretations form a sort of hierarchy or pyramid with the most comprehensive, such as those of logic, at the top, and the least general, such as it swans, etc., at the bottom . . . with this complex system of interrelated concepts, we approach particular experiences and attempt to fit them, somewhere and somehow, into its preformed patterns. Persistent failure leads to readjustment; the applicability of certain concepts to experiences of some particular sort is abandoned, and some other conceptual pattern is brought forward for application. The higher up a concept stands in our pyramid, the more reluctant we are to disturb it, because the more radical and far-reaching the results will be if we abandon the application of it in some particular fashion.

The concepts of a framework prescribed certain kinds of behavior in appropriate circumstances. In short, a concept was a plan of action, a mode of responding to the environment. But it was not true or false: if it was inapplicable, it was withdrawn. Using it made judgements predicting the conjunction of certain elements of the given. Mere awareness of the given—best but inadequately reported in such statements as 'This appears yellow'—was never knowledge. Knowing was ascertaining that some elements of the given related to others in an orderly fashion. It entailed going beyond the immediate, making inferences about patterns in time. A concept always 'must have a temporal spread. What is required to determine its applicability is some orderly sequence in experience, or some set of such.' Employing a categorical framework supposed that elements of the given fell under specific concepts. If the framework was acceptable, then if we responded consistently, certain other elements of the given confronted us. For example, if this yellowish something is a pencil I hold in my hand, then if I attempt to write with it, I will see the appropriate graphite marks. I credited the resulting judgement—that I had a pencil in my hand—only if my possible future activities eventuated, or would eventuate, in a certain pattern of experience.

Knowledge was predictive: it consisted in choosing concepts that used some elements of the given as signs of others. And knowledge was empirical, requiring that claims to truth were at least possibly verifiable. If we were to spell out the full meaning of a statement, we would define an infinite number of experiences that would occur if we acted in specific ways: if this were a pencil, then it would pierce the paper if pushed; appear unidimensional if held at a certain angle; need sharpening if used for a long period; and so on. If we verified a modest number of these hypotheticals we became convinced that the statement was true, but future experience could always fail to substantiate our claims. So, finally, knowledge was probable only.

With varying success we applied alternative categorical frameworks to these given elements, each framework selecting different patterns for consideration. But if any of them yielded knowledge, their application must pick out elements that were genuinely related. That is, if knowledge differed from the lucky guess, a real probability existed that present elements of the given connected to future ones. There must be a ground, a valid basis for applying the concepts. Here Lewis was concerned with Kant's answer to Hume, and the preoccupation underscored his central position in the tradition of Cambridge pragmatism. Royce and then Perry had pioneered lecturing on Kant at Harvard. Lewis continued this effort, and his class became the model for teaching the *Critique of Pure Reason* in the United States.

Could we warrant inferences from the past to the future? This dilemma, Lewis maintained in 1930, 'historically . . . overshadows and colors all the others'. The difficulty ran 'through the whole history of post-Kantian epistemology'. Lewis's critique of pragmatism was just Royce's: 'It was the besetting sin of James . . . to confuse validity with truth; and of Dewey . . . to avoid the issue by the near absence of any distinction between the two.' For Lewis, however, the best descriptions of our claims to truth differed from warranting such claims.

We were aware of the given but did not create it by thinking and in general could not displace or alter it. To interpret certain given items of experience as signs of other possible experience, the given must have a minimal order, or, Lewis added, we must be able to impose this degree of order on it. But Lewis implied that he was proceeding independently of metaphysical commitment. Like the critical realists, he affirmed that he was an epistemologist and not a metaphysician. If we imposed order on the given, we could say that it was mental in nature; if we merely discovered order within it, we could say that it had properties independent of mind. But Lewis wished to leave these metaphysical issues open. Although his usual locution—the given must have a minimal order—might predispose an interpreter to designate Lewis a realist, he was anxious to show that his position was compatible with 'the characteristic theses of idealism'. Idealists rarely asked if thinking created the data of sense. Rather they asked if we could apprehend a real object without the active construction of mind, and both Lewis and the idealists agreed that such apprehension entailed thought. Lewis did not even contest a second idealist thesis that the existence of sense data, as such, was not evidence of an existent independent of mind. The given might exist outside mind, 'that question should not be prejudged'. He would not dispute whether the given existed unknown; we here left 'the analysis of experience and plunged into metaphysics'. He simply wanted to point out that the idealist need not maintain that thought created the given. The crucial point, which Lewis conceded, was that the given, when acknowledged, was known.

Lewis bridled only at the dogmatic and speculative theses of idealism. The fallacy of the dogmatic idealist lay in arguing that because things as known depended on mind, they could not have characters independent of mind. We could not infer that mind determined known objects from the fact that their nature depended on it. The dogmatic idealist neglected the possibility that 'the object as known may be coincidently determined by two conditions and thus relative to both'. The given was a constituent of Lewis's analysis of objects, and they might have 'independent' characters because of its contribution. The speculative idealist explained the existence of the given, why we had the particular experiences we did, and argued that the condition of experience was another spiritual being. Lewis said he could not concern himself with this speculation, but he did venture that the 'particularity of experience is itself an ultimate—if inexplicable—datum'.

Lewis also believed that he could eschew a Kantian commitment. For the Kantian, requirements of intelligibility must limit experience: our forms of receptivity imposed conditions upon what we could experience. But for Lewis, this solution was impossible, for we could only conjecture that these conditions belonged to mind and not to the nature of the independent real or to that portion of reality to which experience had so far been confined. The conditions would appear simply as limitations on what was given, and their continuance in future experience would be as problematic as any empirical generalization. Either we attributed these conditions to the nature of the independent real and consequently had no solution to Hume's problem; or we concluded that these a priori conditions were innate to the mind, although we had no reason for doing so. Kant's work resulted in either skepticism or the view that mind determined the given— dogmatic idealism.

All of these positions were metaphysical, and need not be explored in an examination of epistemology. On the one hand, Lewis's views were compatible with essential idealistic claims; on the other, he wanted to show that arguments for dogmatic idealism were fallacious and that he could avoid speculative idealism in his limited discussion. He concluded that 'between a sufficiently critical idealism and a sufficiently critical realism, there are no issues'. It was this sort of statement that irritated Sellars. Pragmatists were unwilling to go beyond experience. In Sellars' eyes they prejudiced themselves in favor of idealism, and refused to allow that human beings were creatures in a material world.

What was Lewis's non-metaphysical answer? In order for empirical knowledge to be valid the connection between certain given elements and their expected sequences must be probable. But although experience was independent of mind, he argued, experience could not lack this order. If experience had a minimal order, then our world would be one of apprehensible things, 'and to this we could conceive no alternative whatever'. His thesis required 'no peculiar and metaphysical assumption about the uniformity of experience to the mind or its categories; it could not conceivably be otherwise. If this last statement was a tautology, then at least it must be true and the assertion of a tautology was significant if it was supposed that it could be significantly denied.'

Suppose 'We must conceive the world to be one of things' was a tautology, a priori true, and thus on Lewis's normal construal of the a priori, analytic. From this premiss Lewis deduced that the given had a minimal order. But this statement was then also analytic, and he had not shown that knowledge was valid. He had only shown that if we explicated our meanings carefully we learned that the given was defined as that which had minimal order. If the statement was synthetic then Lewis might have shown that knowledge was valid, but the price he would have paid would have been to grant the existence of the synthetic a priori. And, indeed, we could reasonably argue that the statement 'We must conceive the world to be one of things' was not a priori in Lewis's usual sense. The a priori defined concepts, and was thus analytic. But he reiterated that the a priori must have alternatives. This crucial tautology had no alternatives. This was exactly the characteristic of Kant's synthetic a priori: the concepts or principles were necessary in application to experience, and therefore universally applicable to experience be its content what it may. Accordingly, Lewis presumed that our receptivity imposed conditions on sense. From his perspective this was dogmatic idealism.

The distinction between the given and mind's contribution, Lewis contended, coincided with the division between the empirical and the conceptual. But in validating knowledge, Lewis collapsed this distinction: he secured the ground of knowledge only if he did not separate the way the world was from the way we conceived it. The requirements of intelligibility limited the given. Perhaps this is only an admission that Lewis was a pragmatist, but I think it is more accurate to say that Lewis was not free of a metaphysical commitment: he skirted skepticism only by embracing what he called a dogmatic idealism. As Sellars complained about Lewis, he did not escape the idealistic experientialism that Sellars also found in Dewey— if Lewis validated knowledge, nothing existed beyond a world organized by mind.

Wilfrid Sellars

Lewis's work set the standard for systematic thought in mid-century America. Wilfrid Sellars, the son of Roy Wood Sellars, attacked this approach to epistemology. Although Wilfrid himself urged that his position was essentially his father's, the son creatively worked through his ideas—and did so by arguing that Lewis had confused the basic issues.

Wilfrid Sellars was born in 1912 and studied philosophy at Michigan, and then at both Oxford and Harvard but failed to earn an advanced degree. He had difficulty in writing and publishing, and despite his famous father initially had a roving professional career. Wilfrid did, however, establish a band of followers wherever he taught—at Iowa from 1938 to 1943 and at Minnesota from 1946 to 1959. In the late 1940s Sellars found a way to put his thoughts on paper, although his exposition remained dense, and in 1959 he received an offer from Yale, attempting to recapture its position in American thought. Yet Sellars' style of philosophizing divided New Haven's practitioners of less logically oriented thought, and in 1963 he went to the University of Pittsburgh, which he turned into a luminous and exciting philosophical center. He remained there, a professor emeritus, until his death in 1989.

Sellars *fils*, as Wilfrid Sellars wrote, self-consciously echoed the work of Sellars *père:* Wilfrid was 'a second generation atheist' who believed that 'the mind as that which thinks is identical with the brain'. But he made his arguments not in the leisurely and discursive book-length fashion of his father but in a series of obscure essays, which were often the preferred form of publication from the late 1940s to the early 1960s, when Sellars made his most distinctive statements. Lewis had been one of Roy Wood Sellars' many opponents; Lewis's trademark doctrine of 'the given', elaborated again in his *Analysis of Knowledge and Valuation* (1946), became the chief target of Wilfrid Sellars' attack.

In his most famous essay, delivered as a series of lectures in 1956, 'The Myth of the Given', and subsequently published later that year as 'Empiricism and the Philosophy of Mind', Sellars argued that Lewis (and many other even more strict empiricists) had constructed their account of the knowledge of physical objects on a false foundation because they presumed an indubitable basis of immediate sense data. According to Sellars, there was no way to get from particular sensory facts to 'epistemic' judgements—statements of belief or knowledge. Knowledge, that is, was a linguistic affair and consisted in the social practices of giving reasons, elucidating evidence, and inferring connections among propositions. No analysis could elevate particular sensory inputs alone into the 'conceptual space' of knowledge. Whereas Lewis ostensibly distinguished the empirical from the conceptual, Sellars' version of this distinction was between descriptive, sensory, facts and the normative enterprise of reason-giving, which was the realm of knowledge encompassed by language. Whereas Lewis justified knowledge, as I have suggested, only by compromising the empirical–conceptual distinction, Sellars argued that those who adopted the myth of the given could not extract knowledge from these sensory inputs because of this divide between the descriptive and the normative. At other times Sellars intimated too that the supposed given served as the foundation of knowledge only because conceptual elements had been smuggled into it in the first place. The question of justification, for Sellars, was moved from the material world to 'the space of reasons', to discourse.

For Sellars, as *sentient* creatures we could have reliably differential responsive dispositions that were causally keyed to things. We could behave effectively and interact with our environment, but this was not *sapience* or knowledge, which was a matter of developing language to talk about our world and criticizing how others talked about it. An example of sentience but not sapience would be a parrot trained to react differentially to red things in its visual field. I held up a tomato; the parrot squawked 'Red'. I held up an apple; the parrot squawked 'Red'. I held up an orange; the parrot squawked 'Not red'. The parrot was classifying the stimuli according to the repeatable responses the stimuli elicited. But this was not the sort of awareness that could form the basis for knowledge; it was not conceptual.

In contrast to this picture of knowledge, Sellars argued, as his father had, that the human organism was in contact with real physical objects external to it. Because of this fact, our talk of physical objects—'The tomato is red'—was logically prior to our attempts to formulate a language of internal sense impressions—'This tomato appears red' or even 'Red spot, here now'. Indeed, said Sellars, the language of sense data that the idealists and pragmatists privileged *was* epistemic: it depended on physical object language and grew out of it at a certain stage of the organism's evolutionary development. Sense contents, Sellars argued, were akin to theoretical constructs that we devised to explain divergences in the ways physical objects presented themselves to us and that were expressed in what Sellars called 'the logic of "looks" talk'. In this way he acknowledged a role for the internal states that were evidently a part of our mental awareness. Yet he also denied a fashionable behaviorism without giving credence to a dualism between the world and an inaccessible individual mental world.

Sellars still believed that he could generate a naturalistic account of the growth of our linguistic categories. Mind—construed as our ability to have knowledge of things—gradually entered the universe through the slow development of language in evolution. Human beings journeyed from 'the grunts and groans of the cave to the subtle and polydimensional discourse of the drawing room, the laboratory, and the study, the language of Henry and William James, [and] of Einstein'. Unlike the experientialism that his father also disliked, the doctrine that Wilfrid Sellars proposed was that the physical world did not arise from social awareness; rather from the matrix of the physical world our knowledge of it emerged in the social activity of language acquisition. Like his father, also, Wilfrid Sellars believed that our knowledge of the structure of the physical world was continuously being refined and revealed in the ongoing investigations of science, whose conclusions would be formulated in characteristic 'discourses'. Thus, in what Sellars called the 'scientific image of man' he looked forward to a time when science would elucidate microphysical concepts to get at the 'microstructural properties' underlying the physical facts of perception itself. The turn-of-the-century idealists had argued that developmental psychology demonstrated how social awareness created the physical world of objects in space and time; this world was the way finite minds grasped the absolute. By the 1950s and 1960s Sellars turned this vision inside out—the world of objects in space and time had evolved organisms whose linguistic abilities enabled them to know this world and in so doing evidenced a plurality of minds.

Sellars, however, carried a heavy burden. He became disenchanted with his own explanation of how the epistemic arose—how an organism such as a parrot might eventually become an organism such as a human being. In an important lecture series of 1960, 'Philosophy and the Scientific Image of Man', Sellars argued that as human beings we had to see ourselves as irreducibly different from other animals; this sense was a component of the 'manifest image' that privileged a consciousness that came to know the world and our place in it. In the manifest image, mind somehow transcended the natural. This image would yet be compatible with the fully mature 'scientific image' that recognized man as a subject for science, as an object and organism, evolutionarily continuous with the other animals, and part of the causal mechanisms of the natural world. Sellars also said that the scientific image, which might be radically revised and extended beyond present concepts, had 'primacy', although the 'manifest' one was not 'overwhelmed' in the synthesis of the two that he proposed. But his proposal was a puzzle, tentatively formulated in an almost unintelligible series of sentences.

Moreover, Sellars had himself criticized Lewis and other empiricists because they presumed to extract the cognitional or normative from the realm of the causal or factual. Yet Sellars' own story of how mind emerged from nature was just such an attempt. If he could show how language developed, then he compromised the distinction between descriptive and normative—just as (to justify knowledge) Lewis had compromised the distinction between the conceptual and the empirical. None the less, the realists struggled over two distinct concerns. Lewis's was the issue of justification; Sellars' was mind's status in a materialistic world.

Tracing the strategies of realist thought over the first half of the twentieth century shows how philosophers moved away from the religious premisses that had generated idealist theorizing. Yet a century after Darwin, philosophers still worried about how to join the acknowledged special qualities of the human mind to the biological world; and it was difficult to avoid conceding that the physical was contaminated by mind. Philosophers found it problematic with their naturalistic and materialistic proclivities both to guarantee knowledge and to make sense of our moral lives—exactly the troubles idealism had been conceived to solve. In *The Principles of Psychology* James had written that 'Consciousness, however little, is an illegitimate birth in any philosophy that starts without it, and yet professes to explain all the facts by continuous evolution.' Later, in *The Varieties of Religious Experience*, he argued—as had Wilfrid Sellars—that 'two orders of inquiry' existed, and that it was fallacious to reduce questions of meaning or significance to those of existence. 'Consciousness', for James, was primitive. Ultimately the realists were trying to refute James's premiss and to *explain* consciousness. The voluminous technical apparatus of argumentation could not entirely mask the Big Question facing philosophers after Darwin—how might knowledge and faith be justified in a materialistic universe?

12 Europe's Impact on the United States, 1928–1964

Philosophy in the American University

By the 1930s a young man who realistically thought of himself as becoming a philosopher was contemplating graduate school in philosophy. There he learned of the strife of American systems—where idealism, realism, instrumentalism, pragmatism, and naturalism vied for clients.

Harvard had hired Bertrand Russell's senior collaborator, Alfred North Whitehead, in 1924 to advance itself further in logic, but in Cambridge he ironically pursued an audacious program in metaphysics. When Whitehead arrived there at the age of 63, he seemed at the end of a striking but not dazzling scholarly life in which work in what would be called 'the philosophy of science' had capped his earlier interest in mathematical logic. *An Enquiry Concerning the Principles of Natural Knowledge* (1919); *The Concept of Nature* (1920); and *The Principle of Relativity* (1922) tried to show how scientific objects could be connected to the world of everyday experience without mind's imposing its categories on nature. In the United States, however, Whitehead dropped the assumption that mind and nature were distinct, that 'nature is closed to mind'. In a synthetic metaphysical volume of daunting complexity, *Process and Reality* (1929), and other writing he made *process* a key notion, urging that acquaintance with reality grew literally as something akin to drops or beads of perception, teleological structures of activity. Whitehead's philosophy, which had an explicit role for God, attracted students and led in the late 1920s and 1930s to a reinvigoration of metaphysics, varied forms of idealism, and a school of Process Philosophers who looked to Whitehead's work as foundational. The logical tradition in Cambridge became associated with C. I. Lewis. In both empirical and metaphysical thought Harvard continued to be *the* place to obtain advanced training, although other institutions remained credibly independent in their approaches.

Unlike Royce and James, Dewey had not established an effective institutional tradition in either Chicago or New York. At Columbia mediocre

leadership had produced, after Dewey's retirement, a nondescript department. At Chicago matters were more complex.

Despite his failure to publish, George Herbert Mead carried on in the
classroom the exposition of Deweyan ideas, but this point of view was more
weakly expressed after his death in 1931. Moreover, the administration of
Chicago had passed into the hands of educational innovator Robert
Hutchins in 1929, and his elevation altered philosophical instruction at
Chicago. Hutchins disdained professionalism in the academy and imple-
mented a 'great books' curriculum for undergraduates that emphasized the
ethereal nature of speculation. In this endeavor Hutchins relied on a
philosopher he hired from Columbia, Mortimer Adler, who had rebelled
against everything for which Dewey stood. The result injured Chicago's
ability to train graduate students. A weakened group of instrumentalists in
the department of philosophy became permanently embattled with an
educational leadership committed to more traditional, even anti-empirical,
philosophy. A joke of the era had it that Chicago was a place where Jews
(Adler) taught Catholicism (the value-absolute Neo-Thomism favored by
Hutchins) to atheists (Chicago's secular and radical students).

None the less, Chicago and Columbia along with Yale and Princeton
remained pivotal institutions. After Whitehead retired in 1937, broad-
gauged speculative thought was denigrated at Harvard. Departments outside Cambridge now carried the banner of spiritual philosophy. Younger
men such as Richard McKeon and Charles Hartshorne at Chicago often
pitted empiricism against metaphysics, and even Justus Buchler at
naturalistic Columbia scorned the cramped thinking of philosophers who
made science their focus. Yale in particular became, as its idealist Brand
Blanshard noted, 'a bastion of metaphysics', and was even willing to forgo
an entrenched anti-Semitism to advance its ideology. There was an affiliation between non-Christian secularism and scientific empiricism. From
the late nineteenth century, at a continuing cost to its reputation, New
Haven had consistently forwarded philosophies more than usually fla-
vored with the sentiments of its school of theology that Congregationalist
Nathaniel William Taylor had originally made famous. After World War II
Yale continued to build on its speculative strengths in desiring to hire Paul
Weiss from Bryn Mawr, a student of Whitehead's and a wide-ranging
philosopher whose interests hearkened back to the spiritual tastes of the
nineteenth century. The problem, for philosophy at Yale, was that Weiss
was a Jew: in addition to having taught women, he had bad manners that
reflected the cultural impoverishment of his Jewish background, and
might not be suitable in New Haven. Weiss prevailed, however, and at Yale
in 1950 founded the Metaphysical Society of America with an attack on

'most' American philosophers who were not interested in basic, creative thought.

Perhaps more important than the parting of ways between empiricists and metaphysicians, no professionally respected thinker claimed the public mantle of Dewey, who in his seventies and eighties still embodied philosophy for the most ruminative of the college-educated élite, and spoke to its urge for guidance in a corporate world. To the extent that this role was filled, it was taken up by figures of the second rank such as T. V. Smith of Chicago and Irvin Edman of Columbia, while Will Durant, who had no academic affiliation, valiantly presented the history of thought to a wide audience of non-academics. In truth, philosophy in the United States was at a low ebb, forming an inward-looking organization that had its own set of professional questions and that seldom reached out to the wider culture.

Catholic schools of higher learning had, at the end of the nineteenth century, come out of a period of somnolence and developed a commitment to a modern version of the philosophy of St Thomas Aquinas. The Neo-Thomists were about as intellectually prepossessing as the American naturalists or metaphysicians, but they were enthusiastic that they could vanquish the modernism, secularism, and irrationalism that they saw embodied in their true enemy—American pragmatism. In 1926 the Thomists formed the American Catholic Philosophical Association, which they hoped would be the spearpoint of their advance. But their leaders could not even convince Thomist troops to read Dewey and his kind, nor did they engage in a dialogue. On the other side, a joint session of the APA and the ACPA in 1937 resulted in the Catholics being charged with fascism. The meeting, which left bitter feelings in the ACPA, symbolized the isolation of Catholic institutions, and the closed professionalism of non-Catholic philosophers who found their primary enemies not in Berlin or Rome, but at Notre Dame or Catholic University of America.

The collapse of the international system in the late 1930s and the spiral toward war did not go unnoticed by professorial philosophy. In World War I, led by Royce and Dewey, philosophers had—famously or notoriously—supported Woodrow Wilson's declaration of war against Germany and his commitment to internationalism. Now, in 1937, 1938, and 1939, philosophers were tangential to the dialogue about the growth of German power between interventionists and isolationists. Philosophers agonized over their impotence and their retreat from what they saw as their ancient calling, which they blamed on specialization within the profession and occasionally on the implications of an empiricism that downgraded moral and religious thinking. The thinkers worried about how the scientific and democratic society for which Dewey spoke could justify its commitments and maintain an intellectual coherence that, they thought, religion had traditionally imparted. Two examples of this pervasive malaise are worth noting.

In 1940, soon after the beginning of World War II, a wide academic community of humanists, social science theorists, and philosophers, as well as some independent intellectuals, convened a continuing annual Conference on Science, Philosophy, and Religion in their Relation to the Democratic Way of Life. Although heavily weighted to the metaphysicians in professional philosophy, the meetings none the less included a visible group of empiricists, and the conferences' center of gravity was the position Dewey had expressed in *A Common Faith*: that it was legitimate to term 'religious' that ideal way of life promoting democracy and science. The upright leadership of this group was never able to make a significant public or professional impact, and its major legacy was to provide a forum for a young Willard Quine to complain about the strategy of religious thinkers who allied themselves with Dewey. Conservatives, said Quine, had tried to make 'the rest of us' religious through conversion; 'the cardinal method . . . [of] their liberal brethren [was] definition'.

The second example occurred in the middle of World War II, when the American Philosophical Association decided to survey its ranks on the role of philosophy after the war in contributing to liberal education. Prompted by the fears I have sketched above, a wide-ranging committee of philosophers surveyed APA members, as well as a host of interested laymen, and conducted seven conferences around the country on the state of philosophy. In 1945, *Philosophy in American Education* summed up their efforts, and was the most significant expression of the professional worry apparent from the late 1930s to the early 1950s. The philosophers most involved were not entirely on the side of the metaphysicians, or against the Harvard group, but they were high-minded, and looked back to the turn of the twentieth century when, they claimed, philosophy had a more sturdy cultural impact. They lamented professionalization and specialization but only half-heartedly embraced more idealistic philosophies as the solution to what they perceived as the discipline's problems. In the end, they hoped that after the war philosophy might again thrive as a core study clarifying conceptual and methodological matters for other scholars, and as a teaching area central to general education. After the war, as we shall see, their hopes were dashed, as philosophers in America left future developments to three separate groups of Europeans.

The triumph of Hitler in Germany in 1933 had an enormous impact on philosophy in the United States. Even before the Nazis came to power, the New World attracted thinkers in Europe. After the Nazi takeover, both Jews and non-Jews left Germany and neighboring countries, destined mainly for the United States. The first two waves of thought to influence philosophy in America—the Marxism of the Frankfurt School in Germany and the positivism of the Vienna Circle in Austria—consisted of philosophical immigrants to the United States. The third wave—of French existentialism after World War II—resulted from the immigration of ideas rather than of the thinkers themselves.

The Frankfurt School

In 1921 a wealthy German-Jewish businessman had created an Institut für Sozialforschung—Institute of Social research—attached to the University of Frankfurt. A left-leaning organization interested in the problems of labor and socialism, the Institute employed academics to study contemporary problems. In 1931 its directorship was awarded to Max Horkheimer, who taught philosophy at Frankfurt and who was not only a Marxist but also a European intellectual in the style of Wilhelm Dilthey and Max Weber. Horkheimer quickly vitalized his Institute and gathered around him several able collaborators. The one closest to him was Theodore Adorno, but they also included, among others, Erich Fromm and Herbert Marcuse. When the Nazis closed the Institute in early 1933, Horkheimer had already transferred its funds and moved himself to Geneva. By the middle of 1934 the Institute had relocated in New York City and associated itself with Columbia University. Although Adorno did not get to the United States until 1938, by that time Horkheimer and the other members of the Institute were established in New York and ultimately became known as the Frankfurt School.

The Marxism of the Frankfurt School was *critical* in two senses: it was not vulgarly deterministic about economic issues but took a complex view of them; and it condemned capitalist society, whose ills could not easily be meliorated. Thus, the doctrines of 'Critical Theory' emphasized not just the economically exploitative aspects of the social order but also the dreariness of cultural and personal life under capitalism. Part of this analysis was a product of having absorbed the manuscript writings of the young Karl Marx, which left-intellectuals were examining at the time. These recently published reflections had downplayed economics and highlighted the alienation of human beings in advanced industrial life. Part of the analysis was due to an idiosyncratic interest in how Marxism embraced a theory of aesthetics and accounted for complex forms of music and art. Part of Critical Theory, moreover, joined Freud to Marx, urging that the mode of production historically conditioned the traumas of the psyche, which psychoanalysis believed endemic to human nature; a more benign economic system could ameliorate the trials of our affective existence. Finally, the Frankfurt School argued that knowledge of the social world would arise only from the application of their theories to empirical data. Marxist ideas bumped up against evidence that was not always tractable.

At the same time the members of the Frankfurt School betrayed the dilemmas of Marxist speculators in a hostile world. Horkheimer was an entrepreneur and institution builder who operated capably even in a global capitalist economy that was under stress. Although he worried whether the Institute would have money to carry on, he maintained its independent endowment, and acted like an industrial manager. Horkheimer and Adorno were also not unaware of their place in the hierarchy of prestige and perquisites that universities in both Germany and America offered; they wanted position and office, as well as salaries befitting their status.

Conservative in a deeper sense, they also disliked their sojourn in a heterogeneous United States where class authority seemed non-existent, and where, at least in the realm of culture, common folk had their own forms of public pleasure, over which the social élite had no control. The Frankfurt School worried that American mass culture, indeed, was fascistic. Horkheimer and Adorno could only imagine that a healthy cultural life was determined from above; culture for them was aristocratic and was degraded and degenerate if it were not. Their empirical studies of American popular culture were hyperbolic in their negative attitude, and when they returned to Europe in 1950, their view of the United States looked as much like that of gloomy central European conservatives as of anti-capitalist Marxists.

The speed with which the Institute moved back to Germany after the defeat of the Nazis suggested the Frankfurt School's uneasy assimilation in America. While in the United States Horkheimer and his comrades produced a number of important studies on authoritarianism and family structure and, as they were leaving, a major work, *The Authoritarian Personality* (1950), which worried about the possibility of fascism arising in the United States. Overall, however, the Institute made little impact on American thought, and conceived of itself as outside the main currents of American life. Fromm and Marcuse were different.

The Institute broke its ties to Fromm in 1939, but he made a successful independent career as a New York psychoanalyst, while writing a number of popular books—among them *Escape From Freedom* (1941); *The Sane Society* (1955); and *The Art of Loving* (1956). From the start Fromm had been more religiously oriented than the other critical theorists, and his work had less of an anti-American thrust than that of many of his colleagues. It also was less sociological and philosophical. Fromm picked up the benign American view of Freud, and the belief that a form of social psychotherapy could release human creativity and transform the unfortunate elements of American life. A moldable human nature and not entrenched class interest became the central problem in the reconstruction of the social order.

Marcuse, who was also cut from the Institute staff in the early 1940s but who, like Fromm, remained in the United States for the rest of his life, had more of an edge. He worked in the State Department's Office of Strategic Services—the OSS—during World War II and was an analyst in its successor agency, the CIA, until the 1950s when the new Brandeis University in Waltham, Massachusetts, hired him as professor of political science.

Marcuse wrote in turgid English with a heavy German influence but moved away from theoretical problems of Marxism to a unique Marxist appraisal of capitalist—read American—society. In 1941 he had written *Reason and Revolution: Hegel and the Rise of Social Theory* in which he argued that Hegel could not be read as a conservative idealist committed to justifying the status quo in early nineteenth-century Germany. Instead, Hegel was on his way to Marx: the earlier thinker's examination of consciousness showed how social life and structures of authority rooted different forms of culture and held within them the prospect for beneficial cultural transformation. That is, Marcuse adopted the nuanced interpretation of Marx that was a trademark of the Frankfurt School and found his origins in Hegel. In *Eros and Civilization*, published in 1955, Marcuse expounded on the Institute's linking of Freud and Marx. The book, which criticized Fromm's acceptance of the ruling social system, urged that the repression that Freud considered necessary to civilization and extant in all societies was really incidental to capitalism. In such a social order 'surplus' repression weakened the positive elements of human nature and strengthened the destructive elements. What the Marxist revolutionary had to strive for was a civilization certainly free from excess repression, that gave more play to the creative and joyful—the Eros of his title. In 1964 a more strident book, *One-Dimensional Man*, applied this critique of modern corporatism to the United States: repression—crucially of a psychical sort though grounded in class interests—produced a culture that curtailed human freedom. Marcuse understood mass culture as had Horkheimer and Adorno, but his challenge was less theoretical and more directed to the realities of life in the United States in the 1950s and early 1960s. In America Marcuse had developed from an ivory-tower intellectual to an engaged critic.

Logical Empiricism

From the 1930s through the 1950s the Frankfurt school was radically present in America but without any professional influence in philosophy. The second movement, logical positivism, was apolitical and made an enormous professional impact. Logical positivism or logical empiricism or simply positivism was, in Europe, identified with the Vienna Circle. The Circle emerged during the 1920s, led by thinkers trained primarily in the physical sciences who brought to fruition in philosophy strands of thought that emphasized science and mathematics; the positivists were most indebted to the achievement of Russell and Whitehead's *Principia Mathematica*.

Such scientific philosophy had its advocates in the United States. Russell had visited Harvard in 1914, where Royce among others tried to attract him to Cambridge. Harvard had been more successful in 1924, when it hired Whitehead, but he had by then turned away from the austere philosophy that experts in logic often embraced. Lewis had a reputation in logic, but it basically served him and those he influenced as an adjunct to philosophy. On the contrary, the Vienna Circle made logic central. Americans looked upon the positivists from afar as exemplary of the most stringent empirical thought; indeed, the positivists embodied an extreme empiricism, a set of doctrines emphasizing the *exclusive* claim of science to knowledge, and downgrading any philosophical pursuits that did not acknowledge such exclusivity.

The positivists had read not just Russell but his Austrian protégé Ludwig Wittgenstein, who had been schooled in Vienna and had then gone to study with Russell at Cambridge University, England, and returned there as a professor in the 1930s and 1940s when it became known for views similar to those of the Vienna positivists. Wittgenstein's book, *Logisch-Philosophische Abhandlung* (1921), was translated into English in 1922 as *Tractatus Logico-Philosophicus*—'the *Tractatus*'. Later repudiated by its author, this ambiguous text was a cult volume, which many thinkers at the University of Vienna embraced, especially in the late 1920s when Wittgenstein lived in Austria. Groups of allied scientific philosophers existed in Berlin and Lvov, Poland. Perhaps most influential in giving the loosely connected thinkers public esteem, however, was a young Englishman, A. J. Ayer, who promulgated their ideas at Oxford. Ayer's popularizing tract of 1936, *Language, Truth, and Logic*, immediately became a best-seller among philosophers, and in America Ayer's version of positivism gave the anti-metaphysical viewpoint notoriety and an audience even before World War II.

Especially after the *Anschluss* of Austria in 1938, American universities received European positivists. Rudolph Carnap went to Chicago; Hans Reichenbach to the University of California at Los Angeles; and Alfred Tarski to Berkeley. Gustav Bergmann wound up at Iowa, and Herbert Feigl went from Iowa to Minnesota. Two other positivists located at Ivy League universities. Carl Hempel was a professor at Princeton from 1955 to 1973; and Ernest Nagel, who was born in Czechoslovakia but trained by naturalists and instrumentalists in New York City, taught at Columbia. In the 1940s this small faction articulated a clear point of view at a time when professional philosophers in the United States had an uncompelling set of beliefs. The positivists, for some, were the wave of the future; for others, they represented expertise lacking in wisdom.

An early book of Carnap's, *Der logische Aufbau der Welt* (1928), was quickly recognized, even in German, as a key text in understanding the philosophical vision of positivism, and established Carnap as a leader in the United States. Carnap and the positivists saw the 'reductionist' effort of Russell and Whitehead—that mathematics was logic in disguise—as a model for epistemology. If we had concepts or things that were strange or unfamiliar, the rigorous thinker should be able to substitute for them what was familiar and acceptable, if the strange or unfamiliar were acceptable at all. We might, for example, be interested in but puzzled over imaginary numbers, about the referent of 'the square root of -1'. A reductionist program might try to replace other expressions for such numbers wherever they occurred; these other expressions might be considered equivalent to them, or merely substitutes. Carnap was unsure of what was familiar and unfamiliar: it was not clear why the world of ordinary physical objects was more puzzling than that of the momentarily present. But taking some set of ideas as basic and showing how they could replace others more suspect appealed to him and others as a specialized challenge and as a way, it must be admitted, of displaying intellectual ingenuity. Moreover, the *Aufbau*, translated as *The Logical Structure of the World* (1967), confronted an old problem that Hume, for example, had adumbrated.

Carnap accepted for his base the individual world of immediate qualities spread out in two-dimensional space and time. The problem was to build from this basis the 'secondary' common world—the physical world of objects not attached to any single mind. There were also the worlds of physics and of social institutions. Using a limited number of primitive relations and the techniques of the *Principia*, Carnap's project was to construct all these worlds. Many complained that the result in the *Aufbau* was sterile and had none of the interest, for example, of Lewis's attempt to account for knowledge from the given and our categorical schemes.

More prepossessing were the implications of the method. It was easy to argue that Carnap was just a new sort of Humean whose small view of life stemmed from the minimal items that he took as fundamental. But positivists might equally well start from a physicalist basis and construct from it the world of mental appearances that might be said to define the life of each individual; and the world of science that interpreted the physical world. Additionally, positivists would come to dispute the equality of various constructions. When one asked what were the constituents of existence, one answer might be preferable to others—physical things, scientific objects, or momentary sensations. Or one might argue that scientific objects were mere calculating devices, or that they crucially underlay either the phenomenal or physical world.

With a coherent set of puzzles, the positivists held that philosophy was a special discipline whose task was to clarify meaningful concepts and definitions, and thus the nature of science. Meaningful statements were of two sorts only. The necessary truths of logic and mathematics, and 'analytic' propositions of ordinary language were the first kind. Such truths displayed meaning, as in 'All bachelors are men' and were true irrespective of the nature of the world, certainly true, because they were about the relations of concepts, the tautological transformation of symbols. The second kind of meaningful statements were empirical propositions, which could be true or false but were probable only—scientific procedure determined their value.

A centerpiece of logical positivism was the principle of verification: the method of verification determined whether a proposition had meaning. Verifiability was the criterion of meaningfulness. Thus, empirical propositions were true or false, and considered to have meaning because they were verifiable. Propositions not so verifiable were, if they were not analytic, strictly speaking *meaningless*. Thus positivists believed that the traditional metaphysical claims of philosophers could be exposed as nonsense. Or at least propositions such as 'The absolute is eternal' could be held to be without meaning.

Connected to the attack on metaphysics—and by implication all those branches of philosophy that were not concerned with logic or empirical knowledge—was the program of the unity of science. Largely because of their training but also because of the twentieth-century success of the hard sciences, the logical positivists urged not just that physics was the paradigm of knowledge, but that any discipline that made claims to knowledge must embrace the sort of logical structure that the positivists thought physics typified.

The most celebrated statement of this view came in an essay of 1942 by Hempel, 'The Function of General Laws in History'. This article set out the standards that historians must meet if their narratives of the past were to count as knowledge. Hempel proposed the 'covering law model' of explanation. A historical argument for him culminated in the assertion of a fact, in his example, the freezing of an automobile radiator on a cold night. To explain this occurrence the historian must have at his disposal certain putatively true generalizations concerning the behavior of water; generalizations that could be put in hypothetical form—if thus and such is true, then thus and such is true. Then the historian had to have knowledge of 'boundary conditions'—propositions asserting that on a certain night the temperature fell below 32 °F; that there was no anti-freeze in the radiator; that the car was not in a garage. These propositions would instantiate the 'if' clauses of the generalizations, and the historian could then deduce that the radiator had frozen. Hempel allowed that historians might only fabricate 'explanation sketches', which lacked the accoutrements of explanations found in the natural sciences. None the less, the logical form of any explanation that would pass muster, not just in history but in any branch of knowledge, must be of the covering law type; anything else was a pseudo-explanation.

Even early on insuperable troubles shadowed logical positivism. Conditional sentences that expressed ideas 'contrary to fact' were unverifiable but surely not without meaning. 'If Hitler had not come to power, intellectuals would not have fled Europe' was a proposition whose meaning was clear even though its truth or falsity could not be verified. Moreover, many propositions that informed us of the structure of our experience were not true by definition, but neither were they empirical. An embarrassing example was the verification principle itself—what is meaningful is verifiable—which was not supposed to be a tautology but could itself not be verified. Finally, the positivists faced difficulties in their analysis of scientific statements. 'All ravens are black' was a perfectly good empirical statement, but what did we do with 'All ravens are black, or the absolute is perfect'? According to the logic to which the positivists adhered, if one disjunct of a proposition containing two clauses joined by 'or' was true, the entire proposition was true. Hempel, again, insisted that positive instances of a generalization confirmed it, and thus a black raven helped to warrant 'All ravens are black'. But, again according to his logic, the latter generalization was equivalent to 'Non-black things are not ravens', and hence the observation of a white shoe also warranted 'All ravens are black'. This was the 'paradox' of confirmation.

Conundrums such as these delighted the opponents of positivism, but throughout the 1950s its relentlessly rigorous argumentation and the generation of a linked constellation of theses that might be solvable using the techniques of logic made logical empiricism a respected doctrine. Its view of ethics was also feared, and became the most prominent idea in the positivist arsenal.

In 1933, Charles L. Stevenson, a graduate student at Harvard, went to Cambridge University for study. He returned to write a doctoral dissertation with the realist Ralph Barton Perry, also known as a moral philosopher defending the objectivity of moral judgements. Like many others of his era—John Dewey was the most prominent—Perry was an ethical naturalist, who argued that morality was descriptive, about relations in the natural world; fact and value were not severed. In his dissertation of 1935, 'The Emotive Meaning of Ethical Terms', Stevenson rejected the ideas of his mentor and of most of the American tradition of moral thinking. Teaching at Yale by the late 1930s, he made his reputation in some important essays and then, in 1944, published the most significant treatise in ethics by an American philosopher in the twentieth century, *Ethics and Language*. Yale rewarded Stevenson by denying him tenure: New Haven's traditional philosophers recognized that he had 'committed positivism', and he went on to a subsequent career at Michigan. The small fracas testified to the radicalism of Stevenson's outlook; the safe and conservative tradition at Yale that had diminished its influence since the late nineteenth century; and the greater tolerance that had given such influence to Michigan.

Seen in historical perspective, Stevenson's position was ambiguous, owing much to Perry and Dewey, but the younger man had picked up the concerns of Continental positivism and its kinsfolk in Cambridge, England. A cleavage existed between facts and values, our beliefs about the world and our attitudes toward it. Scientific language was distinct from evaluative language. There was no way to get from a series of 'is' propositions to an 'ought' proposition. While science contained true or false statements, morality expressed emotion. For the positivist, ethical discourse was, strictly speaking, meaningless, for it lacked empirical meaning, the possibility of verification. Stevenson promoted the notion of emotive meaning. Statements such as 'X is good' might lack empirical or descriptive meaning, but had an important role; they functioned like imperatives, expressing an exhortation to do X, or they were ejaculations, manifestations of feelings. Stevenson even allowed that ethical language had a factual component. Essential to his argument, however, was that the non-rational was crucial to evaluation. Moral disputes were inherently contestable since they intrinsically implicated feeling, and the interminability of moral argument contrasted with the procedural arguments that defined science. 'Pro-attitudes' might even be smuggled into otherwise descriptive language in Stevenson's idea of 'persuasive definition', which became a permanent part of philosophical English, as did the cleavage between facts and 'value judgements'.

Like that of the positivists in epistemology, Stevenson's work generated a series of puzzles, commentary on which made the careers of many 'ethicists'. Commentators complicated his analysis, building on advances in understanding how language functioned, and critics offered alternative accounts of moral language that allowed for a greater role for reason in moral deliberation. Simultaneously, Stevenson's 'emotivism' was the reference for 'non-cognitivism' in ethics (or 'meta-ethics', as it came to be called) for the rest of the twentieth century, and the paradigmatic position against which 'cognitivist's and later 'moral realists' contended.

Existentialism

The third movement was existentialism, brought to the United States when Americans learned, immediately following World War II, of Jean-Paul Sartre. As Americans saw it, Sartre emerged as a luminary in the French intellectual world writing on the decadence of the fascist ideology that had engulfed Europe in the 1930s and on the struggle for legitimate political authority that had arisen in the ruins of the Continent after the expensive victory over the Germans. By the time the war ended Sartre was a café intellectual in France, and a translation of a popular lecture he had given gained some fame in the United States. 'Existentialism is a Humanism' declared that human 'existence precede[d] essence'. No defining characteristic—such as elected by God or uniquely chosen by the Absolute—could guide people's lives. Nor could they take comfort in social conventions or social pressures to explain their behavior. This was for Sartre *mauvaise foi*, bad faith, because it permitted them to avoid responsibility for their decisions. Instead, individuals had to recognize that nothing was guaranteed to them, nothing was settled or determined. Human nature did not exist, and they had to make themselves into what they were to become. They had a radical freedom of choice that could not be sloughed off.

Scholars later learned that Sartre had drawn much of his thought from his German mentor, Martin Heidegger. In Heidegger, however, who had begun his philosophical life as a Roman Catholic, these themes were more profoundly developed. Human persons were 'thrown' into a particular cultural world, their being defined by their relentless passage in time. The individual's ordinary concern with everydayness was only half able to suppress the inevitable presence of the terror of dying. Life was filled with *Sorge* and *Angst*—care and anxiety—because of death. In light of these hard truths, thoughtful people needed to lead an authentic existence and finally to aim for *Gelassenheit*—serene renunciation. But these Augustinian and Calvinist themes, rephrased in the context of conservative inter-war European philosophy, were not as prominent as they might be in Sartre, and almost inaccessibly rendered in Heidegger's original German. Although Sartre himself was an atheist and secularist, his ideas thus ultimately stemmed from the spiritual malaise in which World War I and then Hitler had left European intellectuals.

In the United States in the same period many thoughtful people appeared less hostile to religion than they previously had been. The magazine *Partisan Review* was the journal of cultural opinion that circulated among New York intellectuals and in two series of contributions to the magazine, 'The New Failure of Nerve' in 1943 and 'Religion and the Intellectuals' in 1950, John Dewey's combative student Sidney Hook railed against the new popularity of religious concerns in the educated community. Hook urged that the newly religious were not those 'professionally interested in ideas from the point of view of their validity' and had not 'earned their right to religious disbelief to begin with', and he rightly saw that the rumor of angels would have little impact on much of his profession. These brooding ruminations in the wider community, however, gave Sartre an appeal in America.

William Barrett, who had a doctoral degree in philosophy from Columbia and taught at NYU was also one of the editors of *Partisan Review*. Barrett was not of the stature of Dewey, nor even of Hook, but by the post-war period was one of a few thinkers with a foot in both the academic philosophical world and the wider intellectual world. In 1947 he wrote an essay for the *Review* introducing Sartre, 'What is Existentialism?' A small cadre of American people of mind joined Barrett in investigating Sartre and his peers.

Sartre's most important port of entry in America was the Yale French Department whose head was the internationally known critic, Henri Peyre. Under Peyre's auspices Sartre lectured twice at Yale in 1945 and 1946. Yale's literary critics urged his significance on some of Yale's philosophers. Also on Roman Catholic thinkers: for the first time they found an interest—in religious interpretations of existentialism—that intersected with ideas outside the Catholic system of higher education. James Collins held a Ph.D. from Catholic University of America, and taught at St Louis University. In 1952 he published *The Existentialists: A Critical Study*, which compared Sartre, among others, to Gabriel Marcel, a French Roman Catholic classified as an existentialist. The book was a first step in giving Catholic thought in the United States a reputation in the non-Catholic professional world.

Other beneficiaries of Sartre's emergence were women, discriminated against within the philosophical profession. Proficiency at European languages and fascination with fringe thinkers such as Sartre served women well as existentialism became better known. Universities grudgingly hired several in this new area—Hazel Barnes of Toledo; Mary Coolidge of Vassar; Maxine Greene of Columbia; Marjorie Grene who had to leave Chicago but had a career in Britain; and Catherine Rau, who was employed for a time by Berkeley.

Coincident with the professorial response to Sartre was the response of students. After World War II the growing number of undergraduates mandated to take philosophy courses as part of their general requirement for the bachelor's degree formed a group whose desires and interests, however inchoately expressed, could not be ignored. Two popular undergraduate texts, *The Portable Nietzsche* (1954) and Barrett's *Irrational Man* (1958), illustrated the demands these students made and the way these demands were satisfied. *Irrational Man*, a *tour de force* in the history of ideas, advanced the effort of Barrett's earlier article. He sketched Sartre's ideas and told the reader why they were popular in France. Then, however, Barrett explained that Sartre's conclusions were not his own; he was part of a tradition of thinkers in Europe concerned about the tragic aspect of human destiny—Heidegger; Edmund Husserl, a more academic scholar who had founded the phenomenological movement out of which came Heidegger and Sartre; and Kierkegaard and Nietzsche, the nineteenth-century European thinkers suspicious of reason who inspired the phenomenological tradition. Some of these men were non-believers, but others were Christians rebelling against rational religion. Barrett had not just written a book on existentialism; he had uncovered for Americans a tradition of 'Continental' thought different from that of logical positivism, but also from English empiricism, pragmatism, and Marxism.

Of the French and German figures, and several more whom Barrett integrated into his account, the most exciting to undergraduates was Nietzsche. In *The Portable Nietzsche* Walter Kaufmann, an eccentric professor at Princeton, translated and introduced many of Nietzsche's writings for students, and the popular reception that greeted this volume heralded the introduction into American philosophy of a new array of forces. Kaufmann took advantage of the trend with another best-selling text of 1956, *Existentialism from Dostoevsky to Sartre*.

Troubles Brew

Logical Positivism and Existentialism had much in common. Each was a European philosophy that had given up on religion. The positivists sought in science and scientific knowledge an alternative guide to human life, while the philosophers of *Existenz* thought that examining life's meaninglessness could render it worth living. Herbert Marcuse, who stood outside each group, thought both positivists and existentialists were 'bourgeois idealists', ultimately conventional in politics and enmeshed in the false troubles of individual consciousness. Indeed, there was a similar 'decisionism' in each—action was based on nothing except the perceived necessity of choice—but, contra Marcuse, the two philosophies had parted ways in real politics. The positivists, who were political centrists or social democrats in Europe and liberals in America, distrusted the cataclysmic thought of the existentialists. They pointed to Nietzsche's nihilism and the insanity of his last years. Later in the century Heidegger's connection to the Nazis became an international scandal—he had been an active party member. But this repellent self-seeking was much remarked upon even in the 1940s and 1950s, and the positivists regarded Heidegger too with contempt and suspicion. Finally, Sartre's sympathy for Stalinism dismayed many.

On the other side, the existentialists derided the positivists. Hannah Arendt, a German thinker who had emigrated to the United States in 1941, asked Barrett why Americans took seriously the 'second-rate European positivists that have come here'; in Europe, she said, Carnap and Hempel were 'jokes'. The positivists abetted this appraisal through their embarrassed refusal to make their left-liberal leanings a public force. Indeed, in his 1954 presidential address to the Eastern Division of the American Philosophical Association, Ernest Nagel felt he had to defend himself and others against the charge of a shallow scientism. He began by saying that 'as a reflective man by profession', the philosopher had to articulate 'if only occasionally, what sort of world he thinks he inhabits, and to make clear to himself where . . . lies the center of his convictions'. Positivists had difficulty in rebutting the accusation that, while political choice might be problematic, they held that it was literally meaningless. Thinkers such as Nagel made illegitimate the only questions worth asking. Their professional blinders and apolitical arrogance did not make the empiricists many friends.

Barrett and Kaufmann hoped for a dialogue in America between these views. Positivism and existentialism, said Kaufmann, were 'completely out of touch with each other', and Nietzsche was 'the last best bridge between them', for Nietzsche was a thinker of clarity who debunked religious and metaphysical foibles, yet wrote compellingly about the human place in a godless universe. More explicitly, Barrett argued that American professional philosophy was parochial; no one had replaced Dewey as a public thinker. Positivism and its adherents in the United States exemplified this defect.

But for a hundred years the existential tradition had been examining the big questions that positivists were now ignoring and would add a needed dimension to the philosophical conversation in the United States. Both positivism and Marxism, wrote Barrett, were relics of the Enlightenment, which overemphasized the rational and technical at the expense of 'the shadow side of human life', 'all that is dark and questionable'. Not just Carnap and Stevenson, but also the Marxists viewed humanity in a 'thin and oversimplified' way that a confrontation with speculators such as Nietzsche and Sartre would enrich.

In 1958, John Wild of Harvard, a realist who had worked in the tradition of Roy Wood Sellars and Lewis, invited a recent Chicago doctorate and Northwestern philosopher, William Earle, to visit Cambridge. Wild had discovered the existentialists, and hoped that Earle, who was interested in European phenomenology, might get a permanency at Harvard. Earle visited and left unheralded, and in 1960 Wild himself went to Northwestern, frustrated by his failure to move Harvard in the direction of the Continent. Quine, a leader in Cambridge of the younger thinkers influenced by scientific philosophies, argued that Wild's departure would allow another logician or philosopher of science to teach at Harvard. Two years later Wild had established at Northwestern a Society for Phenomenology and Existential Philosophy, which brought together many hitherto scattered voices interested in Continental thought. Then Wild himself left Northwestern for New Haven, a more prominent institution consciously assuming an anti-positivist stance.

Although committed to speculative thinking, Yale wanted diversity in its ranks and representation of empiricist–positivist thought, but it had trouble living with its ideal of toleration. It had hired Stevenson out of Harvard but then fired him in 1946. His replacement was Carl Hempel. But in 1955 Hempel was refused a full professorship and left for the position at Princeton he would occupy for almost twenty years. After a few years of searching, Yale hired Wilfrid Sellars in 1959 as Hempel's substitute, but he went to Pittsburgh in 1963 because of New Haven's antagonism toward scientific thought, taking with him some promising philosophers who felt as he did. By the early 1960s, as Sellars' brand of philosophy attracted more and more talent, Yale was forced to hire thinkers of the second rank to maintain its 'humanist ideology', and could not retain those in the other camp. Throughout the 1960s and early 1970s, a series of public disputes left New Haven in disarray, while an internal evaluating committee recognized a major decline in the repute of philosophy at Yale. While its philosophers were only slowly seeking an alliance with the French Department, their hostility to Harvard's priorities was plain.

From a wider perspective, however, the fight was not between Harvard and Yale. Positivism and existentialism were the intellectual products of a Europe that, in politics, thought in destructive extremes. European ideas and ideologies had begun to provoke a contest among American scholars who had shortly before been devotees of compromising pragmatism. Between the two extremes, such naturalists as Sidney Hook were unable to keep alive the legacy of John Dewey.

13 *Harvard and Oxford, 1946 – 1975*

The Institutional Nexus

In 1935 a young philosophy don in Oxford, England, Isaiah Berlin, was browsing in a local bookstore and ran across C. I. Lewis's *Mind and the World-Order*. Intrigued by the volume, Berlin arranged a seminar on it attended by a number of English philosophers, among them A. J. Ayer, Stuart Hampshire, and J. L. Austin, all of whom were impressed by this systematic treatise. Wilfrid Sellars, then a peripetetic graduate student, attended and later recalled the interchanges over the book as 'the highlight' of his year. During World War II Berlin served as an attaché to the British Foreign Office in Washington, DC, and made direct contact with Harvard pragmatism when he journeyed to Cambridge, Massachusetts. This was surely not the first connection between English philosophers and the United States. In the second decade of the century, as I have noted, Bertrand Russell, then at Cambridge University and at the height of his fame, visited Harvard, and in a celebrated case twenty-five years later was denied the right to teach at the City College of New York, because of his radical reputation. In the mid-1920s Harvard, again, obtained the services of Alfred North Whitehead, who left the University of London. Berlin's trip to Cambridge, Massachusetts, however, initiated a much more sustained tie between Oxford University and Harvard, and one in which the English pursued the Americans. Moreover, it endured to shape the dialogue of professional philosophy in the United States for twenty-five years.

Berlin's role in the creation of this tie was that of intellectual middleman, and on the American side of the water a similar middleman, Morton White, a Columbia Ph.D. who went on to a position at Harvard in 1948, assisted him. White struck up a friendship with Berlin when the Englishman returned to Harvard in 1949, and in the spring of 1951, White spent a term in Oxford meeting Berlin's philosopher friends, who were proponents of something called conceptual analysis.

Analysis was a strand of thought originally identified with Cambridge, England, and the views of its thinkers, G. E. Moore and Bertrand Russell, and Russell's student, Wittgenstein, who also taught there, though he wrote in German. Hostile to metaphysics and certainly to the notion that philosophy was a guide to wisdom, analysis rather looked at philosophy as an activity that clarified ordinary talk and the structure of science. The analysts did not try to teach how to live the good life, but to find out how we used a word like 'good' or 'ought'; they defined concepts that might have their own existence but were always expressed in language. We might use these concepts, but it was a more difficult task to spell out what they implied and what the criteria for their employment were. Moore was identified with examining ordinary language. Russell, whose views were far and away the most well known, applied the techniques of the new mathematical logic to philosophy and was himself usually mistaken for a logical positivist and considered, at least, an uncompromising empiricist. By the 1940s Wittgenstein had clearly rejected logical empiricism and pursued 'therapeutic' positivism. These views of the later Wittgenstein were, in the 1940s and 1950s, the most mysterious yet supposedly the most profound. After his death in 1951 they were promulgated by followers who translated him from the German and brought into print previously unpublished writings—aphorisms, questions, suggestions, jokes, snatches of conversation, and arguments with himself. In this work Wittgenstein proposed that the study of how ordinary language worked could dismantle the problems of philosophy, make us aware of how we came to ask its strange questions, and free us from the need to ask them again.

In Oxford a large group of philosophers who, like Berlin, had come to maturity and institutional importance after the war promulgated ideas such as these. They were first led by Gilbert Ryle, half a generation older than most of them, who, not incidentally, had a gruff but friendly interest in Americans. In 1947 he took over the editorship of the premier British journal of philosophy, *Mind*, and in 1949 published his major work, *The Concept of Mind*. This book derided the traditional view of the mind as an inner entity and argued instead, as had the American instrumentalists, that it was to be understood as a function of behavior. But Ryle couched his program for behaviorism in linguistic terms. He explicated consciousness as a form of speaking; suggested that we understand the mental as the human capacity for language; and discussed ideas as inclinations to action—intimating that we had to unpack, for example, notions such as intelligence *via* the understanding of conditional sentences such as, 'If she were presented with a math problem, she would solve it quickly'.

Among the Oxford élite, Ryle enlisted Paul Grice and J. L. Austin, two men even more involved in the study of language but whose reputation for genius was more local because of the paucity of their publications. Through ordinary language, Austin wanted to promote a mundane understanding of our place in the world against various philosophical theories. He believed that ordinary language made distinctions minute enough to circumvent philosophy's puzzles, and deprecated notions such as that of sense-data that found the existence of a common-sense universe of objects peculiar. Grice's student P. F. Strawson had more traditional interests but was also the one Oxonian who could pass as a logician. A. J. Ayer was by far the most wide-ranging and famous of the group and indeed had been to the United States in the 1930s, but insiders regarded his logical-empiricist views as passé, and by the 1950s he had taken a chair at London. None the less, Ayer was rooted in the Oxford milieu and returned there in 1959. In London he ran his own international philosophical salon that, while indebted to Oxford, was more cosmopolitan.

At Oxford, philosophy—usually referred to as 'analysis' or 'philosophical analysis'—was more a manner than a program, although it must be admitted that it was stuffy and sometimes arid in the range of its concerns. Yet the dons had studied Lewis's *Mind and the World-Order* and knew his later work of 1946, *An Analysis of Knowledge and Valuation*. Although not adherents of his abstemious pragmatism, they were susceptible to Berlin's favorable reports on the even more disciplined leanings of a younger group of Harvard philosophers and the careful, not to say finicky philosophizing that White practiced when he was there in 1951. Ironically, Berlin and White himself soon lost interest in these ideals but two of White's peers exemplified them.

Willard Quine was a logician who had been a graduate student at Harvard and never left Cambridge, rising through the ranks to the professorship that Lewis had occupied. Although Quine had been a student of Whitehead's, he had studied Lewis's pragmatism and begun a friendship with Rudolph Carnap when he visited Europe in 1932–3 before Carnap fled the Continent. Nelson Goodman was Lewis's student and a professor for much of his career at the University of Pennsylvania—where White, teaching there briefly in 1946 and 1947, had met him—before his appointment to Harvard.

Both of these men carried on the tradition of Cambridge pragmatism that Peirce first exemplified. In the second half of the twentieth century it was called pragmatic analysis. Technical essays in logic and in the closely reasoned philosophical style that Lewis had popularized typified pragmatic analysis. Substantively, however, Goodman and Quine rejected Lewis's mentalistic language—expressions that depended on our intuitions of meanings—especially of modal ideas of what was necessarily true or false. They were also suspicious of hypothetical sentences, the contrary-to-fact conditionals that delineated the possible but not actual—'If the Nazis had not over-run Europe, American philosophy would have been more meta-physical.' The 'ontological commitment' of Goodman and Quine—their view about whether such things as meanings or possible experiences existed —was more strict than that of other philosophers and expressed a cautious view of what could be known.

In the context of Oxford philosophy, the work of several other talented academics, and the contributions of scores of lesser scholars, pragmatic analysis became part of the more diffuse movement of American analytic philosophy. Some analysts modeled their work on an idealized view of science; others were more interested in unpacking the meaning of concepts. In general, what joined them was an apolitical, secular temper that saw philosophy as a professional field of study connected only tangentially to problems of life and death.

For the analysts, including Goodman and Quine, symbolic logic was a tool necessary for philosophic reasoning. Although they were suspicious of any absolutistic comprehension of science, and were frequently skeptical in their leanings, analytic philosophers often elevated scientific under-standing as the only kind, and indeed, with the logical empiricists, made 'the philosophy of science' a central subfield that was almost coterminous with epistemology. In focusing on the careful explication of how language was used, or should be used to avoid obfuscation, or could be restructured to be transparent, analytic philosophers invented 'the philosophy of language', another central subfield to go along with the philosophy of science. In part this 'linguistic turn' reflected a denigration of the status of the philosopher. The classic pragmatists had thought philosophy might change the world; the inter-war generation had worried that it was not changing the world; by the 1950s philosophers had stopped agonizing about their shrunken role, and even embraced it. In emphasizing that phi-losophy was about language, philosophers were noting a new impotence. A dimension of this impotence was the trivializing of other fields of philoso-phy. Although analysts did not dismiss more traditional areas of philoso-phy as meaningless as did logical positivism, by ignoring them they implied that these fields could be ignored.

The sort of public philosophy that Dewey had promoted almost van-ished. In the 1920s and 1930s Dewey had engaged with non-philosophers of the likes of Reinhold Niebuhr, Walter Lippman, and Harold Lasswell (a policy scientist), in conversations that were considered by professionals to be an essential aspect of what philosophy was about. By the 1950s profes-sional thinkers rarely thought of such conversations as part of philosophy at all. From 1940 to 1970 Dewey's most prominent follower, Sidney Hook, was an active participant in many intellectual debates outside the academy, and spoke to issues that involved Niebuhr and Lippman, as well as Hannah Arendt, John Courtney Murray (a Roman Catholic thinker), Paul Blanshard (a social commentator), Milton Friedman (an economist), and Arthur Schlesinger, Jr. But these debates did not count for promotion in the profession of philosophy, and few people who were known as philosophers participated in them. Just as political options shrank for Americans during the high tide of the Cold War against communism from 1945 through the early 1960s, so did options that could be construed as 'real' philosophy. Analysis narrowly defined the boundaries of philosophy, delimiting the few questions that were taken as constitutive of university thinking, and marginalizing many others. Analysis was the philosophy of the democratic imperial West, with Great Britain in a junior partnership with the United States. Not only the politically active, but also the metaphysicians were shunted to the sidelines, as soul-searching about the nature of philosophy disappeared.

At the same time the connection between Harvard and Oxford maintained and augmented the prestige of each school, and study in one or both was often imperative for preferment in the United States. It is, however, difficult to say what sort of intellectual influence the English actually had on the Americans. Lewis had made a restrained mode all-important, and his students were enamored of logical positivism. Oxford was less formal in its emphases. While reinforcing the clubby ethos of American philosophy, the English may have directed American analytic philosophy away from an even greater logical and scientific focus that it otherwise might have had.

After Berlin and White made the first contacts in 1949 and 1951, the Harvard and Oxford groups exchanged ideas through the 1950s. In 1953 Goodman delivered in London the lectures that would become his book, *Fact, Fiction, and Forecast* (1955). A few months later Quine went to Oxford, where he worked on his important *Word and Object* (1960) and attended a seminar by Grice and Strawson that took up some of his views. Alluding to American aid to Europe after World War II, Berlin reported that Austin, self-consciously the leading Oxford thinker, treated Quine 'like a Marshall Plan ambassador, not to be affronted on any possible grounds'. The next year Austin went to Harvard to deliver the lectures that would become *How to do Things with Words* (1962), and the next year Wilfrid Sellars, who was (idiosyncratically) making a reputation as an analytic philosopher independent of Harvard, went to Ayer's London to deliver 'The Myth of the Given', his attack on Lewis (and others). At the end of the decade Paul Grice delivered the William James lectures at Harvard, which, though long unpublished, had a great readership circulating informally. White, Quine, and Goodman went back to Oxford, and Berlin also returned to Harvard.

Nelson Goodman

Like Quine's, Goodman's intellectual life was indebted to Carnap. In 1930, shortly after the publication of the *Aufbau*, Goodman set to work on his own constructionalist project in which, with ultimately greater success than Carnap, he used a single primitive relation to build a simulacrum of our common physical world from a phenomenalist basis. This project eventuated in a Harvard dissertation of 1940, 'A Study of Qualities', and a book of 1951, *The Structure of Appearance*, which was substantially revised and (from Goodman's view) perfected in a second edition of 1966. This elaborate effort, which had comparatively few admirers, testified to what critics called the 'fussiness' and 'formalism' of Goodman's approach.

Yet in other areas, Goodman captured the imagination of philosophers. Central to Lewis's work in both logic and epistemology was the idea of modality. In order to philosophize we needed not only a sense of the true, but also of the necessary; of the false, but also of the impossible. This was the basis for Lewis's distinction between analytic and synthetic statements. The latter, or empirical ones, were simply true or false; the former, which displayed relations of meaning, *could not* be false (or, if they were contradictory, true). Following the path of Peirce, James, and Royce, Lewis also spoke of possible experience—what *would* happen to confirm or disconfirm the truth of a statement even if it did not occur—delineated in 'counterfactual conditionals'. With many American philosophers who preceded him, he believed that their meaning was clear and that some conjectures of possibilities were more legitimate than others—were I in the field now, I would see black cows and not green ones, although in fact no one was there now. Other philosophers assumed the innocence of contrary-to-fact hypotheses in grasping the dispositional predicates that frequently made their way into speculation. When Dewey, for example, analogized 'is red' and 'is desirable', he treated both predicates as dispositionals—what was red would appear red under certain standard conditions, whereas what was desirable would be desired in agreed circumstances. On the contrary, Goodman found contrary-to-fact conditionals mystifying rather than clarifying, and also distrusted philosophers, such as Ryle on the mind or Hempel on the nature of scientific law, who relied on counterfactuals.

In the 1870s when Charles Peirce elaborated his pragmatism, he worried that science was identified with skeptical empiricism and nominalism—the view that only individuals existed. Ostensibly the scientist observed and grouped phenomena on the basis of practical calculations and dismissed the characteristics that individuals had in common and that permitted categorization based on genuine similarities. But if science were a rational enterprise, Peirce said that individuals shared certain features and underlying structures that science uncovered. He defended epistemological realism. Goodman attacked this sort of realism and denied that there were any essential connections among separate individuals. Science could not demonstrate that either the constructive power of the mind or connections of objects themselves ordered the world. To the extent that we could justify induction, Goodman held, we would not reassess Kant's reply to Hume but refine Hume's own modest discussion. All we had to work with were actual individual occurrences, and thus nominalism had to satisfy us.

Beginning with his article of 1946, 'The Problem of Counterfactual Conditionals', Goodman argued that, as usually stated, the problem of induction was insoluble. If all the coins in my pocket were silver, that generalization did not support the counterfactual: if a coin were to be put in my pocket, it would be silver. Yet the generalization that all butter melted at 150 °F did support the counterfactual: if this stick of butter had been heated to 150 °F, it would have melted. The first generalization was accidental; the second lawlike. How could we discriminate between the two sorts, and thus warrant lawlike generalizations that buttressed the work of science and illuminated the scientist's search for causal regularities? How did we distinguish a legitimate prediction from a lucky guess?

Goodman essayed a multitude of answers to these questions and found all of them wanting. More important, he devised pointed examples to show the failures inherent in standard approaches. In fact, he invented predicates—the most famous of which was 'grue'—whose behavior generated specialized essays in the journals for a generation. Something was grue if it was green before time *t*, and blue thereafter. Before time *t*, Goodman asked, why did we believe that the generalization 'All emeralds are green' was perfectly acceptable in its support of the prediction that an emerald found after time *t* would be green, while 'All emeralds are grue' lent no support to the prediction that an emerald found after time *t* would be grue?

Such predictions were neither reports of experience nor logical consequences of it, so how could we privilege the green over the grue? Goodman urged that the answer could not lie in our having in the present knowledge of the future that we indeed did not have, or in our trying to account for such unattainable knowledge. Rather we must follow Hume, who had told us that we accepted one prediction rather than others because it best accorded with past regularities, which had established within us habitual expectations. For Goodman this answer did not miss the point and merely give us the origin of our predictions instead of their justification. Rather, Goodman said, we could not distinguish a justification of induction from a careful description of how we successfully predicted. If we could make explicit the criteria we used in inductions, we would have gone a long way in solving the problem of induction. The conformity of principles of inductive inference to standard inductive practice justified them—they would accord with the inductions we sanctioned. But if a principle yielded unacceptable inferences, we would drop it as invalid. Predictions were acceptable if they conformed to valid canons of induction; and the canons were valid if they accurately codified practice. This reasoning was not circular; we worked in spirals: 'The process of justification is the delicate one of making mutual adjustments between rules and accepted inferences; and in the agreement achieved lies the only justification for either.'

Goodman generated his rules of inductive inference from a primitive notion of linguistic 'entrenchment': the predicate 'green' was better entrenched in the language than 'grue' and so, other things being equal, was a better candidate to project as a basis for reliable predictions or for constructing generalizations. And Goodman worked out how we could construct degrees of projectibility to give some preference to entrenched predicates but not rule out new predicates that would allow us to alter our practices and introduce novel concepts.

We sought the roots of inductive validity in language. The line between valid and invalid predictions was 'drawn upon the basis of how the world is and has been described and anticipated in words'. When we talked about what we might legitimately predict, as opposed to what we believed would not happen, we need not transgress the boundaries of the actual. 'What we often mistake for the actual world is one particular description of it. And what we mistake for possible worlds are just equally true descriptions in other terms.' How did knowledge and a lucky guess differ? The difference did not lie in the structure of the world, or in the power of the mind to shape our experience, but in the way language worked. We could not escape language and somehow grasp the world as it was and thus learn how it would be in the future. We could not find beyond language an indubitable basis for knowledge. Rather, all we had was our language, and philosophy should figure out how it worked in practice.

The relativism of which Goodman was accused was heightened later in his career, particularly in his *Languages of Art* (1968), but his view did reflect the aesthetic practices with which he had been engaged in his early life as an art critic, dealer, and connoisseur. In that book and subsequent publications Goodman continued to deny anything beyond the actual, and to dismiss even the idea of a world that could be described in one crucial and basic (i.e. scientific) manner. Instead, language provided us with many sets of interwoven and related terms by means of which we might organize our experience for different purposes. But we did this because of practical demands. No one constellation of descriptions of the world—no one vocabulary—could be said to be more true than the others; different descriptions might prove more or less efficacious, depending on our changing aims and practices. Many of these themes were debated at the annual American Philosophical Association Meeting in a much noted plenary symposium of 1951, 'The Experiential Element in Knowledge', that included Goodman, Lewis, and the logical positivist Hans Reichenbach. Over fifty years before, at a similar high-profile gathering—the Great Philosophical Discussion at Berkeley in 1895—George Holmes Howison had stated that all the participants assumed the truth of philosophical idealism—that the mental was the only truly real. Now times had changed. Reichenbach began the proceedings by saying that 'Kant's thesis' was fallacious. Reichenbach took 'for granted' the 'common [anti-Kantian] presumption' that there was no 'rational' source for knowledge and that the discussants shared 'a common empiricist basis'.

But just as Howison had acknowledged that idealists could disagree, so Reichenbach too acknowledged that empiricists could disagree. Both he and Goodman went after Lewis's view that there was a given that uniquely warranted knowledge. Against Goodman and Lewis, however, Reichenbach argued that observation reports of the momentarily given were dependent on references to physical objects. This was the argument that Wilfrid Sellars made against Lewis a few years later in 'The Myth of the Given'. More important, Reichenbach asserted that no reports of experience were certain; knowledge was based on shifting coalitions of reports about physical objects and about observations, which had varying degrees of credibility, but none of which was immune from revision. Science might be the only true form of knowledge, but it did not have an uncriticizable ground.

Goodman was respectful of his mentor Lewis, whom he ranked with Kant in the stream of modern philosophy. Kant had exchanged the structure of the world for the structure of mind, and Lewis had exchanged the structure of mind for that of concepts. Goodman also believed with Lewis that the building blocks of knowledge were momentarily grasped instants of experience, but Goodman now thought that we had to exchange the structure of concepts for that of 'several symbol systems'.

Like Reichenbach, Goodman denied certainty. No guaranteed connection of the sort Lewis wanted existed between our conceptual apparatus—language—and the world. Rather, said Goodman, we must treat utterances as *part* of the given patches of experience. To explain the connection between non-linguistic experience and linguistic experience, Goodman intimated that we think of a signaling relation. The appearance of black smoke and a toot followed 'The train is coming'. But Goodman rejected Lewis's quest for empirical certainty, and the idea that one set of signals might be better than any other. Instead he considered various languages as tools for accomplishing certain limited sets of collective aims. Linguistic experience assisted us practically in interpreting the non-linguistic.

In his reply Lewis took no prisoners. He said, as he had said for over twenty years, that the issue was the justifiability of knowledge, which had to be distinguished from an analysis of the content of knowledge. Justifiability depended on an empirically certain basis. Without justification the philosopher had to hold that any empirical judgement was as good as any other because none could be warranted. The sort of skepticism Goodman was advocating was 'worse than unsatisfactory'; it was 'nonsense', 'an intellectual disaster'.

Van Quine

Quine gained repute in the recondite field of symbolic logic, a recognized expertise by the 1940s. In the late 1940s, however, he made his mark as a theorist of knowledge, blending a concern for alternative conceptual schemes and a commitment to the primacy of physical science. In 1951 *Philosophical Review* published 'Two Dogmas of Empiricism', a paper Quine had read at the Eastern Division meetings of the APA the preceding year; it proved to be the most influential philosophical essay written by an American in the second half of the century and demonstrated how he would join pragmatism and positivism. Quine first repudiated the 'dogma' of distinguishing analytic and synthetic statements, conceptual and empirical judgements, those that displayed meanings and those that experience verified. As we have seen, this distinction was essential to the positivists who restricted the meaningful to logical tautologies and the propositions of natural science; and to Lewis who distinguished between the contribution of mind to knowledge and the empirically given.

Quine maintained that this dogma connected to a second, that to each synthetic statement 'there is associated a unique range of possible sensory events, such that the occurrence of any of them would add to the likelihood of truth of the statement, and that there is associated also another unique range of possible sensory events whose occurrence would detract from that likelihood'. On the contrary, Quine claimed, we could not separate a statement's truth into its factual and linguistic components; the unit of empirical significance was the whole of science. There was no way to distinguish between verifying statements within a system and choosing alternative systems. Thus Quine declared in a widely quoted passage:

As an empiricist I continue to think of the conceptual scheme of science as a tool, ultimately, for predicting future experience in the light of past experience. Physical objects are conceptually imported into the situation as convenient intermediaries—not by definition in terms of experience, but simply as irreducible posits comparable, epistemologically, to the gods of Homer. For my part I do, *qua* lay physicist, believe in physical objects and not in Homer's gods; and I consider it a scientific error to believe otherwise. But in point of epistemological footing the physical objects and the gods differ only in degree and not in kind. Both sorts of entities enter our conception only as cultural posits. The myth of physical objects is epistemologically superior to most in that it has proved more efficacious than other myths as a device for working a manageable structure into the flux of experience.

This 'holism' meant that 'the totality of our so-called knowledge or beliefs' was a 'man-made fabric which impinges on experience only along the edges'. Expressed in sentences, knowledge faced corroboration as a 'corporate body'. It was 'misleading to speak of the empirical content of an individual statement', and 'folly to seek a boundary between synthetic statements, which hold contingently on experience, and analytic statements, which hold come what may. Any statement can be held true come what may, if we make drastic enough adjustments elsewhere in the system.'

Perhaps the most important consequence of denying the analytic–synthetic distinction was what happened to the separation between the conceptual analyst and the empirical researcher. We could not philosophize about the structure of knowledge without an acquaintance with that knowledge itself. The philosopher must emphasize not the reflective individual but collective investigation; philosophy was 'continuous with science'. Epistemology had to be 'naturalized'. Philosophy could not function as a discipline beyond science; it had rather to take its cues from what physicists actually did. To formulate a theory of knowledge—as indeed James and Dewey had first suggested—the pragmatist must investigate how the psychologist, anthropologist, and natural scientist worked.

'Two Dogmas' thus reiterated themes that Peirce and James had first stressed, but Quine, almost simultaneously with Goodman, also rang changes on this tradition. Peirce, James, Royce, Dewey, and Lewis had made human choice crucial in determining what existed, but had all assumed that science would provide us with one agreed answer to the question: what is there? Quine went further: there was a practical dimension of choice *among* various systems, and he intimated that, for example, a religious world-view, in addition to a scientific one, might have some justifiability. Pragmatists such as Peirce and Dewey had saved the religious by ultimately identifying it with science. James had argued, in a different accent, that both science and religion were defended in the same way and might both be true. Quine (and Goodman) took this tack too but added that such world-views might be *alternative*. We might, said Quine, need to be skeptical about all claims—even scientific ones—to the complete truth. The 'obvious counsel', he commented, was 'tolerance and an experimental spirit' that looked to human practices for criteria of what different world-views were acceptable.

On the other hand, Quine did not escape his long tutelage with Carnap and a commitment to natural science as the only legitimate form of know-ledge and to a certain basis for this knowledge. Even in the early 1950s, this dimension of Quine's thought was evident. If both the gods and the physi-cal objects were myths, fictions, or cultural posits, we could speak of them as such only if we had some idea of what was non-mythic, factual, or given. Quine recognized that the 'quality of myth' was relative to our viewpoint and purposes and asked what viewpoint we adopted in philosophy. Among the various conceptual schemes best suited to various pursuits, Quine said that the phenomenalistic one claimed 'epistemological priority'. If we con-cerned ourselves with the theory of knowledge, which for Quine was an extension of physical science, we must take as basic 'the disordered frag-ments of raw experience'—Lewis's given, Carnap's or Goodman's phenom-enalistic basis. These were the elements by which the philosopher must analyze how we attained and justified knowledge. Choice of a conceptual scheme was relative to our purposes; but once a purpose was specified—to find out what was true—choice vanished.

When Quine philosophized in this mode, he was anti-pragmatic and positivistic. The phenomenalistic conceptual scheme, which as epistemol-ogists we took as basic, entailed a belief in natural science. As a naturalist, he said that 'physical objects are real, right down to the most hypothetical of particles . . . I . . . hold this ontological line of naïve and unregenerate realism'. 'Cultural relativists' in science who preached 'epistemological nihilism' disturbed him.

Yet even as Quine focused on science as the one best way, his pragma-tism reasserted itself: we might not be able to decide among alternative sci-entific views. In his important book, *Word and Object* (1960), dedicated to Carnap, this Quine was paramount. He was there concerned to analyze meaning so as to avoid postulating mental entities, thus indirectly address-ing the pragmatic program of understanding mind as a form of behavior. There was, said Quine, nothing in meaning that was not in behavior, and he theorized that public linguistic experience defined meaning. Quine imagined a linguist faced with penetrating and translating a hitherto unknown language, but assisted by a well-intentioned native speaker or informant. No one had undertaken this task in its extreme form, and thus Quine called it 'radical translation'.

A rabbit ran by, and the native, pointing to the rabbit, said 'Gavagai'. The linguist concluded that 'gavagai' referred to the rabbit, and that 'Gavagai' meant 'There's a rabbit.' The linguist could test this conclusion by pointing to some other rabbit and saying 'Gavagai' and waiting for the native's assent. Was the translation correct?

Quine said we could not know: our word 'rabbit' referred to a physical object, but 'gavagai' might refer to temporal rabbit slices, or to undivided rabbit parts; or it might mean 'It is rabbiting,' analogous to 'It is raining.' In all such cases, Quine argued, the native would assent to the linguist's use of 'gavagai' just where the English-speaker would use 'rabbit'. If the linguist could ask the native which of these was meant, the problem would be solved, but the linguist did not have the ability to ask such questions in the native tongue; and indeed was trying to learn how to ask such questions. Moreover, the resources at the linguist's disposal were of no help in making the appropriate discrimination. If the native meant by 'gavagai' temporal rabbit slices, he would take the linguist's question 'Is this gavagai identical with yesterday's?' to mean 'Is this rabbit slice a member of the same series as yesterday's?' and the linguist could not tell the difference. Understanding the native language in part involved postulating the entities in the native's world, and the available evidence was not enough to rule out any number of different ways of construing the basic entities in that world—one's 'ontology'. The linguist imputed the English ontology of physical objects to the native language and the native's life world, because that was the natural thing to do; it was how we thought. But this imputation had no grounds but convenience.

In sum, 'indeterminacy of translation' turned into an argument for the 'inscrutability of reference' and Quine's famous 'ontological relativity'. Our understanding of a language's subject-matter—its ontology, the world it was taken to describe—was relative to our choice, which was at least partially arbitrary, of how to translate that language in terms of another.

In the 1970s and 1980s the indeterminacy of translation gave way to a related doctrine, the underdetermination thesis, which Quine expounded in various versions, with a varied technical background. He envisioned a situation where we had assembled all possible observations and then argued that we could imagine two (or more) theoretical formulations of the evidence but would not be able to find an observation that would decide between them. The competing theories would be 'empirically equivalent', but we could not rule out that they were 'irreconcilable' or 'incompatible'. Scientists would not be surprised that a theory was underdetermined by the evidence—for that was what made it a theory and not a mere summary of the data. Nor would it disturb them that for a fixed amount of evidence, different and incompatible theories could be generated to account for it. Indeed, the standard view of experimentation proceeded on the assumption that successive experiments—observations—could be devised to distinguish competing theories—some would be able to account for the observations, others not. Quine's argument had its bite because he created a situation in which all observations formed a fixed totality, and represented it as what went on in science.

Quine hedged the expression of his thesis, once declaring it 'modest and vague', and only asserting that 'our system of the world' was bound to have 'empirically equivalent alternatives' that we could not reconcile. None the less, this was only modest if we were allowed to conduct experiments in the future that would allow us to throw out the weak sisters among the competitors; if experimentation was forbidden, we might have alternative physics, say of Newton or Einstein, neither of which could claim truth.

Quine was rhetorically devoted to the *practice* of scientists—'actual endeavors and activities old and new, exoteric and esoteric, and grave and frivolous'. His advocacy of the naturalization of epistemology meant that an acceptable theory of knowledge could be no more than 'a generalization of the sciences'. If we wanted to know how knowledge was possible and how it was justified, we could do no more than to look at the premises that underwrote the scientific enterprise. When Quine did focus on actual science, he was at his most positivistic: the world was the way physics told us it was—'a multitude of twitches in the void', and no evidence existed for believing in God or in anything else, like free will, that was at odds with a causally determined natural world. Critics might deplore the depth of this vision, but it was consistent with a disposition to regard physics as the core area of knowledge.

At the same time, Quine ironically sustained his indeterminacy and underdetermination only when he discarded the practice of science. His radical translation was an a priori thought experiment; it did not examine the way anthropologists, linguists, or translators learned a language, studied language acquisition, or translated from one language to another. Scholars did not gain knowledge of other languages in the way he suggested, and the way they did gain such knowledge persuaded them to rule out the sort of indeterminacy Quine preached. Then he claimed that his underdetermination thesis was about science, but it was not about the practice of science. In a limited way Quine explored science as a body of knowledge but he ignored the role of enquiry among actual scientists; for them it was a process in which theories were generated to account for observations, tested by observation and experiment, and revised indefinitely in terms of the results of such tests. Instead, Quine wrote from a post-scientific perspective in which there was nothing to do except generate alternative theories. He came to his indeterminate and underdeterminate conclusions when he philosophized from his armchair, engaging in a style of thought that other pragmatists, and Quine himself in his more positivist moods, found to be dogmatic, unconcerned with the practices of scientific communities.

Analytic Philosophy

American philosophy in the 1930s had lacked a coherent set of programs and, by the 1940s, any figure who transcended the academic world. In this context many younger thinkers looked to logical empiricism or philosophical analysis as the desirable next step, following the pragmatism of James and Dewey as a secular, scientifically oriented creed that would advance in a rigorous way and avoid the extravagant claims of older thinkers such as Royce (and some of the more amorphous claims of Dewey and his followers). Yet to other younger thinkers—trained by extravagant and amorphous scholars—and to many older philosophers, analysis and positivism were enemies not just to traditional philosophy but to wisdom and the good life; to philosophy's title to be the Queen Discipline in the university; and to the philosopher to be the spokesperson for intellectuals to the world outside the academy. Indeed, C. I. Lewis, the American grandfather of analysis, was one of these older philosophers. A dreaded antagonist, Lewis was also self-righteous and disapproved of the work of Goodman and Quine as immoral in its implications. For a long time Lewis's veto kept Goodman from Harvard. Early on, even Morton White worried that analysis had unnecessarily constricted philosophy's boundaries. Before he gave it up entirely, he had tried to expand it in his book of 1956, *Toward Reunion in Philosophy*. The volume cajoled analytic philosophers to use their skills but to broaden their vision, but did not effect the desired reunion. Other opponents, most prominently at Yale, self-consciously designated themselves as metaphysicians or humanists. The Harvard–Oxford axis became ideologically dominant in the Anglo-American philosophical world, but also generated anger at its technocratic craftsmanship.

The institutional alliance between the two schools was extraordinary for the growth of professional thought in the quarter-century after World War II. Among prominent philosophers for whom the Harvard–Oxford connection was strategic were Donald Davidson (Berkeley), Daniel Dennett (Massachusetts Institute of Technology), Burton Dreben (Harvard), Saul

Kripke (Princeton), David Lewis (Princeton), Robert Nozick (Harvard), Martha Nussbaum (Chicago), Sydney Shoemaker (Cornell), and Paul Ziff (University of North Carolina). Additionally, a number of American nationals did their doctoral degrees at a Harvard-tainted Oxford, and returned to teach in the United States: among them Stephen Schiffer (City University of New York, Graduate Center), John Searle (Berkeley), and Peter Unger (New York University). Finally the visits of Oxford philosophers continued to Harvard—H. L. A. Hart in 1957, A. J. Ayer in 1970, and Bernard Williams in 1972.

Late in the century, as the British standard of living declined for professionals, the Harvard–Oxford connection was crucial in launching a philosophical brain-drain from England to America, as older Oxford philosophers sought greener pastures in their declining years, and as newly minted ones looked for brighter futures in the United States. Stuart Hampshire was first, going initially to Princeton and then to Stanford, as did J. O. Urmson. And most Englishmen sought out pleasant climates— among them, Richard Wollheim went to the University of California at Davis and then Berkeley, Paul Grice to Berkeley, Ninian Smart to Santa Barbara, R. M. Hare to Florida, Gainesville. Notable among younger thinkers were John McDowell at Pittsburgh and Crispin Wright at Michigan. The relation between Harvard and Oxford also helped to construct a new association among a leading group of philosophy departments that Harvard dominated—among them Princeton, Pennsylvania, Cornell, Stanford, Berkeley, and the University of California at Los Angeles.

14 The Tribulations of Professional Philosophy, 1962–1999

Higher education expanded after World War II, in part to meet the needs of tens of thousands of returning servicemen, in part to respond to the federal government, which began to fund education deemed essential to the nation's defense in the period of Cold War with the old Soviet Union. But despite this growth the structure of prestige in the academic world in general, and in philosophy in particular, remained intact. As one historian has pointed out, the 'Harvard model' became standard: even schools that served regional needs or catered to specialized groups of students downgraded service and teaching and hired and promoted faculty on the basis of credentials beginning with the doctoral degree and eventuating in productivity evidenced by writing. In philosophy Harvard maintained its distinctive rank, and leadership flowed to its fellow Ivy League universities; to other fortunate private institutions on the East Coast, such as Johns Hopkins; to the great public institutions of the Midwest and the University of Chicago; to select liberal arts colleges; and to a few large schools on the West Coast.

A continued expansion in the 1960s, accompanied by more private and public money that eventually found its way into the pockets of academics (including philosophers) altered this system irrevocably. First of all, the number of institutions multiplied. Especially dramatic were the increases in schools funded by individual states. For example, New York, Ohio, Wisconsin, and California enlarged the number of public universities under their purview. Many states—Michigan and California being two outstanding examples—also added another tier of institutions, state colleges.

When these establishments created philosophy departments, older schools trained more philosophers, and the new ones themselves opened graduate programs. In 1920 the membership of the American Philosophical Association was about 260; in 1960 it was 1,500; in the 1990s it was well over 8,000. One observer noted that in the first half of the twentieth century the United States, Britain, and Canada founded thirty philosophy journals. Fifteen more were added between 1950 and 1960, and forty-four in the 1960s—as many as in the previous sixty years—and then about 120 in the next twenty years! By 2000 close to ninety institutions in the United States awarded students the doctoral degree in philosophy. At the end of the twentieth century the sheer number of publishing 'philosophers' had changed the activity and made it impossible for philosophers to monitor what when on in their profession.

As important as an augmented number of schools promoting research and a veritable flood of professionally trained scholars were shifts that made more schools desirable destinations for philosophers. More money in the system meant that many universities could offer enormous salaries and perquisites to thinkers they wanted on their faculties. Research budgets, reduced teaching loads, helpful assistants, frequent leaves of absence, and subventions for travel became available. Universities created research centers to make their schools attractive to outsiders, and entrepreneurially minded philosophers might find it desirable to run such centers or to be given the power to hire more people in their fields.

Far greater mobility resulted. Prior to the 1960s philosophers of originality might be 'called' to professorships in institutions perceived to be more desirable than the ones from which they came. By the 1960s philosophers were more peripatetic. The common use of the jet plane made geographic locus less a consideration than it previously was. The California schools, for example, benefited from coast-to-coast air travel. Philosophers might also relocate because of climate or a promised lifestyle—in addition to schools in California, for example, those in Florida and Arizona were more sought after than they had previously been.

Suddenly the old hierarchical system in philosophy was modified by the intrusion of schools that previously would not have been imagined to be of the first rank. State universities themselves outside the Midwest and California—Florida, Texas, the State University of New York—now challenged wealthy Eastern institutions. For the first time in American history Southern colleges became prominent in philosophy—Virginia, Duke, the University of North Carolina. Sectarian institutions, which had refused the secular revolution and had been written off the map of higher education since the end of the nineteenth century, made a modest comeback as capable thinkers were attracted to such places as Calvin College of Michigan and Wheaton College of Illinois. More important, universities with a historic commitment to Roman Catholic teaching were at last recognized as part of the philosophical scene. For years, such schools pursued the study of medieval or Thomistic thought, and commented on pragmatic ideas as if from a foreign country; now Fordham, Catholic University, and Notre Dame succeeded in attracting noteworthy philosophers and placed their doctoral students in non-Catholic institutions.

In the 1960s and 1970s these structural changes accentuated three coincident struggles in philosophy itself. One concerned the fragmentation of analytic philosophy. A second concerned the challenge to analysts by assorted non-analytic philosophers. A third concerned the opposition of other disciplines to philosophy as the discipline that would 'do' philosophy. In the background to all these struggles—and sometimes in the foreground—were the political upheavals of the 1960s, precipitated by the drama of the civil rights movement, the war in Vietnam, and their cultural residue.

Analytic Philosophy Fragments

In the first intra-systematic confrontation with Harvard and the schools in its orbit, a number of institutions gathered together thinkers leaning to common research projects of high profile. The Massachusetts Institute of Technology, the University of California at Irvine, and New York University, for example, became distinctive centers of analytic philosophy that altered the old honorific network. In the work of Hilary Putnam, Cambridge developed its distinctive brand of pragmatic analysis, adding to the remarkable tradition that had begun with Peirce, but by the end of the century Harvard was not even the department *primus inter pares*.

Analysts versus Pluralists

Another and more serious sort of challenge came from institutions that promoted a different brand of philosophy entirely. In the 1960s analytic philosophers could not head off accusations of narrowness and irrelevance. The Vietnam era unleashed rage against all ruling orders.

In part the strength of the rebellion derived from the support of undergraduates. The leaders of the students who formed the armies that rocked the academy had, first of all, studied existentialism. Although they probably knew the novels of Sartre's one-time friend, Albert Camus, better than 'Existentialism is a Humanism', they certainly rejected the apolitical positivism, which they identified with conventional American philosophy. Sartre's issues of autonomy, responsibility, and integrity were just those of students defining their identities within the confines of family, peers, the adult world—and now the clamor about American racism, at home and abroad. The Port Huron Statement of 1962, credited with formulating the vision of the New Left, adopted an existentialist idiom in outlining its radical views.

The undergraduates had also come across Herbert Marcuse, who briefly made the Frankfurt School prominent in the United States. In 1964 he had written *One Dimensional Man* and in 1965 a crucial essay, 'Repressive Tolerance'. *One Dimensional Man* analyzed American life, and argued that the social system smothered dissent by making the satisfaction of material needs all-important and creating a capitalist juggernaut that supplied these needs. The American people were one-dimensional in having their lives reduced to consumerism and in embracing a culture devoid of creativity and choice. Commercialized society offered fake choices. Making a further moral distinction that found American capitalism wanting, Marcuse argued that the violence necessary to overthrow this system was more noble and acceptable than the violence state authorities used to maintain the system in power. 'Repressive Tolerance' claimed that the intellectual pluralism in the United States guaranteed the triumphs of the capitalists, because it downgraded claims of any social theory to be *the true* analysis of the poverty of spiritual life in America; tolerance of various opposing ideas assured the victory of conservative ones. Marcuse advocated *intolerance* of conservative ideas, and a climate of erudition that would stifle anti-revolutionary life. A left-wing scholarly dictatorship was necessary in the United States. Although Quine was a minor part of the critique, Marcuse excoriated Quine's writing as exemplary of the aridity of conventional philosophy, of its distance from significant social concern, and of its complicity in a 'manipulative-technological' system.

Marcuse's more philosophical prose was well-nigh unintelligible, and even his work of 1964 and 1965 was not easy reading. And Marcuse himself, at Brandeis and later in the 1960s when he left Brandeis for the University of California at San Diego, was hardly a zealous activist—he was 70 in 1968. But readers got the apocalyptic and romantically revolutionary side of the message, and suddenly he became the theoretician of the student left, not just in the United States but in Europe as well. In the late 1960s and early 1970s his books were academic best-sellers exploring 'the system' that undergraduates were rejecting. The phrase '*drugstorisation* of Marcuse' captured his celebrity status in France, and in the United States, too, he was a man of nationwide controversy. Indeed, Ronald Reagan, then governor of California, was involved in Marcuse's struggles in the system of higher education until after 1970, when the latter's contract was not renewed—he was 72. It was perhaps the greatest renown an American philosopher had achieved since Jonathan Edwards had led the Great Awakening almost 250 years before.

Analytic philosophers spoke to wider issues during this same period. A new magazine, *Philosophy and Public Affairs*, founded in 1969, signaled the efforts of some thinkers to escape the stereotypical view of the American philosopher as unconnected to philosophy's perennial interests. More important was the publication of John Rawls's *A Theory of Justice* in 1971.

Rawls taught at Cornell when he printed his pathbreaking essay, 'Justice as Fairness', in the *Philosophical Review* of 1958. He first presented his views as an examination of concepts embedded in the language and not as a 'normative' undertaking. The idea was to uncover what we would *call* justice, to reach 'a higher order of abstraction'. To unpack this concept Rawls conducted a thought experiment for his readers. He suggested that they imagine a group of rational intelligences founding a society; they could not be actual people for they had no idea in advance what role they themselves would play—young or old, rich or poor, male or female, white or black. This was 'the original position' in which creatures acted from 'a veil of ignorance'. The philosopher had to figure out what rules they would draw up. Rawls hoped to reveal that members of this putative society would behave so that a modicum of benefits might accrue to the least advantaged. A rational mind would always be open to the thought: under the veil of ignorance, I could be one of the least advantaged. Justice *meant* being fair.

By the time *A Theory of Justice* had fully outlined Rawls's ideas and made him famous for reinvigorating political philosophy, Harvard had attracted him, and he was associated not merely with the analytic philosophy practiced there, but also with the substantive commitments of political liberalism. A wide audience took up Rawls because his conclusions were consonant with a belief in compensatory justice that was a heritage of the 1960s. He gave an academic and non-Marxist imprimatur to egalitarian proposals acceptable on other grounds. Yet despite Rawls's influence as one of the prominent practical philosophers of the second half of the century, he also shared the disregard for the study of practices that were often supposed to dominate the naturalized epistemology of philosophy at Harvard. Rawls was uninterested in the history of political economy and the attempts of politicians in critical periods to build a just state. The American Founding Fathers of the 1780s, the French Revolutionaries of a decade later, and the Bolshevik leaders of the early twentieth century meant little to Rawls. To talk about justice, he created a scenario that could not possibly involve human beings; he was investigating rationality, not politics. Just as Quine had eschewed linguistics when he spoke of translation, so Rawls ignored the collective experience of attempts to construct a just society. In real life, ignorance of one's actual cultural locus—one's sex, age, social status, and race—would disqualify one from politics; Rawls made such ignorance the *sine qua non* of acceptable participation. Perhaps this conclusion intimated only that Harvard's pragmatic philosophers were still philosophers, who as a matter of practice preferred the conceptual to the empirical.

None the less, Rawls failed to satisfy the growing enemies of analytic philosophy. At the top of the hierarchy of the 'old' university system, even analysts who did moral and political philosophy found themselves derided. Proud of their rarefield intelligence and commitments to formalist research, they were attacked as much for their pride as for the substance of their work. By the end of the Vietnam War (1975) analysts were opposed by many scholars who were perhaps less intellectually gifted but who were convinced of the parochialism of analytic philosophy. These scholars commanded hiring at many colleges with no tradition of analytic philosophy— or indeed no tradition of philosophizing at all—but with resources that could make them viable trainers of graduate students and pleasant places of employment often on a par with more settled schools.

At first metaphysicians, the philosophers who had worried from the 1940s that scientific philosophy was insufficient, fought empiricists, who were the precursors to analytic philosophers. As the conflict escalated in the 1970s, commentators described it as that between the pluralists—a wider group including the older metaphysicians—and the analysts. As one commentator put it, the pluralists focused on 'immediate grievances, the general theme being the arrogance of the philosophical establishment'; while this establishment perceived the pluralists as 'second-rate philosophers who seek to gain politically what they have been denied on the basis of merit considerations'. Yale, now a bastion of *ressentiment*, and a few other older institutions linked to New Haven—Emory and Northwestern—led the attack on analytic philosophy. The dispute continued until the end of the century, and was reflected in hiring and tenure decisions; the biases of journals; and election to positions in the three divisions of the American Philosophical Association. The fight was made more complex by the struggle to attract faculty, which turned not just on doctrine and personality, as it had done when white males were the only figures in the academy, but also on sex, race, and sexual preference.

Pluralists did not merely resist analysis. They represented forces that prior to the 1960s had been minor competing voices in philosophy; social upheaval gave them an identity and common enemy. The metaphysicians formed the base of opposition, but more important were expounders of what came to be called Continental Philosophy, which along with metaphysics found a headquarters at Yale. Continental speculation represented the maturation of the impulse that had claimed Sartre for an American audience after World War II. Its adherents focused on scholarly studies of Husserl and Heidegger, and wrote academic treatises about topics that these thinkers had made popular. Americans also commented on more recent French and German thought, but none of them emerged as independent interpreters of this tradition as had, say, the Europeans Hans Georg Gadamer and Jurgen Habermas.

Unremarked upon was the remarkable impact not of Continental Europe, but of Catholic Europe. The existential tradition in Sartre had been atheistic, but many of his European peers were struggling to find a basis for faith as intellectual Christianity declined. In the United States Continental Philosophy often had a religious blush: only a commitment to the spiritual could save us from life-denying science, logic, and analysis. Roman Catholic institutions of higher learning, or strategically placed Catholic believers at non-Catholic institutions, innovatively attacked the secularism of analytic philosophy.

In addition to Continental philosophers, feminist, Marxist, and African-American thinkers, among others, swelled the ranks of the pluralists, arguing that color, class, and gender determined certain aspects of the supposed neutral study of epistemology. Examining the cultural stance of the knower challenged the standard claims of the theory of knowledge. Finally, the pluralists ushered in a revival of interest in classic American philosophy. According to them the tradition of thought that had seemingly ended with Dewey and extended back to Peirce, James, and Royce—and on some accounts to Ralph Waldo Emerson—was far more concerned with the world beyond the academy than was analysis, and had a far less provincial conception of philosophy. Professors who evaluated the canon of American thought believed that analytic philosophy had betrayed the tradition from which it sprang and also leagued themselves on the side of the pluralists.

One long-term publishing venture reflected this state of affairs. The series *Library of Living Philosophers* was the lifetime publishing project of Paul A. Schilpp, a professor of philosophy at Southern Illinois University. In the late 1930s Schilpp determined to honor great thinkers while they were still alive, and contracted with them and with many critics to produce a bibliography of writings; an autobiography; a collection of essays; and a response to them by the philosopher who was selected for this particular canon. The orientation was not American but displayed rather the way Schilpp saw the philosophic world refracted in the United States. He began with John Dewey (1939); George Santayana (1940), who had left the United States permanently in 1912; and Alfred North Whitehead (1941).

Over the next sixty years Schilpp and his successor from 1981, Lewis Hahn, produced handsome volumes commemorating the living ideas of some thirty thinkers. Schilpp and Hahn had a changing board of editors who chose the philosophers and made selections that represented the competing factions in American philosophy and the European resources on which they drew. Thus, *The Library of Living Philosophers* printed volumes on Carnap, Lewis, Quine, and Donald Davidson; and their interlocutors G. E. Moore, Ayer, and P. F. Strawson; but also on Hartshorne, Weiss, and Marjorie Grene; and their interlocutors Sartre, Gadamer, and Paul Ricœur, among many others. The different volumes of the *Library of Living Philosophers* were produced in different universities, and demonstrated that in the United States there were many non-overlapping professional conversations.

The APA abetted the chaos. In 1994 its Board of Officers denounced all attempts at ranking departments of philosophy. On the one hand, the APA conceded that departmental esteem and reputation were not 'utterly undeserved'. On the other hand, in reasoning that imbibed the relativism of the 1960s and obvious disagreements on what constituted quality, the organization questioned the 'justice' of 'impressions' of esteem and reputation. The APA argued that no polling of philosophers could generate a reasonable ranking; that quantitative measures based on survey data were untrustworthy; and that the very idea of rankings might be 'fundamentally unreliable'. All this flew in the face of the fact that everyone knew that some departments were better than others, and that national rankings, while always contestable, did accurately portray the academic landscape. In officially throwing out rankings, the APA was throwing up its hands at the disorder in its own house. If it could not advise students where to look for philosophical instruction, who could?

A flood of books by philosophers ruminated on the crisis in the profession and proposed various nostrums for revitalizing American thought. Two of these books illustrated the split. In *Post-Analytic Philosophy* (1985) the editors selected essays by thirteen thinkers who, they suggested, might take analytic philosophy into greener pastures. The institutions represented by these philosophers were: Berkeley; Columbia; Harvard (4); Massachusetts Institute of Technology; New School for Social Research; New York University; Princeton; Stanford (2); and Yale. Another volume, *Portraits of American Continental Philosophers* (1999) contained autobiographical statements of twenty-two thinkers. Institutions: Boston College (2); DePaul; Duquesne; Empire State College; Emory; George Mason; Georgetown; Hunter College; Northwestern; Penn State University (4); Purdue; Rice; State University of New York, Stony Brook (2); University of California at Riverside; University of Memphis; University of Texas, Austin; and Villanova.

'Theory' Outside Philosophy

A third and final challenge to philosophy complicated the intra-professional fights. In the first half of the twentieth century American philosophers had lived off the social capital created by the thinkers at Harvard on the one hand, and Dewey at Chicago and Columbia on the other. These men had positioned philosophy as a central scholarly discipline: it spoke to educated disquiet about the human condition and provided, to other disciplines, expert counsel on how investigation might be carried out, or on the methods requisite for obtaining warranted belief. Philosophers in the 1940s and 1950s effectively purveyed versions of positivism and instrumentalism as the premises out of which legitimate enquiry grew.

In the second half of the century, the APA asserted officially that philosophy was of constant use to realize wisdom and had incalculable benefits for the public life of citizens, but for its 100th anniversary in 2001 it appointed a committee 'to plan activities to raise the visibility of philosophy'. But analytic philosophers did not aspire to be public figures, and were content with successful professional lives. Their lack of aspiration was consonant with the general view, made a point of contention by the logical empiricists, that matters of morals and politics were not anyway in the cognitive domain. Thus, philosophers began to write themselves out of subsidiary careers as what would become known as 'public intellectuals'. As Quine put it in a striking piece in *Newsday* in 1979, the student who 'major[ed] in philosophy primarily for spiritual consolation is misguided and is probably not a very good student'; philosophy did not offer wisdom, nor did philosophers 'have any peculiar fitness for helping . . . society'.

By the 1960s the problems of analytic philosophy had grown enormously complicated and their application to other disciplines uncertain. The willingness of practitioners to speak to non-philosophers also declined— philosophers disdained much of the rest of the academy and had little interest in what other practitioners wanted. This was true for both analytic philosophers and their opponents. While analytic philosophy was unintelligible to many because of its often forbidding use of mathematical symbolism, non-analytic philosophy was not known for its clarity; Heidegger was as incomprehensible as Sellars. Except for the public standing of Marcuse, notable non-analytic philosophers sank into the same relative obscurity as, say, Ernest Nagel and Nelson Goodman. A comprehensive survey by the American Philosophical Association in the mid-1990s showed that 40 per cent of all schools of higher education did not teach courses in either twentieth-century analytic *or* Continental philosophy, and another 40 per cent offered such courses only every two years or 'occasionally'. The demand for such courses I would best estimate as 'low moderate'. The report by the 'Committee on the Status and Future of the Profession' ranked twentieth-century analytic philosophy as one of two courses whose demand was reported as 'low' by at least 30 per cent of responding departments. The other such course was medieval philosophy. But the preparer of this report was identified with the pluralists and, in truth, their flagship courses did not fare much better. Philosophy departments at the end of the century were isolated, with few scholars knowing or caring what they were doing, let alone educated people outside the academy.

In these circumstances scholars in other fields philosophized for themselves, doing philosophy out of whole cloth, or teaching themselves in philosophy. The result was that, certainly in the harder social sciences, positions were retained for theorists or methodologists who may or may not have had any philosophical training, but were 'the philosophers' in these departments. Similar roles were found for people in departments of history, other humanities departments such as religion, and in the softer social sciences such as anthropology. While the ideas expounded in these disciplines varied, one striking consequence could be found in departments of political science, sociology, and economics: long after even the most committed of scientific philosophers rejected logical empiricism, this philosophy gained a new lease of life when defended by scholars in other disciplines.

Another development of this sort was the invention of 'applied philosophy'. Professional schools of business, law, and medicine favored courses in 'business ethics', 'legal ethics', or 'medical ethics', and budding professionals in those areas, which often grew their own expert faculty who were not professional philosophers, taught them. The philosophers themselves were confused. Sometimes they refused to have anything to do with the interlopers, but just as frequently—lured by the prospect of increasing enrollments—philosophers of 'meta-ethics' tried to dominate these courses while distancing themselves from the tainted practicality of the professional schools.

By the 1980s departments of English were doing the most significant philosophy outside philosophy departments. English department philosophers took up any one of a number of versions of cultural relativism, or the relativism of meaning and interpretations more generally, often connected to the pragmatists. By the 1990s, when academics thought of acquainting themselves with 'theory', they turned to departments of literature. These departments often looked to Europe for inspiration and sometimes found allies in American Continental philosophers. But the latter group differed from the literary theorists who sought guidance from more contemporary

French thinkers, for example Michel Foucault and Jacques Derrida, and who themselves became part of a tradition outside the discipline of philosophy. Edward Said of Columbia; Frederic Jameson of Duke; and 'the Yale Critics', Harold Bloom, Paul DeMan, Geoffrey Hartman, and J. Hillis Miller, were not merely scholarly commentators on a European tradition, but themselves figures in that tradition. They were more valued than American Continental philosophers.

In 2000 the *Concise Routledge Encyclopedia of Philosophy* announced that it had contributions from more than 1,200 of the world's contemporary leading thinkers. Who was one to believe? To whom should one listen? Was Richard McKeon 'one of the most profound and brilliant philosophers of the twentieth century'? Were Paul and Patricia Churchland 'towering figures' in philosophy? Was Hector-Neri Castaneda 'one of the most important philosophers of the late-twentieth century'? Was Edward Said 'among the truly important intellects of our century?' Was John Kekes's *Against Liberalism* a book that 'deserves a place on the same shelf with Burke, Tocqueville, and Hayek'? The historian sorting through hard questions about the quality of thought that plague the history of philosophy had an impossible time. Analytic philosophy itself had split. But pursued by talented if abstract thinkers, it had to be judged not only by whatever common standards it had but by the standards of many antagonists who might be intellectually less prepossessing and might disagree among themselves but who accurately saw a lack of breadth in analytic philosophy. Quine himself wrote that it was hard to separate philosophers into 'sages and cranks' and that philosophical writing was often 'incompetent'.

In grasping these issues, I have discerned the wide influence, in all the competing camps, of the new philosophy of science of Thomas Kuhn; and a consensus on materialism that prompted the work of Richard Rorty.

Thomas Kuhn

Harvard had educated Kuhn as a physicist in the 1940s, but Quine in the Philosophy Department had also influenced him. After Kuhn taught in the sciences in Cambridge, Berkeley recruited him in 1956 where he held a joint appointment in philosophy and history. In 1957 he published a book on astronomy, *The Copernican Revolution*, which, along with other writing, exhibited the blend of philosophy and history that he brought to his work on scientific thought. In 1961 Ernest Nagel published his masterwork *The Structure of Science*. Carl Hempel's collection of his most formidable essays, *Aspects of Scientific Explanation*, followed in 1965. Kuhn's second book, *The Structure of Scientific Revolutions*, a slim volume published in 1962, was thus sandwiched between what later appeared to be two positivist dinosaurs. It was the most influential philosophical volume of the last third of the century, and Kuhn himself became, as one historian put it, 'one of the most widely discussed academic intellectuals of the century'.

Focusing on the actual practice of science, the book depicted how two kinds of changes occurred in scientific belief, that which was part of 'normal' research and that which developed when a 'scientific revolution' took place. Normal scientific research progressed within a paradigm, or disciplinary matrix. A paradigm defined a scientific community and had three elements. The first were symbolic generalizations—the laws, theories, and definitions to which the scientists were committed. The classic example of this aspect of a paradigm were the three laws of motion and the conceptualizations dependent upon them that Newton propounded at the end of the seventeenth century. Indeed, for Kuhn, symbolic generalizations were tied to a specific achievement, like Newtonian mechanics, that made them convincing in a specific era. The second element Kuhn termed models— large-scale beliefs about the universe, analogies, and heuristic maxims. The faith of the nineteenth century that all change was continuous and a mixture of historical and logical factors, and the belief that the structure of the atom was like the solar system were both exemplary models. Lastly Kuhn spoke of exemplars, shared problem experiences or standard initiations, for example the high-school test for oxygen that heated potassium chlorate in the presence of the catalyst manganese dioxide. Scientists had performed this experiment so often that it was almost inconceivable that it should go wrong, and they learned nothing from it. Rather, its function was ritualistic: it socialized students to correct procedure and a common conception of how to do laboratory work.

The science done within such a tripartite disciplinary matrix was directed toward classes of problems significant in its terms; the work also assumed as a basis for further research the prior results obtained by practitioners within the paradigm. Such normal research, the first kind of scientific change, elaborated, applied, or tested this way of seeing the physical world.

In contradistinction to this 'progress', Kuhn analyzed a 'scientific revolution'. A revolution occurred when scientists perceived anomalies still unsolved by normal research not as inadequately explained puzzles or yet-to-be-understood phenomena, but as counter-examples calling into question the paradigm itself. When scientists viewed anomalies in this way, Kuhn argued, a crisis took place in normal science. Out of such a crisis, a new paradigm might arise, one in which a novel set of concepts defined different problems. In fact, from his own studies of science Kuhn asserted that different paradigms implied different views of the world. Dramatic 'paradigm shifts'—such as Einstein's replacement of Newtonian physics—involved progress that was not in any simple sense cumulative. A new theory displaced an old one; it did not simply build upon it. The old and new paradigms were incomparable as well as incompatible.

Kuhn gave the anti-positivist elements in Quine a practical illustration. Quine's 'holism' and indeterminacy theses had intimated that alternative conceptual frameworks could equally well account for the data of experience. Now Kuhn said that this was true of succeeding scientific paradigms. He favorably contrasted a thick analysis of scientific practice to the abstract scientific studies of Hempel and Nagel. Philosophers of science were encouraged to look at what was actually going on, rather than to impose some logical scheme on the messy reality of human behavior.

Although Kuhn's work was paradigm-shattering, its style was common in the 1960s. The iconoclastic thinker Paul Feyerabend echoed many of Kuhn's views at the time, and the same sort of reasoning can be found in such works as Norwood Russell Hanson's *Patterns of Discovery* and Michael Polanyi's *Personal Knowledge* of 1958; Peter Berger and Thomas Luckmann's book of 1966, *The Social Construction of Reality*; and Clifford Geertz's *Interpretation of Cultures* of 1973. Their popularity through the 1960s and beyond must, I think, be attributed in part to the same fevered social scene in the United States in which Sartre and Marcuse flourished. The 1960s not only put the positivists at risk but also valorized romantic and subjective views. Many philosophers who knew little about the hard sciences, including the burgeoning American Continental philosophers, found comfort in Kuhn's willingness to dislodge science from its privileged claim to objectivity. Religious thinkers also relished Kuhn's attack, since if science was an acceptable belief system even if it did not progress, theological paradigms might come back; and social scientists rallied around Kuhn by explaining that they *would become* scientific by adopting a paradigm in their own fields.

The Structure of Scientific Revolutions was really remarkable in its caution. At the end of the book, a chapter entitled 'Progress Through Revolutions' seemed to argue that the 'evolution' of science ruled out 'progress toward truth'. But Kuhn used evolution in a way different from its use in the biological world, where a vast proliferation of life-forms existed. One might analogize this sort of evolution to the development of theology where, for example as we have witnessed in America in the nineteenth century, competing schools of thought grew up, each with its own paradigm. Scientific evolution was different. As Quine put it, science developed 'a manageably narrow spectrum of visible alternatives' and a 'narrowing of sights'; it had a 'tunnel vision'.

Although Quine viewed Kuhn as a 'relativist' enemy rather than as a follower in his footsteps, Kuhn echoed Quine's view of scientific evolution and said that paradigm change 'invariably produce[d] an instrument more perfect in any sense than those known before'. None the less, progress did not move us closer to the real and instead consisted of growth in the number of problems solved by successive scientific communities and the precision of individual problem-solutions. Such a view underscored the 'very special communities from which scientific production' came and 'the wonderfully adapted set of instruments we call modern scientific knowledge'. The scientific enterprise was precious to Kuhn, and the 'tenuousness of humanity's hold' on it was apparent to him. But he could not say what nature, including humanity, had to be like in order that science be possible. For Kuhn the positivist view of the progress of knowledge might be wrong, but various 'relativistic' alternatives that sprang up after the publication of *The Structure of Scientific Revolutions* might not be right.

In 1960–1, when Kuhn was putting the finishing touches to *The Structure of Scientific Revolutions*, Berkeley took up his elevation to a full professorship. Influenced by positivism, the senior philosophers there agreed to Kuhn's promotion only if it were made in the History Department. Although the philosophers did not inform Kuhn, they argued that he had few pretensions to being a philosopher, and that his history of science had little connection to philosophy. The History Department at Berkeley embraced Kuhn, but two years after what was termed his 'eviction' from Philosophy, and a year after the publication of 'the book', he left for a position in the History of Science at Princeton. The Berkeley decision— arguably the worst in the American academy in the twentieth century— underscored the constipated arrogance of analytic philosophy, and its suspicion of practice.

'Analytic Metaphysics'

The second set of developments meriting consideration concerned a central field of analytic philosophy that comprised the overlap of work in the philosophy of mind, the philosophy of science, and the philosophy of language, and that reached out even to certain areas of linguistics, physiological psychology, evolutionary biology, and the novel discipline of Cognitive Science. This set of developments was indebted to Sellars and Quine and found an extreme representative in Richard Rorty.

For Lewis and to a lesser extent the positivists, epistemology distanced itself from metaphysical commitment, in part because metaphysics had become identified with the 'excesses' of absolute idealism. For some time

Sellars' courting of materialism was a minority position. As the pragmatism of Quine replaced that of Lewis, however, the sense of options changed. For many thinkers Quine's arguments for the inscrutability, or indeterminacy, of reference, made epistemology impossible and skepticism unavoidable. In the 1960s, however, two sorts of criticisms were made against Quine's complaints about reference.

Noam Chomsky had been a student of Goodman's at Pennsylvania, and had worked with Quine as a fellow at Harvard before going on to a professorship in linguistics at the Massachusetts Institute of Technology. Contra Quine, Chomsky argued that linguistic ability was innate and reflected the deep structure of the mind, an a priori conceptual framework. Chomsky's book of 1957, *Syntactic Structures*, was at first limited in its influence to the separate but related discipline of linguistics, but by the 1960s he had located himself in the rationalist philosophical tradition, referring to his views as 'Cartesian linguistics'. He countered Quine's argument that the mind could be reduced to verbal behavior, and his work easily allowed the inference that referring was a respectable but as yet unexplained connection between mind and a world beyond it.

The second set of claims made against Quine had their own contested history. His studies in logical theory had led to the triumph of the views of Russell and Whitehead in the *Principia Mathematica* over the attempt by Lewis and others to make modal notions of impossibility and necessity integral to logic. After Quine's work, Lewis's ideas did not occupy center stage among logicians, although Lewis certainly had supporters. One of them was Ruth Barcan Marcus, a formidable thinker who challenged Quine and who struggled for years in a field dominated by men, rising at last to a chaired professorship at Yale in the 1970s.

In her critique of Quine, Marcus was joined by Saul Kripke, a peculiar man who had been educated at Harvard and Oxford, and had begun writing in modal logic as a teenager in 1959, long before he went on to the McCosh Professorship at Princeton. For over thirty years, however, allies of Marcus and Kripke, respectively, had disputed over which of them had devised a lethal attack against Quine. A memorable meeting of the Boston Colloquium for the Philosophy of Science in February, 1962, had pitted Quine, as a commentator, against Marcus, assisted by remarks from a twenty-two year old Kripke in the audience. Over thirty years later, in an acrimonious meeting of the APA in 1994, philosophers were still bickering over whether what became known as 'the new theory of reference' had originated in Marcus or Kripke.

According to 'the new theory', proper names picked out their referents directly and independently of any descriptions that might be associated with them. A primal dubbing of an object grounded the use of names by speakers, and a causal chain running back to the initial tagging sustained the subsequent use. In this analysis the notion of intending to refer was taken as a given in starting the chain and in keeping it going. It was thought to follow that certain properties were essential to a person or thing; reference was something that occurred in experience but also could be said to be necessarily true—things with essences were out there for us to find. Philosophers took these ideas in many directions, and Kripke's work proved to be especially rich. In time, the new theory and Chomsky's philosophy of language assisted thinkers in combating the skepticism inferred from Quine's arguments in 1960 for inscrutability. Although neither Chomsky nor Kripke and Marcus could be associated with Sellars' project, a new respect for his materialistic metaphysics grew up, and for projects similar to his in giving a positive account of the relation of the materialistic world to its offspring, the knowing mind.

By the end of the twentieth century most thinkers in this field were materialists or, as they called themselves, 'physicalists'. They explored how the nature of the mind as we ordinarily thought of it could be reconciled with a materialist view of the world and with what science told us of neuro-physiology. Of special importance was the connection of mind to the organisms in the natural world. But of equal importance was the connection of mind to physics, usually regarded as the paradigmatic study of the way the world 'really' was. Overall, physicalists were defending a version of the claim of both Sellarses but one that now was more consensual: these thinkers placed human beings in the natural world as biological creatures; they accepted physics as our best knowledge of the way the world was; they asked, first, what was the exact connection of the mental to its material environment; and then how various aspects of this environment that we studied were related to physics.

Many positions were staked out. Eliminative materialists argued that there was no such thing as the mental, and that our 'folk psychology' would just have to be replaced by a more adequate scientific view. Reductive materialists gave a certain reality to the mental but urged that it could be reduced to the physical. Non-reductive materialists struggled to make coherent more subtle points. Functionalists postulated that mental states were intermediary between stimuli and behavior. Other non-reductive materialists said that the mental emerged or derived from the physical but did so in a strong sense of 'emerge' and a weak sense of 'derive'. These philosophers brought back into circulation the technical term 'supervenience' to assert that the mental necessarily co-varied with the material in a way that was dependent on the material but not deducible from it. Most of these thinkers could be described not just as physicalists but as traditional realists: an external world existed, and one task was to show how it became known.

Another connected position was called 'internal realism', and opposed itself to what it took to be the traditional aims of other physicalists. The most outstanding representative of this outlook in the late 1970s was the influential thinker Hilary Putnam, who was educated at Pennsylvania and the University of California at Los Angeles, where he did a doctorate with Hans Reichenbach, and taught at Northwestern, Princeton, and the Massachusetts Institute of Technology before taking a position at Harvard in 1965. With wide interests and high self-regard, Putnam shifted his ideas many times throughout a long career, but his argumentative powers were such as always to carry thinkers of merit along with him.

Putnam urged that traditional 'external' realism presupposed that a description might be true of the world irrespective of any point of view. But this supposition was incoherent, for to assert that some truth is true irrespective of viewpoint is to adopt a perspective from which the truth is asserted; otherwise the position cannot be intelligently proposed. In other words, Putnam said, truths were only true *'within* a theory of description', only as *'represented in our belief system'*. In order to make claims about the world, we had to adopt a conceptual system, and once we did this there was a correspondence between the world and truths about it, but the realism was internal to our selection of a conceptual framework: we were able to refer because in adopting a conceptual framework—in deciding how to organize sense inputs—we established the preconditions for reference. The intentionality of reference was compatible with 'internal' but not external realism.

Putnam did not deny that there were experiential inputs to knowledge; we also had, he said, causal interactions with the objects in our world. Moreover, although 'a certain pluralism' was opened up in selecting frameworks, some frameworks were better than others; it was just that our concepts to some extent shaped all inputs. Putnam considered himself to be writing as a Kantian, at least as Putnam interpreted Kant. There was some mind-independent reality but it functioned like Kant's noumenal world, which was a *Grenz-Begriff*, a limiting concept lacking clarity. But Putnam also apparently placed us as biological creatures in a physical world.

Enter Rorty

Rorty did an undergraduate degree at Chicago, and his doctorate at Yale with Paul Weiss in 1956, early on hearing complaints about analytic philosophy. Rorty none the less began his professional life as an analyst influenced by Wilfrid Sellars and even more by Quine, though Rorty became one of only a few prominent figures without a Harvard connection. In 1967, at the beginning of the twenty years he spent in the Princeton Department of Philosophy, he edited, with a skillful introduction, *The Linguistic Turn*, an anthology of analytic philosophy emphasizing the philosophy of language. Rorty was deeply knowledgeable about this movement, believing that its achievements were 'sufficient to place . . . [it] among the great ages of the history of philosophy'. At the same time, however, he had initiated an argument that came to fruition in a book ten years in the making, *Philosophy and the Mirror of Nature* (1979), and that would, in effect, attempt to hoist analytic philosophy on its own petard.

More than most analysts, Rorty was interested in the history of philosophy and, even more, in philosophy's diminished role in post-war culture. *Philosophy and the Mirror of Nature* learnedly situated analytic philosophy in what Rorty called the epistemological project that had engaged philosophers since Kant. For Rorty the thrust of analysis had been to ground knowledge, usually to justify the labors of science and distinguish it from other endeavors that were less rational, more subjective. In this respect, he intimated, philosophers had assumed the mantle that theologians in the United States had only recently given up—of guardians of that which made humanity special. But because of its technical virtuosity, which Rorty both exhibited and lamented, philosophy in its university setting had often lost its audience.

More important, analytic philosophy had failed in its mission. Looking at the main positions, which we have just explored, Rorty seemed to adopt the view of a layperson who might ridicule philosophical experts unable to agree on how many angels could dance on the head of a pin: what was the point of all the ceaseless argument? Would it ever be possible to decide which physicalist position was correct? Rorty was unequaled in the journals in seeking out weaknesses in the various constructive programs of his peers. *Philosophy and the Mirror of Nature* concentrated on the work of Sellars and Quine to indict the very idea of analytic philosophy. According to Rorty it needed one of two distinctions to get off the ground. The distinction between empirical and conceptual truth was crucial to the scientism of the positivists, but when Quine urged that it was illegitimate, we were led to a vision of alternative conceptual schemes and the views of Kuhn. None the less, Quine defended a scientific philosophy by sometimes maintaining the other critical distinction, between what was given—Quine's 'raw fragments of experience', 'the flux of experience'—and what was interpreted. But, said Rorty, in attacking the given Sellars had demolished this distinction, and without it Quine and other late twentieth-century naturalists had no defense against the true consequences of Quinean argumentation. Indeed, Rorty urged that we could not truly honor the scientific community, as had Quine and Kuhn; it was no more or less exceptional than other communities that told us how to negotiate the world. Accepting Sellars' view that knowledge was linguistic, Rorty said that essential to human life was a series of sometimes competing, sometimes co-operative dialogues, that enabled human beings to cope more or less effectively with the problems and troubles of existence. But it was illegitimate to speak of any statements as being true about the world or to give pride of place to the scientific community; to puzzle about justifying our beliefs was the wrong worry.

Rorty could not quite assert his conclusions. In a much-cited essay, 'The World Well Lost', he dismissed the notion that we could talk of a primary physical world at all. The critical philosopher, he wrote elsewhere, had to take Sellars' view of knowledge as linguistic and 'strip' it of the 'accidental accretion' that it was fundamentally knowledge of the world of physics. Yet Rorty regularly allowed later in asides that he was a materialist; that mind was no more than behavior—a version of 'eliminative materialism'; and that everything fell into a causal nexus about which science was our only guide. In a book of 1989, *Contingency, Irony, and Solidarity*, Rorty said, 'with common sense', that 'most things in space and time are the effects of causes which do not include human mental states'; he held 'a bleakly mechanical description of the relation between human beings and the rest of the universe'. At the end of the twentieth century Rorty argued that Darwin's *Origins of Species* was 'the most troubling' book of the second millennium. Human beings would probably take another 1,000 years 'to give up the last remnants of the idea that they contain a spark of the divine'. A 'thorough-going secularism' meant that we had to abandon all hope of 'getting in touch with something safer and more stable than the wobbly and endangered human community'. Like Roy Wood and Wilfrid Sellars, Rorty, finally, said he was an atheist.

Classic pragmatism was a transitional set of commitments leading away from a religious view of the universe to a secular one. Indeed, even Quine, *qua* pragmatist, was more ambivalent about the truth of materialism than were philosophers like Sellars and Rorty. In long perspective, they did not have the religious hue that can be found in even the pragmatic analysis of Lewis and Quine. Rorty's materialistic claims, however, were just true and not to be defended by philosophy. There was, it seemed, the world, which—like the *Ding an sich*—we could barely talk about but always pre-supposed, as had Putnam. Rorty agreed with Wilfrid Sellars that a causal connection existed between this world and sensory appearance. But Rorty did not think this naturalism was compatible with Sellars' view that we could explain how knowledge was possible; or rather Rorty dissented from Sellars' position that there was anything extraordinary about the scientific language employed to tell us about the world. Various descriptions of the world existed or, better, various conversations could be judged by their efficacy in meeting certain limited human aims. Yet, it seemed, none of these conversations could justifiably assert that Rorty's bleak, Darwinian, godless world was the real one, although Rorty sometimes made this asser-tion. He did not address the concern implicit in Sellars: that if we could not show that the language of science had a special status, no language could make sense. Rorty seemed to think that our biological condition only made conversation about truth illegitimate, but the larger question was whether we could talk sense at all if we were just animals. Rorty later intimated this himself: the role of philosophy might just consist in promoting the hope that it was worthwhile to keep conversing.

Philosophy after Dewey seemed *both* increasingly secular *and* increas-ingly relativistic—at least if one asked its leadership. Lewis propounded alternative conceptual schemes yet perceived a disgraceful retreat from objectivity in Quine and Goodman. But Quine, with his 'ontological rela-tivity', also thought himself a scientific materialist and Kuhn a cultural relativist. Rorty too was a materialist, and could not understand why Kuhn, who knew Rorty at Princeton, thought him a subjectivist.

Rorty argued that the palaver of the scientists, overall, was acceptable just because it was accepted and uncontested. Philosophy could not fortify this palaver, nor show that it had any greater justifiability than it appeared to have. Instead, philosophers should admit they were involved not with a quest for truth but with an examination of discourses and vocabularies; and thinkers would be more illuminating if they attended to those conversa-tions of a moral and literary sort that had more surprises and—in Kuhnian terms—more revolutionary and abnormal turns in them than what we saw in the 'normal' community of natural scientists. Philosophers had to give up their self-image of assisting various people of knowledge to legitimate their endeavors, just as they earlier had had to give up their claim to be the last-ditch defenders of religion. Instead the philosopher, said Rorty, must think of himself as an 'informed dilettante' who fashioned a 'hermeneutic' salon to facilitate or mediate different 'discourses'.

Rorty desired to give philosophy a new high-profile intellectual role after analysis had forfeited such a role. He was very much like the nineteenth-century theologian Horace Bushnell. Focusing on language, Bushnell had lambasted his professional discipline for over-technicality, for splintering into sects and losing its audience and calling. But, like Rorty 150 years later,

Bushnell's critique of his field went hand in hand with an urge to recon-struct it, and to give himself a status as a significant social commentator.

The great bulk of *Philosophy and the Mirror of Nature* was analytic philos-ophy, though the book's end delineated his new philosophy of 'edification' that relied on the thinking of Continental philosophers, most notably Sartre. In his own less dramatic way, using the resources of Anglo-American thought, Rorty was articulating existentialist ideas. In a world bereft of meaning, human beings had to make themselves, and they did so through their conversational gambits, which allowed them to shape whatever purposes they had. In the United States Rorty melded the scientific, anti-religious views of European positivists, on the one hand, and ruminations about human life characteristics of *Existenz* philosophy, on the other. In a compromising American style Rorty had brought together the antitheses so striking in twentieth-century European philosophies that had come to these shores.

Philosophy and the Mirror of Nature cited Dewey as one of his 'heroes', and Rorty's interest in him increased in the 1980s and 1990s, as did his interest in Continental thinkers other than Sartre. Some analytic philoso-phers thought the resulting combination of pragmatism and materialism obviously contradictory, and were infuriated by Rorty's perceived lack of seriousness in confronting the contradiction. But a part of the analytic community responded positively to Rorty's well-grounded critique of it, and Continental philosophers, although dismayed at his interpretation of several members of their tradition, grudgingly acknowledged his serious concern for people such as Heidegger. When classic American pragmatism was honorifically reassessed in the 1980s and 1990s—partly through Rorty's efforts—other pluralists who specialized in the history of American thought recognized his contribution to their historical work. They too suspected his interpretations—especially of a Dewey whose biggest mistake was a taste for reform based on social science—but anointed Rorty as the latest thinker in this American tradition—now writ large as Peirce, James, Dewey, and Rorty. His ability to bring so many philosophers into his own conversational development contributed to his striking influence among those intellectuals who denominated themselves theorists, whether or not in the discipline of philosophy. The secret to Rorty's appeal was the respect he received from some members of all the warring factions.

In the 1990s Rorty focused on literary criticism as the discipline best able to enlighten us about the different ways it was possible to be human, and so to expand our tolerance for diversity and our compassion for others con-ceived as different. The interest in literary studies was of a piece with the large role that an almost passive aestheticism had played in Rorty's outlook.

For him the literary critic had replaced the philosopher in 'the conversation of the west', and so explained why philosophy had almost lost out in the academy to English departments. The core area in which to look for wisdom was literature—'plays, poems, and, especially, novels'. To foster this interest, Rorty first supported pluralist efforts within the American Philosophical Association, but eventually, like Kuhn, gave up on the discipline of philosophy. His ideas had carried his fame beyond that profession. He left Princeton's department in 1982 for a position in the Humanities at Virginia, and, in 1998, for one in Comparative Literature at Stanford.

At the same time, now in his late sixties, like many American philosophers before him, Rorty could not resist examining public affairs, an area he had always made secondary to the private worlds of individuals that, he believed, literature explored. Responding to critiques of those who saw him as an apolitical professorial élitist, he adopted the commitments of a public intellectual and set aside the indifference of the spectator residing in a Darwinian universe. His ruminations appeared in *Achieving Our Country* (1998).

This slim, large-print volume, written in seven months to a year, applied Rorty's ideas to politics, with which he was familiar as a child of leftist intellectuals in the 1930s and 1940s. Taking up the patriotic themes of Royce's *Philosophy of Loyalty*, Rorty despaired that the left since the 1960s had focused on cultural issues rather than the social and economic priorities of his youth. He urged that we recall to mind the activists of that earlier era: 'we'—by which he meant left-liberals in the humanities and the softer social sciences—had to reinvent the radical political language of the first part of the twentieth century; we had to redescribe our current notions by reinvigorating older and more forceful ideas. Such a reconstrual would allow these intellectuals more appropriately to appreciate the United States and to guide them to views that Rorty believed were more efficacious.

Rorty's effort was much criticized, and he later apologized for his 'amateurish' ignorance. His loosely written exhortations contrasted with the careful reasoning of his earlier essays and with *Philosophy and the Mirror of Nature*. The didactic and simplistic account of the politics of the twentieth century bore little resemblance to what knowledgeable scholars believed, reflecting more his early memories and nostalgia, which he incorporated into the text of *Achieving Our Country*, than a grasp of American politics or history.

The Poverty of Applied Philosophy

Peirce had no political or social philosophy, and neither did William James. That of Royce, as I have suggested, was insubstantial. Dewey's sensitivity to political and social issues was different and more credible, and displayed the Hegelian deposit in his thinking. None the less, Dewey's great strength was his active commitment in national and international politics. He did not turn his scholarly attention to politics until he was in his seventies when he wrote a series of brief books in the 1930s, but they did not match the expositions of instrumentalism of the 1920s, or his bigger book of the 1930s. The only one of his political books that received attention, the earliest of 1927, *The Public and Its Problems*, was often cited as an example of a floundering Dewey.

In the 1950s C. I. Lewis continued the Harvard tradition. In his retirement, he berated his philosophic peers for offering up emotivism in ethics when, as Lewis thought, 'the moral core of Western civilization falls under the most severe challenge it has ever had to meet'. Worried about the evils of Joseph Stalin's Soviet Union and the mean and widespread anti-communism of Joseph McCarthy, Republican senator from Wisconsin, Lewis still had little to offer: he had spent his life doing logic and epistemology, and was ill prepared to think about public issues. Quine and Goodman (and Sellars) had the good sense not to speak out on an American culture about which they knew little. One remarkable exception who tested the generalization was Noam Chomsky. The 1960s galvanized him to attack the imperial order he saw at work in the United States. Beginning with a striking and widely noted essay in 1967, 'The Responsibility of Intellectuals', Chomsky wrote, along with his studies of theoretical linguistics, political and historical works, which denounced the American security state for over thirty years.

Like Chomsky, Rorty was idiosyncratic as an American philosopher in being self-consciously on the left, but more conventional in his failure in the political realm. His expository style had had a long career in American pragmatism, disappointing only to those who wished philosophers to have something to say about the world. Why would someone who spent most of his career cogitating over Quine, Sellars, and Heidegger, and who wrote on social and political life as if it derived from this cogitation, be able to speak about this life? No matter what philosophy claimed about the importance of practices, it remained an enterprise that favored not the lived world but the seminar room, yet still assumed that the latter could tell us of the former.

Conclusion

Over a 300-year period American philosophy was distinctive in being touched by national historical developments—by America's status as a colony of Great Britain and as an intellectual province of Europe; by the Revolutionary and Civil Wars, World Wars I and II, the Cold War, and Vietnam; by the rise of the university system, its relation to the wealth produced in the industrialization of the country, its specialized professionalism, and by the twentieth-century developments that made American thinkers the most privileged on earth. But this broad socio-economic and political context was not so important in shaping philosophy as the overwhelming Protestant character of the dominant culture, and the deep Christian commitment that extends to the present and distinguishes the United States from the other nations of the North Atlantic West.

The peculiar ahistoric religious individualism that had its birth in Jonathan Edwards especially shaped the outlines of American thought. Philosophy in America began with worries about the relation of the single believer to a God whose purposes were not ours, a spiritual anxiety. The end of the nineteenth century reaffirmed these worries when the first pragmatists constructed a new religious world-view that embraced evolution. In the twentieth century, as religious commitment declined, philosophers wrestled with the question of how a biological organism could know about itself.

The individualist, contemplative heritage had led early on to a division of labor between philosophers and thinkers on social affairs. None the less, through the nineteenth century, philosophical theologians and religiously inclined philosophers had an important public role in making the ways of God known to Americans. When intellectual life turned away from literalist Protestantism at the end of the nineteenth century, philosophy achieved its greatest prominence as thinkers were able to combine ostensibly modern scientific views with ideas that had a Protestant spiritual hue— the many varieties of pragmatism. In the twentieth century, however, philosophers (and many academics) became more secular, outdistancing public culture. Their subsequent isolation was partly a function of academic professionalism but also of the space between their own non-religious views and those that were acceptable even among the educated upper-middle class.

Unable to offer advice on religious perplexities, philosophers had a diminished civic presence. Since the eighteenth century they had devoted little effort to the study of our communal involvement—our engagements with the social or political order. This lack stemmed from the fact that a comprehension of the soul's link to the cosmos was generally approached through cogitation; in the long history of philosophy in America Dewey was a minority voice in intimating that understanding politics and society might require epistemological strategies different from the abstruse exploration advanced by most thinkers in the United States. Moreover, after Dewey, as the full materialist import of Darwin became clear, political and social philosophy may well have been rendered more dubious for philosophers: what could be its point?

As a genre of intellectual work, the body of American political and social theory from the Federalists onward differs almost in kind from what has been done, for most of their lives, by the philosophers standardly treated in this book and others. When philosophers tried their hands at this different genre, they brought to the task different skills and competencies, and fashioned variants on the genre that presumed that knowledge of the polity and social order was not different in form from knowledge in general or knowledge in the physical sciences; and was, in any case, less difficult to get a handle on. The results displayed the view that political and social philosophy was easier to comprehend than the theory of knowledge, and that the former could be read off from one's conclusions about the latter. Despite claims to master practices and to deny distinctions between theory and evidence, the conceptual and the empirical, and the like, even pragmatic philosophy in the twentieth century was a largely armchair enterprise. It was almost an occupational hazard of philosophers that their work had in it a heavy, not to say overwhelming, dose of the a priori. Reasoning, thinking, and talking had primacy of place.

Philosophers made their points with thought experiments—deciding to have a runaway trolley kill one good person or five not-so-good persons; a native believing that it is 'rabbiting'; brains in a vat hooked up to think they are perceiving the world; a parable about a Twin Earth; a man in Barn Façade County, where there are 999 red façades and one real barn; what it was like to be a bat; a tree struck by lightning but reconstructed as a philosopher killed by the same lightning; the color grue; and makers of a new society ignorant of their sex, race, and age. Philosophers did not take seriously the claims of history, politics, or social thought to generate insights that theorizing alone could not provide. That is why, for example, even Rawls, a more influential political philosopher than Marcuse, Rorty, or Chomsky, was a carrier of abstract ideas.

Many commentators have found in American ideas a practicalism—often identified originally with Benjamin Franklin—that distinguished the thought of the New World from the Old. But Franklin represented a rendezvous with life that was outside the experience of most philosophers in America. It was the less religious Europeans in the traditions of Mill, Marx, and Weber who, in the twentieth century, were more interested in the social and political world. But since the politicians employing the rationales provided by European thought led their countries to repeated disasters, perhaps we should not scorn American philosophers for their comparatively lesser interest in politics. Those commentators interested in 'public intellectuals' and the retreat of philosophers from the 'public sphere' in the twenty-first century need to reflect on these ambiguities.

At the end of the twentieth century, analytic philosophers trying to make sense of their field regularly worried over their withdrawal from much social contact, but had few resources to explain it. One of the fascinations of Rorty's work was that he took the unabashedly secular orientation of many American philosophers and went out in the open with it, while they remained in the cloister; he tried to appeal to the best instincts of a democratic public and to mobilize its opinions. The result was, again, ambiguous, certainly so when Rorty declaimed against religion as 'a conversation stopper'. The lasting impact of Calvinist Protestantism on American philosophers has been that so long as they were religious they might influence public debate albeit in an abstracted way, but they could not think very well about social and political life in empirical or historical terms and were in any event dismissed when they turned from the religious. Thus, the more committed spirituality of American culture has meant that in the twenty-first century any secular dialogue in which philosophers might want to engage was problematic.

Many pundits at this time claimed that philosophy was 'over', but this lament or exultation appeared dubious when examined from a more careful historical perspective. Rorty and the postmodernists, with whom he occasionally identified, made it most often. Yet philosophers other than the postmodernists, including Kant and Hegel and analytic philosophers, had proclaimed that their thought had closed certain speculative strategies. At the same time, what they were doing looked continuous with what came before and after them. If philosophy were to become poetry, dialogue, and conversation, this would not take us far from people like Plato, Berkeley, Nietzsche, and James, all of whom have been easily fit into narratives of the traditions of Western thought. Closer to home over the last 300 years, Locke and Newton and then Darwin had revolutionary impacts on American philosophy, yet the concerns of Jonathan Edwards are as recognizable to us as are those of Peirce, James, and Royce. It might be true that certain research programs have reached a dead end. But such a result is not much different from what happened, for example, to American theology, post-Darwinian idealism, or logical positivism. The 'end' of these projects did not mean the end of philosophy, nor did it mean that what followed was severed from what had gone before. Indeed, the weight of tradition is so heavy that it is more likely that the defining ideas of the last three centuries in this country will dominate the future.

Whatever the perplexities of formulating 'practical philosophy', the difficulties for philosophers remained their audience, and those who have proclaimed the end of philosophy would have a stronger argument if they pointed out the shrinking audience for the professional discipline and the truism that a practice cannot survive without one. This weakness is mitigated by the fact that, ensconced in the university system, a discipline can exist for a long time with a minimal audience, although even the leadership of the institutions of higher education may catch on after a time. But reflective people throughout American history have needed something like philosophy. They have wanted its synthesis of instruction and argumentation, and in all likelihood they will find a way of extracting this mix from the cultural system in which they find themselves.

METHODS, SOURCES, NOTES

Although I have tried to make this volume interpretatively weighty, I have designed it as a textbook. I have minimized the citations below that are keyed to the relevant chapters and pages in the book, but indicated the variety of sources on which a cultural and social history of ideas must draw. Other pertinent information precedes the notes in many chapters.

This history of philosophy depends, initially, on the standard histories of American theology: George Nye Boardman, *A History of New England Theology* (1899); Frank Hugh Foster, *A Genetic History of the New England Theology* (University of Chicago Press, 1907); Joseph Haroutunian, *From Piety to Moralism* (Henry Holt, 1932); H. Shelton Smith, *Changing Conceptions of Original Sin* (Scribners, 1955). Primarily, however, I have been indebted to the conventional histories of philosophy: I. Woodbridge Riley, *American Thought from Puritanism to Pragmatism and Beyond* (Henry Holt, 1923); H. G. Townsend, *Philosophical Ideas in the United States* (American Book Company, 1934); Joseph Blau, *American Philosophic Addresses, 1700–1900.* (Columbia University Press, 1946); Herbert Schneider, *A History of American Philosophy* 2nd edn., (Columbia University Press, 1963); W. H. Werkmeister, *A History of Philosophical Ideas in America* (Ronald Press, 1949); Morton White, *Science and Sentiment in America: Philosophical Thought from Jonathan Edwards to John Dewey* (Oxford University Press, 1972); and Elizabeth Flower and Murray G. Murphey, *A History of Philosophy in America* (Putnams, 1977).

My version of the story that each of these histories tells in its own way fundamentally premises that there is indeed a story to be told. On the one hand, however, I have stressed the integrity of philosophy as a coherent intellectual discipline, more than have some of the histories listed above. On the other hand, I have simultaneously tried to contextualize the ideas more than these histories: I have looked at the changing locus of intellectual activity, and its religious and political environment, as well as the thought itself. I share the view that 'the history of ideas' is an abstract and rarified enterprise. I also share the view that 'the social history of ideas' may tell us far more about society than about thought. And I finally believe that the connection between the two is mysterious—so mysterious that claims to go much beyond my admittedly rudimentary attempts to connect the two are not persuasive even if my own are unsatisfactory. In taking this position, I have tried to steer between the Scylla of philosophers' suspicion of history and the Charybdis of historians' suspicion of philosophers.

For biographical information on my many subjects, I am indebted to the

Dictionary of American Biography; for philosophers in the second-half of the twentieth century, I have consulted Stuart Brown, Diane Collinson, and Robert Wilkinson, eds., *Biographical Dictionary of Twentieth-Century Philosophers* (Routledge, 1996).

There are now standard editions, complete or in progress, for many of the people I have written about—Edwards, Emerson, Peirce, James, Santayana, and Dewey. Where at all practical, I have cited them from these editions, but since these editions often depart from readily available reprints of first editions, or from other conventionally cited editions, I am not sure that my practice has been correct, especially since the standard editions are not always easy to find or to use. The Harvard edition of William James, which I have cited, is a case in point: James was a writer of essays, which for close to 100 years have appeared in easily obtainable editions that are deficient from a scholarly point of view. The Harvard edition corrects some obvious problems, but its editorial project introduced others that make the volumes difficult to use.

Recently, historians of American thought have successfully examined archival material to supplement the published record that they had more usually consulted. This has led to a subtle appraisal of ideas based on manuscript evidence. In addition, especially in the twentieth century, the exclusive locus of philosophy in the university and the generation of institutional record-keeping have given us a new source for understanding the context of thought. In a text of this sort I have not felt the need to deal with the minute details of the writings of philosophers. To show the importance of institutions, however, I have tried to give the reader a sense of the richness of this approach by using material from Yale University, the home of unique developments in American thought. The fruits of this research appear in relevant parts of the text, and in the notes.

I have freely taken from my own work and have often cited it in the notes, but three sources that have permeated the writing of this book need to be noted here: *The Rise of American Philosophy* (Yale University Press, 1977); *Churchmen and Philosophers* (Yale University Press 1985); and 'The Transformation of Philosophy', in Mary Kupiec Cayton and Peter W. Williams (eds.), *Encyclopedia of American Cultural and Intellectual History* (2001).

PR is the abbreviation for *Philosophical Review*, *JP* for *Journal of Philosophy*, and *M* for *Mind*.

Introduction

xiii   **William James quoted**: Henry James (ed.), *Letters of William James*, 2 vols. (Little Brown & Co., 1926), i., 205.

1. *Calvinism and Edwards*

6   There are many recent studies of **Edwards** as a philosophical theologian. Among them are Sang Hyun Lee, *The Philosophical Theology of Jonathan*

Edwards, exp. edn. (Princeton University Press, 2000); Stephen H. Daniel, *The Philosophy of Jonathan Edwards: A Study in Divine Semiotics* (Indiana University Press, 1994); and Leon Chai, *Jonathan Edwards and the Limits of Enlightenment Philosophy* (Oxford University Press, 1998). Michael McClymond's *Encounters with God: An Approach to the Theology of Jonathan Edwards* (Oxford University Press, 1998) has the best historiographical discussion of how Edwards has been treated as a systematic thinker since the publication of Perry Miller's pathbreaking *Jonathan Edwards* (Meridian, 1949, 1959). All these books, however, accentuate in Edwards his theological philosophizing and undervalue the premodern Calvinist biblicism and revivalist preaching that was at the core of his understanding of the world.

Even in a study such as this one, which traces Edwards's role in a story that comes up to the end of the twentieth century, due regard must be paid to the actual context in which he put forward proto-modernist arguments in philosophical theology. This literature on Edwards is much less rich but includes Patricia J. Tracy's *Jonathan Edwards, Pastor* (Hill and Wang, 1980); and, for the nineteenth century, Joseph A. Conforti's *Jonathan Edwards, Religious Tradition, and American Culture* (University of North Carolina Press, 1995). For New England Calvinism itself, of course, this literature is immense, and a good place to get a grip on it as it touches Edwards is in David D. Hall's Introduction, to *Ecclesiastical Writings*, vol. xii of *The Works of Jonathan Edwards* (Yale University Press, 1994). Finally, mention must be made of this edition of Edwards's writings, being published by Yale University Press in twenty-seven volumes, which for the first time provides a clear sense of all that Edwards wrote and when, and authoritative introductions to the various sorts of writing that engaged his attention. The edition has a web site on which much information is available: yale.edu/wje.

6–7   **Theological and Ministerial views**: Darren Staloff, *The Making of an American Thinking Class* (Oxford University Press, 1998), interprets these views within a social-history framework that I believe to be wrong, but refers ably to the enormous secondary literature on the Puritans, some of which I have used in my description; also useful are the more balanced Stephen Foster, *The Long Argument* (University of North Carolina, 1991), and Peter S. Field, *The Crisis of the Standing Order: Clerical Intellectuals and Cultural Authority in Massachusetts, 1780–1833* (University of Massachusetts Press, 1998).

7–8   **Newton and Calvinism**: Norman G. Fiering, *Jonathan Edwards's Moral Thought and its British Context* (University of North Carolina Press, 1981), 272–7.

8   **Edwards and Yale**: Edwards, *Scientific and Philosophical Writings*, ed. Wallace E. Anderson (Yale University Press, 1980), 17–27, 52–136.

8–10   **View of the history of modern philosophy**: An excellent starting point is Arthur Kenyon Rogers, *A Student's History of Philosophy* (Macmillan, 1901), pt. III.

10–11 **Edwards in 'Notes on the Mind'**: Anderson (ed.), *Philosophical Writings*, 65–73; **God only substance**: 215; **infinite idea**: 344; **experiencing God's ideas**: 97–8.

12 *Creatio continua*: Douglas J. Ellwood, *The Philosophical Theology of Jonathan Edwards* (Columbia University Press, 1960), 35–50; James Carse, *Jonathan Edwards and the Visibility of God* (Scribners, 1967), 89.

12 **Mirror analogy**: David Lyttle, 'Jonathan Edwards on Personal Identity', *Early American Literature*, 7 (1972), 168–9.

12–13 **Existence and perception**: Anderson (ed.), *Philosophical Writings*, 398.

13 **Sin and grace**: Edwards, *Letters and Personal Writings*, ed. George S. Claghorn (Yale University Press, 1998), 759–804.

13–14 **Edwards as pastor**: Tracy, *Jonathan Edwards, Pastor*.

14 **Edwards as premodern**: Bruce Kuklick, 'An Edwards for the Millenium', *Religion and American Culture*, 11 (2001), 109–17; **Cape Breton example**: Edwards, *Apocalyptic Writings*, ed. Stephen J. Stein (Yale University Press, 1977), 444–60.

15 **Stewart and Fichte**: Stewart, *Dissertation, Exhibiting a General View of the Progress of . . . Philosophy . . .* (1829), 384; Fichte quoted in Clyde A. Holbrook, *The Ethics of Jonathan Edwards* (University of Michigan Press, 1973), p. ix.

16 **Religion consists in affections**: . . . *Religious Affections*, ed. John E. Smith (Yale University Press, 1959), 119.

17 **Sense of the heart**: Edwards, 'Ideas, Sense of the Heart, Spiritual Knowledge or Conviction Faith', ed. Perry Miller, *Harvard Theological Review*, 41 (1948), 129–45; Smith (ed.), *Affections*, 96–9, 197–214.

17 **Varying accounts**: Murray G. Murphey and Elizabeth Flower, *A History of Philosophy in America*, 2 vols. (Putnams, 1977), i. 181–2; Lee, *Philosophical Theology of Edwards*, 34–114.

18 **New sense**: Smith (ed.), *Affections*, 205, 272.

19 **Christ and history**: Edwards quoted from Elwood, *Philosophical Theology*, 46–7.

19–20 **Christian experience and practice**: Smith (ed.), *Affections*, 450.

20 **Saints as fixed stars**: Smith (ed.), *Affections*, 373–4.

20 **Calvinists, determinism, and freedom**: William K. B. Stoever, 'A Faire and Easy Way to Heaven': Covenant Theology and Antinomianism in Early Massachusetts (Wesleyan University Press, 1978), 110–11, 195.

20 **Locke on the will**: *An Essay Concerning Human Understanding*, ed. Peter H. Nidditch (Oxford University Press, 1975), Bk. 2, ch. 21, paras. 5–48.

20–21 *Freedom of the Will*: Edwards, *Freedom of the Will*, ed. Paul Ramsey (Yale University Press, 1957), 152, 158, 171–4. See the discussions of Ramsey, 'Introduction' to Edwards, *Freedom*, 8–118; A. E. Murphy, 'Jonathan Edwards on Free Will and Moral Agency', *PR* 68 (1959), 181–202; and

Roland Delattre, 'Beauty and Politics', *American Philosophy from Edwards to Quine*, ed. Robert W. Shahan and Kenneth R. Merrill (University of Oklahoma Press, 1977), 29–32.

21–3 **Edwards on self determination**: Ramsey (ed.), *Will*, 163–4; **traveler's tale**: 346; **greatest apparent good**: 142; **connected terms**: 158.

2. *Philosophy and Politics*

26 **New England culture**: Jack P. Greene, *Pursuits of Happiness* (University of North Carolina Press, 1988), 2–80.

26 **Puritan dilemma**: Edmund S. Morgan, *The Puritan Dilemma: The Story of John Winthrop*, 2nd edn. (Little Brown & Co., 1999), esp. pp. xi–xii.

26–8 **Calvinism and politics**: the issue was raised in a fundamental way by Alan Heimert, *Religion and the American Mind: From the Great Awakening to the Revolution* (Harvard University Press, 1966), and I have used the large literature that has been produced since then. Two excellent historiographical overviews appear in Philip Goff, 'Revivals and Revolution: Historiographic Turns since Alan Heimert's *Religion and the American Mind*', *Church History*, 67 (1998), 695–721; and Derek H. Davis, *Religion and the Continental Congress, 1774–1789* (Oxford University Press, 2000). I have also relied on Mark Noll's manuscript, 'America's God from Jonathan Edwards to Abraham Lincoln' (December 2000). On Edwards especially see Gerald R. McDermott, *One Holy and Happy Society: The Public Theology of Jonathan Edwards* (Penn State University Press, 1992), 178–84; and on his followers, Mark Valeri, *Law and Providence in Joseph Bellamy's New England: The Origins of New Divinity in Revolutionary America* (Oxford University Press, 1994).

28–32 **American republicanism**: I have a brief bibliography in my edition of *Thomas Paine: Political Writings*, rev. edn. (Cambridge University Press, 2000), pp. xxvii–xxvix. Up-to-date interpretations of the Founders may be found in the series American Political Thought, edited by Wilson Carey McWilliams and Lance Banning, issued by the University Press of Kansas.

33 **Political theory and philosophy**: the same sort of point is made indirectly by Thelma Z. Lavine, 'Have Pragmatists Rejected Classical American Philosophy?', *Transactions of the Charles S. Peirce Society*, 36 (2000), 385–92.

33 **Pitt quoted**: Davis, *Religion*, 58.

33 **Franklin**: Max Farrand (ed.), *The Records of the Federal Convention of 1787*, 3 vols. (Yale University Press, 1937), i. 450–2.

34 **Adams quoted**: Davis, *Religion*, 69.

35–7 **Franklin's *Dissertation***: in addition to the original texts, my discussion relies on two sources: Elizabeth Flower and Murray G. Murphey, *A History of Philosophy in America*, 2 vols. (Putnams, 1977), i. 100–7; and Kerry S. Walters, *Benjamin Franklin and his Gods* (University of Illinois Press, 1999), 43–64, 170. See also Kuklick, 'The Two Cultures in

Eighteenth-Century America', in Harry S. Stout and Barbara B. Oberg (eds.), *Benjamin Franklin, Jonathan Edwards, and the Representation of American Culture* (Oxford University Press, 1993), 101–13.

3. *Theology*

38   In addition to the older works on theology I have cited in my introduction to the historiography above, more recent syntheses are: James Hoopes, *Consciousness in New England: From Puritanism and Ideas to Psychoanalysis and Semiotic* (John Hopkins University Press, 1989); and Allen Guelzo, *Edwards on the Will: A Century of Theological Debate* (Wesleyan University Press, 1989).

38–9   **New England Theology**: Bruce Kuklick, *Churchmen and Philosophers* (Yale University Press, 1985), 43–5.

39   **Educated clergy**: Kuklick, *Churchmen*, 45–8, 264–5; James W. Schmotter, 'Ministerial Careers in Eighteenth-Century New England', *Journal of Social History*, 9 (1975), 249–69.

39–40   **Outlines of New Divinity**: William Kern Breitenbach, 'New Divinity Theology and the Idea of Moral Accountability', Ph.D., Yale University, 1978.

41–2   **New Divinity men quoted**: Samuel Hopkins, *Works*, ed. Edwards Amasa Park, 3 vols. (1852), i. 40, 135, 139, 153–4; iii. 356; Nathaniel Emmons, *Works*, ed. Jacob Ide, 6 vols. (1842), iv. 144–7, 344, 348, 383; v. 120; Bellamy, *Works*, ed. Tyron Edwards, 2 vols. (1853), i. 260, 578–82; ii. 26–7, 43.

42–4   **Hopkins on the means of grace**: *Works*, iii. 183–275, 276–497; **on disinterested benevolence and Newton**: ii. 742; iii. 16, 33.

44   **Sin necessary to good and God author**: Hopkins, *Works*, ii. 493–545; Bellamy, *Works*, ii. 20–2, 32–5, 60, 64; Emmons, *Works*, iv. 455–6.

45   **Taste scheme**: Hopkins, *Works*, i. 191, 200–1, 367–8, 375–6; iii. 225, 553–4.

45–7   **Emmons' views**: Kuklick, *Churchmen*, 56–9, 265–6.

47–8   **Rise of Princeton**: Mark Noll, *Princeton and the Republic, 1768–1822* (Princeton University Press, 1989); and Noll (ed.), *Princeton Theology, 1812–1921* (Baker Books, 1983, 2001).

48   **Witherspoon and Smith on Berkeley**: Witherspoon, *Works . . .*, 9 vols. (1815), ii. 106, 108; vii. 21–3, 34, 37–8; viii. 116–18, 122; Smith, *Lectures on the Evidence of Christian Religion*, 2 vols. (1809), i. 20–4, 127–48.

48–9   **Reid and Stewart**: S. A. Grave, *The Scottish Philosophy of Common Sense* (Oxford University Press, 1960).

50   **Religious liberalism**: Conrad Wright, *The Beginnings of Unitarianism in America* (Starr King Press, 1955).

50–1   **Professionalization of divinity**: Kuklick, *Churchmen*, 72–5, 85–7; 'Transformation of Philosophy', *Encyclopedia of American Cultural and Intellectual History*, ed. Mary Kopiec Cayton and Peter W. Williams (Scribners, 2001).

51 **Stuart and Dwight**: Daniel Day Williams, *The Andover Liberals* (Kings Crown Press, 1941), 14; John R. Fitzmier, *New England's Moral Legislator: Timothy Dwight* (Indiana University Press, 1998).

52–3 **Hodge**: Bruce Kuklick, 'The Place of Charles Hodge in the History of Ideas in America', in John W. Stewart and James H. Moorhead (eds.), *Charles Hodge Reconsidered* (Eerdmans, 2002).

53 **New Haven**: Ralph Henry Gabriel, *Religion and Learning at Yale* (Yale University Press, 1958).

53–5 **Taylor on concepts**: *Essays, Lectures, Etc. . . . In Revealed Theology* (1859), 2, 50; 'On the Authority of Reason in Theology', *Christian Spectator*, 9 (1837) 151–62; **on taste**: Lyman Beecher, *Autobiography, Correspondence, Etc.*, 2 vols., ed. Charles Beecher (1864), i. 384–8; **on moral government**: Taylor, *Lectures on the Moral Government of God*, 2 vols. (1859), i. 200, 307; ii. 137; **on the will**: Eleazar T. Fitch, *An Inquiry into the Nature of Sin . . .* (1827), 57, 66–7, 83; **Edwards' and Taylor's psychology**: Fisher, *Discussions*, 249–50, 300–12.

55–6 **Taylor on the will**: Edward D. Griffin, *Doctrine of Divine Efficiency* (1833), 8–11, 206; Taylor, 'Concio ad Clerum', in Sydney Ahlstrom (ed.), *Theology in America* (Bobbs-Merrill, 1967), 213–49; and *Moral Government*, i. 290–2.

56–7 **Taylor on sinning**: *Revealed Theology*, 192–201; **on grace**: 373–9; **on best system**: 385, 413.

4. Collegiate Philosophy

59 **On Witherspoon**: William D. Carrell, 'American College Professors, 1750–1800', *History of Education Quarterly*, 8 (1968), 289–305.

60 **Reid and Stewart**: W. R. Sorley, *A History of British Philosophy Before 1900* (Cambridge University Press, 1900), 203–9.

60–1 **Witherspoon and Smith**: Jack Scott (ed.), *An Annotated Edition of John Witherspoon's* Lectures on Moral Philosophy (Associated University Presses, 1982); Smith, *Lectures on the Evidences of the Christian Religion*, 2 vols. (1809), i. 20–4, 127–48.

61 **Harvard and Bowen**: Bruce Kuklick, *Rise of American Philosophy* (Yale University Press, 1977), 32–4.

61–2 **McCosh**: *Intuitions of the Mind*, 3rd edn. rev. (1872), 101–17, 127–8.

62 **Baconian and doxological science**: Theodore Dwight Bozeman, *Protestants in the Age of Science* (University of North Carolina Press, 1977); Charles Hodge, *Systematic Theology*, 3 vols. (1878), i. 1–188.

62–4 **Kant**: the American view is best expressed in Josiah Royce, *The Spirit of Modern Philosophy* (1892), 1–134; and *Lectures on Modern Idealism* (1919, 1963, Yale University Press), 1–30.

65 **Kant and Hamilton**: John Veitch, *Hamilton* (1882), esp. 223–46.

66–7 **Porter**: *The Human Intellect* (1868), 83–104, 127–213, 216–20, 633–45.

67   **Later Bowen**: Bowen, *Gleanings from a Literary Life, 1838–1880* (1880),
        139–40, 159–60, 196, 294–7; *Modern Philosophy from Descartes to
        Schopenhauer and Hartmann* (1877), 30, 42, 77, 150–3, 166, 217, 318–20.
67–9   **Hickok**: *Rational Psychology* . . . (1849), esp. 553; *Creator and Creation* . . .
        (1872); *Humanity Immortal* . . . (1872).
69   **Kant and his successors**: Royce, *Spirit*, 135–264, 483–506; *Lectures*,
        31–259.
70   **Newton and theologians on space**: Allen, 'Notes on Taylor's Lectures',
        128, Yale Divinity School Library; Henry Boynton Smith, *System of
        Christian Theology*, ed. William S. Carr, 3rd. edn. (1886), 19–20; Hodge,
        Systematic Theology, i. 383–8, 595–6.
71   **Hamilton's presentationalism**: Thomas Reid, *Works*, with a Preface etc.
        by Sir William Hamilton, 6th edn., 2 vols. (1863), ii. 746–8, 816–17.
71   **McCosh**: *Intuitions*, 167–208, 232.
71   **Bowen**: 'Mr. Mill and his Critics', *American Presbyterian Review*, 1 (1869),
        362–5.
72   **Porter**: *Human Intellect*, 645–62.
72–3   **Moral Philosophy**: Donald Meyer, *The Instructed Conscience* (University
        of Pennsylvania Press, 1972); H. Wilson Smith, *Professors and Public Ethics*
        (Cornell University Press, 1956).
73   **Self-caused will**: Noah Porter, *Elements of Moral Science* (1885), 72.
74   **Critic on public philosophy**: Robert Charles Post, 'Studies in the Origins
        and Practice of the American Novel', Ph.D., Harvard University, 1980, 19.

5. *Amateurs*

75   **Marsh's impact**: Joseph Torrey, *The Remains of the Rev. James Marsh* . . .
        (1843), 75–6, 244–6, 492 ff.; Coleridge, *Aids to Reflection . . . with a prelimi-
        nary essay . . . by James Marsh* (1829), pp. xvi–xvii; Peter Carafiol,
        Transcendent Reason (University Presses of Florida, 1982), 72–3, 78–9.
76   **Marsh's views**: Marsh, *Aids . . . preliminary essay*, p. x; Torrey, *Remains*,
        142, 197–8, 206, 210, 252–3, 342–6, 393–408, 448–9, 473–99, 554.
76–7   **Marsh's Christianity**: Torrey, *Remains*, 485, 500; Woods' quote from John
        J. Duffy, *Coleridge's American Disciples* (University of Massachusetts Press,
        1973), 106.
78–80   **Emerson's *Nature***: in *Collected Works of Ralph Waldo Emerson*, ed. Robert
        E. Spiller, i. *Nature, Addresses, and Lectures* (Harvard University Press, 1971),
        7–45.
80   **'Divinity School Address'** (1838): ibid. 71–93.
80–1   **Parker, 'Discourse'**: in *The Transcendentalists*, ed. Perry Miller (Harvard
        University Press, 1950), 260–83.
81–2   **Transcendentalism as a cultural movement**: Anne C. Rose,
        Transcendentalism as a Social Movement (Yale University Press, 1981);
        Lawrence Buell, *Literary Transcendentalism* (Cornell University Press,

1973); and Joel Porte and Saundra Morris, *The Cambridge Companion to Ralph Waldo Emerson* (Cambridge University Press, 1999).

83   **Bushnell on Christian nurture**: Bushnell, *Christian Nurture* (1861), 9–64; Conrad Cherry, 'The Structure of Organic Thinking: Horace Bushnell's Approach to Language, Nature, and Nation', *Journal of the American Academy of Religion*, 40 (1972), 3–4.

83–4   **Hodge on Bushnell**: Hodge, 'Review of *Christian Nurture*,' *Princeton Review*, 19 (1847), 502–39.

84   **Transforming experience**: Mary A. Bushnell Cheyney, *Life and Letters of Horace Bushnell* (1880), 192, 208, 499.

84   **'Life, or the Lives'**: in Bushnell, *Work and Play* (1903), 273, 294, 301–12.

84   **'Science and Religion'**: in Mary Bushnell Cheyney (ed.), *Spirit in Man* (1903), 266–75.

85   **Theological formula**: Bushnell, *Christ in Theology* (1851), 33; *God in Christ* . . . (1849), 69–71.

85–6   **On the 'Preliminary Dissertation'**: see the discussion in Jerry Wayne Brown, *The Rise of Biblical Criticism in America, 1800–1870* (Wesleyan University Press, 1969), 171–9.

86   **British and German metaphors**: Bushnell, *An Argument for 'Discourses on Christian Nurture'* . . . (1847), 39; *God in Christ* (1849), 140–2.

86   **Christ as metaphor**: *God in Christ*, 146, 156, 203–4, 251–68; *Christ in Theology*, 110, 225, 240–56; 'Our Gospel a Gift to the Imagination' (1869), in Bushnell, *Building Eras in Religion* (1881), 259.

86   **Bushnell on the church**: *God in Christ*, 146, 156, 208–9.

86–7   **Bushnell on systematic theology and ministry**: *God in Christ*, 48, 330; *Christ in Theology*, pp. v–vi.

87–8   **Supernaturalism**: *Nature and the Supernatural* (1858), 177, 205; 'Dudleian Lecture' (1852), as reprinted in H. Shelton Smith (ed.), *Horace Bushnell* (1965), 245.

88   **Porter on Bushnell**: 'Review of *Nature and the Supernatural*', *New Englander*, 17 (1859), 224–58.

88–9   **Overview of Mercersburg**: James Hastings Nichols (ed.), *The Mercersburg Theology* (Oxford University Press, 1966).

89–90 **On the organic church**: John W. Nevin, *The Mystical Presence and Other Writings* . . ., ed. Bard Thompson and George H. Bricker (United Church Press, 1966), 160–76; 'The Apostle's Creed' (1849), in Nichols (ed.), *Mercersburg Theology*, 71, 310.

90   **Nevin and Schaff's critique of Protestantism**: Nevin, 'Catholic Unity', in Nichols (ed.), *Mercersburg Theology*, 46; Schaff, *The Principle of Protestantism*, ed. Bard Thompson and George H. Bricker (United Church Press, 1964).

90–1   **Mercersburg's significance**: Robert Clemner, 'Historical Transcendentalism in Pennsylvania', *Journal of the History of Ideas*, 30 (1969), 579–92.

91–2   **Introduction to St Louis**: William Goetzman (ed.), *The American Hegelians* (Knopf, 1973).

92–3 **Hegelians on the Civil War**: Denton J. Snider, *The American Ten Years War, 1855–1865* (Sigma Publishing Co., 1906).

93–4 **Concord School**: Lewis S. Feuer (ed.), 'Letters of H. A. P. Torrey to William T. Harris', *Vermont History*, 25 (1957), 215–19; Denton J. Snider, *The St. Louis Movement . . .* (Sigma Publishing Co., 1920), 262–77.

94 **Amateurs and institutions**: the most recent survey of the system of higher education in this period is Roger L. Geiger (ed.), *The American College in the Nineteenth Century* (Vanderbilt University Press, 2000).

Introduction to Part II

95 **On pragmatism**: Thoemmes Press is printing an unparalleled selection of primary sources in its publishing program in the History of American Thought. Its web site is: thoemmes.com/american/cover.html. The Society for the Advancement of American Philosophy and the Charles S. Peirce Society are both organizations dedicated to promoting the study of American thought, mainly since the Civil War, and focus on pragmatism. The books on pragmatism are legion, and conventional. John Diggins, *The Problem of Pragmatism* (University of Chicago Press, 1994) offers a brooding analysis, and James Kloppenberg, *Uncertain Victory: Social Democracy and Progressivism in European and American Thought, 1870–1920* (Oxford University Press, 1986), puts pragmatism in an international context.

96 **'The Thirteen Pragmatisms'**: authored by Arthur O. Lovejoy, *JP* 5 (1908), 5–12, 29–39.

6. Shape of Revolution

97–8 **Mill on Hamilton**: *An Examination of Sir William Hamilton's Philosophy* (1865), 12–16, 85–7.

98–9 **Darwin**: for an introduction see Thomas F. Glick and David Kohn (eds.), *Charles Darwin on Evolution* (Hackett Publishers, 1996).

99 **Darwin in America**: among recent books are: Ronald L. Numbers, *Darwinism Comes to America* (Harvard University Press, 1998); Paul K. Conkin, *When All the Gods Trembled* (Rowman & Littlefield, 1998).

100–1 **On the new university system**: the standard work is Lawrence R. Veysey, *The Emergence of the American University System* (University of Chicago Press, 1965). More recent syntheses include George M. Marsden, *The Soul of the American University* (Oxford University Press, 1994), and Julie A. Reuben, *The Making of the Modern University* (University of Chicago Press, 1996).

101–2 **Rise of the social sciences**: Dorothy Ross, *The Origins of American Social Science* (Cambridge University Press, 1991); Ronald G. Walters (ed.), *Scientific Authority and Twentieth-Century America* (Johns Hopkins University Press, 1997).

102–4   **Biblical criticism**: Peter J. Thuesen, *In Discordance With the Scriptures: American Protestant Battles over Translating the Bible* (Oxford University Press, 1999); Jerry Wayne Brown, *Rise of Biblical Criticism in America, 1800–1870* (Wesleyan University Press, 1969); R. E. Clements, *A Century of Old Testament Study*, 2nd edn. rev. (Lutterworth, 1983); 'Julius Wellhausen and his *Prolegomena to the History of Israel*', Special Issue of *Semeia*, 25 (1982); and for a specific example, William James, *The Varieties of Religious Experience* (Harvard University Press, 1985), 12–14.

104–5   **Social history of late-nineteenth century America**: Nell Irvin Painter, *Standing at Armageddon: The United States, 1877–1919* (W. W. Norton, 1987); Susan Curtis, *A Consuming Faith: The Social Gospel and Modern American Culture* (Johns Hopkins University Press, 1991), Sheldon Stromquist, *A Generation of Boomers: The Patterns of Railroad and Labor Conflict in Nineteenth Century America* (University of Illinois Press, 1987); Elizabeth Sanders, *Roots of Reform: Farmers, Workers, and the American State* (University of Chicago Press, 1999).

109   **Hodge on Darwin**: *What is Darwinism?* (Baker Books, 1994), 156.

7. Idealism

112   **Morris on the English mind**: *British Thought and Thinkers* (1880), 7–29.

112   **Idealists study Kant**: Morris, *Kant's Critique of Pure Reason* (1882); Schurman, 'The Genesis of the Critical Philosophy', *PR* 7 (1898), 1–22, 135–61, 225–47, and 'Kant's Critical Problem: What is it in Itself and for Us?', *PR* 8 (1899), 129–66; Fullerton, 'The Doctrine of Space and Time', *PR* 10 (1901), 229–40.

113   **Symposium**: 'Comments by Professor Howison', in Josiah Royce *et al.*, *The Conception of God* (Thoemmes Press, 1897, 2000), 84.

113   **Bowne's argument**: Bowne, *Theory of Thought and Knowledge* (1897, 1899), pp. iii–iv.

113   **Schurman and Creighton as absolutists**: Creighton, *Studies in Speculative Philosophy*, ed. Harold R. Smart (Kraus Reprints, 1925, 1970); Schurman, *Agnosticism and Religion* (1896).

113   **Self–realization ethic**: Ladd, *Philosophy of Conduct* (Scribners, 1902); *What Ought I to Do?* (Longmans, Green, 1915), esp. 255–7; Bowne, *Principles of Ethics* (1892), 304.

113–14   **Mulford**: *The Nation: The Foundations of Civil Order and Political Life in the United States* (1870), esp. 340–1.

114   **Howison, Fullerton, and Bowne against absolutism**: Howison, 'Comments', in Royce *et al.*, *Conception*, 91, 94, 98, 113; Fullerton: *The Philosophy of Spinoza* (1891) and *On Spinozistic Immortality* (1899); Bowne, *Thought and Knowledge*, 306.

114   **Howison's and Morris's alternatives**: John Wright Buckham and George Malcolm Stratton, *George Holmes Howison* (Kraus Reprints, 1934), esp. 136; Marc Jones, *George Sylvester Morris* (D. McKay Co., 1948), 315–17.

114–15 **Bowne's position:** *Studies in Theism* (1879), 145, 261, 324; *Metaphysics*, rev. edn. (1898), 43, 97–103; **Kantianized:** 423; **private dream:** *Theory of Thought*, 281.

115   **Royce's life:** John Clendenning, *The Life and Thought of Josiah Royce*, rev. and exp. edn. (Vanderbilt University Press, 1999).

115–16 **Royce on purpose of thought:** Royce, *Fugitive Essays*, ed. Jacob Loewenberg (1920, 1968, Books for Libraries Press), 199–204, 347–8, 373; **dialectical argument:** 249–53; Royce, 'Kant's Relation to Modern Philosophic Progress', *Journal of Speculative Philosophy*, 15 (1881), 378; **inadequate response:** *Fugitive Essays*, 256.

117   **Individual and absolute consciousness:** Bruce Kuklick, *Josiah Royce* (Hackett, 1972), 20–1, 244.

117–18 **Tensions in view:** Royce, *Fugitive Essays*, 112–13, 338; 'Mind and Reality', *M* 7 (1882), 30–54.

118–22 **Possibility of error:** Royce, *Religious Aspect of Philosophy* (Peter Smith Publishers, 1885, 1965), 300–2, 339–54, 370–405, 422–5.

119   **Causation and belief:** Royce, *Studies in Good and Evil* (1898), 158.

122   **My self and this world of objects:** *Studies*, 162; *Spirit of Modern Philosophy* (1892), 360–74.

122   **Royce's domination of epistemology:** an excellent place to start is Randall E. Auxier (ed.), *Critical Responses to Josiah Royce, 1885–1916* (Thoemmes Press, 2000), 3 vols., esp. vol. ii.

123   **Dewey's conventional ideas quoted:** 'Ethics and Physical Science', *Andover Review*, 7 (1887), repr. in Jo Ann Boydston (ed.), *Early Works of John Dewey* (Southern Illinois University Press, 1969), i. 205–6 (hereafter: *EW*, followed by date of publication in parentheses and volume number); 'Soul and Body', *Bibliotheca Sacra*, 43 (1886), *EW* i. 115.

123–4   **New psychology:** 'The New Psychology', *Andover Review*, 1 (1884), *EW* i. 53, 56–7, 58; *Psychology*, *EW* (1967), ii. 254.

124–5   **New psychology against the British:** 'Psychology as Philosophic Method', *M* 11 (1886), *EW* i. 148, 149, 151, 157, 160; 'Illusory Psychology', *M* 12 (1887), *EW* i. 172–3, 175.

125–6   **Dewey on Caird and Green:** 'On Some Current Conceptions of the Term Self', *M* 15 (1890), *EW* (1969), iii. 56–74; 'Caird's *Critical Philosophy of Immanuel Kant*', *Andover Review*, 13 (1890), *EW* iii. 181–3.

126   **Dewey writes later:** 'Green's Theory of the Moral Motive', *PR* 1 (1892), *EW* iii. 171–3.

126–8   **Dewey's rationale for experimental idealism and neo–Hegelianism:** 'Self-Realization as the Moral Ideal', *PR* 2 (1893), *EW* (1971), iv. 53; 'The Study of Ethics' (course syllabus) 1894, *EW* iv. 262–4.

8. *Pragmatism in Cambridge*

129   The magazine, *Transactions of the Charles S. Peirce Society*, is the best place to start to sample the work and influence of Peirce. A biography is Joseph

Brent, *Charles Sanders Peirce: A Life*, rev. and enlarged edn. (Indiana University Press, 1998). The Peirce Edition Project, which is publishing a comprehensive edition of Peirce's writing, has a website with much of interest: iupui.edu/~peirce.

129 **Metaphysical club**: the standard work is now Louis Menand, *The Metaphysical Club* (Farrar, Straus, 2001).

130 **Green's role**: Philip Wiener, *Evolution and the Founders of Pragmatism* (Harvard University Press, 1949), 152–71; Jerome Frank, 'A Conflict with Oblivion: Some Observations on the Founders of Legal Pragmatism', *Rutgers Law Review*, 9 (1954–5), 425–63.

130 **Holmes's role**: Frank, 'Conflict', 435, 444–6; Max Fisch, 'Justice Holmes, the Prediction Theory of Law, and Pragmatism', *JP* 39 (1942), 86–7, 93–4.

130–1 **Holmes and Wright on evolution and law**: Max Fisch: 'Evolution in American Philosophy', *PR* 56 (1947), 368–9; 'Alexander Bain and the Geneaology of Pragmatism', *Journal of the History of Ideas*, 15 (1954), 413–44.

131–2 **James's contribution**: Fisch, 'Bain', 441–2, and 'Evolution', 362–6; James, *The Will to Believe* (Harvard University Press, 1979), 71–2, 184–5.

132–3 **Kant quoted**: from Wiener, *Evolution*, 23.

134–5 **Peirce's New List**: *Writings of Charles S. Peirce: A Chronological Edition*, ed. Christian J. W. Kloesel (Indiana University Press, 1984), ii. 49–58. (Hereafter *WCP* followed by date of publication in parentheses and volume number.)

135–40 **Peirce on Descartes**: *WCP* ii. 211–12; **on Berkeley**: 462–87; **on community**: 239; **on the absolute ego**: 203; **on induction**: 264–72; **on morality of science**: 485–7.

140–1 **Peirce's relationalism**: Murray G. Murphey, *Development of Peirce's Philosophy* (Harvard University Press, 1961), 153–4.

141–4 ***Popular Science Monthly* series**: *WCP* (1986), iii. 247 ff.; 263 ff.; Murphey, *Development*, 168–71.

146–7 **Peirce's position as semiotic**: my discussion is taken from the perceptive account in James Hoopes (ed.), 'Introduction' to *Peirce on Signs: Writings on Semiotic by Charles Sanders Peirce* (University of North Carolina Press, 1991), 7–9.

147–9 **History of the Peirce papers**: Nathan Houser, 'The Fortunes and Misfortunes of the Peirce Papers', *Signs of Humanity*, ed. Michel Balat and Janice Deledalle-Rhodes, (1989), iii. 1260–75; Victor F. Lenzen, 'Reminiscences of a Mission to Milford, Pennsylvania', and W. F. Kernan, 'The Peirce Manuscripts and Josiah Royce—A Memoir, Harvard 1915–1916', in *Transactions of the Charles S. Peirce Society*, 1 (1965), 3–11; and 90–5, respectively.

9. Pragmatism at Harvard

150–1   The most recent biography of William James is Linda Simon, *Genuine Reality: A Life of William James* (Harcourt, Brace & Co., 1998).

151–3   **James's early voluntaristic idealism**: James, 'Spencer's Definition of Mind' (1878) in *Essays in Philosophy* (Harvard University Press, 1978), 21; 'Are We Automata?' (1879) and 'Feeling of Effort' (1880) in *Essays in Psychology* (Harvard University Press, 1983), 43, 45–6, 51–2; and 101–23, respectively; *Will to Believe* (Harvard University Press, 1979), 91–2, 94–5.

153   **Relation to realism and idealism**: 'Feeling of Effort', in *Essays in Psychology*, 118.

153   **Inconclusivity of arguments and tolerance**: James, 'Spencer', *Essays in Philosophy*, 17–18, 21; 'Review of Bain and Renouvier' (1876) in *Essays, Comments, and Reviews* (Harvard University Press, 1987), 326; *Will to Believe*, 18–20, 92–3.

154   **Royce's views**: Royce, *Religious Aspect of Philosophy* (Peter Smith Publishers, 1885, 1965), 441, 454, 468, 475–7; Royce *et al.*, *Conception of God* (Thoemmes Press, 1897, 2000), 49–50, 135.

154–5   **James on Germans and English**: James, 'German Pessimism' (1875) *Essays in Philosophy*, 13; *Will to Believe*, 196–221.

155   **James does psychology**: James, 'The Function of Cognition', in *The Meaning of Truth* (Harvard University Press, 1975), 13–32.

156   **Metaphysics leaks in to psychology**: James, *Psychology: Briefer Course* (Harvard University Press, 1984), 400.

156   **James and Peirce**: James, 'Philosophical Conceptions', in *Pragmatism* (Harvard University Press, 1975), 258–9.

157   **Pragmatism and method**: James, *Pragmatism*, 34, 38, 98.

157   **Psychology and logic in pragmatism**: 'Humanism and Truth' is published in *Meaning*, 37–60; quote from 'A Word More About Truth' (1907) in *Meaning*, 85–6.

158   **James on elementary drag**: 'Knowing of Things Together' (1894) in *Essays in Philosophy*, 72–8; *Meaning*, 81–2.

158   **James on Royce**: *Pragmatism*, 126; *Meaning*, 23 n. 6, 80–1, 84.

158   **Nominal essence of truth**: James, *Meaning*, 89, 106–7.

158   **James and Peirce**: James, *Meaning*, 87–8, 130–1, 142–4.

158–9   **James's description of truth as useful**: *Pragmatism*, 32–4; *Meaning*, 54–5; **and verification**: *Pragmatism*, 97, 99–100; *Meaning*, 56–7, 129; **and compatibility**: *Pragmatism*, 35–6; **and elegance**: *Pragmatism*, 104.

159–60 **Historical development**: *Pragmatism*, 83–4, 122.

160   **James and Kant**: *Pragmatism*, 117–20; *Meaning*, 37–51, 105–7, 122, 146–8, 157–8.

161   **James on the possible**: *Pragmatism*, 116, 125, 135–6; 'Controversy about Truth' (1907), in *Essays in Radical Empiricism* (Harvard University Press, 1976), 152–3.

162–3 **Absolute pragmatism**: Royce, *Philosophy of Loyalty* (Macillan, 1908), 324–48; Daniel S. Robinson (ed.), *Royce's Logical Essays* (William C. Brown Co., 1951), 78–86, 116–18, 336–7.

164–5 **James on religion**: *Varieties of Religious Experience* (Harvard University Press, 1985), especially Lectures II, III, XVIII, XIX, and XX; Henry Levinson, *The Religious Investigations of William James* (University of North Carolina Press, 1981).

165–6 **Royce on value and loyalty**: 'Royce's Urbana Lectures', ed. Peter Fuss, *Journal of the History of Philosophy*, 5 (1967), 64–5, 70–1; Royce, *Philosophy of Loyalty*, 16–17, 19–20, 52, 124–6, 116–22, 162–6, 313–15, 336.

167 **Santayana on James and Royce**: *Character and Opinion in the United States* (Scribners, 1920), 44, 61–2.

168 **Royce on public issues**: *Philosophy of Loyalty*, pp. vii, xi; *Race Questions, Provincialism, and Other American Problems* (Macmillan, 1908), 111–65, 57–108.

168–9 **James's humanism**: James, *Talks to Teachers on Psychology* (Harvard University Press, 1983), 4, 149–51, 165–7.

169–70 **James on war**: 'Moral Equivalent' (1909), *Essays in Religion and Morality* (Harvard University Press, 1982), 162–73.

170–1 **Problems of practical philosophy**: Bruce Kuklick, *Rise of American Philosophy* (Yale University Press, 1977), 311–14. Antithetical views are George Cotkin, *William James: Public Philosopher* (Johns Hopkins University Press, 1990); Joshua Miller, *Democratic Temperament: The Legacy of William James* (University of Kansas Press, 1997).

171–2 **Neutral monism**: James, *Radical Empiricism*, 3–5, 264–5.

172 **Pragmatism and metaphysics**: ibid. 14.

172–4 **Radical empiricism**: ibid., 22–3, 42, 66, 100; 'Philosophical Conceptions and Practical Results', in *Pragmatism*, 268–70; 'Review of *Personal Idealism*,' *Essays, Comments, and Reviews*, 544–5; Ralph Barton Perry, *The Thought and Character of William James*, 2 vols. (Little Brown & Co., 1935), ii. 549–50, 591–2, 749, 751–2, 756.

174 **James abandons logic**: Perry, *Thought*: ii. 764; James, *A Pluralistic Universe* (Harvard University Press, 1977), 95–7; Bergson's critique, ibid., 101–22; continuity: ibid., 125–35.

174–5 **Autobiographical sections**: James, *Pluralistic Universe*, 83–100.

175 **Human and divine substance**: ibid., 137–49.

175–6 **Royce's final religious thought**: see John E. Smith, 'Introduction' to Royce, *The Problem of Christianity* (University of Chicago Press, 1968), 1–36.

176 **Reputations of Royce and James**: Kuklick, *Rise*, 338–50, 435–7.

177 **James on empiricism and religion**: *Pluralistic Universe*, 137–49.

177–8 **James's greatness**: Craig R. Eisendrath, *The Unifying Moment: The Psychological Philosophy of William James and Alfred North Whitehead* (Harvard University Press, 1971), 213–14.

10. *Instrumentalism in Chicago and New York*

There is an outstanding biography of Dewey, Robert Westbrook, *John Dewey and American Democracy* (Cornell University Press, 1991); John R. Shook's *Dewey's Empirical Theory of Knowledge and Reality* (Vanderbilt University Press, 2000) has a full historiographical discussion.

179   **Pragmatism in Chicago**: Darnell Rucker, *The Chicago Pragmatists* (University of Minnesota Press, 1969).

179–80 **Dewey and Social Gospel:** Jo Ann Boydston (ed.), *The Early Works of John Dewey* published by Southern Illinois University Press (hereafter *EW*, *MW*, or *LW*—for this edition of the *Early*, *Middle*, or *Later Works* respectively—followed by date of publication in parentheses and volume number); (1969), i. 227–49; (1969), iii. 187–90; (1971), iv. 3–10, 99, 101–2.

180–1   **Dewey and Chicago**: Andrew Feffer, *The Chicago Pragmatists and American Progressivism* (Cornell University Press, 1993).

181–3   *Studies in Logical Theory*: *MW* (1976), ii. 137, 333, 334, 336.

183–4   **Dewey's Darwinism**: *MW* (1977), iv. 1–14.

185   **Mead**: Mitchell Aboulafia (ed.), *Philosophy, Social Theory, and the Thought of George Herbert Mead* (State University of New York Press, 1991); Hans Jonas, *George Herbert Mead* (MIT Press, 1997).

186   **The method of intelligence**: Dewey, *Reconstruction in Philosophy* (1920) in *MW* (1982), xii. 147, 159–61, 182–3.

186–7   **Logical conditions of scientific morality**: Originally published in 1903 in *MW* (1977) iii. 3–35.

187   *Human Nature and Conduct*: Murray G. Murphey, 'Introduction' to *Human Nature and Conduct, MW* (1983), xiv. xxii.

188   *Quest for Certainty*: *LW* (1984), iv. 207–16.

188–9   **Politics in the 1920s and 1930s**: William E. Akin, *Technology and the American Dream* (University of California Press, 1977); Guy Alchon, *The Invisible Hand of Planning* (Princeton University Press, 1985); R. Alan Lawson, *The Failure of Independent Liberalism* (Capricorn Books, 1972); Edward Purcell, Jr., *The Crisis of Democratic Theory* (University of Kentucky Press, 1972); Westbrook, *John Dewey*.

189–90 *Public and its Problems*: *LW* (1984), ii. 304–14, 333–4, 364–72. See the discussion in Brett Gary, *Nervous Liberals: Propaganda Anxieties from World War I to the Cold War* (Columbia University Press, 1999), 18–39.

190–1   **Naturalism**: Peter Rutkoff and William B. Scott, *New School* (Free Press, 1986); David A. Hollinger, *Morris R. Cohen and the Scientific Ideal* (MIT Press, 1975); Yervant H. Krikorian (ed.), *Naturalism and the Human Spirit* (Columbia University Press, 1944); Sidney Hook, *Out of Step: An Unquiet Life in the Twentieth Century* (1987). And see 'A Humanist Manifesto', from *The New Humanist* (1933), reprinted in the excellent sourcebook edited by Paul Kurtz, *American Philosophy in the Twentieth Century* (Macmillan, 1966), 368–71.

192   **Niebuhr and Dewey**: Niebuhr, *Moral Man and Immoral Society* (Scribners, 1932), and 'A Footnote on Religion', *The Nation* (26 September, 1934), 358–9; Dewey, *A Common Faith, LW* (1989), ix. 3–5, 11–12, 20, 35–6, 50–1, 53–4.

193–6   **Science, the supernatural, and religion**: John Hermann Randall, 'Epilogue', in Krikorian (ed.), *Naturalism*, 354–82; Sidney Ratner, 'The Evolutionary Naturalism of John Dewey', *Social Research*, 18 (1951), 435; John Oliver Crompton Phillips, 'John Dewey and the Transformation of American Intellectual Life, 1859–1904', Ph.D., Harvard, 1978, 309.

196–7   **Dewey's Legacy**: recent appraisals are: James Pettigrew, 'Introduction', and James T. Kloppenberg, 'Pragmatism: An Old Name for Some New Ways of Thinking', in Pettigrew (ed.), *A Pragmatist's Progress: Richard Rorty and American Intellectual History* (Routledge, 2000), 1–17, 19–59, respectively.

Introduction to Part III

199   The American Philosophical Association, the crucial professional association in the twentieth century, has sponsored a history of itself, although information about it cannot be accessed directly from the APA's web site: udel.edu/apa.

11. *Realism*

201   **Professionalism**: Bruce Kuklick, *Rise of American Philosophy* (Yale University Press, 1977), 233–58; Roger L. Geiger, *To Advance Knowledge: The Growth of American Research Universities, 1900–1940* (Oxford University Press, 1986), 191–233.

201   **James on professionalism**: Henry James, Jr. (ed.), *The Letters of William James*, 2 vols. (Little Brown & Co., 1920), ii. 228–9; James, *A Pluralistic Universe* (Harvard University Press, 1977), 118.

202   **Royce on realism**: *World and the Individual*, 2 vols. (Dover, 1899, 1901; 1959), i. 70.

202   **Montague and Perry on Royce**: Montague, 'Professor Royce's Refutation of Realism', *PR* 11 (1902), 49–55; Perry: 'Professor Royce's Refutation of Realism and Pluralism', *Monist*, 12 (1902), 458.

203   **'Program and First Platform'**: *JP* 7 (1910), 373–401.

203–4   **Perry's Neo-Realism**: 'Cardinal Principle of Idealism', *M* 19 (1910), 325–6, 330–1; 'Ego-Centric Predicament', *JP* 7 (1910), 8–9; 'Division of the Problem of Epistemology', *JP* 6 (1909), 716.

204–5   **Holt's Neo-Realism**: Montague, 'Story of American Realism', *Philosophy*, 12 (1937), 146; Edwin Bissell Holt, *et al.*, *New Realism* (Macmillan, 1912), 328, 346–55, 358, 368–70; Holt, *Concept of Consciousness* (Macmillan, 1914), 231–4.

206–7   **Montague's Neo-Realism**: Montague, 'Story', 151–5.

207   **Further co-operative work**: Holt, *et al.*, *New Realism*, p. v.

207–8   **Santayana in *Life of Reason***: 5 vols. (Scribners, 1905–6) i. 9–47, 103, 126, 140, 161–83, 202–7; Henry Levinson, *Santayana, Pragmatism, and the Spiritual Life* (University of North Carolina Press, 1992).

209   **Santayana's critical realism**: Durant Drake *et al.*, *Essays in Critical Realism* (Macmillan, 1920), 4–5, 20–1, 117.

209–10   **Ideas of critical realists**: Drake *et al.*, *Essays*, 4 n., 96–7, 104, 108–10, 200–2.

211   **Temporalistic realism**: Lovejoy, 'The Anomaly of Knowledge', *The Thirteen Pragmatisms and Other Essays* (Johns Hopkins University Press, 1963), 236–86; Thomas English Hill, *Contemporary Theories of Knowledge* (Ronald Press, 1961), 126–34.

211–12   **Sellars' views**: C. F. Delaney, *Mind and Nature: A Study of the Naturalistic Philosophies of Cohen, Woodbridge and Sellars* (University of Notre Dame Press, 1969), 145–202.

212   **On logical separation**: Sellars, *Evolutionary Naturalism* (Open Court, 1922), 182, 185; **on construction of world and causal theory**: *Philosophy of Physical Realism* (Macmillan, 1932), pp. vi, 122–3; **on appearances and objective content**: *Evolutionary Naturalism*, 27; 'Knowledge and Its Categories', in Drake *et al.*, *Essays*, 206; *Critical Realism* (Rand McNally, 1916), 269, 275.

212–13   **Sellars on knowledge as linguistic**: 'Knowledge', in Drake *et al.*, *Essays*, 197–8; **on facts and structure of knowledge**: *Physical Realism*, 80; *Evolutionary Naturalism*, 35, 68; *Critical Realism*, p. vi; *The Essentials of Philosophy* (Macmillan, 1922), 115–16.

213   **Emergent materialism and the brain-mind**: *Evolutionary Naturalism*, 238, 298, 311; *Critical Realism*, pp. vi, 252.

213   **Behaviorism**: Sellars, *Evolutionary Naturalism* 301, 315–16.

213   **Critique of Dewey**: Sellars, *Physical Realism*, 2, 9, 50, 105, 410; *Evolutionary Naturalism*, 56; *Reflections on American Philosophy from Within* (University of Notre Dame Press, 1969), 37–8.

214   **Social philosophy**: Sellars, *The Next Step in Religion: An Essay Toward the Coming Renaissance* (Macmillan, 1918), 7–8, 217; *Religion Coming of Age* (Macmillan, 1928), 194, 201, 244, 288.

214   **Lewis's role and biography**: Murray Murphey's forthcoming book, *C. I. Lewis*, is outstanding.

215   **Lewis as neo-pragmatist**: Sellars, *Physical Realism*, 146.

215   **Royce's leading ideas**: Bruce Kuklick, *Josiah Royce* (Hackett, 1972), 132–5.

215   **Lewis on definitions**: *Collected Papers of C. I. Lewis*, ed. John D. Goheen and John L. Mothersheard, Jr. (Stanford University Press, 1970), 231, 233, 244; Lewis, *Mind and the World-Order* (Dover, 1929, 1956), 101–2, 268.

215–16   **On the given**: Hill, *Contemporary Theories of Knowledge*, 379–80.

216   **Applying frameworks**: Lewis, *Mind*, 305–6.

216–17   **Meaning and predictability**: Lewis, *Mind*, 274–308.

217   **On the justification of knowledge:** Lewis 'Review of Keynes, *Treatise on Probability*', PR 31 (1922), 185; *Collected Papers*, 264; Schilpp (ed.), *The Philosophy of C. I. Lewis* (Open Court, 1968), 11.

217–20 **Lewis avoids metaphysical commitments:** Lewis, *Mind*, 45–8, 64–6, 196, 230; **dogmatic and speculative idealism:** 184–94, 213–19; **Lewis's answer:** x–xi, 320–1; **Lewis's failure:** 213–36, 321, 368–85, and Henry Veatch, *Two Logics* (Northwestern University Press, 1969), 136–7, and Schilpp, *C. I. Lewis*, 284.

220   **Sellars on Lewis:** *Physical Realism*, 185.

220   **Wilfrid Sellars and father:** Wilfrid Sellars, 'Physical Realism' (1954) in *Philosophical Perspectives* (Charles C. Thomas, 1967), and 'Autobiographical Reflections', in *Action, Knowledge, and Reality: Critical Studies in Honor of Wilfrid* Sellars (Bobbs-Merrill, 1975), 281, 282.

221–2   **Sellars' views in 'The Myth of the Given':** from the published version, *Empiricism and the Philosophy of Mind* (Harvard University Press, 1997), with an 'Introduction' by Richard Rorty, and 'Study Guide' by Robert Brandom. The parrot example is taken from Brandom, 150–1.

222   **Sellars on growth of mind:** *Empiricism and the Philosophy of Mind*, 117.

223   **Sellars' scientific image:** Sellars, 'Philosophy and the Scientific Image of Man', in *Science, Perception, and Reality* (Ridgeview Publishing Co., 1963, 1991), 34.

223   **Sellars' reconciliation:** ibid. 6–9, and the last sentence on p. 37.

223–4   **James:** *Principles of Psychology*, 2 vols. (Harvard University Press, 1981) i. 152; *Varieties of Religious Experience* (Harvard University Press, 1985), 17–24.

12. *Europe and the United States*

226   **Chicago:** Harry S. Ashmore, *Unseasonable Truth: The Life of Robert Maynard Hutchins* (Little Brown & Co., 1989), 88–105, 153–64.

226   **Blanshard:** see his 'Epilogue', in Arthur Pap, *An Introduction to the Philosophy of Science* (Free Press, 1962), 429.

226–7   **Weiss:** Hendel to Blanshard, 2 October, 1945; and Yale News Bureau Release, 15 April, 1950, Charles Seymour Papers, Series I, Box 127, Folder 1077, Yale University Archives.

227   **Smith, Edman, and Durant:** George Cotkin, 'Middle-Ground Pragmatists: The Popularization of Philosophy in American Culture', *Journal of the History of Ideas*, 55 (1994), 283–302; Joan Shelley Rubin, *The Making of Middlebrow Culture* (University of North Carolina Press, 1992).

227   **Catholic thought:** William M. Halsey, *The Survival of American Innocence* (University of Notre Dame Press, 1980), 145, 207–8, n. 31.

227–8   **Professorial indifference to public life:** compare the two anthologies, *Contemporary American Philosophy*, 2 vols. (Macmillan, 1930), ed. George P. Adams and William Pepperell Montague, and *American Philosophy*

Today and Tomorrow (L. Furman, 1935), ed. Horace M. Kallen and Sidney Hook, and see esp. pp. v–vi of the latter.

228   **Philosophy on the eve of war**: Van Wyck Brooks, 'Conference . . .', in *Science, Philosophy, and Religion: A Symposium*, no author (Harpers, 1941), 1–10.

228   **Quine**: comment in *Science, Philosophy, and Religion, Second Symposium* (Harpers, 1942), 238–9.

228   **Philosophy in World War II**: Brand Blanshard *et al.*, *Philosophy in American Education* (Harpers, 1945), pp. vii–xii, 3–65.

228–9 **Intellectual migration from Europe**: Donald Fleming and Bernard Bailyn (eds.) *The Intellecual Migration: Europe and America, 1930–1960* (Harvard University Press, 1969).

229–30 **Frankfurt School**: Martin Jay, *The Dialectical Imagination: A History of the Frankfurt School and the Institute of Social Research, 1923–1950* (Little Brown & Co., 1973); Rolf Wiggershaus, *The Frankfurt School* (MIT Press, 1994).

231   **Marcuse**: the most interesting study has been done by another idiosyncratic American philosopher: Alasdair Macintyre, *Herbert Marcuse* (Viking Books, 1970).

232   **Logical positivism**: see A. J. Ayer (ed.), *Logical Positivism* (Free Press, 1959).

232   **American view of positivism**: see Ernest Nagel, 'Impressions and Appraisals of Analytic Philosophy in Europe', *JP* 33 (1936), 5–24, 29–53.

233   **Carnap's *Aufbau:*** J. Alberto Coffa, *The Semantic Tradition from Kant to Carnap* (Cambridge University Press, 1991), 208–22; Alan W. Richardson, *Carnap's Construction of the World* (Cambridge University Press, 1998).

234   **Positivist views**: the best summary is still A. J. Ayer, *Language, Truth, and Logic*, 2nd edn. (Dover, 1936, 1946, 1952).

234–5 **'Function of General Laws'**: the essay was published in *JP* 39 (1942), 35–48, and has been reprinted in Hempel's *Aspects of Scientific Explanation* (Free Press, 1965), 231–44.

235   **Positivist problems**: Hempel's expanded treatment is outstanding in 'Empiricist Criteria of Cognitive Significance: Problems and Changes', *Aspects*, 102–22.

236   **Stevenson at Yale**: Arthur W. Burks, 'Preface', *Values and Morals: Essays in Honor of William Frankena, Charles Stevenson, and Richard Brandt*, ed. Alvin I. Goldman and Jaegwon Kim (D. Reidel, 1978), p. xii.

236–7 **Stevenson's views**: see particularly his early essays reprinted in *Facts and Values: Studies in Ethical Analysis* (Yale University Press, 1963), 1–54.

237   **Sartre in America**: Ann Fulton, *Apostles of Sartre* (Northwestern University Press, 1999); Jeffrey C. Isaacs, *Arendt, Camus, and Modern Rebellion* (Yale University Press, 1992).

237   **'Existentialism is a Humanism'**: appeared in a 1949 translation by P. Mairet published by The Philosophical Library in New York. It was

reprinted in many places; see e.g. Robert C. Solomon (ed.), *Existentialism* (Random House, 1974).

238   **Hook quoted:** 'Religion and the Intellectuals', *Partisan Review*, 17 (1950), 225.

238   **Barrett:** William Barrett, *The Truants: Adventures Among the Intellectuals* (Doubleday, 1982).

238   **Sartre at Yale:** *Yale News Digest*, 20 April 1945; 18 January 1946.

240   **Marcuse and existentialism:** Perry Anderson, *Considerations on Western Marxism*, 4th edn. (Verso, 1984), 26–7, 57–8, 85–9.

240   **Irrationalism and existentialism:** Tony Judt, *Past Imperfect* (University of California Press, 1992); Richard Wolin (ed.), *The Heidegger Controversy* (MIT Press, 1993).

240   **Arendt on positivists:** Barrett, *Truants*, 104.

240   **Nagel's defense:** 'Naturalism Reconsidered', APA, *Proceedings and Addresses*, 28 (1955), 7.

240   **Kaufmann:** 'Introduction', *The Portable Nietzsche* (Viking, 1954), 18–19.

240–1   **Barrett:** *Irrational Man* (Doubleday, 1958), 4–7, 21–2.

241   **Wild and Quine at Harvard:** Fulton, *Apostles*, 121–2.

241   **Yale's hostility:** Seymour Papers, Box 127, Folder 1077; Griswold Papers, Box 79, Folder 712; Box 81, Folder 726; Box 87, Folders 785–88; Brewster Papers, Bernstein Case, Boxes 43, 44; 306, Folder 12, Yale University Archives; Sellars to Albritton, 30 April 1980 (copy of letter in possession of R. B. Marcus).

13: *Harvard and Oxford*

243   **Berlin and Lewis:** Michael Ignatieff, *Isaiah Berlin* (Henry Holt, 1998), 82–7; A. J. Ayer, *Part of My Life* (Harcourt, Brace, 1977), 151–2.

243   **Sellars:** Wilfrid Sellars, 'Autobiographical Reflections', in *Action, Knowledge, and Reality: Critical Studies in Honor of Wilfrid Sellars* (Bobbs-Merrill, 1975), 287.

243   **Bertrand Russell in New York:** John Dewey and Horace M. Kallen (eds.), *The Bertrand Russell Case* (DaCapo Press, 1941, 1972).

243   **Morton White:** his *A Philosopher's Story* (Penn State University Press, 1999), 189–252.

243–5   **Oxford philosophy:** see J. O. Urmson, *Philosophical Analysis* (Oxford University Press, 1956).

246–7   **Constriction of philosophy:** another attempt at understanding these issues is John McCumber, *Time in the Ditch: American Philosophy and the McCarthy Era* (Northwestern University Press, 2000).

247   **Quine as Marshall Plan ambassador:** White, *Story*, 226.

248   **Goodman and the *Aufbau*:** Alan Hausman and Fred Wilson, *Carnap and Goodman: Two Formalists* (Martinus Nijhoff, 1967).

249–50   **'The Problem of Counterfactual Conditionals':** reprinted in *Fact,*

Fiction, and Forecast (Harvard University Press, 1955), 56, 67, 117. For the professional importance of the discussion, see Douglas Stalker (ed.), *Grue* (Open Court, 1994).

251   **Memorable meeting**: 'Memories of Hans Reichenbach', in Maria Reichenbach and Robert S. Cohen (eds.), *Hans Reichenbach, Selected Writings, 1909–1953* (D. Reidel, 1978), i. 35, 42, 67, 83.

251   **Reichenbach**: 'Are Phenomenal Reports Absolutely Certain?', *PR* 61 (1952), 147–8, 155–9.

251–2   **Goodman**: Foreword, *Ways of Worldmaking* (Hackett, 1978), p. x; 'Sense and Certainty', *PR* 61 (1952), 163–7.

252   **Lewis**: 'The Given Element in Empirical Knowledge', *PR* 61 (1952), 174–5.

252   **On Quine**: see Bruce Kuklick, review of Quine's autobiography, *The Time of My Life* (MIT Press, 1985), *Philadelphia Inquirer*, 22 December 1985.

252–3   **'Two Dogmas'**: in *From a Logical Point of View* (Harvard University Press, 1953), 41, 43, 44, 45.

253   **Philosophy continuous with science**: Quine, 'Has Philosophy Lost Contact with People?', *Theories and Things* (Harvard University Press, 1981), 191.

254   **Quine's tolerance**: 'On What There Is', *Logical Point*, 19.

254   **Epistemological priority**: ibid., 15–17.

254   **Quine's naturalism**: Quine, 'The Pragmatist's Place in Empiricism', in *Pragmatism: Its Sources and Prospects*, ed. Robert J. Mulvaney and Philip M. Zeltner (University of South Carolina Press, 1981), 32–3.

254–5   **Quine on translation**: *Word and Object* (MIT Press, 1960), 26–79; George D. Romanos, *Quine and Analytic Philosophy* (MIT Press, 1983), xiv.

255–6   **Underdetermination**: Quine, 'On Empirically Equivalent Systems of the World', *Erkenntnis*, 9 (1975), 313–28, quote at 326–7; and see the discussion and citations in Murray G. Murphey, *Philosophical Foundations of Historical Knowledge* (State University of New York Press, 1994), 224–61.

256   **Quine on practice**: Quine, 'Has Philosophy Lost Contact?', *Theories and Things*, 190; **on ultimate particles and materialism**: his contribution to *What I Believe*, ed. Mark Booth (Crossroad, 1984), 71.

257   **Lewis's hostility to Goodman**: White, *Story*, 104, 109.

14. *Tribulations*

In appraising American philosophy in the last part of the century I have depended on four journals: *JP*, *PR*, *Philosophy and Phenomenological Research*, and *Review of Metaphysics*. Also important are the various publications of the American Philosophical Association.

259   **On the academic world**: Richard M. Freeland, *Academia's Golden Age* (Oxford University Press, 1992).

259–60 **Size of the APA**: *PR* 29 (1920), 158–64; APA, *Proceedings and Addresses*, 1960, 1991–1999, Membership Lists.

260   **Estimate of journals**: Susan Haack, *Manifesto of a Passionate Moderate* (University of Chicago Press, 1998), 197.

260   **Doctoral training**: APA, *Guide to Graduate Programs in Philosophy* (1998).

261   **MIT, Irvine, NYU, and Harvard**: ibid.

261   **Sartre**: Ann Fulton, *Apostles of Sartre* (1999), 75, 130.

262   **Marcuse on Quine**: *One Dimensional Man* (1964), esp. 149, 216–17; 'Repressive Tolerance', in Marcuse, R. P. Wolff, and Barrington Moore, Jr., *A Critique of Pure Tolerance* (Beacon, 1965), 81–117.

262   *Drugstorisation*: Alain Martineau, *Herbert Marcuse's Utopia* (Harvest House, 1986), 7–26.

263   **Rawls**: *A Theory of Justice* (Harvard University Press, 1971), p. viii.

263   **Rawls' popularity**: Lenn Goodman, 'Political Philosophy', in Oliver Leaman (ed.), *The Future of Philosophy* (Routledge, 1998), 63–6.

264   **Pluralists versus analysts**: A. J. Mandt, 'The Inevitability of Pluralism', in Avner Cohen and Marcelo Dascal (eds.), *The Institution of Philosophy* (Open Court, 1989), 79.

266   **Ranking**: 'Ranking of Departments and Programs' (1994) in APA, *Statements on the Profession* (1997), 33–4; on the other hand, 'The Philosophical Gourmet Report'—www.blackwellpublisher.co.uk/gourmet— displays an obsession with ranking largely prejudiced in favor of the analytic tradition.

266   **Split in profession**: John Rajchman and Cornel West (eds.), *Post-Analytic Philosophy* (Columbia University Press, 1985); and James R. Watson (ed.), *Portraits of American Continental Philosophers* (Indiana University Press, 1999). A companion to the latter book is Walter Brogan and James Risser (eds.), *American Continental Philosophy: A Reader* (Indiana University Press, 2000).

267   **APA on wisdom**: APA, *Philosophy, A Brief Guide for Undergraduates* (1982), 8, 12; APA e-mail to membership, 10 October 2000.

267   **Quine**: 'Has Philosophy Lost Contact with People?', repr. in *Theories and Things* (Harvard University Press, 1981), 193; an earlier statement of similar views appeared in 1964 in *The National Observer*, reprinted as 'A Letter to Mr. Osterman', in Charles J. Bontempo and S. Jack Odell (eds.), *The Owl of Minerva: Philosophers on Philosophy* (McGraw Hill, 1975), 227–30.

267–8   **APA survey**: APA, *Philosophy in America 1994: Summary and Data* (1997), 28, 41.

268–9   **Philosophy in English departments**: Gerald Graff, *Professing Literature: An Institutional History* (University of Chicago, 1987); Robert Scholes, *The Rise and Fall of English* (Yale University Press, 1998).

269   **Who to believe**: Advertisements for *Encyclopedia, New York Review of Books,* 13 April 2000; Churchlands, ibid., 39; Castaneda, ibid. 15 July 1999, 25; Said, *New York Times Book Review,* 7 November 1999, 34; Kekes, jacket cover; McKeon, Vanderbilt University Press Catalogue, Spring 2000.

270   **Historian quoted**: David A. Hollinger, in 'Afterword', in Gene A. Brucker,

Henry F. May, and David A. Hollinger, *History at Berkeley* (University of California Press, 1998), 43.

270–1   **Kuhn's relativism:** *Structure of Scientific Revolutions*, 2nd. edn., enlarged (University of Chicago Press, 1970), 160, 167–73.

271   **Quine on science:** 'The Nature of Natural Knowledge', in Samuel Guttenplan (ed.), *Mind and Language* (1975), 81; 'Epistemology Naturalized', in *Ontological Relativity and Other Essays* (Columbia University Press, 1969), 87.

272   **Quine on Kuhn's relativism:** 'Has Philosophy Lost Contact', in *Theories and Things*, 192.

272   **Kuhn's Berkeley promotion:** Hollinger, 'Afterword', 43–5, 48–50; 'A Discussion with Thomas S. Kuhn', from Kuhn, *The Road Since Structure*, James Conant and John Haugeland (eds.) (University of Chicago Press, 2000), 301–2.

272–3   **Analytic metaphysics:** to follow the issues that I narrate as leading to Rorty, a good source is Robert B. Brandom (ed.), *Rorty and his Critics* (Blackwell, 2000).

273   **On Marcus and Kripke:** see Paul W. Humphreys and James H. Fetzer (eds.), *The New Theory of Reference and its Origins* (Kluwer Academic Publisher, 1998).

273–4   **The new theory of reference:** from Kripke, *Naming and Necessity* (Harvard University Press, 1980), the ideas of which date from the late 1960s and early 1970s.

274–5   **Varieties of physicalism:** a good introduction is Georges Rey, *Contemporary Philosophy of Mind* (Blackwell, 1997). Jaegwon Kim's collected essays in *Supervenience and Mind* (Cambridge University Press, 1993) are outstanding.

275   **Putnam:** for the flavor of the man see his 'A Half Century of Philosophy, Viewed from Within', in Thomas Bender and Carl E. Schorske (eds.), *American Academic Culture in Transformation, Fifty Years, Four Disciplines* (Princeton University Pess, 1997), 193–226.

275   **Putnam's internal realism:** drawn from his *Reason, Truth, and History* (Cambridge University Press, 1980), quotes at 50, 54, 73.

275–6   **Rorty on Yale:** Derek Nystrom and Kent Puckett (eds.), *Against Bosses, Against Oligarchies: A Conversation with Richard Rorty* (Prickly Pear Pamphlets, 1998), 50–4; **Rorty on analytic philosophy:** Rorty, ed. *The Linguistic Turn . . . with Two Retrospective Essays* (University of Chicago Press, 1992), 33, 371; **Rorty spends ten years writing book:** *Philosophy and the Mirror of Nature* (Princeton University Press, 1979), xiv.

276   **Failure of the mission of analytic philosophy:** Rorty's most gifted student, Robert Brandom, has attempted to carry out the program of Sellars, if not Rorty himself, in *Making it Explicit: Reasoning, Representing, and Discursive Commitment* (Harvard University Press, 1994) and *Articulating Reasons: An Introduction to Inferentialism* (Harvard University Press, 2000).

276   **Quine on raw experience and the flux of experience:** Quine, 'On What There Is' and 'Two Dogmas of Empiricism', *From a Logical Point of View* (Harvard University Press, 1953), 16, 44.

277–8   **Rorty's ambivalence:** 'The World Well Lost' (1972), repr. in *Consequences of Pragmatism* (University of Minnesota Press, 1982), 3–18; **Rorty corrects Sellars:** in his 'Introduction' to Wilfrid Sellars, *Empiricism and the Philosophy of Mind* (Harvard University Press, 1997), 8 n. 10; **his materialism:** *Philosophy and the Mirror of Nature*, 382, 384, 387–90; *Contingency, Irony, and Solidarity* (Cambridge University Press, 1989), 5, 17; **Rorty on Darwin:** 'International Books of the Year and the Millenium', *Times Literary Supplement*, 3 December 1999, 11; **Rorty as atheist:** Rorty, 'Religion as a Conversation Stopper', *Philosophy and Social Hope* (Penguin Books, 1999), 169; **Rorty hopes conversation will keep going:** ibid., esp. xii–xxxii.

278   **Rorty on Kuhn:** 'Thomas Kuhn, Rocks, and the Laws of Physics', *Social Hope*, 187–8.

278   **Rorty as dilettante:** *Philosophy and the Mirror of Nature*, 317–18.

279–80 **Rorty in 1980s and 1990s:** Rorty, 'Comments on Sleeper and Edel', *Transactions of the Charles S. Peirce Society*, 21 (1985), 39; **Rorty on literature:** *Contingency*, 93.

280   **Rorty criticized as apolitical:** Richard Wolin, *The Terms of Cultural Criticism: The Frankfurt School, Existentialism, Poststructuralism* (Columbia University Press, 1992), 157–60.

280   **Rorty writes book on patriotism in year:** Nystrom and Puckett, *Bosses*, 2; *Achieving Our Country* (Harvard University Press, 1998), 3–4, 153.

280   **Rorty's apology:** 'Afterword', in James Pettigrew (ed.), *A Pragmatist's Progress: Richard Rorty and American Intellectual History* (Rowman & Littlefield, 2000), 207.

281   **Lewis:** in his essays *Values and Imperatives*, ed. John Lange (Stanford University Press, 1969), 19.

281   **On Chomsky:** the latest hagiographic book is Neil Smith, *Chomsky* (Cambridge University Press, 1999); 'The Responsibility of Intellectuals' was first published in a Harvard student journal, *Mosaic*, in 1966; then to wide acclaim in the *New York Review of Books* in 1967; it was reprinted in *American Power and the New Mandarins* (Vintage Books, 1969).

Conclusion

282–4   **On the ambiguities of political philosophizing:** for another, thoughtful, perspective, see Thomas Bender, *Intellect and Public Life* (Johns Hopkins University Press, 1993). An excellent survey of the views I am questioning can be found in James Pettigrew (ed.), *A Pragmatist's Progress: Richard Rorty and American Intellectual History* (Routledge, 2000).

284   **Analytic philosophy's withdrawal**: Tyler Burge, 'Philosophy of Language and Mind: 1950–1990', *PR* 101 (1992), 3; Sydney Shoemaker, 'Philosophy in the Last Twenty Years 1979–99', typescript (1999), 8; Avrum Stroll, *Twentieth-Century Analytic Philosophy* (Columbia University Press, 2000), 247–50, 267–70.

ACKNOWLEDGEMENTS

I am indebted to Peter Momtchiloff at Oxford University Press for first suggesting this project, and then for his work in bringing it to completion. For help with the manuscript I would like to thank Richard Beeman, Elizabeth Block, Robert Fogelin, Ruth Marcus, Murray Murphey, Mark Noll, Leo Ribuffo, Richard Rorty, and John Slater. Two scholars, Paul Coates and David Hollinger, have enabled me to work out the shape of the argument, and I especially thank the former for assisting me in understanding deviant causal chains.

INDEX